Realism and the American Dramatic Tradition

Realism and the American Dramatic Tradition

Edited by
William W. Demastes

The University of
Alabama Press
Tuscaloosa and London

Library of Congress Cataloging-in-Publication Data

Realism and the American dramatic tradition / edited by William W.
  Demastes.
      p.   cm.
  Includes bibliographical references and index.
  ISBN 0–8173–0837–7 (pbk. : alk. paper)
    1. American drama—20th century—History and criticism.
  2. Realism in literature.   I. Demastes, William W.
  PS338.R42R43   1996
  812′.50912—dc20   96–4682

British Library Cataloguing-in-Publication Data available

The illustration on the cover is from *Fool for Love* by Sam Shepard,
world premiere production (1983) at the Magic Theatre, San Francisco, directed by Sam Shepard. Pictured are Kathy Baker as May
and Ed Harris as Eddie. Photograph by R. Valentine Atkinson. Used
by permission of the Magic Theatre.

For Michael Quinn,

too soon taken from us

Contents

Preface:
American Dramatic Realisms,
Viable Frames of Thought

William W. Demastes

The tyranny of realism. This phrase summarizes the impression expressed in numerous critical analyses of twentieth-century American drama. It is true that since the beginning of the twentieth century, realism has been the dominant mode of theatrical expression. While it is also true that America has produced the occasional nonrealist success—*The Adding Machine, Our Town, Camino Real,* and *Angels in America*—even such playwrights as Eugene O'Neill and Sam Shepard, who resisted the call to realism and experimented with other forms, returned to this form if for no other reason than that American audiences have been more willing to accept realist drama than any other form. Their careers demonstrate a cultural feedback loop wherein dramatists write realist plays for American audiences, and audiences in turn come to expect realism of authors. Why American audiences hunger for realism when other national theatres have opened themselves to other forms is a difficult question, but perhaps dispelling several myths about the form will suggest why Americans prefer this much-criticized but nevertheless popular form.

The charge that realism is a tyrant stems from the conclusion that realism is a structurally unambitious, homogeneous, tunnel-visioned form, its every product churning out the same fundamental message and denying creation of a more open, pluralistic theatre. From all that has been written about realism in the theatre, and based on the widespread use of the term, one would assume the term itself had been sufficiently identified, its conditions and parameters established, and its opposites marked. But the fact of the matter is, this term has a chameleon-like existence, changing colors at almost every turn and blending into a context appropriate to whatever needs a particular practitioner or critic deems appropriate for his or her goals. Opponents often reduce the term to signifying use of real refrigerators, food, or other props on stage. Others identify it by observing common, unadorned language, and "common" themes. Similarly guilty of oversimplification, proponents often argue that realism is predicated on "objectivity," a faithful rendering of existence without biased impositions on the part of its creators.

It seems we will likely never have a fully delineated and universally satisfactory definition of realism—at least, we will never have a *single* satisfactory definition. If any critic or lexicographer sat down to create a prescriptive definition, much of theatrical and literary history would simply have to be rewritten, for it is unlikely that any prescribed definition would be sufficient to embrace the many past and current applications of the term. In turn, a descriptive definition would need to be so inclusive that the term *definition* itself would need redefining.

What this book attempts to demonstrate is that realism is a term identifying a rich and varied confederacy of theatrical products bound only by a limited set of prescriptions and utilized by a heterogeneous group of artists. In many cases realism is not so much the tyrant as is the limited critical apparatus of reviewers and audiences who quickly identify superficial qualities in a play and instantly identify the work as being of a type that is intellectually unambitious, aesthetically primitive, and culturally irrelevant. To be sure, this confederacy of realist artists has occasionally created mediocre fare, but so has it created powerful, moving, and stimulating art. One simply cannot condemn the whole lot, as one cannot offer unqualified applause to realist drama as a genre. Each brand of realism, created by each practitioner, has corresponding strengths and weaknesses that should be addressed at different levels and from different perspectives. What one must constantly recall is that instant fallacy occurs when one tries to defend or attack *realism* without first identifying the particular permutation under scrutiny.

Among these various realisms, there are of course various points of convergence. Minimalization of theatricality is very much a central gauge of realism, upon which rests a fundamental criterion of the realist mode. Theatricality is craft, and craft needs a crafter to manipulate material. A realist product minimizes theatricality because theatricality implies a fabrication by a crafter/playwright that belies realism's very essence—"objective intentions." There appears to be no playwright present because forces of "nature" are designed to replace the playwright as the controller of events. So goes the argument, at least.

Of course, a crafter is very much alive and present in realist drama despite the illusion of absence. In many ways, in fact, creating an untheatrical theatre is the height of theatrical illusion. The realist playwright *does* control events and *does* manipulate action (or inaction), as does a creator of any theatrical piece. More frequently than one might expect, fundamentally realist plays even break with realist practice and slip into moments of overt theatrical manipulation. *Death of a Salesman* and *The Glass Menagerie* come quickly to mind. Too much overt theatricality, however, ultimately results in the play being labeled something other than realist. The point is that realism is not an either/or proposition. Rather, there is a sliding scale in effect, and depending on critical leanings, an audience may accept certain levels of theatricality but still identify the work as fundamentally realistic. So while realism can be said to be a form that minimizes theatricality, theatricality does have its place to a certain, and always debatable, degree in the realist product. But the restraints under which this realist crafter/playwright operates are more clearly—even if only generically—articulated: the realist playwright is restrained by "nature," is essentially required to operate according to "rules of reality," whatever they may be at any given moment. What for one generation may be realistic could be for another the height of artifice.

To break with the rules of reality is to create something other than realism. When melodrama transforms a villain into a reformed penitent without sufficient preparation, it has broken accepted rules of psychological credibility. When a letter magically arrives exactly when the plot requires it—to save the farm at the last moment—temporal credibility is shattered for most of us. We usually deride poetry from the mouths of dock workers. When sudden confessions of love resolve apparently irreconcilable conflicts, we usually call it romantic comedy and write it off as unrealistic. And when an innocent suddenly dies, we want a reason. In fact, for all of the above, we need reasons, which must themselves satisfy our rules of reality. For some of us, our rules of reality might allow us to accept the above events; for others such events are disallowed.

There are countless borderline events, the "reality" of which would come under question depending on the observer. Such events could acceptably—for some element of an audience, at least—become part of, even central to, a realist text. For some, sudden "unexplainable" events confirm the mystery of life. Still others accept that love can instantaneously thaw the frozen heart. This leaves us, then, with a second level of subjectivity within a form that attempts to create an aura of objectivity. First, the playwright is there, actively filtering and realigning elements of action while trying to produce an illusion of noninvolvement or objectivity on the stage. This first level of deluded objectivity would probably be less problematic if we all agreed on the objective truth or reality of the filter that a playwright chose. If the crafter were filtering through and ordering events that displayed a universally acceptable—that is, consensus-derived—objectivity, then realism, despite the fact of its being subjectively crafted, would still remain an essentially "objective" form. But realism is doubly subjective in that it is controlled by a crafter who is *not* some shamanistic revealer of *the* rules of reality. The rules of reality are themselves subjects of debate, and the realist form attracts just the type of confederacy that can present this plurality of visions. If the crafter is faithful to the set of rules established as a premise, and if an audience accepts the premises, then the result is an acceptably realist text.

Interestingly, this fact of a debatable subjectivity/objectivity in realism—which at first glance looks to be a betrayal of goals and intentions—is precisely what I would argue is realism's strength in that its potential pluralism defeats the very tyranny it has been charged with creating. Alternative realities *can* be presented in realist form. Alternative perspectives can be empowered. The problem here involves the question of whether or not audiences are ready (intellectually capable) and willing (sufficiently open-minded) to consider the alternatives. Here we move from an abstracted argument about the *possibilities* of realism to the very grounded problem of the likely *realization* of these possibilities.

Realism is faced with the problem of being identified as a monolith, a problem stemming in large part from the fact that, to this day, realism has not been able to separate itself from naturalism. While naturalism, as propounded by Emile Zola, is clearly a *type* of realism, more often than not its unique epistemological and ontological foundations are identified as belonging to realism in general. This conflation appears to be a primary reason many critics condemn realism as a single-visioned, tyrannical oppressor of alternative visions of reality. Naturalism, after all, is a very specific vision with a cornerstone epistemology fundamentally Newtonian in its belief in inescapable/unalterable causality, that all actions lead to necessary and predictable reactions. Though there is much more to making a naturalist play, its legacy of causal precision in comprehending human events has marked realism, leaving in the minds of many the belief that realism must adhere to this delimiting vision of universal comprehension. But realism is not necessarily bound to causal/linear invariance. Realism is free to offer such visions but free to offer others as well.

What realism centrally owes to naturalist thought is an increasingly focused insistence—initiated by many earlier artists but rigorously "perfected" by the naturalist realists—on actual study and presentation of human and existential detail, to be true to one's observations. But it must be made clear that realism does not subscribe to any single philosophical overlay, naturalist or otherwise. A single existential formula or worldview just does not exist, for each creator/crafter/playwright inserts a unique vision into the material he or she creates and presents. Each crafter may feel bound to pursuing truth as honestly as possible, but in each case "truth" has its variations. Realism becomes a highly individualistic form in the hands of any number of individual artists.

Once the distinction between realism as a means of presentation and realism as a philosophy becomes clear, we begin to see the potential diversity of the realist form. Given the potential richness and variety of the realist form, I believe we have, in part, an explanation of why realism has endured on the American stage. Interpreting reality, after all, is a democratic and pluralistic process; working from life experiences, all individuals develop singular critical apparatuses and evolve visions of reality. In the process of developing this philosophy of experience, we develop criteria that allow us to distinguish "real" behavior, appearance, custom, etc., from artifice and illusion. Realism onstage allows audiences to utilize criteria developed in the process of living. It may be a "low" art form, requiring minimal training and aesthetic expertise, but it is accessible to a large public that can use its life training to assess the virtues and weaknesses of the product onstage. Furthermore, because realism lacks a central authority, because its standards are created through the highly individualistic process of actually living, it needs to be responsive to multiple and variable interpretations of existence, in ways suitable both to a wide range of artists and to a multiple and pluralistic community whose insistence on preserving the right to individual pursuits of truth is confirmed in a form offering the widest possible latitude for pursuing that truth.

It seems that, in order to avoid esoteric eclecticism, American theatre has evolved in a manner truly appropriate to its pluralistic culture: a nation of many faces, perspectives, and beliefs, united rather tenuously as a "single" culture, has adopted a theatrical form likewise of many faces, perspectives, and beliefs, also rather tenuously united—under the term *realism*.

Inasmuch as is possible in a single volume, the essays that follow collectively trace the development of American dramatic realism in the twentieth century, from the late nineteenth-century playwright James A. Herne to currently active contemporaries like Shepard, Mamet, and Norman. Together the subjects of the essays demonstrate the diversity of the realist form while the essayists demonstrate the variety of critical perspectives available to those confronting the realist form. The essays also function as separate entities, concentrating on the efforts of single writers or distinct groups of writers.

Brian Richardson's introductory essay discusses a wide range of oppositional American drama as it explores a number of the theoretical and practical paradoxes of realism, the most salient being that realism can help refute idealistic or romantic worldviews, though its own alternative vision can never be definitively established.

With Patricia D. Denison's essay, the volume turns to studies of individuals or distinct groups. Denison opens with a discussion of James A. Herne, the "American Ibsen." Focusing on Herne's 1897 manifesto "Art for Truth's Sake in the Drama" and his controversial play *Margaret Fleming* (1890), Denison explores how aesthetic truths become intertwined with cultural truths, dramatic agenda with social agenda, aesthetic theory with social practice. Central to the concerns of the essay is the complex relationship of theatrical melodrama, social realism, and cultural configurations in late nineteenth-century America.

Yvonne Shafer looks at the work of Rachel Crothers, perhaps the most significant American woman playwright in the first quarter of the twentieth century, whose works present a society that restricted women's opportunities to traditional family roles. In fact, Crothers's own efforts in the theatre reflect those restrictions. Shafer looks at Crothers's 1910 play, *A Man's World*, and Augustus Thomas's 1911 rebuttal of Crothers, *As a Man Thinks;* the conclusion Shafer draws is that Crothers's play contributed to both social and theatrical advancement while Thomas's work is reactionary on both counts.

Moving in a similar way to understand feminism and realism, J. Ellen Gainor's essay selects examples from the Provincetown Players to revisit recent developments in feminist critical theory and to identify several deficiencies and problems with that perspective, one which challenges the value of realism in the feminist agenda.

Robert F. Gross suggests that American high comedy in the 1920s cannot be understood by reference to realism alone, but needs acknowledgment of the intersecting demands of realism as the dominant theatrical style, the strong idealizing impulse within the genre, and the requirements of a theatre that showcased star performances. These plays cannot be considered merely as literary works; they are the relics of theatrical events that were dominated by performers such as Laurette Taylor, Francine Larrimore, and the Lunts.

Turning to a different American stage, Patricia R. Schroeder looks at the women of the Harlem Renaissance, who utilized realism on the stage, she contends, for three purposes: to depict and so protest the social oppression of African Americans; to replace demeaning stereotypes of African-American women with fully human, developing female characters; and to recover the lost history of African-American women in America. To illustrate these goals at work, Schroeder analyzes four plays by African-American women: Angelina Weld Grimké's *Rachel* (1916), Mary P. Burrill's *They That Sit in Darkness* (1919), Georgia Douglas Johnson's *Safe* (1929), and Shirley Graham's *It's Morning* (1939).

Frank R. Cunningham's essay on Eugene O'Neill works to capture the monumental efforts of this most prolific playwright, who as Cunningham notes attacked the orthodoxies of his age on every front. The

result is a body of work concerned with creating a humanly responsive, imaginative realism merged with a spiritual quest which exposes
his characters as both victims of and responsible for the increasingly
coarsened conditions of their culture.

Turning to a lesser luminary, Clifford Odets is reevaluated by John
W. Frick. Frick identifies Odets's current critical standing as too reliant
upon the playwright's reputation as a member of the Communist
Party, noting that Odets's own early enthusiasm for communism further complicates the matter. As an alternative suggestion, Frick works
to reveal Odets as a romantic sensitized to the suffering and disen-
franchisement of the average American, and to demonstrate how
Odets's symbolic realism was designed to reflect the average American's hunger for humane community, ultimately free of any formal
leftist or political agenda.

Despite the commercial advantages attached to writing realist plays,
not all American playwrights succumbed to the urge. Christopher J.
Wheatley argues that Thornton Wilder rejected realism because its
emphasis on the probable eliminated the possible implicit in faith,
while realism's emphasis on causality insulates the audience from vital dramatic action. Moreover, the paternal assumptions of realism
are, in Wilder's view, un-American. Ironically, Wilder's challenge has
resulted in his body of work being identified as fundamentally "European"; American realism readily adjusted itself, as is evident among
the works of his contemporaries, even as Wilder was attacking the
form.

Lillian Hellman is a good case in point. With Hellman's most famous work, *The Little Foxes,* Judith E. Barlow returns to the question
of feminism and realism, testing the materialist feminist claim (and
Wilder's as well) that realistic drama necessarily reinforces the established social order, even when attempting to critique it. Barlow explores the complexity and power as well as the limitations of realism,
a dramatic form that clearly plays a crucial role in American women
writers' theatrical heritage.

Brenda Murphy examines Arthur Miller's complicated relationship
with theatrical realism in the context of his bifurcated interest in
dramatizing the individual as experiential subject and the individual
as citizen. His fifty-year search has led him from the development of
the complex theatrical idiom of subjective realism in *Death of a Sales-*

man (1949) to a stripping away of theatrical semiosis to create starkly simple, rhetorically structured dialogic series in *The Last Yankee* (1993) and *Broken Glass* (1994).

Thomas P. Adler draws on Antonin Artaud, Virginia Woolf, and Tennessee Williams's own notion of "personal lyricism" as a way of sketching out the differences between Williams's realism and that of virtually every other American realist playwright. The resulting form—which Adler terms *androgynous*—situates realistically conceived and handled characters within a nonrealistic, poeticized stage space, allowing Williams to unlock integral aspects of human existence that audiences of the time generally demanded remain closeted.

Janet V. Haedicke looks at the recent efforts of women playwrights such as Henley, Howe, Norman, and Wasserstein, successful contemporary realists who have become the current focus of debate on the viability of realism within the feminist agenda.

Eric Bergesen and I turn to two contemporary African-American playwrights, LeRoi Jones/Amiri Baraka and August Wilson, who are identified as paradigms of two opposing factions in the African-American theatre world, respectively the political and the aesthetic theatre. Using *Dutchman* and *Ma Rainey's Black Bottom,* the essay addresses the strengths and weaknesses of the realist form when applied to these opposing agendas.

The late Michael L. Quinn argues that David Mamet confronts the traditional concept of unmoderated realism, presenting plays that are not representative but expressive, focusing on performed actions rather than mimesis, as they reflect Mamet's direct involvement in the construction of the plays.

My concluding essay with Michael Vanden Heuvel looks at the works of David Rabe and Sam Shepard, two playwrights who have introduced epistemological and ontological challenges to the dominant linear ideology traditionally expressed by realist predecessors. Their "chaos-informed" realism may very well have paved the way to a revitalized and revolutionary American theatre for the twenty-first century, conceptually challenging and culturally relevant.

Realism and the American Dramatic Tradition

Introduction: The Struggle for the Real—Interpretive Conflict, Dramatic Method, and the Paradox of Realism

Brian Richardson

The concept of realism has recently taken a series of beatings at the hands of a large and varied group of critical theorists. Todorov, for example, archly states that a work is described as having verisimilitude insofar as it tries "to make us believe that it conforms to reality and not its own laws. In other words, the *vraisemblable* is the mask which conceals the text's own laws and which we are supposed to take for a relation to reality."[1] Robert Scholes asserts that "it is because reality cannot be recorded that realism is dead. All writing, all composition, is construction. There is no mimesis, only poesis. No recording, only constructing."[2] Jonathan Culler similarly observes that "reality" is "only a tissue of socially agreed conventions as to what is the case; thus the correspondence of a text with reality turns out to be only the correspondence of . . . one sort of text with another."[3] It should not be surprising that realism has no place in current literary theory. Almost every type of formalism denies any connection between the world and the literary text; most varieties of poststructuralism deny the distinction between factual and fictional narratives: every text is for them necessarily fictional. Given such presuppositions, it is only to be expected that realism is disavowed: these paradigms cannot in principle comprehend even the theoretical possibility of realism.

1

To be sure, many aspects of the recent critiques of the concept of realism are impossible to deny. Pictorial analogies to the contrary, literary realism is never an unambiguous reproduction of the external world, but always entails numerous interpretive strategies and significant ideological self-situating. In the early Renaissance, Leon Battista Alberti painted a view from a window and then hung his painting next to that window. Spectators could glance back and forth between the representation and the reality, and judge exactly how realistic the painting was. There is however no comparable, unmediated slice of reality to which any fictional narrative can be juxtaposed. There is at best a more or less contradictory set of texts and fragments that may be repeated or altered. A realistic novel or play never reflects but instead reconstitutes its object; no text or performance can ever attain the status of a definitive reproduction of the real. As René Wellek has pointed out, literary realism strives to be " 'the objective representation of contemporary social reality.' It claims to be all-inclusive in subject matter and aims to be objective in method, even though this objectivity is hardly ever achieved in practice."[4] One thing we have learned in the twentieth century is that nothing is more subjective than individual notions of objectivity.

Does this mean then, as the majority of theorists aver, that literary realism is merely another mode of fabrication or narrative convention, neither more nor less accurate a depiction of experience than any other mode, neither more nor less realistic than a fairy tale, a gothic romance, or an account of a journey to Hades or to the Hesperides? It is difficult to acquiesce to such a position for a number of reasons. First, unlike most other modes, literary realism situates itself as verisimilar: unlike the tale of chivalry, it purports to depict salient features of the world of our experience. This implicit truth claim is frequently averred and systematically defended in realist works, and for this reason deserves our scrutiny. Second, since the origin of the drama, playwrights have regularly critiqued what they perceived to be unrealistic scenes and conventions precisely because of their implausibility. In his *Electra*, Euripides parodies the unlikely scene of the tokens' recognition in Aeschylus' *Choephoroe*, and Aristophanes in the *Thesmosphoriazusae* mocks the dubious Euripidean device of sending a message written on oar blades. Such deflations are a hallmark of modern realism; in *A Doll's House*, Krogstad knows that Nora won't commit suicide because, as he points out, such things happen only in books. Finally, it should be noted that the compelling power of realism is and always has been its ability to expose and demystify impoverished and inaccurate worldviews. As James Joyce stated, "in realism you are down to facts on which the world is based: that sudden reality which smashes romanticism into a pulp. What makes most people's lives unhappy is some disappointed romanticism, some unrealizable or misconceived ideal. . . . Nature is quite unromantic. It is we who put romance into her, which is a false attitude, an egotism, absurd like all egotisms."[5] It is this opposition that underlies the fundamental drive toward realism, and that is at times explicitly avowed as such. In *Long Day's Journey into Night,* Edmund castigates his father's vision in just these terms, and thereby articulates the realist suspicion of and challenge to romantic beliefs: "facts don't mean a thing, do they? What you want to believe, that's the only truth!"[6]

Realism can refute a variety of dubious or inaccurate worldviews and ideologies, especially those based on some form of idealism. In this, it provides a kind of epistemological catharsis. Just this kind of interpretive drama is frequently staged in many of the most celebrated works of American realism, as one character's romantic or sentimental vision is shown to be contradicted by the recalcitrant world of facts that only another, darker version of experience is able to comprehend.

This leads us to the paradox of realism. It is a *Weltanschauung* that can never be fully verified, though any of its examples can always be falsified (unlike works which make no ontological claims, such as pastorals or fairy tales). It exposes false ideologies even as it is necessarily highly ideologically coded itself. It claims to depict life as really lived even though the artifactuality of the conditions of its own production precludes so close a correspondence; even the dialogue of "superrealistic" drama is extremely artificial when compared to actual human conversation. In short, realism can expose falsehood but cannot reveal the truth. This, I believe, is why realism has provoked such heated and contradictory theoretical debate, why successive authors can legitimately feel they are being more realistic than their immediate predecessors in the mode, and why the methods of realistic depiction undergo continuous transformation.

Literary realism should be viewed not as a mirror, and not as a delusion, but as a synecdoche, a model that attempts to reconstruct in an abbreviated but not inaccurate manner the world that we inhabit. A model as such is neither true nor false, but it can be determined to be more or less adequate, accurate, and comprehensive, and one model can be seen to be more effective than another. This is in principle equally true of models of the universe, of recent history, or of human behavior (though these disciplines, at least since the Renaissance, have not been able to claim an equal degree of poetic license). In adjudicating between rival literary models of human experience, three elements emerge as signally important: the function of interpretation, the construction of the typical, and the status of probability. None of these terms is unproblematic, and all carry with them certain metaphysical and ideological assumptions. But this only serves to make the study of realism more urgent—as urgent, perhaps, as the study of history.

Susan Glaspell's *Trifles* is, I believe, an exemplary realist text, and one that can fully reveal both the great potential and the significant stakes of the realist enterprise. Glaspell's play begins with the investigation of a murder, as the sheriff and the county attorney examine the farmhouse of John Wright, the murder victim, in an attempt to discover evidence. A male neighbor, his wife, and the sheriff's wife are also present. The men's examination of the kitchen (where the play is set) is cursory; they are convinced that nothing of any importance could exist among the conventional implements of a woman's domestic space. Once the men are gone, the two women tidy up the kitchen, and in the process uncover some items that appear curious to them, such as a bird cage with a broken door; later they find a dead bird, its neck broken. Soon they are able to reconstruct a series of events to explain these oddities. Though this narrative remains unspoken, it is clear to the audience that Mrs. Wright had been driven to desperation by her husband's sullen indifference and rigid domination. The one source of joy for her, the canary, was killed by the husband, who had ripped open its cage and throttled the bird. That night, she prepared a little coffin for the bird, strangled her husband with a rope, and washed her hands. It is the women who are able to deduce this series of events, who are able to determine what actually constitutes evidence; and, because they so keenly appreciate the motivation of Mrs. Wright—the very motive sought in vain by the county attorney—they decide to keep their knowledge to themselves. This probably ensures that Mrs. Wright will go free; the men never will understand, and consequently will be unable to apply their laws to the woman.[7]

The struggle for interpretation in this play is both an instance and an emblem of a characteristic feature of the enterprise of realism. Rival hermeneutic stances find themselves in conflict over the reading of a set of events. Each attempts to generate a narrative model to explain what its subscribers believe to be the relevant facts. The play does not end in an epistemological impasse but validates one reading over the other—the superior model can explain more, and explain more convincingly. More precisely, the women's account of the entire sequence of events, including the range of social and psychological elements that form the unfortunate causal skein and lead to a more lenient judgment of the fatal act, is a more complete and accurate interpretation than the men can muster.

In European realism, the hermeneutic battles are frequently between an idealistic and a realistic reading or model of events, as characters espousing some variety of the former stance (Gregers Werle, Hedda Gabler, *Candida*'s Marchbanks, and almost all of the characters in Chekhov's plays) are shown by the course of events to have misperceived the world they inhabit. The paradigmatic example of this might be what Raymond Williams termed "Strindberg's definition of naturalism as the exclusion of God";[8] indeed, the depiction of the cunning yet slavish pastor in *The Father* is a quintessential expression of the realists' attack on the possibility of supernatural agency.

In American realist drama, the focus is often less metaphysical and more directed to social and psychological issues, as playwrights contest the official optimistic master narratives of American society, including different versions of the romance of "the American dream"—perhaps most blatantly in Sam Shepard's *Buried Child,* in which a visitor to the midwestern family farm first laughingly describes it as being "like a Norman Rockwell cover or something,"[9] but rapidly discovers the multiple horrors and degradation that lie just beneath the surface.

It is significant that the most celebrated American realist playwrights—Eugene O'Neill, Tennessee Williams, Lillian Hellman, Arthur Miller, and later Sam Shepard—all confront major aspects of this mythic vision of American society and offer instead rival versions of experience that are presented as not merely different but more realistic, that is, more accurate versions of social existence. O'Neill is particularly adept in chronicling the vast range of self-serving illusions with which his characters delude themselves—*The Iceman Cometh* is a kind of sustained deflation of twelve popular varieties of self-deception, or "pipe dreams," as Hickey calls them. At the same time, O'Neill invariably points out the larger social structures that influence or determine the characters' failures and consequent delusions.

This conflict—and it seems to be fundamental in American realist drama—is starkly presented in the dialogue of *A Streetcar Named Desire*. As Mitch removes the paper lantern from the light bulb, Blanche asks, "What did you do that for?" He responds, "So I can take a look at you good and plain!" She counters, "Of course you don't mean to be insulting!" He answers, "No, just realistic." To this Blanche responds, "I don't want realism. I want magic! Yes, yes, magic! I try to give that to people. I misrepresent things to them. I don't tell truth, I tell what *ought* to be truth. And if that is sinful, then let me be damned for it!—*Don't turn the light on!*"[10]

Williams is notable for giving explicit voice to the specifically ideological claims of realism. The narrator at the beginning of *The Glass Menagerie* states that the ensuing memory play "is sentimental, it is not realistic."[11] Its temporal setting is furthermore stated to be "the thirties, when the huge middle class of America was matriculating in a school for the blind. Their eyes had failed them, or they had failed their eyes . . . " (p. 23). Not surprisingly, the illusions that nourish the main characters are thoroughly exposed by the drama's end.

What is perhaps an even more sustained struggle for the real occurs in *Cat on a Hot Tin Roof*. Surrounded by characters either consumed by self-delusions or constantly intriguing to improve their fortunes, Brick and Big Daddy stand out as figures who will not lie and cannot be lied to. Their common struggle against the dishonesty all around them brings them together just long enough for each to expose the one illusion that the other harbors. As Brick states: "Mendacity is a system that we live in. Liquor is one way out an' death's the other."[12] It might be noted that a similar pattern of deception and self-deception permeates Hellman's *The Little Foxes*. As Gerald M. Berkowitz observes, the Hubbard siblings, given the opportunity to become rich, "stop at nothing—theft, blackmail, double-crossing, murder—to succeed,"[13] all beneath the veneer of southern cordiality. Comparable reconstructions of the American myth underlie much of the work of Arthur Miller, as Berkowitz documents (pp. 77–82); a particularly stark contemporary treatment can be found in Mamet's *Glengarry Glen Ross.*

For much of the twentieth century, African Americans were largely excluded from all but the most tawdry versions of the American dream; consequently, it should be of some interest to see how contemporary African-American playwrights negotiate this theme. In August Wilson's *Ma Rainey's Black Bottom,* set in the 1920s, the major characters express radically different views concerning the situation and possibilities of blacks in the United States. The character Slow Drag tends to accept social reality more or less uncritically and without seeming to be able to imagine an alternative vision of how things might be. Cutler has a profound belief in Christianity and feels that eventually God's justice will be done. Toledo espouses a vaguely separatist, proto–Pan-African nationalism, and suspects that the best future prospects for blacks lie in developing their own community. Levee is an ambitious individualist and a firm believer in his potential to rise to success through entrepreneurial capitalism; he has no doubt that the system will fully reward his talent and vision. Ma Rainey is utterly cynical, convinced of the ruthless and predatory nature of the unjust society that surrounds her.

Referring to the record producers that Levee believes will help make him rich, Ma states: "They don't care nothing about me. All they want is my voice. Well, I done learned that, and they gonna treat me like I want to be treated no matter how much it hurt them. They back there now calling me all kind of names. . . . But they can't do nothing else. They ain't got what they wanted yet. As soon as they get my voice down on one of them recording machines, then it's just like if I'd be some whore and they roll over and put their pants on. Ain't got no use for me then. I know what I'm talking about. You watch."[14] By the end of the play, Ma Rainey's explanatory abilities prove all too successful as Levee, after being mercilessly exploited by the white record producers, vents his rage by killing Toledo, and the pattern of exploitation completes its full vicious circle.

Lorraine Hansberry's *A Raisin in the Sun,* set in Chicago in the 1950s, documents the tremendous struggle of a black family to achieve what whites would consider to be an ordinary, even typical existence. Here the barriers are predominantly racist, with one crucial exception—Walter Lee's attempt to better the family's prospects through capital investment. This ends in a financial fiasco and makes the family's struggle all the more difficult. At the same time, by offering a range of sympathetic and believable African-American characters almost entirely absent from Euro-American drama of the period, Hansberry succeeds in transcending, via realism, the impoverished conceptions of popular stereotypes.

Alice Childress, in *Wedding Band,* similarly charts the all but unattainable goal of what elsewhere might be the beginning, rather than the arduous telos, of an American realist play—the desire of two single adults, in love with each other, to marry and live together. By attempting to depict typical and even mundane central characters, this powerful drama of interracial love in the South is also careful to reject and demystify the potentially sensationalistic elements that frequently accompanied the subject of such forbidden love in more popular media. Taken together, these works should help to indicate a distinctive African-American contribution to realism's contestation of the master narrative of American culture as they disclose how fragile, limited, deceptive, or illusory that narrative has been.

Other works critique an equal and opposite illusion, that white supremacy is either completely insurmountable or utterly ubiquitous. In Wilson's *Fences,* Troy Maxson cautions his son Cory not to aspire too high, not to hope for example for a college education, since white America would only crush such extravagant ambitions. But Cory feels that Troy has misread the evolving social code; a series of transformations were under way in the fifties that not only allowed but demanded such desires, he argues, and the events of the play validate Cory's interpretation. Turning to another drama of the investigation of a murder, we may conclude this section with a glance at Charles Fuller's *A Soldier's Play.* The setting is an army base in the deep South in 1944; the victim is the black sergeant of an all-black unit. Every character in the play is convinced that the Ku Klux Klan is behind the murder, but the hypothesis fails to explain fully all the available evidence. In the end, it is revealed that Sergeant Waters was killed by one of the black enlisted men he commanded, as the drama uncovers numerous layers of stereotyping, misprision, retribution, and identity construction.

Running through all of these plays is the clash of incompatible interpretations of the social world—the world jointly inhabited, according to the realist postulate, by both characters and spectators. In each case, the more conventional and, usually, more rosy-tinted *Weltanschauung* is demonstrated to be inadequate, to be in other words an insubstantial dream, if not a systematic lie. The problem of course is that one can never definitively prove the validity of an image of society; to test the theory of gravity, one may conduct any number of experiments, but to document O'Neill's vision, one can at best marshal additional corroborating documents, narratives, and visions. Such dramas can set forth vivid, incontrovertible counterexamples that defy and confound more idealistic worldviews, though they can never definitively establish a totalized alternative. They counter ideologies even as they are steeped in opposing ideologies; they claim to be true but can never be neutral. Their objectivity is perhaps comparable to the strained disinterestedness of a jury during an emotional trial, from whom much important information has been withheld but who must pass judgment on the few incontrovertible facts and the many contested interpretations of the case.

Additional paradoxes are inherent in realism's basic claim to represent the world as it is: one concerns the stability of the world; the other attaches to the *depiction* of that world. Our conceptions of what really exists continue to evolve, and a wide array of divergent techniques steadily emerge to reproduce those conceptions, each claiming greater fidelity and verisimilitude. A key category of both the aperception of the world and of realist aesthetics is that of causality. The hidden source of the strength of realism's appeal is that it accurately reproduces the same canon of probability that also governs everyday existence. This is perhaps the foundation of concepts like "the typical" and "the lifelike" that, from Engels and Howells to contemporary reviewers, have seemed indispensable parts of the critical idiom. Since the invention of realism in the middle of the nineteenth century, causality has been a foundational element that has never ceased undergoing continuous transformation. A large part of the original appeal of realism was its disavowal of the excessive "happy coincidences" that vitiated both romantic plays and nineteenth-century melodrama. Ibsen's works (and later, James A. Herne's) were intended to depict an unbreakable chain of causally connected actions, though even here one can perceive a few carefully buried yet utterly improbable juxta-positions of unlikely correspondences that do wonders for the work's emplotment even as they undermine its pretentions to verisimilitude: think, for example, of the melodramatic timing of the events sur-rounding the letter-box episode in *A Doll's House*.

A little later, Zola would attempt to tighten further the screws of a totally naturalistic determinism in *Thérèse Raquin*. In 1888, Strindberg argued in the preface to *Miss Julie* for a much more expansive and what we would now call overdetermined notion of cause.[15] Later yet, realist authors were deliberately introducing occasional chance events into their works in order to give them a greater aura of realism.[16] Such thinking is not unprecedented; according to Aristotle, Agathon once remarked that it is likely that many unlikely things should happen. Nevertheless, tightly connected sequences of causes and effects, in the name of an accurate representation of reality, served as the corner-stone of realistic drama.

In 1941 Vladimir Nabokov, in his essay "The Tragedy of Tragedy," articulated the feelings of a number of modernists when he observed that modern drama is "so hypnotized by the conventionally accepted rules of cause and effect that it will invent a cause and modify an effect rather than have none at all."[17] He attacks this strategy not only on aesthetic grounds but in the name of verisimilitude as well: "The tragedies of real life are based on the beauty or horror of chance—not merely on its ridiculousness. And it is the secret rhythm of chance that one would like to see pulsating in the veins of the tragic muse" (pp. 340–41). Modern developments in philosophy, physics, probabil-ity theory, and chaos theory have tended to confirm this modernist perspective, and mechanistic, billiard-ball notions of causation have been abandoned. Contemporary playwrights like Sam Shepard, who routinely incorporate apparently unlikely infusions of chance events, can now do so in the name of the real. In the past hundred years, our concept of probabilism has undergone radical transformation, and re-alistic playwrights who ground their work in the probable have had to reconstruct the causal lines within their plays as reality itself is repeatedly redescribed. As our understanding of nature changes, so must the methods by which it is depicted.

Contemporary American drama has recently produced three exemplary instances of vital reinventions of the realist project that ironically point to the necessary limitations of every realist undertaking. The first is the phenomenon of superrealism, dramatic spectacles that strive for a minimum of artifice or mediation. For the superrealist playwright, such as Terry Curtis Fox, the early Edward Bond, Wolfgang Bauer, or Franz Xaver Kroetz (and, we might add, David Mamet), "the only way to see the world as it is, is to render it with as little distortion and personal overlay as possible," writes Carol Gelderman.[18] She affirms that the most noticeable difference between this and earlier kinds of realism lies in the dialogue. The language of the superrealistic play "is not a convention; it is real in the sense that it is based on actual speech with all of its repetitions, silences and pauses, [and] the slips in language which reveal ignorance and lack of thought" (p. 360). Gelderman's general description of the superrealist project, it will be observed, sounds very similar to Zola's claims for the naturalistic playwright: "the facts are produced, in order to be absolutely thorough, and so that his inquiry may belong to the world's comprehensive view and reproduce reality in its entirety."[19] Likewise, Gelderman's depiction of superrealist speech brings to mind Strindberg's remarks on dialogue in the preface to *Miss Julie*.[20] And, as the rhetoric of realistic theory remains largely constant, its practice has many fundamental similarities as well. The dialogue Gelderman adduces to display the superrealist difference, speeches from the beginning and end of Bond's *Saved*, is in fact much better ordered, more coherent, and less redundant than ordinary conversation. Keir Elam has discussed this subject quite convincingly in his *Semiotics of Theatre and Drama*, where he contrasts a superreal snatch of Sam Shepard's dialogue with a transcript of actual café conversation. We may substitute a passage from Bond cited by Gelderman and compare it to Elam's example of "real" conversation:

Len: Somethin up?
Pam: Can't I blow me nose?
Len: Wass yer name?

Pam: Wass yourn?
Len: Len.
Pam: Pam
Len: O . . .
Len: 'Ow often yer done this?
Pam: Don't be nosey.[21]

C.: Excuse me. I hate to do this but I'm bringing it back 'cause it's stale.
S.: Ow well I'll make you another one.
C.: OK. Thanks a lot. I kinda feel bad doing this but.
D.: I guess so eh (laughter) Well it's your own fault.
C.: I do.
S.: Is that more to your liking?
C.: Yeah okay well I fell rotten bringing it back.
D.: Well no.
S.: Well if you're not satisfied you should why should why should you eat something you've paid for.
C.: I know.
S.: If you.
C.: I know.
S.: Don't want it cause it's not . . . fresh.[22]

One hardly needs Elam's scrupulous linguistic analyses to see at once how different any stage speech, however realistic, is from actual conversation and to determine why this must be the case: so much of actual conversation is vacuous, repetitive, contradictory, redundant, and most importantly, inconsequential that a dramatist succeeds in being realistic at the expense of being interesting. That is, insofar as drama is an artifact intended for an actual audience, it must work against the suffocating boredom of ordinary existence; to succeed, it must be more than merely realistic. Mere verisimilitude is always inadequate.

This points to another paradox: the term *realistic drama* must always be something of an oxymoron. That is, insofar as a performance is a drama (say, with coherent dialogue, significant issues, dramatic pace, and a tolerable closure), it ceases to be perfectly realistic. On the other hand, too much realism may preclude drama (who would want to pay to see an enactment of the café dialogue inscribed above?); total realism may indeed fail to be drama at all. One is reminded of Howell's warning, cited by Murphy, that "realism becomes false to itself when it heaps up facts merely, and maps life instead of picturing it" (p. 28).

Another fascinating development in contemporary drama is present in David Henry Hwang's *M. Butterfly,* a play that, like *The Glass Menagerie,* investigates a number of realism's traditional concerns from the framework of a psychodrama. Ignoring Aristotle's judicious observation that what is impossible but can be believed is preferable to what is possible but unconvincing, Hwang has constructed a play out of the most improbable of events—a Frenchman cohabiting for several years with a Chinese man whom he believes to be a woman. Here two of the cornerstones of realism—the actual and the probable—are placed in opposition. Hwang also states, perhaps paradoxically, that "given the degree of misunderstanding between men and women and also between East and West, it seemed inevitable that a mistake of this magnitude would one day take place."[23] Interestingly, Hwang's text begins with a *New York Times* account of the episode that authenticates the relationship and situates it historically. The unfolding drama thus becomes a kind of archeology of cupidity, as the audience marvels at Gallimard's vast capabilities of self-deception, while perceiving the cultural forces that dictate his blindness. At the play's conclusion, however, the illusions can no longer be maintained; Gallimard must choose between his beatific vision and the real thing. He tells his imaginary Butterfly, "Get away from me! Tonight I've finally learned to tell fantasy from reality. And, knowing the difference, I choose fantasy." When his partner asserts that he is Gallimard's fantasy, the Frenchman responds, "You? You're as real as hamburger" (p. 90). The epistemological drama ends as Gallimard finally identifies himself as the dying Butterfly, and Hwang's interrogation of the limits of the improbable is finally circumscribed by a compelling dramatic form.

In Sam Shepard's recent work, in addition to the superrealism of the dialogue and sets, there is a continuing fascination and probing of favorite American myths.[24] One of the most compelling is the interrogation of the concept of the West in the ironically titled *True West,* where the most impoverished and cliché-ridden notions of this imaginary space jostle incongruously with the frustrating experiences of life in suburban Los Angeles. The quest for an authentic image of this elusive vision is regularly derided as foolish: "There's nothing real down here."[25] Nevertheless, Lee, a poorly educated hustler, is convinced he can write a screenplay that is different, that is real: "true-to-life-stuff" (p. 15), "Based on a true story" (p. 18), "too much like real life!" (p. 21). His scenario is little more than a vague vision of a couple of guys chasing each other around Texas' Tornado Country. Ironically, this simplistic scene, which is little more than a failed Hollywood cliché, captures the imagination of a Hollywood producer who offers to bankroll the project, "the first authentic Western to come along in a decade" (p. 30). Here, we are in the presence of what Baudrillard calls the "hyperreal": "the real is not only what can be reproduced, but *that which is always already reproduced.* . . . The hyperreal transcends representation . . . only because it is entirely in simulation. . . . Hyperrealism is made an integral part of a coded reality that it perpetuates, and for which it changes nothing."[26] The simulation displaces the real, the representation consumes and negates its referent. Shepard's critique of popular culture's mythmaking then takes an unusual turn: the protagonists of the play *True West* end up in pursuit of each other, locked in a bitter struggle, resisting any form of closure, exactly like the two characters of Lee's unfinished script, as life comes to mimic a debased version of art.

These three examples of what might be called postmodern realism demonstrate the vitality and innovation of contemporary writers' quest for the real. It is now a more self-conscious and audacious enterprise, scrutinizing a wider range of potential fictions and ruthlessly interrogating residual devices of mediation inherent in even those dramatic forms born of suspicion. Perhaps most remarkable is that so vast an array of playwrights choosing to contest society's master narratives select realism as the mode in which to stage their critiques. It is not a coincidence that generations of African-American playwrights, from Langston Hughes to August Wilson, regularly employed realism to give voice to previously suppressed words, acts, and histories. It is equally true that early twentieth century writers and spectators found in realism a literary strategy well suited to feminist political struggles, as Sheila Stowell has recently pointed out;[27] contemporary female playwrights like Wendy Wasserstein, Tina Howe, and Marsha Norman also continue to employ the methods of realism to explore women's issues. When Puerto Rican author Miguel Dinero decided to depict the brutal facts of prison life, he chose to do so within a realist poetics. Furthermore, almost every American drama that attempts to educate the public about AIDS uses realism as its vehicle. This in turn suggests that realism has an epistemological power and social efficacy far beyond that of the mere "fabrication" that contemporary theory insists on calling it.

Though utilizing fictional characters and plots, realism makes epistemological claims about our social world by challenging existing models and offering alternative ones. Nevertheless, realism as we have seen can never be definitively embodied. There will always be struggles over the means and the content of dramatic representation. Realism will continue to strive for objectivity, typicality, and totality, and it will always fail to achieve these goals. It will never cease to attempt to provide a more plausible model of the world than that set forth by idealist programs, but will always be susceptible to a still more thoroughgoing realist critique.[28] Realism will endure, and so will the conflicts that invariably surround it.

Notes

I wish to thank my colleague James Robinson for his helpful comments on an earlier version of this essay.

1. Tsvetan Todorov, "Introduction," *Communications* 11 (1968): 3. Here I use Jonathan Culler's translation of Todorov's passage in Culler's *Structuralist Poetics* (Ithaca: Cornell UP, 1975), p. 139. This citation and the two that follow it are discussed by A. D. Nuttall, "Realistic Conventions and Conventional Realism in Shakespeare," *Shakespeare Survey* 34 (1981): 33, and by Barbara Foley, *Telling the Truth: The Theory and Practice of Documentary Fiction* (Cornell UP, 1986), p. 11, two scholars who are trying to move beyond what Foley calls modern theory's "anxiety of reference" (p. 267). Foley is extremely deft in countering the arguments of those, particularly deconstructionists, who deny the concept of the real (pp. 9–19).

2. Robert Scholes, *Structural Fabulation: An Essay on the Fiction of the Future* (South Bend: U of Notre Dame P, 1975), p. 7.

3. Here I cite Nuttall's summary ("Realistic Conventions," p. 33) of Culler's position, which is itself a condensation of familiar views of a number of contemporary French theorists.

4. René Wellek, "The Concept of Realism in Literary Scholarship," in *Concepts of Criticism*, ed. Stephen H. Nichols, Jr., pp. 222–55 (New Haven: Yale UP, 1963), p. 253.

5. Arthur Power, *Conversations with James Joyce* (New York: Barnes and Noble, 1975), p. 98.

6. Eugene O'Neill, *Long Day's Journey into Night* (New Haven: Yale UP, 1955), p. 127.

7. It is revealing to look at Mamet's *Oleanna* in the light of *Trifles,* since Mamet is seeking to deny the possibility of a female hermeneutics, even as Glaspell attempts to demonstrate its necessity. In Mamet's drama of interpretation, however, what counts as evidence is agreed upon by the opposing parties. It is the meaning, the narrative, and the use of that evidence (regardless of its truth or falsity) that provides the grounds of the conflict.

8. Raymond Williams, "Realism and the Contemporary Novel," in *Twentieth Century Literary Criticism,* ed. David Lodge (New York: Longman, 1972), p. 582.

9. *Buried Child,* in *Seven Plays* by Sam Shepard (New York: Bantam, 1981), p. 83.

10. Tennessee Williams, *A Streetcar Named Desire* (New York: Signet, 1947), p. 117.

11. *The Glass Menagerie* (New York: New Directions, 1970), p. 23. Subsequent references are cited in the text.

12. *Cat on a Hot Tin Roof* (New York: Signet, 1955), p. 94. In this context, it may be remembered that *Summer and Smoke* contains a particularly stark materialist critique of religion, illusion, and decorum in the eighth scene's "anatomy lesson," and the prominent mirror at the beginning of the last act of *Sweet Bird of Youth* turns out to reveal the fortunes, not the features, of the main characters.

13. Gerald M. Berkowitz, *American Drama of the Twentieth Century* (New York: Longman, 1992), p. 52. Subsequent references are cited in the text.

14. *Ma Rainey's Black Bottom* (New York: Penguin, 1985), p. 79.

15. "Author's Foreword to *Miss Julie*," trans. Elizabeth Sprague, in *Playwrights on Playwriting,* ed. Toby Cole (New York: Hill and Wang, 1961). For additional discussion, see Brenda Murphy's excellent survey of the varieties of early realist theory and practice in *American Realism and American Drama, 1880–1940* (Cambridge: Cambridge UP, 1987), pp. 24–49. Subsequent references are cited in the text.

16. The origin of this practice may be in Ibsen's *Master Builder.* See William Demastes, "Reinspecting the Crack in the Chimney: Chaos Theory from Ibsen to Stoppard," *New Theatre Quarterly* 10, 39 (Aug. 1994): 242–54, for a perspicacious analysis of the role of coincidence in this and subsequent realist drama.

17. Vladimir Nabokov, "The Tragedy of Tragedy," *The Man from the USSR and Other Plays,* trans. Dmitri Nabokov (New York: Harcourt Brace Jovanovich, 1984): p. 326. Subsequent references are cited in the text.

18. Carol Gelderman, "Hyperrealism in Contemporary Drama: Retrogressive or Avant-Garde?" *Modern Drama* 26.3 (Sept. 1983): 357–67, at 358. Subsequent references are cited in the text.

19. Emile Zola, "Naturalism on the Stage," trans. Samuel Draper, in *Playwrights on Playwriting,* ed. Toby Cole (New York: Hill and Wang, 1961), p. 11.

20. Strindberg writes: "In regard to the dialogue, I have departed somewhat from tradition by not making my characters catechists who ask stupid questions in order to elicit a smart reply. I have avoided the symmetrical, mathematical construction of French dialogue, and let people's minds work irregularly, as they do in real life where, during a conversation, no topic is drained to the dregs, and one mind finds in another a chance cog to engage in. So too the dialogue wanders, gathering in the opening scenes material which is later picked up, worked over, repeated, expounded, and developed" (in *Playwrights,* p. 178).

21. Cited in Gelderman, "Hyperrealism," p. 361.

22. Keir Elam, *The Semiotics of Theatre and Drama* (New York: Methuen, 1980): p. 179.

23. David Hwang, *M. Butterfly* (New York: New American Library, 1988), p. 98. Subsequent references are cited in the text.

24. See Toby Silverman Zinman, "Sam Shepard and Super-Realism," *Modern Drama* 29.4 (Dec. 1986): 423–30, for a lucid account of popular mythologies and the nature of realism in a number of Shepard's later plays.

25. Sam Shepard, *True West,* in *Seven Plays,* p. 49. Subsequent references are cited in the text.

26. Jean Baudrillard, *Simulations,* trans. Paul Ross, Paul Patton, and Philip Beitchman (New York: Semiotext(e), 1983), pp. 146–47.

27. Sheila Stowell, "Rehabilitating Realism," *Journal of Dramatic Theory and Criticism* 6.2 (Spring 1992): 81–88.

28. See George Levine, *The Realistic Imagination* (Chicago: U of Chicago P, 1981), pp. 4–15, for an excellent account of the repeated cycle of innovative realistic strategies ossifying into stubborn conventions that must themselves be dismantled in the name of realism.

TWO

The Legacy of James A. Herne: American Realities and Realisms

Patricia D. Denison

When James Herne announced in his artistic manifesto the need for a serious American social drama, he was voicing a concern that had been heard before. His manifesto, "Art for Truth's Sake in the Drama" (1897), now considered the central statement of late nineteenth-century American dramatic theory, reflected a century of concern that America was producing too few "native" plays worthy of serious attention. More than fifty years earlier, Anna Mowatt had pointedly declared that homemade dramas should no longer require "the *London* stamp" to succeed.[1] Though many nineteenth-century American dramatists shared her desire for American artistic autonomy, the widespread availability of unprotected plays from abroad encouraged them to appropriate European dramatic texts and theatrical techniques. Not until Dion Boucicault led a campaign for enforceable copyright laws did this widespread borrowing (for which actor/manager Boucicault was himself notorious) gradually cease. And with revised copyright laws came altered performance spaces and shifting cultural contexts, which generated new possibilities toward the end of the century for a specifically American approach to dramatic theory and practice.

Herne's 1897 manifesto offered a new conception of "truth" in the theatre, one that gave priority to realistic rather than melodramatic structures and to natural rather than mannered performance. The contrast Herne draws between "standard" melodramatic drama that merely amuses and realistic drama that "gets to the bottom of a question" provides a reminder that our tendency to equate melodrama with escapism has a long history.[2] But the alternative he advocates of a truthful realism leaves unexplored the complexities implicit in any appeal to truth. As truth always implies being true to some notion or other of what is real or authentic in the world around us, melodrama, and other dramas that "amuse," might well claim to have their own engagement with truth. In effect, Herne's arguments renew interest in the old question of aesthetic truth and its relationship to social truth but in the complicating context of a rapidly changing world, and this leads us, as it led Herne, directly to questions about theatrical change and its relationship to social change in the "new" world ever coming into being in America.

For forty years, Herne was actively involved in the American theatre as a respected actor and playwright. William Dean Howells, renowned novelist, critic, and advocate of American literary realism, described Herne as "a dramatist of remarkable and almost unequalled performance" whose work is "American to the finger-nails."[3] Hamlin Garland, Pulitzer Prize–winning writer, and B. O. (Benjamin Orange) Flower, respected editor of *The Arena,* offered similar ringing endorsements in a Boston circular promoting, as "An American Play without a Soliloquy," Herne's most innovative play, *Margaret Fleming.* Convinced that a "growing number of people to whom melodrama no longer appeals" would welcome "serious studies of American life," they endorsed the play as one that moves toward "an intellectual atmosphere unreached . . . in any other American play."[4] Written in 1890, this "epoch-making"[5] drama of understated yet disruptive social realism provides an exemplary instance of the complicated interaction of aesthetic theory and dramatic practice in nineteenth-century theatre.

"Realism" is, of course, an elusive category with ever shifting boundaries and a complex relationship to its own legacy. Herne's realism, however, takes the form of a social drama that provocatively examines the nature of human rights, responsibilities, and relationships. His work, often compared to Ibsen's, compels audiences to confront the contingent nature of cultural constructs, often including the oppressive constraints of gender configurations. But his realism is not one that rejects theatrical convention. In spite of Herne's unkind words about melodrama, his attempts to display "truth" and "humanity" in a new realism involve him in a recurring struggle to reconcile the competing claims of social realities and melodramatic structures. And it is Herne's legacy, in particular, that affects the subsequent development of twentieth-century American drama.

Just as twentieth-century drama is more fully understood when situated in the context of nineteenth-century conventions which it both replicated and replaced, so too is Herne's work more fully appreciated when situated in the context of the cultural standards and theatrical conventions from which it emerged. Herne began his life in the theatre in 1859, and later described that time in enthusiastic terms: "Twenty years old—an actor and six dollars a week—why I had reached the summit of earthly bliss."[6] However, this reaction was not shared by his father, whose response to his son's leaving factory work for the stage was somewhat different. His remark, "The fools are not all dead yet,"[7] spoke of a not uncommon attitude in mid-nineteenth-century America toward theatre folk, who were widely regarded as vagabonds wandering on the margins of society. Herne's efforts to reform the theatre were thus aimed at changing not only its dramatic focus but also its social function and status. And this involved him in a steady expansion of his theatrical responsibilities. Young Herne began as a "general utility" in the theatre, playing minor roles and gaining considerable practical knowledge while working at such theatres as the Adelphi, Troy; the Gayety, Albany; the Holliday Street, Baltimore; Ford's, Washington, D.C.; and at a variety of performing spaces on cross-country tours. By 1869, however, he was stage manager of the New York Grand Opera House and then stage director of the Baldwin Theatre, San Francisco, with its illustrious company which included James O'Neill. And there he met a young actor, Katharine Corcoran, whom he wed in 1878, and who would be his lifelong partner in personal and professional endeavors.

His successful playwriting career began a year later in San Francisco as he collaborated with the young David Belasco on *Hearts of Oak*. That highly popular play was widely regarded as registering the general movement in American drama from melodramatic spectacle toward realistic presentation that was to prove so crucial to Herne's career. The play includes a real baby and real supper onstage and nothing as melodramatic as a stage villain. Herne's early plays continued to blend romantic extravaganza and prosaic detail, but in his later work he seeks increasingly to develop a restrained and detailed realism. The transition was a subtle one, however, as both Herne and American theatre in general were struggling to find a balance between old and new. Herne continued, for example, to admire the considerable talents of the older generation of actors, like Edwin Forrest and Edwin Booth, with whom he had worked, but his pursuit of a greater realism drove him, as playwright and manager, to replace the old "star system" with a less histrionic and more subtle ensemble playing.

The move toward ensemble playing marked an important change in the organization and presentation of American theatre, and Herne soon stood at the forefront of late nineteenth-century dramatists and theatre practitioners who were moving in this direction. Seeking to reduce conventional reliance on large spectacle, histrionic gesture, strong curtains, stock scenes, and type characters, they gave greater emphasis to local detail, subtle exchange, quiet curtains, intimate settings, and psychologically complex characters. And Herne's search for a new dramatic method included not just new features but a new conception of how these various features were related. A special July 4, 1900, "James A. Herne Edition" of the *Sag Harbor Pilot* indicated the importance of this effort: "Mr. Herne is the apostle of realism. . . . He regards not only the *individual* but the *class* in his portrayals; not only the class but its *environment*" (my emphasis).[8] It is just this combination of individual psychology and cultural enquiry that made *Margaret Fleming* his most controversial play. But the exploration of such social realities runs right through his celebrated and less-celebrated work.

In 1890s America, it was, as Herne ruefully acknowledged in "Art for Truth's Sake in the Drama," "pretty hard work to get a hearing" (p. 3)[9] for innovative plays. But he was a risk taker, as evidenced by his constant experimentation with dramatic structure and his recurring examination of social conventions, particularly those of small New England towns. His first successful play, *Hearts of Oak* (1879), moves away from large-scale spectacle toward small-scale presentation in a detailed study of the whaling village of Marblehead, Massachusetts. *The Minute Men of 1774–75* (1886) reconstructs a famous historical moment, Paul Revere's ride and the battles of Lexington and Concord. *Drifting Apart* (1881) is populated by Gloucester fishermen and addresses the issue of temperance. Then comes *Margaret Fleming* (1890) with its exploration of gender and class in Canton, a Massachusetts mill town, followed by *Shore Acres* (1892), a study of family conflict and land speculation along the Maine coast. *The Reverend Griffith Davenport* (1899) returns to another historical moment, the Civil War and the problematics of slavery. Herne's final play, *Sag Harbor* (1899), takes us full circle in certain respects, for it began as a reworking of *Hearts of Oak*. The location has shifted, though, from a small fishing village in Massachusetts to one in New York, not far from Southampton, Long Island, where Herne and his family settled.

Though a determined innovator in theatrical practice, Herne openly acknowledges his own dramatic legacy in "Art for Truth's Sake in the Drama." There he gives particular credit to Boucicault and Dickens: Boucicault for his skill at displaying the "common things of life," and Dickens for his talent in creating "representative" characters "full of human sympathy" (pp. 5–6). It may, at first glance, seem rather odd that Herne, reputed to be an "American Ibsen" and "apostle of realism," would choose to emulate Boucicault and Dickens, both of whom rely strongly upon melodramatic structures and high sentimentality in their work. As we have noted, Herne often attacked melodrama and regarded it as deplorably old-fashioned: "Seen under the analytical microscope, it [melodrama] is false to almost every aspect and color of life. . . . Like crimps and crinoline, or the different stock tie of our periwig-pated grand parents, the melodrama has outlived its usefulness."[10] But dramatic fashions, not unlike clothing fashions such as crinolines, are often adopted and adapted as they move from one generation to the next, and from one country to another. In spite of their iconoclastic attitudes, both Ibsen and Herne developed their theatrical skills as stage managers of theatres producing numerous melodramas and well-made plays, and this early experience left its mark on their work. For both playwrights, subsequent innovation became less a matter of repudiating the old than of reconfiguring it in order to create anew. And it was a similar kind of refashioning that enabled Herne to use the "representative" characters of Dickens's novels as models from which he would create new character studies in the American theatre. Herne insisted in "Art for Truth's Sake" that reading Dickens's novels and acting in their stage adaptations "helped materially in [his] dramatic development" (p. 5).

This amalgam of the old and the new in Herne's plays has, not surprisingly, prompted wide-ranging critical response that is as mixed in the twentieth century as it was in his day. His contemporaries generally applauded, although some derided, his experimental dramatic techniques. William Dean Howells praised *Margaret Fleming* as "wholly and perfectly true in our conditions" and with "the same searching moral vitality as Ibsen's best work."[11] Hamlin Garland described the play in similar terms: "Without question it was the most naturalistic, the most colloquial, and the most truthful presentation of a domestic drama ever seen on the American stage up to that time."[12] The *New York Spirit of the Times* reviewer, on the other hand, asked, "When is this Ibsenism nonsense to stop, and how many more otherwise respectable people are to be infected by it?"[13] Ibsen was the natural point of reference for those wishing to compare American and continental drama, for a volume of his plays had just been translated and a matinee performance of *A Doll's House* had been presented. And it was the case with both playwrights that their innovations were more apparent to their contemporaries than was their reliance upon conventions, while later audiences and critics have tended to see more clearly the conventional components. The controversy surrounding the work of both playwrights, however, fed directly into debate about the need for an independent American theatre, for the conventions Herne was alternately rejecting and adapting were those of the European melodrama. Arguments about dramatic structure, stage management, and performance space thus involved competing social visions of "old" European worlds and their relationship to the "new" American world in the making at the turn of the century.

If we acknowledge that America's sense of its own reality is, and was from the outset, contested, then we can see why the sense of "truth" in Herne's artistic manifesto might implicitly be multiple and why the aesthetic and cultural truths in *Margaret Fleming* were so disruptive, both in the 1890s and, despite their melodramatic overtones, to this day. Set in the local domain of marital relations in a Massachusetts mill town, the play explores controversial gender configurations and class relations. Herne's work, which was renowned in general for psychologically complex characters rather than formulaic plot mechanics, firmly grounds the "truth" of character, as he notes in "Art for Truth's Sake," in its thickly textured, "peculiar social condition" (p. 3). But it is important to note that social constructs like class and gender function in *Margaret Fleming* not as governing factors but as guiding ones, and whenever the issue of determinism arises, it is raised not to be validated but to be questioned. As Herne reminds us, truth is often "ugly, or at least is not always beautiful," but it is also clear that for Herne it was not finally fixed. In this respect, his work is not a mere imitation of continental naturalism, with its recurring emphasis on the deterministic and disagreeable. "In expressing a truth through art," Herne writes, "it should be borne in mind that *selection* is an important principle. If a disagreeable truth is not also an essential, it should not be used in art" (p. 2). In such a comment, Herne both affirms his commitment to realism and complicates its relationship to social reality. If "essential" realism relies upon aesthetic choosing, we might well wish to enquire about Herne's principle of selection.

A reexamination of *Margaret Fleming* may clarify the kind of "truth" that Herne explored in his drama, and its implications for American theatre history. As the play begins, we meet Philip Fleming, a seemingly carefree and prosperous mill owner, and Margaret Fleming, an elegant and spirited woman, who are celebrating the birthday of their baby daughter, Lucy. The opening set, with family portraits—those of Philip's wife, baby, and father—displayed in the mill office, serves to remind us that Philip's motto, "Live and let live,"[14] governs not only business affairs but family affairs, not only his public life but also his private life. And when Philip faults his old foreman, who *"chew[s] tobacco and speaks with a quick, sharp New England accent,"* for his "poor economy," the audience wonders what kinds of economies will replace the old and in what contexts (pp. 221–22). Such questions are prompted by the closely detailed, thick description in a play that foregrounds intricate social relationships in the town and daily interaction at the mill. We share the characters' concern for the minute details of their daily life, such as the need to replace the main supply belt in the finishing room and the reliance upon a "fast express" either from the Harry Smith Company, New York, or the "Boston people," White and Cross (p. 230). But even as we recognize Philip Fleming's eagerness to take care of such details, we discover that his diligence may be too late, for the Cotton Exchange Bank is threatening to call in its loans on his family-owned business.

Philip, it turns out, is living on credit in more ways than one. When Doctor Larkin, the traditional *raisonneur,* enters and says to him, *"(Hotly.)* I used to respect you" (p. 227), the play moves from the realm of financial balances to that of moral reckonings. Philip's good-natured banter ceases abruptly when Doctor Larkin announces that he has just returned from the bedside of a young woman who, having refused Philip's money for an abortion, has given birth to his child and now lies near death. When the doctor insists that Philip behave honorably and visit the dying woman, he rushes off to what he describes to his wife as a "business engagement" (p. 229). The high drama of the opening scene ends not with a spectacular melodramatic tableau but with a quiet curtain, as Philip *"while sunk in deep thought . . . takes his umbrella and hat and goes out quietly, shutting the door so that the click of the latch is heard, as the curtain falls"* (p. 230). And the audience, like Philip, readies itself for "deep thought" rather than light entertainment, as the full impact of Herne's stagecraft is subtly but firmly established.

Just as Herne's play challenges the audience to think deeply about the nature of personal responsibility and cultural conventions, his manifesto phrase, "art for truth's sake in the drama," serves as shorthand for similarly complicated aesthetic issues. As Herne himself points out, careful attention must be paid to every dramatist's "selection" of representative truths. Herne reveals some of his own principles of selection when he calls for a new American drama that "gets to the bottom of a question" by striking at "unequal standards and unjust systems" (p. 9). Here aesthetic truths become openly intertwined with cultural truths, dramatic agenda with social agenda, aesthetic theory with social practice. In *Margaret Fleming*, it is no accident that Lena Schmidt, the young woman, who dies soon after giving birth to Philip's child, is of a different social class than the father of their child. Philip has had affairs with "so many [mill] girls," but he would never consider marrying "out'n the mill" (pp. 224–25). Like many impoverished young women of immigrant status who worked in nineteenth-century industrial settings, Lena risked financial and sexual exploitation when she met her "boss." This is the kind of ugly truth that American drama had generally avoided, and Herne thought the costs of such avoidance were high, as he notes in "Art for Truth's Sake": "It is not sufficient that the subject [of a play] be attractive or beautiful or that it does not offend. It must first of all express some large truth. That is to say, it must always be representative" (p. 2). But rather than taking the "representative" in Herne's work as given, one must also ask, representative of what, for whom, and for what purpose? To what extent can the realist's fascination with minute details be reconciled with the goal of expressing some large representative truth when the society to be represented is itself complex and changing?

The relationship between Herne's aesthetic theories and his dramatic practice directs attention to local contexts in which large cultural values are not so much given as contested. Consequently, the representative can prove to be not so much a descriptive inevitability as a prescriptive necessity for those seeking to shape a society in flux. When the raisonneur, Doctor Larkin, prescribes cures for the physical ills of individual patients, they seem rather oddly to be intended for society as a whole. And when he voices outrage at Philip and his affair, it is again in terms of the representative status of the people he selects for attention:

> *Doctor:* God Almighty! If we can't look for decency in men like you [Philip]—representative men—where in God's name are we to look for it, I'd like to know? (pp. 228–29)

For the doctor, the word *representative* gives the local instance a larger social status, but it is not so much a claim for universality as it is a claim for historical necessity; not so much a claim that Philip can stand for all people all of the time in all places but that he has representative status for the "we" who occupy a particular historical time and social space. The "truth" of everyday commonplaces is thus revealed as contestable, and the tensions that surround it permeate the action, linking various social groups, times, and places. Philip, a "rich man" in the new world, is accorded deferential, and grudging, respect by recent immigrants from "de olt country," whose very presence speaks of unbridged social difference (p. 232). The picture of his father and even a picture of the mill itself, prominently displayed in the opening set, remind the audience that Philip is not just working for material interests but has inherited the rights and responsibilities of a family business functioning in a larger social sphere. And in "New" England, just over a century old and still very much in-the-making, the relationship between such rights and responsibilities is still very much open to question. In dealing with his wife and his lover, for example, Philip seems to have two quite different standards. As Philip points out, his wife Margaret shares his continuing social status and social rights, while Lena (the first-generation, German working-class woman he seduced) belongs to a past period of "foolishness," the conclusion of which terminates whatever brief rights she enjoyed:

> *Philip:* I've sowed my wild oats. . . .
> *Joe:* Ye've turned over a new leaf, eh?
> *Philip:* Yes—married. . . . and got a baby.
> *Joe:* Thet so! Did ye marry out'n the mill?
> *Philip:* Oh no. She was a Miss Thorp, of Niagara. (p. 224)

Describing his wife as "more than I deserve," Philip "*becomes serious for the first time and a shadow flits over his face.*" And at this point, detailed realistic presentation reverts intriguingly to old-fashioned melodramatic declamation: "If my wife left me," declares Philip, "I'd kill myself" (p. 225).

This shift in technique serves as a classic instance of Herne both selecting from and transforming the dramatic legacy he inherited. European dramatic conventions dictate that in domestic melodramas, courtesan and magdalen plays, and formulaic well-made plays, it is the woman, such as Dumas *fils*'s Camille Marguerite, who dies at the end—usually with a broken heart, at times aided by consumption, and most often by her own hand. In *Margaret Fleming*, though, we have, as Philip's sudden declamation suggests, a surprising gender reversal. It is not a hysterical, fallen "woman with a past" but rather a philandering husband with a profligate past who threatens, and later attempts, suicide.[15] Thus without entirely discarding the melodramatic conventions he inherited, Herne alters their gender configurations—thereby reshaping theatrical modes in order to complicate social norms. Philip becomes, in effect, the victim of social responsibilities he had not fully recognized, and with the recognition comes a self-condemnation both morally justifiable and socially and theatrically surprising. But the point of the gender reversal is not just to surprise the audience about Philip but also to open up new space within which Margaret can begin to function.

It has become a critical commonplace to note that the play exposes the conventional wisdom of the time regarding double standards of sexual morality.[16] When, in the final act, Margaret directly asks her profligate husband, "Suppose—I—had been unfaithful to you?" he responds with *"a cry of repugnance"* (pp. 264–65). And in his artistic manifesto, Herne openly acknowledges the social agenda of the play and even admits that the play was "didactic in places" (p. 7). But in light of Herne's reputation as an early realist, it is important to note that when moral certainties are invoked, they tend to emerge less from Margaret's personal pain than from Doctor Larkin's recurring attempts to tend to the physical and spiritual ills of a society in a state of flux. And what ultimately gives Herne's perspective on the double standard its power and persuasiveness is its location in a context in which standards of various kinds for various groups are persistently in conflict. In such a context any attempt to assert a single standard, new or old, will seem trite and melodramatic:

> *Doctor:* I know just what brutes such men as you are. . . . The girl's not to blame. She's a product of her environment. Under present social conditions, she'd probably have gone wrong anyhow. But you! God Almighty! . . . It is just such damn scoundrels as you that make and destroy homes.
> *Philip:* Oh, come now, doctor, aren't you a little severe?
> *Doctor:* Severe! Severe! Why, do you realize, if this thing should become known, it will stir up a stench that will offend the moral sense of every man, woman and child in this community?
> (pp. 228–29)

These melodramatic, moralistic denunciations, rather than being, as some have suggested, a failing of the play, are instead integral to its internal dynamics—for they raise in cruder form central issues that are then carefully reexamined, not simply casually reinforced. Larkin's large, broad-brushed moralistic judgments and his globalizing determinism, though unconventionally directed at the erring man rather than the erring woman, provide a necessary backdrop against which the particularized, detailed, "powerful but savage truth"—as Herne himself describes the situation in "Art for Truth's Sake" (p. 7)—of the play gains its power.

Many late nineteenth-century American audiences, accustomed to the schematic certainties of conventional melodrama[17] and the conventional judgments of raisonneurs in well-made plays, were highly startled by the "powerful but savage" truth of a play making a polemical and controversial point about male sexual responsibility.

Others, though, were just as intrigued by Herne's new mode of dramatic enquiry and its techniques for situating rather than merely embellishing the pronouncements of its raisonneur. But Herne was right to anticipate the difficulty of getting novelty of any kind on the stage. After premiering in Lynn, Massachusetts, *Margaret Fleming* was staged in Chickering Hall, Boston, because no traditional theatre space in New York or Boston would put on Herne's controversial work. Nevertheless, the play soon became, according to Howells, "the talk of the whole city wherever cultivated people met."[18] "On a stage of planking, hung with drapery," wrote Garland, "was produced one of the most radical plays from a native author ever performed in America."[19] Ironically, this transformed performance space, usually reserved for piano recitals, promoted just the kind of intimacy needed for small-scale realism onstage. The theatre, albeit makeshift, was of the type for which Herne had campaigned: "a new class of theatres . . . parlor-like places, where the audience is brought into intimate relations with the stage."[20] In such a space, plays could be performed that raise more questions than are answered. And, in *Margaret Fleming*, it is, finally, the unsettling questions posed by Margaret's behavior rather than Philip's melodramatic gestures or Larkin's definitive statements that leave a lasting impression.

In the climactic act three, Margaret leaves her elegant home to visit a modest cottage where, unknown to her, the mother of Philip's child has just died. As the curtain closes, *"she unbuttons her dress to give nourishment"* not to her baby but to the crying infant belonging to Philip and Lena (p. 260). Puritan reviewers found the scene sensational, not only for the nearly bared breast but for Margaret's decision to nurse her husband's child by another woman. The stage picture, both quiet and powerful, recalls our first image of Margaret in act one; there the curtain rises with Margaret singing a lullaby and fastening *"the last two or three buttons of her dress"* (p. 231). But the differences, as the puritanical responses suggest, are as important as the similarities between the pictures. In act four, Margaret draws attention to the similarities between these pictures when she speaks, in romantic, idealized terms, of motherhood as "a divine thing" that transcends all contexts (p. 266). But it would be a mistake to regard her solely as a saintly maternal figure, just as it would be a mistake to classify her solely as a melodramatic heroine, as one whose "total goodness and

extreme weakness" provide the "emotional center of the melodrama."[21] To portray her in terms of these black and white dualities,
of the medieval Vice-versus-Virtue schemata found so often in nineteenth-century melodramas, is to overlook Herne's repeated attempts
to achieve his detailed realism by displaying motherhood, families,
and social relationships in a variety of contexts. And to essentialize
her nature thus is to fail to relate her to the multiple social standards
and shifting theatrical modes evoked by the play.

There is clearly more and other to Margaret Fleming than first appears, and that is most evident in the reconfiguration in an ensemble
context of the didactic raisonneur. This is not a conventional, Scribean
well-made play in which the ending is predicted by a single raisonneur who speaks confidently to and for a social consensus. In the pivotal act three Doctor Larkin is replaced by his patient Margaret, whose
eyes, though growing weak, see more clearly than his do, and whose
voice, though much less certain, competes with his for authority.
Gradually she has come to recognize, and to voice, the competing
demands that social life places on individuals. In a startling turn of
events, Margaret acknowledges that she loves not only her husband
but also, in a different way, the physician who brought her child into
the world, and this acknowledgment of divided allegiances leads directly to her announcement that she will henceforth take responsibility for her own decisions:

> *Margaret:* I love you—I have always obeyed your orders haven't I?
> (*She speaks brokenly.*)
> *Doctor:* (*Quietly.*) Always.
> *Margaret:* Then, let me be the doctor now, and I order you to
> leave this house at once.
> *Doctor:* (*Hopelessly.*) You are determined to do this thing?
> *Margaret:* (*With finality.*) Yes. (p. 258)

Determined, in fact, to confront her husband directly and to disregard
the doctor's advice, Margaret is seeking to establish her own balance
between competing rights and responsibilities. In the final act the
doctor and her husband, after his failed suicide, return. But in this
play about social change, decision making is now clearly in the hands
of someone who is herself changing. In both the published version
and the performed versions of the play, Margaret announces that her

relationship with Philip is inescapably altered. In the published version, Margaret gives Philip the chance to earn her respect anew, but in the original version, reconciliation seems unlikely.[22]

What matters, however, is not that there are alternate endings, but that in both endings it is Margaret, the character exhibiting a capacity to adapt to changing circumstances, who is firmly in control of events. When she announces that the "wife-heart has gone out" of her, Philip admits that he had "never realized before, the iniquity—of [his]—behavior" (pp. 264–65). When she tells the amazed Philip that she intends to raise his child by Lena, she asks him to accept the responsibility that he earlier denied: "to make atonement for the wrong you did his mother. You must teach him [the child] never to be ashamed of her" (p. 266). Displaying magnanimity and compassion, Margaret is concerned less for her husband's betrayal of herself than for his mistreatment of Lena and their son. She poignantly draws attention through this particular "iniquity" (p. 265) to the general inequity of "unequal standards and unjust systems" (Herne's phrase in "Art for Truth's Sake" [p. 9]), to the double standard on gender issues being only intensified by prejudices based on class. In doing so, she herself becomes one of those new representative examples by means of which Herne sought to change both American drama and American society.

Few, onstage or offstage, wished, however, to face the unpleasant truths Margaret confronts, but when she insists that there is nothing to forgive, she does so not as a conventionally selfless wife but as an increasingly knowledgeable social critic who realizes, in ways that Philip had failed to realize, the reciprocal relationship between social rights and social responsibilities. When Margaret says it is "not a question of forgetting, or of forgiving" (p. 264), she recognizes that a simple act of forgiveness would facilitate the process of everyone forgetting everything of importance to be learned from his negative example. What Margaret finally offers Philip, and the audience, is not a large, simplifying and summarizing image of the "true" wife and mother to cover all cases for all times but a local, historically situated, complicated instance of one person's adjustment to changing social circumstances. It is important that Doctor Larkin, quick to learn from her example, turns from outrage at the "representative" behavior of Philip to admiration of Margaret as a case upon whom others may, in future, model themselves—adopting and adapting as they see fit:

> *Doctor:* And this world needs just such women as you.
> *Margaret:* What does the world know or care about me? (*The bell rings and the door opens and shuts.*)
> *Doctor:* Very little, but it's got to feel your influence. (pp. 261–62)

The difference between a model to be replicated and a model to be emulated is a difference that allows future generations to be guided by the past rather than governed by it, and it is this evolutionary approach to change that finally emerges from the detailed realism of Herne's work.

The play itself moves from Philip's cavalier motto, "Live and let live," to Doctor Larkin's deterministic philosophy of a person as a "product of her environment," to Margaret's growing belief in the self as a maker of his or her "living future" (pp. 221, 228, 266). It moves from Philip's inability to distinguish right from wrong, from Doctor's Larkin's prescriptive certainty about right and wrong, to Margaret's reexamination of the terms as historical categories, moral guidelines, and social constructs. Margaret, as the "New Woman" of act four, refuses to be fixed by past events but allows, instead, for both her own and other people's future change and growth. Philip's past will surely remain part of him, but whether or not it will be perceived as the decisive part of him will depend on his future actions and on Margaret's response to them. Unlike Doctor Larkin, who believed that one's environment determined one's future, Margaret works to shape her environment rather than let others determine it. Old gender stereotypes may shift, albeit all too gradually, from an era of double standards to one of flexible and multiple standards, but the new social order Margaret envisages might well include an enlightened Philip, an operation to recover her eyesight, and a Doctor Larkin who advises on medical matters and leaves cultural diagnosis to others who see the world not in prescriptive terms but from multiple perspectives. As the final curtain closes, Philip asks for his daughter, Lucy, and Margaret indicates that both his children are in the garden: "PHILIP *goes quickly to the door opening upon the garden and gazes out eagerly. . . . [*MARGARET's*] eyes look into the darkness and a serene joy illuminates her face. The picture slowly fades out as* PHILIP *steps buoyantly into the garden*" (p. 268).

Here, in this final stage picture, the tableau stands not as a diagram of moralistic certainty but as an emblem of potentially successful change, of the emergence of a New Eden in New England. The "truth" advocated in "Art for Truth's Sake in the Drama" and displayed in *Margaret Fleming* is one that details not just "unequal standards and unjust systems" (p. 9) but also the possibilities for regenerative reconfiguration of moral standards and systems in late nineteenth-century America. Herne, as an advocate of change in society and in the theatre, proclaimed that if an artist "must choose between giving offense and receding from his position, he should stand by his principle and state his truth fearlessly" (p. 9). This revolutionary aspect of his art is couched, however, in evolutionary practice. In the dramatic structure of *Margaret Fleming,* bits of high melodrama and light entertainment—such as tipsy Joe Fletcher being tossed through a window by his angry wife, Maria, who draws a pistol when she discovers the seducer of her younger sister, and Margaret becoming blind as a consequence of childbirth and her husband's betrayal—intermingle in a daring drama that also looks to the future and seeks to establish new models for emulation. In terms of its wider social structure, the play refuses to make large definitive moral judgments, as a melodrama traditionally would, for to do so would be to endorse contemporary cultural convictions whose temporary historical prominence needs to be clearly displayed. In a world that has "got to feel [Margaret's] influence," much is still to be learned and much still needs to be done (p. 262).

Herne's influence, not unlike Margaret's, remains with us. His obituary headline in the *New York Herald* (June 3, 1901) draws a fitting analogy between his own character and his dramatic characters: "Rich in Human Sympathy, the Characters He Preferred Were of the Same Nature."[23] His detailed "realism," with its focus on the complex local instance as a means of promoting larger social change, is pivotal to the more general problematics of America's attempt to construct a new world, onstage and offstage. These problematics, which have been well explored by others, focus, as does Margaret's development as a character, primarily on the new country's relationship to its past. For those seeking to establish a characteristically American society, one impulse was to reject the European past and to start again—a procedure that raised the question of whether starting all over again was a one-time occurrence or a constantly recurring process. If the latter were the case, then it would become difficult to characterize America in stable terms or to provide America or Americans with durable roots. If the former were the case, then the danger of producing a repressive past could recur. Another alternative would be to avoid rejecting the past entirely and instead to select from it anew. This would allow the new world to select the most positive parts of the recent European past while rejecting the negative parts, but it would raise the questions raised by Herne's selective realism about who would make those selections and how. Yet another option would be to seek to recover forms of humanity not necessarily European at all, but those that might have existed before large-scale societies debased the human qualities that characterized life in the garden of Eden. Debates over whether America should be a new world without a past, a New England with parts of Europe's past renewed, or a New Eden in which parts of humanity's lost past are revived make it evident that from the outset America's sense of its own reality was contested and that its own sense of truth was inherently multiple.

If we bear in mind the contested nature of American social reality, and if we recall the issue of "representativeness" raised both in Herne's aesthetic theory and in his dramatic practice, it is easy enough to see an analogy between contrasting views of American culture and contrasting forms of American drama. The new drama for the new country could be a new drama relying on radically new dramatic forms, or a new drama based selectively on renewed European models, or a new mythic drama attempting to recover the latent characteristics of transhistorical humanity. As has been noted, American nineteenth-century dramatists tended, by and large, to select the middle option: that of adopting and adapting the conventions of European drama. They modeled upon and reshaped comedies of manners, formulaic well-made plays, heroic dramas, sentimental romances, domestic melodramas, and sensational extravaganzas. But what is not so frequently noted is the evolving relationship between convention and invention that enabled someone like Herne to engage in the radical reshaping of conventionally formulaic plays. The recurring tension in the drama between the formulaic patterns and the competing possibilities in effect registers the tension in American society about America's past, its future, and its nature. The social and dramatic complexities of Herne's nineteenth-century realism continue to trouble us a full century later.

Notes

1. Anna Cora Mowatt, *Fashion,* in *Nineteenth-Century American Plays,* ed. Myron Matlaw (New York: Applause Theatre Book Publishers, 1985), p. 31.

2. James A. Herne, "Art for Truth's Sake in the Drama," *The Arena* 17 (Feb. 1897): 361–70. Rpt. in Alan S. Downer, *American Drama and Its Critics* (Chicago: U of Chicago P, 1965), pp. 3–9. Subsequent references correspond to Downer and are cited in the text.

3. William Dean Howells, "Editor's Study," *Harper's Monthly* 83 (Aug. 1891): 477–79. Qtd. in Brenda Murphy, *A Realist in the American Theatre: Selected Drama Criticism of William Dean Howells* (Athens: Ohio UP, 1992), p. 54.

4. Qtd. in John Perry, *James A. Herne: The American Ibsen* (Chicago: Nelson-Hall, 1978), pp. 151–52.

5. B. O. Flower, "An Epoch-Making Drama," *The Arena* 4 (1891): 247. In "Art for Truth's Sake in the Drama," Herne refers to William Dean Howells's description of the play as "epoch-*making,*" but Hamlin Garland (*Boston Post* [May 12, 1891]) and others use "epoch-making."

6. James A. Herne, "Old Stock Days in the Theatre," *The Arena* 6 (Sept. 1892): 402.

7. Qtd. in Julie A. Herne, "Biographical Note," in James A. Herne, *Shore Acres and Other Plays* (New York: Samuel French, 1928), p. xii.

8. *Sag Harbor Pilot* 2.1 (July 4, 1900): 2.

9. McConachie focuses on the "hegemony of the American bourgeoisie" and attributes Herne's difficulties in getting *Margaret Fleming* produced to the "pervasiveness of business-class ideology in the theatre by the 1890s" (Bruce McConachie, *Melodramatic Formations: American Theatre and Society, 1820–1870* [Iowa City: Iowa UP, 1992] p. 256).

10. New York Public Library of the Performing Arts, Lincoln Center, New York, James A. Herne Clipping File, undated.

11. Qtd. in Julie A. Herne, "James A. Herne: Actor and Dramatist," Herbert J. Edwards Collection (unpublished), Orono: University of Maine, undated, p. 313.

12. Hamlin Garland, "On The Road with James A. Herne," *Century Magazine* (Aug. 1914): 578.

13. Review of *Margaret Fleming, New York Spirit of the Times* (May 9, 1891).

14. James A. Herne, *Margaret Fleming,* in *Nineteenth-Century American Plays,* ed. Myron Matlaw (New York: Applause Theatre Book Publishers, 1985), p. 221. Subsequent references are cited in the text.

15. The resistance from theatre managers unwilling to risk controversy was as prevalent in Europe as in America during the same period. The year before *Margaret Fleming* opened in Lynn, Massachusetts, Arthur Pinero's *The Profligate*

opened in London at the Garrick Theatre. The play caused considerable controversy because of the ending in which the profligate husband commits suicide by taking an overdose of morphine. Because of theatre manager John Hare's fear that audiences would find the ending too strong, Pinero agreed to change the performed ending to one of reconciliation but insisted in retaining the original ending in the published version.

16. Brenda Murphy, *American Realism and American Drama, 1880–1940* (Cambridge: Cambridge UP, 1987), p. 13.

17. Herne, "Art for Truth's Sake in the Drama," p. 3.

18. Howells, "Editor's Study," p. 479.

19. Hamlin Garland, "The Future of Fiction," *The Arena* 7 (April 1893): 543.

20. Qtd. in Perry, *James A. Herne*, p. 150.

21. David Grimsted, *Melodrama Unveiled: American Theatre and Culture 1800–1850* (Berkeley: U of California P, 1968), p. 175.

22. Herne, who often reshaped his plays, rewrote the final act for the 1892 McVicker's Theatre production, but neither this version nor the original is extant. Katharine Corcoran Herne, Herne's wife and collaborator who played the original Margaret Fleming, reconstructed the play in 1914 after a fire in the Hernes' Southampton home destroyed the manuscripts.

23. New York Public Library of the Performing Arts, Lincoln Center, James A. Herne Clipping File MWE2.

THREE

Whose Realism? Rachel Crothers's Power Struggle in the American Theatre

Yvonne Shafer

Rachel Crothers was an active figure in the early twentieth-century movement toward realism in American playwriting. In her plays, she examined a society that stringently limited opportunities for women. In *A Man's World* (1910), Crothers depicted a career woman who rejects the man she loves because she condemns the double standard that he upholds. Most contemporary male critics attacked the play for a lack of realism; playwright Augustus Thomas even went so far as to write a play, *As a Man Thinks* (1911), in rebuttal. Crothers condemned the status quo through the choice her heroine made, but was her heroine a realistic depiction of American women? Thomas, for one, attacked her views. But by defending the conventional viewpoint and utilizing a conventional, even stale, story line, was Thomas actually depicting his society in a more realistic fashion?

Critics were divided, some describing Crothers's play as dealing with a real issue in a real world of real men and women, while others found her conclusion laughably unrealistic. Most critics praised the reality and depth of Thomas's characterizations, but the critic for *Current Literature* said, "They are theatrical property, not being of flesh and blood."[1] Analysis of the plays will be in terms of contemporary criticism, criticism from a decade later, and the view of a present-day reader. In terms of the development of realism in the American theatre, Crothers's play contributed toward its advancement, whereas

Thomas's play looked to the conventional, stereotypical plays of the past.

In the first decade of the twentieth century, the American theatre was dominated by male playwrights such as Clyde Fitch, David Belasco, Langdon Mitchell, and Augustus Thomas, who wrote popular commercial plays with a veneer of realism. Writing the same type of play was a woman named Martha Morton, who attempted to join the American Dramatists Club, of which Thomas was the president. Turned down because she was a woman, she formed the Society of Dramatic Authors in 1907 with Rachel Crothers as a member. Refusal to admit women to the American Dramatists Club was one of the more obvious forms of discrimination that women playwrights had to face.

Crothers had begun her career as a playwright at the turn of the century.[2] An example of the unconventional approach she often took in her early playwriting is *The Three of Us* (1906). Her heroine, Rhy (note that the name does not indicate gender), is an independent, physically strong woman, somewhat masculine, but very attractive to men. Living in a small Nevada silver town, she finds herself in a compromising position because she has been in a man's room. She defies two men when they insist that they should save her honor, pointing out that her honor is in her own hands. The play was unconventional enough to create a stir, but had a conventional, sentimental ending which was satisfying and reassuring to the conventional theatregoer. At the end Rhy turns to her brother for support and assistance and she marries one of the men she earlier defied. Nevertheless, the role of Rhy is unconventional and at least explores the characterization of the new woman. The play was successful both in New York and on tour. With her first professionally produced full-length play, Crothers attracted positive attention from audiences and critics and indicated her interest in exploring the changing world for women in America.

The changes for women were obvious. As Crothers commented, "If you want to see the signs of the times, watch women. Their evolution is the most important thing in modern life."[3] Although many women were content to fulfill their traditional role, others demanded change. As June Sochen wrote in *The New Feminism*, the new woman was questioning "the typical cultural definition of her role in society": "The new woman was better educated than her mother, more interested in experimenting with life, and ready for a career outside the home. More women were going to college in the 1910s than ever before; further, from the point of view of percentages, more women obtained degrees, especially the Ph.D., in 1920 than ever before or since [15 percent]. Six percent of all the doctors in our country were women in 1910."[4] In addition to these changes, women were working to get the vote and to improve circumstances related to marriage and divorce, and to earn equal pay. As more women entered the work force and attitudes changed, more women sought divorce, independence, and an end to the sexual double standard. Unlike most male playwrights, Crothers reflected these changes in her characterizations of women. As the number of women playwrights increased, a more realistic depiction of the concerns of forward-looking women appeared on the stage.

Crothers's play *Myself Bettina* (1908) was a social drama examining sexuality in relation to American women. The central figure is an unmarried woman who has traveled in Europe, seen life, and had an affair. The play is unusual in that the woman does not commit suicide or die because of her past, but Crothers was moving toward the clarity of theme and construction that appear in *A Man's World*. The play was also important in relation to the changing theatre scene. Maxine Elliott bought the play as a starring vehicle for herself and gave Crothers her first chance to direct a professional production—normally a task taken by a man. It was a major breakthrough in that period. Crothers wrote that Elliott "had such an admiration for and faith in the work of women, that she was delighted to find a woman who could shoulder the entire responsibility."[5]

Although the play was important in its subject matter and because Crothers was given an opportunity to direct it, it was a failure, running only thirty-two performances. Following this unsuccessful play, Crothers might well have chosen to take a conservative course and produce the type of conventional characters and plays that the mass of the audience, including women, preferred. Instead, in *A Man's World*, she wrote a play with controversial subject matter and an ending that did not pander to popular taste. The subjects treated are the double standard, the shame of illegitimacy for the woman and child, and the problems of women of the streets.

In *A Man's World*, as in many of her plays, the leading figure is an attractive, successful woman who feels a conflict between her career

and romance. As Florence Kiper commented in 1914, Crothers's heroine is

> a woman who has made a place for herself as a writer. Her writ-
> ings have been largely directed against the abuses from which
> women suffer in the present social arrangement. She is a type of
> the modern feminist. And the conflict of the drama is waged not
> so much without as within her own nature, a conflict between
> individual emotion and social conviction. What many of our
> writers for the stage have missed in their objective drama that
> uses the new woman for a protagonist is a glimpse of that tumul-
> tuous battlefield, her own soul, where meet the warring forces of
> impulse and theory, of the old and the new conceptions of ego-
> tism and altruism. Miss Crothers understands the dramatic inter-
> est of such tumult. The heroine of A Man's World [is] a woman
> whose intellectual power has enriched, not devitalized, her emo-
> tional capacity—(why do certain of our dramatists believe femi-
> nine intellect must inevitably devitalize!).[6]

Crothers's heroine is a novelist who goes by the name of Frank Ware
and has been perceived by the critics as a male writer until the day
the play begins. Her identity has been discovered by a male critic who
writes: " 'The Beaten Path' is the strongest thing that Frank Ware has
ever done. Her first work attracted wide attention when we tho't
Frank Ware was a man, but now that we know she is a woman we
are more than ever impressed by the strength and scope of her work."[7]
With this review, Crothers imitated the male critics whose real reviews often took this condescending tone when praising the works
she and other women playwrights had written.

Like many other women playwrights, such as Susan Glaspell and
Alice Gerstenberg, Crothers was well educated and intelligent, and
through her work became financially independent. In Frank Ware,
Crothers created a character with these same qualities. Her heroine is
an example of a woman who thinks for herself and pursues her goals
with freedom. She leads a decidedly bohemian life, free from any dic-
tation of personal or professional behavior from a man. Her father was
a writer who wanted her to see all sides of life and judge actions independently of conventional wisdom. In this Crothers illustrates a
point of great concern to feminists of the day: a change in American

educational methods. As Sochen has written, "The expansion of woman's roles was tied to another element in the feminist ideology: the re-education of roles in childhood. The new attitude toward women would begin by retraining all children according to the emancipated values of feminism. Crystal Eastman said that, 'it must be manly as well as womanly to know how to cook and sew and clean and take care of yourself in the ordinary exigencies of life.' No role ought to be regarded as solely a feminine role. It should not be womanly to cry when deeply moved, and manly to repress one's tears. It should not be womanly to change a baby's diaper and manly to refuse to do it."[8]

Crothers expresses similar views in explaining her protagonist's background. Her father played the maternal and fraternal roles because her mother had died, and he treated her no differently than he would have treated a son. Frank says, "Natural? Surely, I am nothing but natural. I'm a natural woman—because I've been a free one. Living alone with my father all those years made me so. He took me with him every possible place. . . . Dad wanted me to see—to know—to touch all kinds of life—and I surely did. He developed all his stories by telling them aloud to me. He used to walk up and down the library and talk out his characters. So I began to balance men and women very early—and the more I knew—the more I thought the women had the worst of it" (pp. 34–35).

Her upbringing has led Frank to feel concern for women who, unlike herself, are not independent; women who have had romances and possibly illegitimate children, and are considered "fallen women" by society. Unconcerned about other people's attitudes, she has adopted a child whose mother suffered in this way, and she has a deep hatred for the unknown man who seduced the woman and fathered her child. This feeling goes to the heart of the double standard: he is not blamed, but she died in disgrace, and had she lived, rejection by her family and friends would probably have caused her to become a prostitute as she had no other means of earning. A respectable man would not have married the woman in the case, but a respectable woman is supposed to overlook the man's actions.

The only major weakness in the construction of the play is that the long arm of coincidence figures heavily: the man Frank has come to love turns out to be the father of her adopted child.[9] Frank has resisted love because she wanted independence and because she has felt a bitterness toward men, particularly Kiddie's unknown father. She tells another woman, "Every time I see a girl who's made a mess of her life because she loved a man, I think of Kiddie's poor mother, with the whole burden and disgrace of it—and the man Scott free" (p. 93).

Despite this feeling, Frank has fallen in love with a newspaper writer, Malcolm Gaskell. He represents all that is powerful and respectable in society, in contrast to Frank and her struggling artistic friends. Gaskell can put in a word in the right place and see that a book is reviewed, a musician is hired, or an artist has an exhibition. One of Frank's friends says, "Why the devil won't she marry him? I tell you Malcolm Gaskell's going to be a big man some day. He's got the grip on this newspaper all right, all right, and he's not going to let go till he's got a darned good thing" (pp. 13–14). Gaskell is confident of his power and confident that men are superior to women. He would like to marry Frank, but she seems to put him off, and, more importantly, he fears that she may be the natural mother of her "adopted" child. In an effective scene Crothers dramatizes the differences between Frank and Gaskell. Gaskell says he had thought that she did not mean half of what she said, that she was only talking about ideals, not reality:

> *Gaskell:* I never thought before that you actually believed that things ought to be—the same—for men and women.
> *Frank:* No,—I know you didn't.
> *Gaskell:* But I see that you believe it so deeply that you think it's a thing to go by—live by.
> *Frank:* Of course.
> *Gaskell:* You couldn't get far by it.
> *Frank:* Not far. No. You wouldn't have asked me to marry you— if Kiddie had been my own child.
> *Gaskell:* Oh, I don't—I—I love you. I want you. But when I knew he was not—the greatest change came that can come to a man. A radiance went over you. I wanted to kneel at your feet and worship you. That's the way all men feel towards good women and you can't change it. No woman with that in her life could be the same to any man—no matter how he loved her—or what he said or swore. It's different. It's different. A man wants the

mother of his children to be the purest in the world.
Frank: Yes, and a man expects the purest woman in the world to forgive him anything—everything. It's wrong. It's hideously wrong. (pp. 98–99)

The play sets up a basic incompatibility between the two, which would have been resolved by the final scene in a conventional play. But Frank is unwilling to forgive because she knows Gaskell would not have forgiven her. As Eaton put it, "The traditional treatment of the theme is to devise a situation in which the erring man is forgiven by the woman, who then in her turn asks forgiveness, only to be re-fused" (p. 156). Crothers shows a character who loves deeply, but can-not deny her principles and accept Gaskell's conviction that men have the right to behave as they choose, while women do not; that women are not equal and need the protection of men. He makes his outlook clear when he tells Frank, "When you care for a man you won't give a hang for anything you ever believed then. . . . Why this is a man's world. Women'll never change anything. . . . Women are only meant to be loved—and men have got to take care of them. That's the whole business. You'll acknowledge it someday—when you do love some-body" (p. 43).

But at the conclusion of the play, Gaskell is proved wrong; Frank does love him, but she cannot accept his conservative, narrow-minded opinions and she rejects him. He tries to convince her with various arguments, but has no success because he cannot perceive any value in her standards. In the final scene, he says, "Good God, Frank! You're a woman. You talk like a woman—you think like a woman. I'm a man. What do you expect? We don't live under the same laws. It was never meant to be. Nature, nature made men different" (p. 109). The ending reflected the personal experience of Crothers and other women like her in this period. She never married, giving as a reason the fact that superior women had a very narrow field to choose from. She said she had never met "a man who was big enough, strong enough, and intellectual enough who did not also have the vices of those great qualities. Such a man has been taught by millenniums of generously providing for his women folks that his woman should de-pend on him economically and mentally. The superior man will not have the superior woman—not on the superior woman's terms."[10]

Crothers's ending surprised many critics and audience members. Undoubtedly, as in the case of early performances of Ibsen's *A Doll's House*, there were people waiting for the final scene in which the man and the woman were reconciled and the events ended happily. Crothers was clearly playing off the ending of Ibsen's play, but with a difference—the woman tells the man to go, and, unlike Nora, she is financially independent. Another twist was noted by Eaton, who remarked that the revelation of a shameful past leading to separation but ending in forgiveness and reconciliation was all too familiar in plays. As he noted with pleasure, "This is a new twist to the old situation; this is the new woman, indeed; and this, a woman's play, faces the old problem without cant or sentimentality, and lands a good square blow" (p. 157).

But other critics attacked the ending as unrealistic and improbable, agreeing with the attitude expressed by Gaskell early in the play, that Frank did not really believe all she was saying, that her ideas were not deeply rooted because they were only ideals, which had never been placed in conflict with deep love for a man. The critic for *Hampton's Magazine*, for example, found the conclusion mildly amusing: "Tisket-tasket; a green-and-yellow basket. She took an idea into a play and on the way she lost it. . . . In this newest play, 'A Man's World,' her intention is excellent, but her execution wobbles, and so when Mary Mannering at the final curtain says 'This is the end'—why nobody believes her. . . . 'This is the end.' Fiddlesticks! Prove it. . . . It seems more like the middle."[11] One can well imagine him saying of Nora, "Fiddlesticks. She slammed the door on Torvald, but she'll be back when she calms down." Disbelief was the general response on the part of male critics to the conclusion.

There were, however, some critics who approved both Crothers's attitude toward the double standard and the heroine's decision. *Theatre Arts Magazine* called the ending "true and forceful" and concluded, "Miss Rachel Crothers in her wholesome play, 'A Man's World,' proves her case that there should be a single standard of morals as between men and women. That she refuses to marry the man can be approved without hesitation, and can be accepted as a forcible and final argument in the matter."[12] At least one critic praised Crothers's courage in risking disaster at the box office with her conclusion. After commenting on the fact that most audience members would have a more traditional view of the double standard, the reviewer for *The Nation* concluded, "Whatever may be thought of its philosophy, the fact remains that in 'A Man's World' . . . Miss Rachel Crothers has written one of the strongest, most interesting, logical, and dramatic pieces on the now dominant topic of the relations of the sexes than has been seen in this city for years. . . . For once sense has not been sacrificed to sentiment, or the desire for a happy ending."[13] Finally, the critic for the *New York Times* strongly applauded the play, remarking that the story was "one suggestive of real life." Summing up his impression of the play, the critic stated, " 'A Man's World' is, in short, a remarkably fine little play, and one which helps to justify the hopes that were built upon the author's first work, 'The Three of Us,' so pleasantly remembered. Here is a deeper, broader, more ticklish subject, and it is difficult to see how it could be better handled."[14]

The final three reviewers quoted were in a minority regarding the acceptability of the ending in relationship to the reality of life. They rejoiced in her daring conclusion, but others laughed at it, and some felt it was a dangerous, even subversive, assault on an established code of behavior. Augustus Thomas (1857–1934) belonged to the latter group. He was so disturbed by the message in her play, and possibly by the attempted intrusion by a woman into the field of playwriting, that within a few months he had written what Deborah S. Kolb describes as "a conservative reply to Miss Crothers."[15] At the time he wrote the play, he was considered in the front ranks of American playwrights. His play *As a Man Thinks* (1911) elevated him to the head of his profession. His title was carefully chosen to give an echo of Crothers's title. Additionally, one of his characters makes reference to her play. Thomas wove together three motifs in his play: support of the double standard, the folly of a woman rebelling against the constraints placed upon her by society, and opposition to anti-Semitism. Only the first two concern us here.

The examination of the merit of the double standard arises from a situation in which a woman finds her husband to be a libertine. The husband, like Gaskell, is a powerful newspaperman. Like Crothers's heroine, he is named Frank. Elinor Clayton and her husband were involved in an ugly scandal when the fact that he had a mistress in Atlantic City became public. Elinor has been prevailed upon to forgive him, and although she has done so she is unhappy because she believes he will have other affairs. When she confides both her fear and her disgust with the double standard to the family doctor and friend, Dr. Seelig, he responds, "Frank is important—he influences public opinion with his magazines and papers. He addresses an audience of two millions, let us say. In the great scheme of the world Frank is a factor—a big factor—isn't he? Your abiding love for him made all the difference between success and failure. All the forces radiating from Frank really do so because of your loyalty at a supreme moment. That's a large commission, isn't it? The fates made you their chosen instrument—their deputy. If Frank hadn't needed help, you couldn't have given it, could you? Well, don't regret having been useful."[16] This is the first example of Seelig's wise speeches, which were regarded as the highlights of the play. The reason critics felt the character was so real and admirable is that Thomas put into his mouth in inflated language the standard clichés about morality which were accepted at the time. One critic implied this by saying, "The play cannot fail to touch a sympathetic chord in the heart and mind of any person of average decency and kindliness."[17]

In his next speech to Elinor, Dr. Seelig develops the theme of the double standard and why it is necessary in contemporary society. In this speech, Thomas was suggesting a flaw in Crothers's title as well as her outlook: "All over this great land thousands of trains run every day starting and arriving in punctual agreement because this is a woman's world. The great steamships, dependable almost as the sun—a million factories in civilization—the countless looms and lathes of industry—the legions of labor that weave the riches of the world—all—all move by the mainspring of man's faith in woman. . . . There is a double standard of morality because upon the golden basis of woman's virtue rests the welfare of the world" (pp. 66–67). One critic noted that the didactic speeches in the play were those which pleased the audience the most.[18] In a review titled, "Thomas Wins with a Thoughtful Play," the critic for *Munsey's Magazine* stated, "The central theme is an old one: a woman's plea that there should be the same law for man as for her sex. In one of the most beautiful speeches ever delivered from the stage, Mr. Thomas makes an effective answer to this contention."[19]

However, Dr. Seelig's speeches have not convinced Elinor Clayton and when she finds out that her suspicions are true, she angrily confronts her husband. He is wholly unimpressed and condescending:

Clayton: Don't assume any convenant, my dear. That doesn't exist.
Elinor: Do you deny your promises after the affair of two years ago?
Clayton: I didn't promise to stagnate. I'm a publisher with a newsman's curiosity about the world he lives in.
Elinor: Colossal! But not privileged. Curiosity of that kind in a woman is idle and immoral! And in a man?
Clayton: A man's on the firing line, a woman's in the commissariat.
Elinor: Which is a fine way of saying you have a license for transgression that your wife hasn't.
Clayton: If you will—yes! (p. 45)

In addition to Elinor, there is another woman in the play who objects to Dr. Seelig's viewpoint about women: his wife. However, she is simply a foil who presents Seelig the opportunity to correct her (as well as those benighted women in the audience who might have been affected by Crothers's play). Elinor was seen entering a hotel with a man and although she did nothing improper, her husband has said that he will not continue to live with an adulteress. Noting that Elinor suffered horrible publicity and emotional distress because of her husband's past infidelity, Mrs. Seelig says, "A man that's been forgiven all that shouldn't talk about divorce if his poor wife loses her head for a minute. It's unbearable the privileges these men claim—and the double standard of morality they set up. . . . All of them. And that woman dramatist with her play was right. It is 'a man's world' " (p. 65).

Although Thomas did not intend it, a reader might well conclude that Mrs. Seelig is right! Elinor says, "*He* claims a right to follow *his* fancy and does it—my right is equal" (p. 51). She soon finds out how wrong she is. Simply because she went to a man's hotel room, her relatives insist that she allow her husband to get a divorce and that she then marry the other man, whom she does not love. Her husband is enraged, offers to put her out of the house, claims that their child is not his, and threatens to make her actions public in a divorce suit.

By the end of the play, Elinor has been brought to her knees with a vengeance and is happy to beg her husband for forgiveness and ask to be allowed to stay in her home with the man and child she loves. One critic commented that the audience might find it improbable that her husband would forgive her and take her back but that their child's illness and the sound of Christmas bells in the distance contribute to the feeling that "such a man might be easily moved by sentiment."[20] The following exchange takes place between the husband, who is still in a resentful, aggressive mood, and the wife, whose belief in equality has totally disappeared:

> *Elinor:* When he [our child] is old enough to understand I'll tell him—the truth.
> *Clayton:* What is the truth?
> *Elinor:* That his mother—was a foolish woman who thought her husband didn't understand her. That his father punished her out of all proportion to her offense, but only as *women* must expect punishment.
> *Clayton:* (*sneering*) I know—because men are brutes.
> *Elinor:* Because—God has put into woman's keeping a trust—of which no one—neither husbands nor fathers tell them truly— about which the world in its vain disputes of equality misleads them—of which they learn only through their own suffering.
> (p. 81)

The scene was one that moved the audience of the period. As one critic wrote, "His play has many poignant moments, with tears that will spring naturally to the eyes of any man and woman in whom sentiment is not wholly dead. Better still, his characters are human—every one of them—and they speak and act as human beings to the last."[21] This critic and others perceived Elinor as fortunate to have realized her folly and to have been forgiven. Her new philosophy will have to carry her through her marriage, because Clayton not only feels no guilt for his actions but intends to continue to behave as he pleases while holding the rod of punishment over his wife's head. Thomas's view, as described by one approving critic, was, "The result may be unjust to the woman, but the operation of the law is inexorable, and subject to no alteration."[22]

Of course there were some critics who felt the characterization and the conclusion of the play were neither just nor realistic. The critic for *International Magazine* said that Thomas's reputation as a writer of serious drama was fallacious, that the play was "adultery story ten thousand and one," and that Seelig was a worse *raisonneur* than Dumas ever used. He criticized the ending, saying, "His explanation of the reason for the existence of the double standard of morality is highly sentimentalized and becomes revolting when we see it convince the heroine so that she cries for forgiveness for an uncommitted sin to her truculant lord."[23] Naturally Florence Kiper, writing from a feminist viewpoint, found the play unintentionally satirical, but she felt that the ending was "a fair enough picture of that American home in which the function of the wife is to be the ornamental symbol of her husband's prosperity. Mrs. Clayton, as played by Miss Chrystal Herne, is par excellence the leisureclass American female, graceful, charming, alert, cultured, exquisitely gowned, utterly helpless. When in Miss Herne's tremulous, low voice, the wife announces her undying love for the husband who has just bullied and insulted her, one is not amazed at all, remembering that for the woman dependent on luxury it is a business to cherish and to conserve her provider" (p. 924). Kiper's view was that the situation for the woman was unacceptable, but that it mirrored the reality of many women's lives.

Crothers's play had been successful, but Thomas's play was an immediate and immense hit, running two seasons, and elevating him to the position of the best American playwright. Klauber, for one, noted that the play put Thomas at the top of the American playwrights' list.[24] And the work was widely hailed as the great American play.

In 1910 and 1911 Crothers and Thomas presented their conflicting visions of society. Although there were critics who accepted her conclusion, and her play as a whole, as a realistic depiction of American life, most did not. The response of audiences and critics to Thomas's play make it clear that his viewpoint was widely seen as realistic and acceptable. Even Clayton Hamilton, a perceptive and forward-thinking critic, called Thomas's play the most notable play of the season and described the writing as "brilliantly real."[25]

Within the decade there were tremendous changes in society, in the position of women, in audiences, and in the critics. Plays were increasingly realistic, moving beyond the surface reality of showing onstage shabby boarding houses, cleverly devised sunsets, and soda fountains which actually functioned. With these changes, playwrights such as Rachel Crothers were able to write plays that challenged existing views in society, rather than reinforcing them. With her play *A Man's World*, she established herself as the spokesperson for women in the theatre. With plays such as *He and She, Let Us Be Gay,* and *When Ladies Meet,* she achieved the position of the foremost American woman playwright, and after her play *Susan and God* was produced in 1937, producer John Golden said, "Again she has verified that she is the world's greatest woman playwright."[26]

As for Augustus Thomas, long called the "dean" or "king" of American playwrights, changes in society and a new generation of critics soon revealed his plays as conventional, shallow examples of commercial work. Writing in 1926, George Jean Nathan sneered at the logic displayed in *As a Man Thinks,* calling it a "scholarly treatise in which it was proclaimed that if it were not for men's pure love for women all the factories would shut down and no trains would run on schedule."[27] The immediate cause of Nathan's long denunciation of Thomas's work was his new play, of which Nathan wrote, "With 'Still Waters,' Mr. Augustus Thomas has now at length been officially lowered into the grave in which, apparently unbeknownst to the majority of writers on the American theatre, he has been peacefully resting for the last twenty-five years. In other words, it has taken American dramatic criticism just one-quarter of a century to arrive at the conclusion that Mr. Thomas, the so-called dean of our dramatists, is what he always has been: a playwright utterly without any authentic talent save the most obvious melodramatic kind" (p. 117). By 1941, Thomas merited only a few words in Freedley and Reeves's *History of the Theatre,* where he was described as "more of a newspaper reporter than a dramatist."[28] In contrast, Crothers was described as "the leading popular playwright among the many women who have written for the theatre," and an exponent of the realism which began to appear in the plays early in the century. *A Man's World* was described as one her most significant plays (p. 584).

Throughout her career, Crothers wrote plays in which she attempted to depict realistically the social conditions of American society. In *A Man's World,* she wrote an ending she believed was appropriate, even as Ibsen had done although he knew that in the society of his time the Noras would not leave their husbands and children. In 1910, Crothers reflected the outlook of a minority of her audience, but as changes occurred, she assumed a position in the theatre comparable to that which Thomas held when he presented his vision of the realism of American society. Throughout her career she focused on the position of women. Although in her succeeding plays she never equaled her 1910 strong, clear plea for women's rights, she continued to present realistic depictions of women in a time of great social change. She felt that the theatre could be used to awaken an audience to injustice and inequality, and she attempted to do that. Nevertheless, after twenty-six years of playwriting, directing, and participation in the American theatre, she told a reporter, "It's still a man's world. He made all the rules. When women juggle them and go in for this so-called freedom, they still must lie and cheat and deceive. They can't yet be frank and open and impersonally free as men."[29]

Notes

1. " 'As a Man Thinks'—The Masterpiece of America's Leading Playwright," *Current Literature* (May 1911): 529–36.

2. For a full analysis of Crothers's career, see Yvonne Shafer, *American Women Playwrights, 1900–1950* (New York: Peter Lang, 1994), pp. 15–35.

3. Qtd. in John Tibbetts, "The 'New Woman' on Stage: Women's Issues in American Drama, 1890–1900," *Helicon Nine* 7 (Winter 1982): 8.

4. June Sochen, *The New Feminism* (Boston: D. C. Heath, 1971), p. viii.

5. Rachel Crothers, "Troubles of a Playwright," *Harper's Bazaar* (Jan. 1911): 14, 46.

6. Florence Kiper, "Some American Plays from the Feminist Viewpoint," *Forum* 51 (1914): 924–25.

7. Rachel Crothers, *A Man's World* (Boston: Badger, 1915), pp. 12–13. Subsequent references are cited in the text.

8. June Sochen, *The New Woman: Feminism in Greenwich Village, 1910–1920* (New York: Quadrangle Books, 1972), pp. 31–32.

9. In *At the New Theatre and Others* (Boston: Small, Maynard, and Co., 1910), Walter Prichard Eaton perspicaciously noted this flaw in the play, then went on to say that the play "just misses the *masculinity of structure* [italics mine] and the inevitableness of episode necessary to make it dramatic literature" (p. 156).

10. Qtd. in Lois C. Gottlieb, *Rachel Crothers* (Boston: Twayne, 1979), p. 120.

11. "*A Man's World* [at] The Comedy," *Hampton's Magazine* (March 1910): 570.

12. "A Man's World," *Theatre Arts Magazine* (Mar. 1910): 68.

13. "A Man's World," *The Nation* (Feb. 10, 1910): 146.

14. " 'A Man's World': Fine Theme Well Handled," *New York Times* (Feb. 9, 1910): 5.

15. Deborah S. Kolb, "The Rise and Fall of the New Woman in American Drama," *Educational Theatre Journal* (May 1975): 154.

16. Augustus Thomas, *As a Man Thinks,* in *Modern American Plays,* ed. George P. Baker (New York: Harcourt, Brace, and Row, 1921), pp. 7–8. Subsequent references are cited in the text.

17. "As a Man Thinks," *Pearson* (May 1911): 671.

18. "The Week," *Outlook* (April 1, 1911): 714.

19. "Thomas Wins with a Thoughtful Play," *Munsey's Magazine* (May 1911): 282–83.

20. Adolph Klauber, "As a Man Thinks," *New York Times* (Mar. 19, 1911) sec. 7, p. 2. The setting of the Christmas season with the reunion of man and wife plays off the situation in *A Doll's House,* in which they separate at the Christmas season.

21. " 'As a Man Thinks': An Interesting if Familiar Story Told with Fresh Insight," *New York Times* (14 Mar. 1911): 11.

22. "As a Man Thinks," *Theatre Arts Magazine* (March 1911): 667.

23. "As a Man Thinks," *International Magazine* (June 1911).

24. Klauber, "As a Man Thinks," p. 2.

25. Clayton Hamilton, "The Plays of the Spring Season," *Bookman* (June 7, 1911): 354.

26. Unidentified clipping, Lincoln Center for the Performing Arts.

27. George Jean Nathan, "In Memoriam," *American Mercury* (May 1926): 118.

28. George Freedley and John A. Reeves, *A History of the Theatre* (New York: Crown, 1941), p. 334.

29. Qtd. in Geraldine Sartain, "Women Can't Juggle the Rules of Man's World," *World Telegram* (Oct. 13, 1932).

FOUR

The Provincetown Players' Experiments with Realism

J. Ellen Gainor

In his introduction to *Beyond Naturalism: A New Realism in American Theatre,* William Demastes quotes Eric Bentley on the "tyranny" of realism that critics hoped the " 'little theatre' uprising" of the "early part of the century" might have defeated, but didn't.[1] For critics of the American theatre (and, it might be added, literature in general), realism is the style non grata, a nineteenth-century form that has been the source of critical controversy since at least the 1930s.[2] Recent feminist theatre criticism in particular has identified realism as a mode antithetical to its goals, as Sue-Ellen Case succinctly explains in her groundbreaking study, *Feminism and Theatre:* "Realism, in its focus on the domestic sphere and the family unit, reifies the male as sexual subject and the female as the sexual 'Other.' The portrayal of female characters within the family unit . . . makes realism a 'prisonhouse of art' for women."[3] While Bentley voices an earlier version of the realism/modernism debate—that which championed the avant-garde aesthetically as an advance over the quotidian nature of realism, Case epitomizes a newer, ideological permutation, in which realism, inextricable from mimesis, emblematizes the recapitulation of dominant social structures in patriarchal culture, which can only be circumvented by the use of alternative artistic forms.

For the American theatre, the evolution of the realism/modernism debate is poignantly ironic. Less than a century ago, those artists who sought to create a vital national theatre chose realism as the mode in which to express their most critical and progressive political views. The Little Theatre movement rejected the commercialism of the professional theatre and strove to develop native drama by encouraging open and radical response both to the aesthetics of extant popular drama and to the pressing social issues of the time. For the founders of the Provincetown Players, the foremost of the Little Theatres committed to native drama, social realism proved the style of choice for the presentation of this new, national theatre.[4] Arising in 1915–16 in the bohemian enclaves of Provincetown, Massachusetts, and Greenwich Village in New York City, the Provincetown Players drew upon the resources of a small community, many members of which were prominent in the artistic avant-garde and socialist/communist movements of the era.[5] Although the canon has memorialized mainly Eugene O'Neill, numerous other artists of note, including Wallace Stevens, Edna St. Vincent Millay, Susan Glaspell, and Theodore Dreiser, wrote for the Players between 1915 and 1922.[6] Much of the forgotten drama they produced features frankly oppositional political content and social commentary.

For scholars concerned with the development of the American theatre in the early decades of the twentieth century, the conflict between the subsequent critical appraisals of realism and the historical context of its creation and impact appears stymieing. The work of the Provincetown Players poses a challenge to the current critical consensus on realism from several perspectives. While the anti-realist argument unravels on its own merits (i.e., its theoretical claims are often fuzzy and ill-defined or insufficiently argued), the example of the Players highlights some basic deficiencies and problems in the development of recent theory, as exemplified by feminist theatre criticism.

In what must be a brief overview of this theoretical problem, I would like to summarize this contemporary critical trend, using feminist theatre criticism as my main example; identify some of the problems inherent in this position and hypothesize how they developed; and then return to an analysis of three dramas from the Provincetown Players' repertoire—Susan Glaspell's *Trifles* (1916) and *Inheritors* (1920) and Theodore Dreiser's *The Hand of the Potter* (1921)—to discuss how these "realist" plays work to criticize the formalist position that would automatically denounce them as ideologically suspect. I want to focus in particular on representative statements of the anti-realist position within a discursive matrix of feminist/Marxist/post-structuralist/"Brechtian" theory to analyze how the work of the Players opposes the tenets of that matrix: the codification of realism as an ideological form that suppresses considerations of content; the transhistoricism and universalizing gestures invoked by the theory, which run counter to the supposed spirit of poststructuralism; and the mis- or partial reading of Brecht, which masks elements of his writing coinciding with the actual, historical practice of the group.

Within American feminist theatre criticism, a few prominent scholars have dominated the debate over realism. In addition to Case, Jill Dolan, in her *Feminist Spectator as Critic,* drawing on the work of Catherine Belsey, argues: "Realism . . . reifies the dominant culture's inscription of traditional power relations between genders and classes."[7] Invoking Brechtian theatre by contrast, Dolan states, "Realist theatre imposes a conservative sense of order by delivering its ideology as normative. . . . Realism naturalizes social relations imposed by dominant ideology and mystifies its own authorship" (p. 106). In her essay "Realism, Narrative, and the Feminist Playwright—A Problem of Reception," Jeanie Forte poses a series of rhetorical questions: "If feminism is a struggle against oppression, then is it really possible for feminist playwrights to communicate the working of oppressive ideology within realistic narrative from within? Is the structure so powerful and deeply ingrained that to allow virtually any realistic elements constitutes a capitulation to dominant ideology? If so, then realism must be abandoned altogether in the search for a subversive practice."[8]

These few examples, which represent a widely asserted critical viewpoint, have a number of features in common. First, none actually defines realism. Each assumes, rather, that the reader understands what the author means by the use of the term, despite the notorious critical inability to pin it down. "No genre," writes Eric Sundquist, editor of a recent collection of essays on American realism, "is more difficult to define than realism, and this is particularly true of American realism. In material it includes the sensational, the sentimental, the vulgar, the scientific, the outrageously comic, the desperately philosophical."[9] In other words, by failing to clarify their use of the term, these critics fall back on a logical fallacy that needs to demonstrate exactly that which is assumed in the argument.

Second, these critics treat realism as universal and static, specifying neither region of origin nor time of use. While Case views realism as synonymous with a domestic setting, Dolan and Forte seem to apply the term more broadly. Raymond Williams, in his 1968 discussion of the development of the modern theatre, presciently provides an analysis of this kind of critical gesture: "It is not only that as the names of movements get known . . . they harden, inevitably. They acquire external associations; become a shorthand of classification; tend to blur and confuse essentially different practices, and certain necessary connections."[10]

In anti-realist feminist scholarship, Dolan's discussion most clearly displays a debt to Althusserian notions of ideology,[11] a critical position developed from earlier Marxist debates over realism and modernism.[12] Grounded initially in the question of whether the nineteenth-century bourgeois novel could have critical or politically subversive impact, this discussion expanded to include other genres, particularly the drama, and began to explore increasingly central issues of form and content. These same parameters are of concern for the contemporary incarnation of the debate, although its participants in theatre criticism have not explicitly acknowledged the connection.

It is within this Marxist framework that the theoretical writings and theatrical practice of Brecht are frequently invoked. Elin Diamond most clearly elucidates the connection between feminist theatre and Brechtian principles. Her 1988 essay, "Brechtian Theory/Feminist Theory: Toward a Gestic Feminist Criticism," is often quoted, serving as the basis for much critical discussion of feminist theatre. Drawing on the well-known essays translated in *Brecht on Theatre*,[13] Diamond states: "Realism disgusted Brecht not only because it dissimulates its conventions but because it is hegemonic: by copying the surface details of the world it offers the illusion of lived experience, even as it marks off only one version of that experience. . . . Brechtian historicization challenges the presumed ideological neutrality of any historical reflection."[14] She expands upon her interpretation of Brecht's views by footnoting several passages from Brecht's essays, which she apparently feels self-evidently support her argument. Most significant are the following two passages:

> The individual whose innermost being is thus driven into the open then of course comes to stand for Man with a capital M. Everyone (including the spectator) is then carried away by the momentum of the events portrayed, so that in a performance of

Oedipus one has for all practical purposes an auditorium full of little Oedipuses, an auditorium full of Emperor Joneses for a performance of *The Emperor Jones.*

Also:

The bourgeois theatre emphasized the timelessness of its objects. Its representation of people is bound by the alleged "eternally human." Its story is arranged in such a way as to create "universal" situations that allow Man with a capital M to express himself: man of every period and every colour. (p. 92)

Instead of functioning the way Diamond intended, these passages illuminate the distinctions between what Brecht was actually discussing and the way that he has been employed in subsequent theory. While Brecht identifies and functionally specifies distinct aspects of realism, Diamond's sweeping characterization collapses his notions. The first passage is clearly focused on identification, the phenomenon by which the audience forms a seamless association with character/action. Although often linked to realism, identification is clearly not identical to it, but rather sometimes results from the ideological pressure inherent in certain versions of realist art. As the analysis of *Trifles* will show, artists conscious of the process of identification can actively manipulate it, and its ideological impact, within a realist frame. The second passage highlights the universalizing force integral to what Brecht specifically identifies as bourgeois realism. The Brechtian examples point strongly back to the historical origin of the anti-realist movement, the Marxist debates originally between Ernst Bloch and Georg Lukács, and then Lukács and Brecht, over the political potential of realist literature. Diamond's notion that "realism disgusted Brecht" misrepresents not only his position within the debate but also his view of his own work. Brecht's critical writing on this topic shows that, initially, the focus was on a very narrow body of realist literature, primarily French novels of the nineteenth century. Brecht immediately perceived this as a problem with geographical, temporal, and generic implications—he recognized the inadequacy of statements that universalize from considerations of generically similar texts written at a specific time in specific places under specific social and political conditions—especially as his own creative genres, poetry and drama, were virtually ignored by Lukács's discussion.

In "On the Formalistic Character of the Theory of Realism," Brecht clearly distinguishes the *form* associated with the bourgeois realist novel from realism as a literary mode or performative technique. Speaking of a new work-in-progress, which he wishes to dissociate from formalist strictures, Brecht remarks: "Somehow it does not fit the intended pattern. But this technique has proved to be necessary for a firm grasp of reality, and I had purely realistic motives in adopting it. . . . So far I have written 27 separate scenes. Some of them fit roughly into the 'realistic' pattern X . . . I consider it to be a realistic play."[15] For the purposes of the debate over realism, this is an extremely important clarification of the Brechtian position. Brecht here identifies himself as a realist writer, which he defines as a writer who avoids the political mistake of collapsing form and content—which, ironically, is exactly what those critics who claim they write from a Brechtian perspective often do.

In "Popularity and Realism," Brecht elaborates on how to achieve a different realism, precisely by deformalizing and contextualizing it: "The realistic mode of writing . . . bears the stamp of the way it was employed, when and by which class. . . . We must not derive realism as such from particular existing works. . . . We shall take care not to describe one particular, historical form of a novel of a particular epoch as realistic . . . and thereby erect merely formal, literary criteria for realism. . . . Our concept of realism must be wide and political, sovereign over all conventions. . . . Realism is not a mere question of form."[16] What Brecht is suggesting is a flexibility of generic designation that will allow variety of form without compromising strength of content, particularly political critique: "Realistic means: discovering the causal complexes of society/unmasking the prevailing view of things as the view of those who are in power/writing from the standpoint of the class which offers the broadest solutions for the pressing difficulties in which human society is caught up . . . making possible the concrete, and making possible abstraction from it."[17] This alternative view of a literary mode, emptied of association with other forms or texts, of course includes Brecht's own work, but does not formally limit the definition of realism. Although subsequent criticism has championed Brechtian dramaturgy as the alternative to what we now can identify as formalist realism, Brecht himself clearly saw critical political potential even within realism itself.

The concepts of identification and historicization raised in the Brecht passages quoted by Diamond thus lose the universal quality inherent to formalist analysis, and become tied specifically to a group of texts circulating in the Marxist debate. In related writings, Diamond explores both mimesis and identification further, provocatively blending Platonic and Aristotelian arguments with contemporary psychoanalytic criticism and phenomenology.[18] This line of argument recapitulates her previous technique, highlighting the problem of contextualization that Brecht associates with formalism. Like the positions Brecht disputes, Diamond draws on classical dramatic theory as universally and transhistorically relevant.[19] It seems clear that the issue of context, central to the emerging discipline of Cultural Studies, itself derived extensively from a Marxist tradition, is fundamentally in conflict with many of the gestures of the poststructuralist theory used by scholars like Diamond.

In the conclusion to *Aesthetics and Politics*, Fredric Jameson provides a thoughtful summary of this issue: "Post-structuralism has added yet a different kind of parameter to the Realism/Modernism controversy, one which—like the questions of narrative or the problems of historicity—was implicit in the original exchange but scarcely articulated or thematized as such. The assimilation of realism as a value to the old philosophical concept of mimesis by such writers as Foucault, Derrida, Lyotard or Deleuze, has reformulated the Realism/Modernism debate in terms of a Platonic attack on the ideological effects of representations."[20] Jameson here captures the essence of the critical progression that collapsed the debate over mimesis into that of realism in poststructuralist theory, and demonstrates how these contemporary critical maneuvers have obscured the historical origins of the conflict. He concludes: "We will not fully be able to assess the consequences of the attack on representation, and of poststructuralism generally, until we are able to situate its own work within the field of the theory of ideology itself" (p. 199), adding an important contextualizing coda onto this discourse.

A caveat by Terry Eagleton on the use of recent psychoanalytic theory in the realism/modernism debate provides a related corrective to such critics as Diamond, who invoke this discourse in the campaign against realism. He critiques the psychoanalytic theory of Julia Kristeva, whose championing of certain modernist works establishes her embracing of formalist principles and rejecting realism, regardless of the dangerous potential for her *écriture* to express right-wing ideology, despite its seemingly progressive aesthetic merit. Eagleton explains, "She pays too little attention to the political content of a text, the historical conditions in which its overturning of the signified is carried out, and the historical conditions in which all of this is interpreted and used."[21]

Thus the critical counterperspectives articulated by such scholars as Jameson and Eagleton provide helpful clarifications of the theoretical miasma the debate over realism has become. The issue of context, raised by each, is central to the specific circumstances of the Provincetown Players that make them an ideal example of a theatre which embodies Brechtian principles of realism and simultaneously explodes the formalist arguments about the ideological contamination of realist drama.

In his autobiography *Troubadour*, the poet Alfred Kreymborg recalls an exchange with the artist William Zorach, who had recently become a scenic designer for the newly founded Provincetown Players: " 'We're strong on realism and weak on fantasy,' the Russian [Zorach] confessed. Maybe you can supply the latter."[22] This quotation not only foregrounds one of the stylistic tensions present from very early on in the group's history, but also exemplifies the way that the American avant-garde was playing out the realism/modernism controversy in the early decades of the twentieth century.

The American situation was quite distinct from that of Europe, however, for the strategic reason that the various movements—realism, naturalism, expressionism, symbolism, etc.—we identify with "modernism" did not arise independently, or in response to each other, as they did in Europe, but rather arrived in the United States virtually simultaneously, as Americans who had traveled abroad brought back news and examples of the new movements, or as Europeans came to this country. J. L. Styan explains that critics such as George Jean Nathan started to bring information about the modern theatre to the attention of his readers, and examples of the new European drama began to appear onstage, via both tours and native productions.[23] The result of this plethora of new artistic influences was that American theatre practitioners embraced the dizzying array of creative possibilities this new drama presented, selecting elements from many of the genres and combining them in ways unique to the American theatre. Thus the concepts of realism and naturalism, as analyzed in the context of nineteenth-century Europe, must be reconceived for America. Just as developments in feminist theory have led to the identification of multiple "feminisms," so, in America, there are "realisms" which cannot be considered monolithically.

In helping found the Provincetown Players, George Cram Cook urged that the group commit itself to producing exclusively the work of new American writers. Simultaneously rejecting the commercialism of the Broadway theatre and championing the nationalist movement in American culture, Cook proposed "a stage where playwrights of sincere, poetic, literary and dramatic purpose could see their plays in action, and superintend their production without submitting to the commercial manager's interpretation of public taste."[24] His announcement for the 1920–21 season attests to his belief in their having achieved that cultural goal: "The Provincetown Players have become a national institution."[25]

Cook was referring here not only to the national attention the work of the group had attained, particularly through their productions of O'Neill, but also to the dissemination of their writing throughout the country via productions of their work by other Little Theatre companies. The Provincetown Players, like their counterparts in cities and towns all across the country, were first and foremost a community theatre. As the work of such companies has garnered little attention in recent drama theory, I would like to identify one key element of the structure of community theatre that I believe is central to the consideration of their work in light of the recent anti-realist theory discussed above.

The notions of identification and mimesis take on distinct resonances in the context of community theatre production. By definition, community theatre is by and for a community, and the work of the Players serves as an ideal example of the dynamics of such presentations. In a community where the identities of the actors are known to the audience, where their status as members of the community doubles with their artistic identities as performers, I would argue that it is impossible for the audience to "identify" with the characters, or for the production to convey an unfiltered mimesis, precisely because the audience will not suspend their knowledge of that duality—in fact, it is integral to their enjoyment of the art.[26] Although this is not at all the same phenomenon as Brechtian alienation, it may function in a related fashion, disrupting the link of audience to play. The key distinction, of course, it that this performative structure operates regardless of the style of work being produced.

Similarly, although realism was the dominant type of drama produced by the Provincetown Players, this notion of production environment works against concepts of drama propounded by such theorists as Catherine Belsey, who believes that in "classic realist" drama, "the author is apparently absent from the self-contained fictional world on the stage."[27] I would again argue that the authors' identities and proclivities, known equally well to the audience as are those of the actors, would preclude the suspension of authorial consciousness even within a realist production.

Although this performance theory seems central to the understanding of the context in which many of the Players' works were written and produced—and, I would also argue, is significant to their reception within the community as political drama[28]—the plays themselves merit examination for the ways in which they utilize and manipulate the conventions of dramatic realism imported from Europe.[29] I would now like to discuss aspects of three plays presented by the Players, each of which uses distinctive means of subverting the conventions of realism without completely transgressing its generic parameters.

With the exception of the work of O'Neill, Susan Glaspell's *Trifles* is undoubtedly the best known drama produced by the Players. Widely anthologized, and for many years a staple of the community theatre repertoire, the play has most recently been embraced by feminist critics eager to recover neglected American women writers and to identify the feminist themes in their work.[30] Yet from the perspective of feminist theatre critics who indict the domestic focus of realist drama, Glaspell's work would appear suspect. This drama exemplifies the problems of criticism that privileges form over content, as Glaspell's themes, the undervaluing of women's work—the "trifles" of the title—and the different social and juridical codes valued by women in patriarchal society, are impossible to ignore.

However, Glaspell does more than introduce what might be called feminist themes in her drama. I believe she consciously subverts the codes of realist dramaturgy to break down the very processes of mimesis and identification theoretically integral to the realist form, and uses these same subversions to highlight her feminist agenda.

Numerous critics have observed Glaspell's technique of an absent central character in a number of her plays.[31] In *Trifles*, Glaspell removes two central figures, the murdered husband John Wright and the wife accused of the crime, Minnie Wright, from the play. By entering upon the drama after the death, the audience is precluded from initially siding with either party. The play opens with the arrival of the local sheriff and the county attorney, a neighboring couple, and the wife of the sheriff.[32] Glaspell removes the men from the action for much of the play (they are investigating the scene of the crime upstairs and looking outside the house for clues), again manipulating the audience's "natural" tendency to identify with male authority figures, and leaves the two women in the kitchen to discover the possible truth behind the murder. Glaspell goes to great lengths dialogically to oppose the women initially, setting up the sheriff's wife as the shadow of patriarchal culture. However, the two women slowly form stronger bonds of identification with the absent wife, and as they grapple with a series of realizations about the traumas of her life, they come to empathize with what she may have done. Clearly, Glaspell wants her audience to make this same journey, and by consciously substituting unexpected and traditionally marginal characters and viewpoints for audience identification, she achieves her goal of subverting prevailing notions of legality, justice, and the value of women's experience.

Glaspell presents a related kind of subversion in her transgression of the semiotic codes for a realist setting. Rather than reinforcing images of ideal domesticity, Glaspell represents the breakdown of the ideal, juxtaposing the women's knowledge of how they "should" perform with alternative examples of "reality":

County Attorney: . . . Dirty towels! (kicks his foot against the pans under the sink) Not much of a housekeeper, would you say, ladies?
Mrs. Hale: (stiffly) There's a great deal of work to be done on a farm.

County Attorney: To be sure. And yet (with a little bow to her) I know there are some Dickinson county farmhouses which do not have such roller towels. . . .
Mrs. Hale: Those towels get dirty awful quick. Men's hands aren't always as clean as they might be. (p. 38)

Later, Glaspell repeats the gesture, as Mrs. Hale notices the counter half wiped, and some of Minnie's sewing gone awry (pp. 40–41). She consistently contrasts two versions of reality, that to which women are taught to aspire, which would, in conventional realism, reinforce ideological codes, and that which better represents the actuality of women's lives, which desperately needs to be seen and established. Thus Glaspell uses the codes of realism against itself—we might even say deconstructs them—to reinforce an alternative view of American life. I would maintain that Glaspell's techniques indeed undermine the ideological function attributed to nineteenth-century realism, and that these strategies fulfill many of the goals Brecht established for the representation of the "realistic."[33]

Glaspell's *Inheritors* introduces another device bridging the critical divisions of "Brechtian" and "realist" dramaturgy. In writing a first act prologue set in 1879—forty-one years before the action of the rest of the play—Glaspell uses a similar kind of historical distancing as did Brecht in *The Caucasian Chalk Circle*, for example; he (and the Elizabethans before him) often employed this to create a resonance between the present and the past. In the subsequent action, set in 1920 in the aftermath of the First World War, Glaspell carefully draws parallels between her historic and contemporary settings—the political conflicts of war, the treatment of indigenous peoples, resistance to government policy, and the relation of the family to society. Glaspell juxtaposes the issue of land claims of settlers versus native American Indians in the Midwest to the situation of Indians resisting British imperialism, for instance, intertwining that debate with the anti-imperialist protests of Indians opposed to American support of British policy, and with the campaign of conscientious objectors, exercising free speech, against the First World War. Without breaking a realist frame, Glaspell nevertheless establishes a dialectic within the drama, such that the lessons of the past must be relearned for the future if American culture and its values are to survive. Glaspell is particularly concerned here with issues of democracy and fundamental constitutional rights, such as freedom of speech, on which the country was founded.

Glaspell's editor, C. W. E. Bigsby, has criticized the play for the conflict between its "radicalism of subject and a conservatism of form which is never resolved."[34] But this is precisely the point. Glaspell consciously chose to work with conventions of realism to expose problems of ideology and political perspective in the dominant culture.[35] By establishing a dialectic within her plays, opposing dominant views to alternative perspectives, she forces her audience both to recognize that ideological pressure and to consider different positions for resistance.

Dreiser's *Hand of the Potter* uses theatrical strategies and a sociopolitical viewpoint very different from Glaspell's in his exploration of dramatic naturalism. Analysts of his fiction have questioned whether the social critiques inherent in his novels really have any disruptive power, reinforcing notions of realism's reinscription of ideological codes.[36] Although *The Hand of the Potter* was, in part, a restatement of ideas contained in his novel *The "Genius,"* Dreiser used the dramatic form to break through the confines of the novel, rendering the play a dramaturgical hybrid that exemplifies the flexibility the Provincetown Players' dramatists found within realism.

Dreiser leaves precious little to the audience's imagination in his lurid depiction of sexual perversion, child molestation, and murder. At first, it might appear that the central character, Isadore Berchansky, epitomizes the realist figures "who refuse to cooperate with social definitions of the self and of the nature and range of the self's desires" and thus become the "scapegoats" whose "expulsion . . . has a culturally stabilizing function."[37] Yet the frankness and fullness of Dreiser's representation of his actions seems to contradict his stabilizing potential. In fact, it is the very transgression of codes which limit the representation of desire in conventional realism that gives *The Hand of the Potter* its realist impact and subversive status.

Dreiser's choice to foreground such desire creates a palpable tension in his work with the pressure of social conformity that the "just" death of Isadore would seem to ensure. Had Dreiser chosen to end his play with this character's suicide, it would have stood as a classic example of realist drama's reinscription of the dominant social order.

However, Dreiser adds a final disquisitory scene between two reporters following Isadore's death that radically questions the social forces at work on Berchansky as well as the spectators' potential immunity from the power of perversion. Breaking neither temporal continuity nor the realist frame, Dreiser nevertheless introduces an entirely different series of perspectives on the action that has just concluded, invoking the latest theories of Freudian psychology and scientists to consider the sexual behavior of the deceased. Here, as with Glaspell, Dreiser employs tactics related, but not identical, to Brecht's. The use of the reporters functions similarly to the techniques Brecht described in his "Street Scene," complete with commentary, analysis, and the retelling of events.[38]

Although, from a feminist perspective, the consistent imposition of blame on Berchansky's female victims is highly problematic—"I'm guilty, and I'm insane, caused by the beautiful make-ups of girls that has set me very passionate"[39]—it is individual psychology and its connection to contemporary society that are Dreiser's ultimate concern. Through the final discussion scene, he refuses to allow his audience to feel safe in their assumed distinction from his antihero, implicating everyone in the downward spiral he has represented. Working with two related realist narratives, he creates a variant of naturalist drama that transcends the containment of his nineteenth-century models.

Although he does not invoke poststructuralist criticism directly, Raymond Williams rejects the formalist application of universal principles of dramatic theory, such as Platonic and Aristotelian concepts of mimesis, to postclassical dramaturgy: "We cannot usefully apply, to any modern art, the critical terms and procedures which were discovered for the understanding of earlier work. . . . Its inherent notions—of hierarchy, separation, fixed rules for each kind—belong to a social and philosophical order built on exactly those principles."[40]

Focusing specifically on the Brecht/Lukács debates, Eugene Lunn summarizes Brecht's ideas on the potential for realist writing that similarly suggest a theoretical position opposed to extant reliance on form: "What was needed . . . was a wider concept of realism as a confronting of a many-sided, contradictory (and often hidden) historical reality, whatever the formal means which facilitated this. 'Realism is not a matter of form. . . . Literary forms have to be checked against reality, not against aesthetics—even realist aesthetics.' "[41] Thus in the reconsideration of American dramatic realism, it appears ever less useful to rely on the methodologies of ahistorical, universalizing, and formalist theoretical principles to evaluate a theatre firmly grounded in concrete material and cultural conditions for its creation. Although the process of canonization values texts with putative transhistorical or "universal" significance, it now seems more compelling to claim that "universality" resides in the complex specificities of a local historical moment, as well as to deconstruct the critical ideology that relegated significant, experimental national drama to virtual obscurity. I would like to close this essay with a quotation from Fredric Jameson that, for me, lucidly encapsulates elements of the theoretical debates with which I have been grappling, and contextualizes this struggle for its future permutations:

> Other conceptions of realism, other kinds of political aesthetics, obviously remain conceivable. The Realism/Modernism debate teaches us the need to judge them in terms of the historical and social conjuncture in which they are called to function. . . . In such extinct yet still virulent intellectual conflicts, the fundamental contradiction is between history itself and the conceptual apparatus which, seeking to grasp its realities, only succeeds in reproducing their discord within itself in the form of an enigma for thought, an aporia. It is to this aporia that we must hold, which contains within its structure the crux of a history beyond which we have not yet passed. It cannot of course tell us what our conception of realism ought to be; yet its study makes it impossible to us not to feel the obligation to reinvent one.[42]

Notes

I am most grateful to David Bathrick, David Faulkner, and Patricia Schroeder for their invaluable suggestions for deciphering the theoretical axes of this debate, and to David Faulkner for his editorial expertise.

1. William W. Demastes, *Beyond Naturalism: A New Realism in American Theatre* (Westport, Conn.: Greenwood Press, 1988), p. 1.

2. For purposes of this essay, I do not intend to engage the complex debate that attempts to distinguish realism and naturalism. As Demastes's title *Beyond Naturalism* suggests, within American theatre theory and criticism, there has been

little segregation of these terms, and although attempting such a distinction might prove illuminating, space limitations preclude that study here.

3. Sue-Ellen Case, *Feminism and Theatre* (New York: Methuen, 1988), p. 124.

4. For a discussion of the forms of theatre produced by the Provincetown Players under the leadership of George Cram Cook, see Gerhard Bach, "Susan Glaspell—Provincetown Playwright." *Great Lakes Review* 4.2 (Winter 1978): 31–43.

5. For a thorough discussion of the intersecting lives of individuals in those communities, see Steven Watson, *Strange Bedfellows: The First American Avant-Garde* (New York: Abbeville Press, 1991).

6. For a history of the Provincetown Players, listing all productions and playwrights, see Robert Karoly Sarlos, *Jig Cook and the Provincetown Players: Theatre in Ferment* (Amherst: U of Massachusetts P, 1982).

7. Jill Dolan, *The Feminist Spectator as Critic* (Ann Arbor: UMI Research Press, 1988), p. 84. (Subsequent references are cited in the text.) Like many feminist theatre critics, Dolan uses Belsey's essay, "Constructing the Subject: Deconstructing the Text," in *Feminist Criticism and Social Change: Sex, Class and Race in Literature and Culture,* ed. Judith Newton and Deborah Rosenfelt (New York: Methuen, 1985), pp. 45–64, as the source of theoretical considerations of realism. However, Belsey's full-length study, *Critical Practice* (London: Methuen, 1980), is a much more comprehensive and detailed exploration of the position of realism in contemporary theory.

8. Jeanie Forte, "Realism, Narrative, and the Feminist Playwright—A Problem of Reception," *Modern Drama* 32.1 (March 1989): 115–27, at 119.

9. Eric J. Sundquist, "Preface," in *American Realism: New Essays,* ed. Sundquist (Baltimore: Johns Hopkins UP, 1982), p. vii. The specific problem of defining realism and tracing its origins for the American theatre will be discussed below.

10. Raymond Williams, *Drama From Ibsen to Brecht,* 1968 (London: Hogarth Press, 1987), pp. 331–32.

11. For a brief overview of these theoretical concepts, see Terry Eagleton, *Literary Theory: An Introduction* (Minneapolis: U of Minnesota P, 1983), pp. 186–87.

12. For full discussions of these historical arguments, see Ernst Bloch, ed., *Aesthetics and Politics* (London: NLB, 1977), and Eugene Lunn, *Marxism and Modernism: An Historical Study of Lukács, Brecht, Benjamin, and Adorno* (Berkeley: U of California P, 1982).

13. John Willett, ed., *Brecht on Theatre: The Development of an Aesthetic* (New York: Hill and Wang, 1964).

14. Elin Diamond, "Brechtian Theory/Feminist Theory: Toward a Gestic Feminist Criticism," *The Drama Review* 32.1 (Spring 1988): 87.

15. Bertolt Brecht, "On the Formalistic Character of the Theory of Realism," in *Aesthetics and Politics,* p. 70.

16. Bertolt Brecht, "Popularity and Realism," in *Aesthetics and Politics,* pp. 81–82.

17. Brecht, "Popularity and Realism," p. 82.

18. See Elin Diamond, "Mimesis, Mimicry, and the 'True-Real,' " *Modern*

Drama 32.1 (March 1989): 58–72; and "The Violence of 'We': Politicizing Identification," in *Critical Theory and Performance,* ed. Janelle G. Reinelt and Joseph R. Roach (Ann Arbor: U of Michigan P, 1992), pp. 390–98.

19. It must be noted that Diamond, in the latest piece, "The Violence of 'We,' " does seem to be moving in the direction of contextualization in her discussion of the work of Elizabeth Robins, when she presents the possibility of rethinking identification within the "highly gendered cultural context" in which her work takes place. See "Violence," pp. 396–97.

20. Fredric Jameson, "Conclusion," in *Aesthetics and Politics,* p. 199.

21. Eagleton, *Literary Theory,* pp. 190–91.

22. Alfred Kreymborg, *Troubadour: An Autobiography* (New York: Liveright, 1925), p. 305.

23. J. L. Styan, *Modern Drama in Theory and Practice,* vol. 1: *Realism and Naturalism* (Cambridge: Cambridge UP, 1986), p. 113.

24. George Cram Cook, Provincetown Players Season Circular, 1916–17, Berg Collection, New York Public Library.

25. George Cram Cook, Provincetown Players Season Circular, 1920–21, Berg Collection, New York Public Library.

26. A similar experience might be remembered by many readers in the phenomenon of the school play, where parents, friends and classmates are acutely conscious of their relations with and knowledge of those onstage.

27. Belsey, *Critical Practice,* p. 68.

28. The political affiliations and activities of such founding Provincetown Players members as John Reed were well known within the Greenwich Village community, and the political content of many of their productions would also be easily contextualized by an audience familiar with authors' beliefs.

29. The writers are also, of course, responding to developing realist conventions within America. For a background study of American drama prior to this moment, see Brenda Murphy, *American Realism and American Drama, 1880–1940* (Cambridge: Cambridge UP, 1987).

30. Much of the criticism has focused on the short story counterpart to the play, "A Jury of Her Peers," which Glaspell wrote the year following the composition of *Trifles.* For examples of readings of the work by prominent feminist critics, see Annette Kolodny, "A Map for Rereading: Gender and the Interpretation of Literary Texts," in *The New Feminist Criticism: Essays on Women, Literature, and Theory,* ed. Elaine Showalter, pp. 46–62 (New York: Pantheon Books, 1985); Judith Fetterley, "Reading and Reading: 'A Jury of Her Peers,' 'The Murders in the Rue Morgue,' and 'The Yellow Wallpaper,' " in *Gender and Reading: Essays on Readers, Texts, and Contexts,* ed. Elizabeth A. Flynn and Patrocinio P. Schweickart, pp. 147–64 (Baltimore: Johns Hopkins UP, 1986).

31. See, for example, Christine Dynkowski, "On the Edge: The Plays of Susan Glaspell," *Modern Drama* 31.1 (March 1988): 91–105.

32. Susan Glaspell, *Trifles,* in *Plays by Susan Glaspell,* ed. C. W. E. Bigsby (Cambridge: Cambridge UP, 1988), p. 36. Subsequent references are cited in the text.

33. Brecht, "Popularity and Realism," p. 82.

34. C. W. E. Bigsby, "Introduction," in *Plays by Susan Glaspell,* p. 19.

35. Brenda Murphy also criticizes the play, explaining, "Glaspell tends to sacrifice the mimetic illusion for polemical effect" (*American Realism,* p. 169). I would suggest that this critique represents an aesthetic hierarchy of critical values related to, but not identical with, the formalist notions of Bigsby.

36. See, for example, W. M. Frohock, "Theodore Dreiser," in *Seven Novelists in the American Naturalist Tradition,* ed. Charles Child Walcutt (Minneapolis: U of Minnesota P, 1974), p. 106.

37. Leo Bersani, *A Future for Astyanax: Character and Desire in Literature* (New York: Columbia UP, 1984), pp. 68–69.

38. Bertolt Brecht, "The Street Scene," in Willett, ed., *Brecht on Theatre,* pp. 121–29.

39. Theodore Dreiser, *The Hand of the Potter* (New York: Boni and Liveright, 1918), p. 183.

40. Williams, *Drama from Ibsen to Brecht,* p. 331.

41. Lunn, *Marxism and Modernism,* p. 86.

42. Jameson, "Conclusion," p. 213.

FIVE

Servant of Three Masters: Realism, Idealism, and "Hokum" in American High Comedy

Robert F. Gross

The history of critical writing on American realism has been, by and large, a celebration of high seriousness. It has largely been writing about drama, not comedy. Its canon is a solemn one, from Eugene O'Neill to Marsha Norman. The farces of Avery Hopwood and George Abbott, the satires of Claire Booth Luce and George S. Kaufman, and the high comedies of Robert Sherwood, Philip Barry, and S. N. Behrman are either relegated to the margins or ignored completely, despite the fact that they exhibit the salient characteristics of realistic drama: the use of box sets, maintenance of the fourth-wall convention, colloquial prose dialogue, and verisimilitude in character and setting. A perusal of the table of contents for this volume will quickly give evidence of this prejudice. In other volumes, writing about American realism tends to ignore comedy altogether, as in William B. Worthen's *Modern Drama and the Rhetoric of Theater,* or to marginalize it as something that stands in the way of realistic representation. This latter approach can be seen most clearly in Brenda Murphy's *American Realism and American Drama, 1880–1940,* in which realism is seen as fundamentally antigeneric, working to dissolve established genres into "the larger rhythms of life."[1] So, for example, Murphy praises Rachel Crothers's *When Ladies Meet* for its "realistic subversion of the expected comic ending" (p. 168). Here, comedy is seen as a partial truth at best, one that must give way to realism's superior claim to wider and more comprehensive truth. One is led to infer that realism can only be achieved at the expense of comedy.

This neglect of the realistic comic tradition in the United States is of a piece with the desperate attempts of the American professional theatre to exalt its status by producing American "tragedies" (from *Metamora* to *M. Butterfly*), and the American theatre scholar's exclusion of authors of comedies, farces, and musicals from his or her canon. Such behavior manifests a current of the puritan tradition, one that sees life as a deeply earnest endeavor and finds levity suspect. To these critics, *Long Day's Journey into Night* is a far more accurate and there-fore "realistic" depiction of middle-class domesticity than *You Can't Take It with You,* and the truth about marriage can be found in *Who's Afraid of Virginia Woolf?* but not in *Paris Bound.* True to the puritan tradition, critics of American drama tend to assume that unpleasant truths possess greater moral and consequently higher aesthetic value.

There is, moreover, another reason for the neglect of comedy in dis-cussions of realism. The development of realism, with its darkened auditoria, elimination of soliloquies and asides, and observance of the fourth-wall convention, is seen by critics and historians as a set of strategies to render the spectator passive, creating a *voyeur* whose pres-ence is never overtly addressed by realistic actors deeply immersed in Stanislavskian given circumstances. Worthen best encapsulates this view of realism: "The spectator is cast as an impartial observer, con-strued outside and beyond both the drama and the theatrical activi-ties—including his or her attendance, participation—that produce it."[2] There is little place for laughter here, for laughter not only proves that the audience is *within* the theatrical event, and an active part of it, but also pierces the fourth wall, giving the actors an immediate and active response to what has just occurred onstage. Each outburst of laughter, each titter, makes the spectator an active participant in the event. Watching a comedy, we are not only aware of how actors pause to let a laugh crest, but also how they begin the dialogue afresh after the laugh has begun to die down. The comic actor depends heav-ily on what Bert O. States has called "the collaborative mode" of per-formance, in which the actor works "to break down the distance be-tween actor and audience and to give the spectator something more than a passive role in the theatre exchange."[3] Any reliance on the collaborative mode undermines the neutralization of the audience that, Worthen argues, realism seeks to produce. If he is correct, "comic realism" would be a contradictory and self-defeating dramatic style.

The nature of realistic comedy is better understood if we view realism as a tendency within dramatic presentation that rarely appears in an unadulterated form, and for good reason. Northrop Frye has noted that the representation of "human life without comment and without imposing any sort of dramatic form beyond what is required for simple exhibition" is very rare indeed.[4] The reason for this rarity, he rightly observes, is that "we usually find the spectacle of 'all too human' life oppressive or ridiculous" (p. 285). To be theatrically effective, the realistic impulse demands the alloy of stronger stuff, whether satire, farce, romance, comedy, tragedy, or melodrama. These forms provide the *mythoi* that organize and heighten realistic elements. After all, who would want those masters of realism, Eugene O'Neill and Arthur Miller, without their flair for melodrama? Mere verisimilitude leaves an audience unmoved.

The realistic impulse works most strongly in the theatre when it exists in creative tension with other elements. This tension between realism and the nonrealistic is part of the very tension between the real and the conventional that lies at the basis of theatrical art. As Michael Goldman has observed: "Drama is always poised between the real and the conventional, and the presence of the two, each imposing different conditions, is part of the most elementary dramatic excitement. The pure or 'consistent' convention as Eliot called it, is impossible in drama, would be fatal if possible, because it would suppress entirely the living presence of the actor. Theater is here and now, difficulty being overcome before our eyes."[5] Rather than viewing realism as a critical monad, or as a stylistic rubric under which entire works can be subsumed, it is more profitable to analyze the presence of realistic elements in a play as they exist in tension with other elements. After all, generations of "realistic theatre" in America have not yet led to the obliteration of that most active moment of the so-called "passive" spectator's participation in the theatrical event—the curtain call.

Nowhere can we see the tendency toward stylistic hybridization in American realist drama more clearly than in the high comedies of Philip Barry, S. N. Behrman, and Robert Sherwood. They are shaped by three differing, and sometimes contradictory, forces: (1) the impetus toward realism in all forms of legitimate theatre; (2) the tendency toward idealism in the form of intellectual abstraction, which had come to define high comedy; and (3) the demands of the Broadway system, which viewed plays as vehicles for stars.

The tension between realism and idealism in these plays can best be seen as a tension between particularity and type. One of the simplest ways to chart the rise of realism on the western stage has been to note the growing emphasis on the depiction of highly individualized phenomena rather than of types, whether in the movement from stock scenery to specially designed sets for each production, from conventionalized stage dress to historically accurate costumes, or from character types to portraits of unique individuals.[6] In realism, verisimilitude tends to be defined less as truth to a generalized type than as truth to the unique individual or milieu. As "an expression of modern liberal humanism,"[7] realism situates value in the painstaking depiction of individuals, however atypical (Blanche DuBois), unexceptional (Linda Loman), or limited (Lenny Small). When it constructs types, they are not the universalized types of neoclassicism but more highly particularized social types, often with some individualizing detail; the southern demagogue (Boss Finley), the Jewish mother (Bessie Berger), or the prostitute with the heart of gold (Kitty Duval).[8] In this respect, realist art is the bourgeois art *par excellence,* as defined by Roland Barthes: "Bourgeois art is an art of detail. Based on a quantitative representation of the universe, it believes that the truth of an ensemble can only be the sum of the individual truths that constitute it."[9] Realistic characterization, then, works through the accretion of discrete details to create the illusion of individuality.

Characterization in high comedy, on the other hand, is defined through the articulation of an idea. Thus, the most famous and influential discussion of the nature of high comedy, George Meredith's *Essay on Comedy,* faults most Restoration comedy for being overly realistic and, thus, bereft of ideas, while he praises Molière as the master of the form because "he did not paint in raw realism. He seized his characters firmly for the central purpose of the play, stamped them in an idea, and by slightly raising and softening the object of study (as in the case of the ex-Huguenot, Duc de Montausier, for the study of the Misanthrope, and according to Saint-Simon, the Abbé Roquette for Tartuffe), generalized upon it so as to make it permanently human."[10] In Meredith's view of high comedy, characters do not exist for their own sake, but for the sake of an idea: "the life of the comedy is in the idea" he writes of *The Misanthrope* (pp. 23–24). If the realist accumulates details to construct a character, the high comic writer takes an attitude toward life and embodies it. *Dianoia*, not *ethos*, is the guiding principle in high comedy. Its purest manifestation, however, is not found in the theatre but in the philosophical symposium, in which plot and character are most strongly subordinated to the development of ideas.[11] In this sense, Plato's *Symposium*, Castiglione's *The Courtier*, and Kierkegaard's "In Vino Veritas" chapter in *Stages on Life's Way* can be accounted among the "highest" of high comedies. It is important to note, however, that the symposium quickly becomes untheatrical. Dialogue gives way to a succession of monologues; ideas become the full extent of characterization; and the real space and real bodies of theatrical presentation can only distract from the verbal play of ideas. The philosophical symposium is complete as a literary text; it does not ask, as the dramatic text does, to be concretized in production.[12]

Successful high comedy in the theatre, contrary to Meredith, tends not to be exclusively the expression of an idea but anchors its ideas in a more particularized, realistic world. The author of high comedy must balance the requirements of the idea with the details of lived experience. High comic characterization as an embodiment of an idea not only requires less elaboration of detail than realistic characterization, but the clarity of the idea can actually be blurred by individualizing detail. The characters in *The Misanthrope*, for example, virtually exist only in the present tense; they are given no biographies to explain their behavior. They spring, rather, fully grown from the brow of the Ideal. Such essentialized characters cannot change. Whereas the realistic protagonist is established through a variety of qualities, different ones of which may be actualized by the course of the plot, the idealist portrait tends to be established by reference to a single quality. If that quality is abandoned, the character vanishes. As a result, authors of high comedy usually need elements of realistic portraiture to effect character transformations. Some of George Bernard Shaw's least realistic high comedies tend strongly toward the symposium, and are populated by static characters (*The Apple Cart, In Good*

King Charles's Golden Days), while his more realistic plays tend toward protagonists who have more facets and exhibit change (*Widowers' Houses, Major Barbara*).

Neither realism nor idealism is in itself intrinsically theatrical. They are opposing poles within all representational art forms. Indeed, as we have seen, the pure extreme of either impulse tends to be unatheatrical. The tension between realism and high comic idealization manifests itself as easily in the novels of Iris Murdoch and Ivy Compton-Burnett as it does in a play. It is only when we turn to the demands of the star system that we encounter an intrinsically *theatrical* set of demands being placed on the American authors of high comedy in the 1920s and '30s, such as Barry, Behrman, and Sherwood.

In his 1928 preface to *The Queen's Husband,* a self-admitted vehicle for the talents of Ronald Colman, Robert Sherwood reflects upon the strengths and weaknesses of contemporary American playwriting. Its primary strength, Sherwood explains, is reportage—a photographic realism that is insufficiently theatrical to excite and move an audience. He finds it ironic that these playwriting reporters claim to imitate Ibsen, Chekhov, and Shaw—imaginative dramatists who present greatly heightened and theatricalized realities. Unlike Meredith, however, Sherwood does not oppose the term *realism* to *idealism,* but adopts a slang term free of any lofty philosophical connotations— *hokum* (and its near-synonym, *buncombe*)—to define theatricality: "It may be as well to eliminate hokum from the novel (though none of the great novelists, including Samuel Butler, Thackeray, Dostoievsky, Hardy and Conrad have done it); but the elimination of hokum and buncombe from the theatre would result in the elimination of the theatre itself. Hokum, as the term is applied in these disillusioned states, is the life-blood of the theatre, its animating force, the cause and the reason for its existence."[13] By drawing on American slang, Sherwood implies that theatricality is coarser, less literary, and more popular in its appeal than realism. It is also more vital, primarily affecting the emotions (p. xviii). Most importantly, however, hokum is the theatre of *actors,* the direct inheritors of a nineteenth-century, pre-realistic theatre; "the theatre is and forever will be the theatre of Rose Trelawney and Fanny Cavendish and the Crummels family" (p. xviii). This tradition is opposed to the theatrical "reforms" of the modern theatre, which saw itself as subordinating the unruly, egotistical, and naive impulses of actors to the benign control of the playwright or director.[14] Indeed, the star actors of the prerealist tradition had been presented as the main opponents of realism, egomaniacal individuals whose performances refused to submit to the self-effacing discipline of realistic representation.

John Gassner, a contemporary of Sherwood's, provides us with a good example of this prejudice against stars as he describes the contradictions to be found in many realistic productions: "The scenery provides an environment (in the physical sense), but the actor nullifies its value by thrusting into the limelight the glamorized personality of the star actress or matinee idol. The actor, who is presumably in a realistic environment (in the box set consisting of three 'walls' formed by lashing together a number of flats), manages to turn the set into the semblance of a platform for himself [sic]. And more often than not, the result is a tremendous box-office success. It would be a mistake, of course, to assume that the average audience cares a straw whether the rules of realism are observed or violated" (p. 26). For Gassner, it is the actor who bears the responsibility for violating the self-effacing canons of realism; he never considers that the director or even the playwright might want such a thing to happen. This violation "nullifies" the value of the production not by acting but by aggressively "thrusting" a "glamorized personality" into the set, and perverting the realistic stage design. The hoi polloi, unaware that true art functions according to rules, is hoodwinked by this wanton display of ego. Although Gassner argues in the same essay that the single most dominant idea of the modern theatre is "freedom," and that "today the flexibility of dramatic and theatrical conventions is recognized everywhere," it is clear that he considers this flexibility and freedom to be the playwright's, not the actor's (pp. 7, 10).

Despite their differing evaluations, however, both Sherwood and Gassner show that the prerealist aesthetic, founded on the display of star performers, continued into the twentieth-century American theatre. This should not surprise anyone who has read the plays produced on Broadway between the world wars, or has looked at the news stories, theatrical reviews, or theatrical advertisements in the daily newspapers. For a theatre public whose sense of presence was not yet substantially modified by the development of motion pictures, the live appearance of a beloved actor onstage was a reaffirmation of the actor's art and aura, an aura that required the actor's *physical* presence onstage. Michael Goldman, drawing on Freud's theory of the genesis of play in *Beyond the Pleasure Principle,* has observed that "the theater springs from the games we play with fear and loss" (p. 37). For the Broadway audiences of the 1920s and '30s, this game of disappearance and reappearance was played out not only within the dramatic texts but in the careers of their favorite stars. For them, an opening night was the "return" of a star to the Broadway stage. It is not unusual, therefore, to see theatrical reviewers make such comments as Alexander Woollcott's on Laurette Taylor's opening night performance as Lissa Terry in Philip Barry's *In a Garden.* He reports, "Laurette Taylor renewed her right to be known in her own land and time as a great actress."[15] Woollcott's choice of verb implies that an actor's reputation needs to be continually reaffirmed through acts of live performance; it is not the building of a canon that is important, as it is for a writer, but a physically immediate reassertion of her artistry. Brooks Atkinson's appreciation of the Lunts in Sherwood's *Reunion in Vienna* gives an unusually full account of this awareness of alternating absence and presence:

> Whenever the Lunts appear behind the footlights, flying the pennant of the Theatre Guild, we are all delighted to discover that they are brilliant actors. For it is discovery, in spite of their long and lucent record. When they are out of town, carrying their "images of magnificence" round about the East, their brilliance is a matter of record. By conjuring up fragments of *The Guardsman, The Second Man,* and *Caprice,* we can remember how their brilliance irradiates a play, lighting up the corners of characters and hidden pockets in dialogue. But a knowledge of brilliance is a paltry thing by comparison with an experience of brilliance. And so when the Lunts come back to town we discover them all over again.[16]

As artists of hokum, Barry, Behrman, and Sherwood worked to maximize the sense of event that surrounded the live appearance of a star actor and the energy generated by it. To present the star as acting alone, selfishly perverting otherwise realistic productions, is to ignore the dominant theatrical aesthetic of the period.

This does not mean, however, that star performances ran roughshod over the conventions of realism and high comedy. Subject matter and actor were meant to work in tandem, each giving different kinds of pleasure. But not only did the appeal of the subject matter enhance the evening's seductive appeal; it also gave a structure to the performances that they could not provide by themselves. Hokum has no plot, no patterns of probability or necessity, and no structuring principle. It can become the string of vaudeville acts or the succession of monologues at an audition. The display of acting in a play requires that the play be *about* something, and that "something" is provided by the dramatist, whether realist, idealist, or some mixture of the two.

Realism, idealism, hokum. The first two are opposed, as movements toward the concrete particular and the intellectual abstraction. The third, through the actor, not only moves between the two in the moment-to-moment unfolding of the production but can transcend that dichotomy for its own purposes of display. Take, for example, the first act of Behrman's 1931 comedy, *Brief Moment,* which starred Francine Larrimore as Abby Fane, a blues singer in a nightclub who marries Roderick Deane, the melancholy heir to a great fortune.[17] The stage directions of the printed text begin by placing the play firmly within realistic conventions. Roderick Deane's sitting room is described, its location in Manhattan given, and the month and time of day noted. The dialogue begins with Roderick and his friend Harold Sigrift in the midst of an intense discussion. It is written in colloquial prose and adheres, as does the entire play, to the fourth-wall convention. It is an expository scene that functions realistically by establishing Roderick as an individual; the twenty-five-year-old son of a powerful tycoon, disenchanted and uncertain of himself, who has fallen in love with a nightclub singer. The relationship between Roderick and his father (who never appears onstage) is quickly sketched in and could easily illuminate Roderick's sense of failure and inferiority. Interestingly, however, Behrman barely develops this information in later dialogue or dramatic action; it is a realistic detail that is quickly passed over. In a more sentimental comedy, the tycoon's reaction to his son's infatuation with a lower-class woman could be the central conflict; in *Brief Moment,* it is brought up and discarded.

As high comedy, this scene begins to lay out the central ideas of the play. *Brief Moment* is a variation on *The Misanthrope,* played across class boundaries. Roderick is an Alceste, a malcontented and introspective sophisticate who is looking for a vital simplicity that he can find neither in himself nor in his society. He believes he has found it in the person of Abby Fane; "she's unspoiled by civilization" he declares.[18] Abby, it turns out, is far from the *naïf* he imagines her to be. She is a Célimène, a social chameleon who can enjoy high society for precisely the superficial pleasures it offers and can learn how to play its games with almost frightening rapidity. In the opening scene, Behrman uses Sigrift's complacent, elitist cynicism as a foil for Roderick's discontented, romantic infatuation.

As hokum, the play begins from its second line to heighten the audience's desire to see the leading lady. "He'll adore her!" says Roderick (p. 3), and there is no question that he means his father and Abby. Throughout the scene, Roderick's romantic infatuation not only reveals his character and establishes Abby's but also celebrates the star. She is "luminous" (p. 5), has "electricity" (p. 5) and "vitality" (p. 6), "glamor" and "poetry" (p. 8). Thus begins a lengthy build to Abby's first entrance halfway through the first act. During this time, not only Roderick but his sister Kay and the gangster Manny Walsh sing Abby's praises as well, with only Sigrift undercutting their effusions. Of the thirty-four pages leading to her entrance, only seven do not contain direct references to her. Everything leading up to Abby's first entrance is one extended exposition of her and her circumstances. This opening invests the presence of Abby Fane with incredible fetishistic power and endows her later comings and goings with great importance. These comings and goings, in turn, are all related to the development of her relationship to Roderick, which is both the focus of the realistic plot line and the embodiment of the play's central idea.

A mere four pages after her entrance, the dramatic action stops cold as Abby sings Jerome Kern's ballad, "Bill"—an action that can be realistically justified as proof of her professional skill as a *chanteuse,* and idealistically justified as an exhibition of Abby as Proteus; but it is, first and foremost, hokum. It exhibits the star of a "legitimate" Broadway show as a participant in a popular form of entertainment—the nightclub performer. Like Sherwood, Behrman momentarily situates his heroine in a tradition that has not submitted to the control of realistic dramaturgy.

Abby's chameleonic nature both helps express the central idea of *Brief Moment* and provides excellent opportunities to show off the skills of the actor. In Act I, she is a saloon singer, given to slangy lines like, "Oh, swell! What a place for a party!" (p. 45). This stands in immediate contrast to her first line at the beginning of the next act, as she serves tea to a Russian film director: "I've always been fascinated by Russia. It's the one country I've always wanted to see. I can imagine it and yet—I can't imagine it. You know what I mean?" (p. 79). The effect is not unlike seeing Eliza Doolittle first at the curbside and later at the ambassador's ball, but with all the intervening scenes removed. Abby's versatility, if well performed, immediately displays the actor's versatility. At such moments, hokum and high comedy become indistinguishable, and realism takes a back seat. Although Behrman makes a concession to realism in his stage directions, which tell the reader that eighteen months elapse between acts one and two, the effect on the audience is as if Abby's transformation has been accomplished over intermission.

Barry's *In a Garden* (1925), Behrman's *Brief Moment* (1931), and Sherwood's *Reunion in Vienna* (1931) not only are constructed from the interplay of realism, idealism, and hokum—they thematize it through characters that represent the different values of dramatists and actors. In this thematization, however, the argument tends to polarize between idealism and hokum, with no character to speak for the values of realism. Therefore, although realism is constantly present in the setting, dialogue, and conventions of these plays, it remains in the background—omnipresent, but never discussed.

In a Garden takes an author of high comedy as its protagonist and dramatizes the destructiveness of using the tenets of high comedy as guides for living. Adrian Terry is a forty-year-old playwright who believes that the phenomena of life only have meaning insofar as they express an idea: "they must contribute something—express something—relate somehow to the *idea*—the idea upon which the whole plan builds it—think! There's no limit—no horizon! The whole world—life itself—*everything* is transformed! . . . Exactly as it is in the theatre!"[19] When Adrian discovers that his wife, Lissa, may have loved another man before they met, and that this previous lover is about to reenter her life, he deals with the discovery as if it were the subject of a high comedy. He has a stage set erected in his library that resembles the garden in which the couple's tryst took place, and works to elicit a reprise of the past event, on the assumption that "romantic incidents don't bear repeating" (p. 21). This plan destroys his marriage, as he deals with his wife not as an equal but as an author would deal with one of his characters. From the beginning, Lissa opposes Adrian's penchant for dealing with life through ideas. Idealized formulations, Lissa argues, ignore the complexity of human beings:

> "Send a telegram to 'any man' of forty, saying 'Flee. All is discovered.' Ten to one he'll flee."—Only he won't. " 'Most men' lead lives of quiet desperation." Only they don't. " 'Every wife' is at heart another man's mistress." Only she isn't. Plays are plays, my dear—and life's life. Don't try to mix them. They won't. People are too unexpected. (p. 26)

A woman who believes that everything in her life has been planned for her, and suffers from the disconcerting feeling that she possesses no more freedom than a character in a play, Lissa looks upon her evening in the garden as the one autonomous, unplanned moment in her entire life. When the setting and circumstances of that evening recur, this does not disillusion her but reconfirms that tryst as a privileged moment. Adrian's epigram about repetition and romance does not kill Lissa's feelings for Norrie Bliss but reawakens them.

In an attempt to save her employer's marriage, Adrian's secretary, Miss Mabie, disillusions Lissa by revealing that Norrie was not acting spontaneously in the garden but on the suggestion of a novelist, Roger Compton. This destroys Lissa's romantic memory, which was itself an idealization of unpremeditated experience, but it does not reconcile her to her manipulative husband. She removes herself from Adrian's library *cum* stage set, to set out on a life of her own. Adrian is left in despair: "I know no one!" he finally admits (p. 133).

"The play is designed to turn against itself," observes Frank Bradley in his treatment of *In a Garden*,[20] and it does so in a way that leaves both sides of the argument undermined. Adrian's idealism can only deal with generalities and leaves no place for interaction with individuals. Lissa prizes the unique and individual, but she is always thrown back on generalized formulations to explain who she is and what she wants. Her memory of Norrie Bliss is as idealized as any of her husband's high comic generalizations, and her final exit from the stage in search of individuality removes her from the world of theatrical representation entirely. By the end of *In a Garden*, there is no way for a play to be a valid representation of reality. Either it can be idealized, that is, *theatrical*, but untrue, or it can be realistic and impossible to represent. Adrian Terry's approach to life falsifies it, but Lissa's makes it invisible.

Although the play on the page can be seen as the story either of Adrian or of Lissa, the play in performance belongs to Lissa. Like *Brief Moment*, the play builds to her entrance, and is structured around the question of whether or not she will leave Adrian, whose library is the play's one setting. Her role is more sympathetic, shows more emotional range, and reaches the highest levels of verbal eloquence to be found in the play. The reviews of the original production show no reservations about the cast, but give little attention to the actor who played Adrian. Lissa, on the other hand, as played by Laurette Taylor, is written about at length.[21] With Lissa as the starring role, the play can be seen as an allegory of the star system, in which an author tries to subject the actor to verbal constraints that she ultimately transcends through her performance. Thus, although the intellectual argument of the play reveals both Lissa's and Adrian's positions to be flawed, the play in performance liberates Lissa from Adrian (and Philip Barry's text). The star performance triumphs over the limits of the text.

As a struggle between a playwright and an actor, *In a Garden* exhibits the same schematic structure as *Brief Moment* and *Reunion in Vienna*. In all three, a male "playwright" establishes a scenario to control the desire of a woman (the leading lady), based on some idealistic notion of the woman that does not correspond to her complex reality. In each case, this playwright's scenario is proved to be inadequate. Only in Barry's play, however, does the leading lady elect to leave the stage—an American Nora. In Behrman's play, she triumphs over the playwright figure and makes the "doll house" her own. In Sherwood's play, she is tranformed into an enigmatic icon, withholding her inmost thoughts from both playwright and audience.

In *Brief Moment*, she chooses to stay, against the playwright's objections. Roderick Deane marries Abby Fane because he believes that she possesses a simple vitality that he lacks. After a year and a half of marriage, he realizes that she is far from simple. She is an actor, so sophisticated in her role playing that he is unable to comprehend her intellectually: "You pick up every argot, you're mixed up in a hundred sets. Underneath these layers of adaptive coloring—what are you? I thought I married a simple person. My God, I married a Grand Duchess" (p. 118). Abby, rather than being tormented by the complexity of life, accepts the ambiguities and mysteries of the real world:

> *Sigrift:* Abby, I sometimes wonder if you know where mimicry ends and sincerity begins?
> *Abby:* Not always. But I don't think anybody knows—always. I think the charm of life is in its uncertainties—and half truths— the charm and the pain too. (pp. 199–200)

Like Lissa, Abby values experience over intellectual formulations about it. Unlike Lissa, her sense of her own strength is so great that it is not threatened by her husband's idealism. Rather, his sense of intellectual superiority is challenged by her complexity. But when a past romantic infatuation resurfaces in Abby's life, in the person of Cass Worthing, Abby pretends to respond to his advances only to frustrate him, repeatedly calling off rendezvous, as he used to do to her. Roderick, unable to accept this as merely a childish revenge on her part, concludes that Abby still loves Cass. Despite her protestations, Roderick goads her into leaving him for Cass. As a result, Abby and Roderick's separation makes the tabloids, divorce seems inevitable, Cass proposes to Abby, and Roderick plans to renounce his fortune and go to the Soviet Union.

When Abby and Roderick meet again, however, their irresolvable temperamental and intellectual differences are overridden by their completely inexplicable attraction to each other. Despite the fact that they can agree on nothing, the curtain falls on their embrace, "their incompatibility swallowed up in their passion" (p. 235). Their mutual attraction runs athwart the intellectual pattern of the play, suggesting depths that cannot be reduced to an idea. The end of *Brief Moment* celebrates the momentary triumph of passion over ideas. Unlike *In a Garden*'s Lissa Terry, Abby Fane does not need to leave the play, because she and Roderick have odd and unknowable internal dimensions that defy knowledge and resist intellectual manipulation, even in front of an audience. The epigraph Behrman took from David Hume for his novel, *The Burning Glass*—"The powers by which bodies operate are entirely unknown"[22]—could easily be taken as the epigraph not only for *Brief Moment* but for all of Behrman's major works. It is an intelligent and skeptical approach, but one that tends to undermine the clarity of high comedy in favor of more realistic portraiture, and more ambiguous playing.

Reunion in Vienna is the sunniest play of these three, largely because the role of "playwright" in this play is the slightest. Here the plot is set into motion by Anton Krug, a distinguished Viennese psychoanalyst who has married Elena, a woman who once had been the lover of the Archduke Rudolph Maximillian. When it appears that the exiled Archduke may illegally return to Vienna to attend a party commemorating the hundredth anniversary of the birth of Emperor Franz Joseph, Krug insists that his wife attend, believing, like Adrian Terry, that any confrontation with the past she has so glamorized in her memory will disillusion her. (Having the same day prescribed the same therapy of disillusionment to a female patient, he obviously believes in this as a general therapeutic principle.) Sherwood does not present his psychoanalyst as a realist, deeply immersed in the particularities of his patient's lives, but as an idealist, who invokes general truths as a way of dealing with individual problems.

In *Reunion in Vienna,* designed as a vehicle for the combined talents of Alfred Lunt and Lynn Fontanne rather than for those of a single lead performer, the need for two separate star entrances effects the basic structure of the play. Instead of introducing the star halfway through the first act, as in *Brief Moment* and *In a Garden,* Sherwood introduces Elena (Lynn Fontanne) almost at once and retards the entrance of Rudolph Maximillian (Alfred Lunt) until several minutes into the second act. Then, knowing that the audience wishes to see the Lunts together, Sherwood teases the audience until more than halfway through the second act. We first confront a decidedly unstarlike Elena, who passes through the room, inventorying her husband's underwear. This is in marked contrast to the extravagant hokum of her second-act reunion with Rudolph, in which champagne is drunk, waltzes are danced, banter is exchanged, faces are slapped, and Elena escapes from the hotel still faithful to her husband, but without her wedding ring and evening gown.

Rudolph is the purest expression of hokum in the three plays. Years after the end of the Hapsburg Empire, he persists in behaving as if it existed. Reduced to driving a taxicab in Nice, he still has all the self-assurance of an aristocrat. Even when Krug's triumph seems complete, and he is arranging with the authorities to return Rudolph to France, and even as the Archduke's megalomaniacal self-confidence seems utterly deflated, Elena becomes his mistress again. Rather than being disillusioned by the spectacle of the defeated Hapsburg, with his torn coat (as her husband predicted), she is more touched by Rudolph in his defeat than in his overconfident swaggering. In the morning, she asks her husband to retrieve her wedding ring from Rudolph at the border, and sits quietly at the breakfast table. When her father-in-law proclaims that he has never had so much fun as during the Archduke's visit, she replies, "Neither have I," and smiles as the curtain falls.[23] The comment is enigmatic. Has her husband's cure ultimately worked, or not? Is she contentedly disillusioned, or has the lure of hokum reestablished itself more strongly than ever? The ambiguity of the ending was much discussed at the time of the play's Broadway run, and Sherwood felt that it contributed to the play's success.[24] As with Lissa and Abby, Elena's complexity ultimately destroys any certainty that her feelings can be identified and contained within an intellectual scheme. This ambiguity is highly effective theatrically, even though it tends to blur the play's intellectual argument. Sherwood said that the initial concept of *Reunion in Vienna* was "science hoist with its own petard,"[25] and published a lengthy and somber preface to the play, but neither Rudolph nor Elena is given a strong intellectual position to counter Anton's scientific modernism. Idea confronts hokum, and hokum carries the theatrical day. The idealized intellectual pattern of the play is eclipsed by its sheer theatricality.[26] Indeed, the play *celebrates* the triumph of theatricality over Krug's intellectual formulae.

In a Garden, Brief Moment, and *Reunion in Vienna* tell stories of detached intellectuals whose abilities to understand other people are limited by their allegiance to abstractions. Adrian Terry prizes taste over passion and can only deal with his wife through artifice. Roderick Deane flees from his guests to muse over whether this is the "final flicker of civilization" (p. 151)—a reprise of the fall of Rome—and will not act on the emotional impulses that could save his marriage. Abby expertly diagnoses his failure to act passionately: "This isn't control, this is anemia" (p. 230). At first, Anton Krug seems different; we are told he opposed the aristocratic rule of the Hapsburgs and spent time in prison. Yet he, too, is a captive of his dignity, distance, and reliance on psychoanalytic theory. The idealizing assumptions of high comedy are linked in all three plays to a lack of intimacy, distance in human relationships, imperfect knowledge of others, and elitism. These plays present idealism as a view of life that unduly limits human possibilities, something that presents human nature as set and predictable. More than the tuxedos, evening gowns, and opulent drawing rooms of American high comedy, it was this essentializing approach to human nature that bothered these playwrights.

Adrian, Roderick, and Anton exhibit the stance of the detached American intellectual whose view of the implications of democracy "especially its cultural implications—[is] unhappy and whose experiences of the intellectual life of the American democracy [are] painful."[27] These are the American intellectuals historian Richard Hofstadter described as "engaged in incompatible efforts. They have tried to be good and believing citizens of a democratic society and at the same time to resist the vulgarization which that society constantly produces."[28] Similarly, the critics and historians of American drama take their places among the alienated intellectuals of these high comedies. In the tradition of John Gassner, Brenda Murphy, and W. B. Worthen, the fixity of dramatic text is preferred to the vigorous fluidity of theatrical event, and the history of American realistic drama is misrepresented as a theatre of neutralized audiences and self-effacing stage personalities. Roderick Deane's exasperated question "Underneath these layers of adaptive coloring—what are you?" (p. 118) finds its equivalent in critic Jonas Barish's jeremiad: "Playwrights in every age including our own have turned away, nauseated, from the insatiable narcissism of the actors to whom they have confided their texts" (p. 349). In passages such as this, the difference between the intellectual and the theatre is expressed as a dignified distance from hokum; the reality of performance must be either disciplined or expunged. Rudolph Maximillian's presence in Vienna is a criminal act in the world of Anton Krug. Roderick admits that Abby has "the eternal glamor of the illicit" (p. 233). Both in the plays and in the critical literature, the attitude of the intellectual toward the actor tends to be suspicious and censorious.

Barry, Behrman, and Sherwood partake in this detachment, insofar as they present their intellectual characters sympathetically and write in the intellectual mode of high comedy. They do not, however, embrace the position of alienation. Although these playwrights were contemporaries of the expatriate "Lost Generation," they chose to remain in the United States, write for the popular stage, and showcase the stars beloved by its audience. As such, they do not try to resist what Hofstadter describes as the "vulgarization" of democratic culture; they seek a compromise with it. They wed glamor and presence of the star performers to characters who are less intellectual and more intuitive, who seek to obliterate the distance between themselves and others. These characters—Lissa, Abby, Elena, and Maximillian—struggle to go beyond any scripts that are set out for them. In these plays, hokum becomes the most democratic mode of expression, transcending the literary controls of both realism and idealism. Their dedication to hokum celebrates the mysterious, the confused, the unpredictable and, above all, *free* element in human beings. Idealism is identified with alienated intellectuals; hokum, with the popular allure of glamorous stars. This is best seen in *Reunion in Vienna,* in which the intellectual, Anton, claims to be democratic, but which reveals the Hapsburg Archduke to be the true democrat, smacking bottoms, brawling, and striding about without his trousers. The democratic impulse is identified not with class position but with an ability to play, and an ability to partake in the modes of popular entertainment, whether the Archduke's slapstick comedy or Abby Fane's nightclub ballads. Yet the result is not anti-intellectual. Abby can sing in a speakeasy and be the intellectual equal of Roderick Deane; the Archduke can hold his own with Vienna's leading psychoanalyst. The balance between democracy and intellect that Hofstadter judges "incompatible" is achieved through the range and virtuosity of its star performances.

In this complex negotiation between intellectuals and stars, American high comedy makes continual use of realistic conventions, but never questions the assumptions behind them. Realism becomes an unquestioned arena in which idealism and hokum play out their problematic courtship. Like the air the characters breathe, realism is held in common and taken for granted. As servants of three masters, Barry, Behrman, and Sherwood reflected at length on the claims of idealism and hokum, but did not dare to question the power of realism in their high comedies. That "third master" was both too useful a means of achieving coherence in an otherwise divided world and too powerful to be questioned.

Notes

I owe much to Stephanie Barbé Hammer, of the University of California–Riverside, and Jim Gulledge, for their valuable suggestions and help in the writing of this article.

1. Brenda Murphy, *American Realism and American Drama, 1880–1940* (Cambridge: Cambridge UP, 1987), p. 114. Subsequent references are cited in the text.

2. William B. Worthen, *Modern Drama and the Rhetoric of Theater* (Berkeley: U of California P, 1992), pp. 20–21.

3. Bert O. States, "The Actor's Presence: Three Phenomenal Modes," *Theatre Journal* 35.3 (Oct. 1983): 365.

4. Northrop Frye, *The Anatomy of Criticism: Four Essays* (Princeton: Princeton UP, 1957), p. 285. Subsequent references are cited in the text.

5. Michael Goldman, *The Actor's Freedom: Toward a Theory of Drama* (New York: Viking Press, 1975), p. 86. Subsequent references are cited in the text.

6. For an example of this narrative, see Oscar G. Brockett, *History of Theatre* (Boston: Allyn and Bacon, 1970), pp. 442–47.

7. John Gassner, *Form and Idea in Modern Theatre* (New York: Dryden Press, 1956), p. 91. Subsequent references are cited in the text.

8. I am indebted to René Wellek ("The Concept of Realism in Literary Scholarship," in *Concepts of Criticism*, ed. Stephen H. Nichols, Jr., pp. 222–55 [New Haven: Yale UP, 1963]) for his distinction between realist and classicist types (p. 246). I differ from him, however, in his stress on the centrality of types to a definition of realism (pp. 242–53).

9. Roland Barthes, *On Racine*, trans. Richard Howard (New York: Performing Arts Journal Publications, 1983), p. 142.

10. George Meredith, *Essay on Comedy* (New York: Chapman and Hall, 1877), p. 10. Subsequent references are cited in the text. Meredith's *Essay on Comedy* was the single most influential critical text on high comedy during this period. Critic Joseph Wood Krutch, theatrical reviewer for the *Nation*, clearly shows Meredith's influence. See, for example, his "Drama: the Kinds of Comedy," *Nation* (Dec. 2, 1931): 621–22, and "The Comic Wisdom of S. N. Behrman," *Nation* (July 19, 1933): 74–76. Through Krutch's mediating influence, Meredith's *Essay* becomes a key text in interpreting Behrman's plays. Behrman himself, in a notebook at the Wisconsin Center for Theatre and Film Research, while detailing plans for *No Time for Comedy*, quotes a passage from the *Essay on Comedy*. See Robert F. Gross, *S. N. Behrman: A Research and Production Sourcebook* (Westport, Conn.: Greenwood Press, 1992), pp. 168–70.

11. Although Northrop Frye uses the term *social comedy* rather than *high comedy*, he makes a similar observation. See Frye, *Anatomy*, pp. 285–87.

12. See Roman Ingarden, *The Literary Work of Art: An Investigation on the Border-lines of Ontology, Logic, and Theory of Literature,* trans. George G. Grabowicz (Evanston: Northwestern UP, 1973), pp. 377–79.

13. Robert Sherwood, *The Queen's Husband* (New York: Charles Scribner's Sons, 1928), p. xvi. Subsequent references are cited in the text.

14. Jonas Barish, in *The Anti-Theatrical Prejudice* (Berkeley: U of California P, 1981), pp. 343–49, documents the widespread disparagement of actors by nine-teenth-century reformers. (Subsequent references to Barish are cited in the text.) For contemporaneous points of view similar to Sherwood's, see Charle Parker Hammond, "Hopkins Sees a New Era," *New York Evening Post* (Feb. 25, 1933), and Sidney Howard, "Preface," *Lucky Sam McCarver: Four Episodes in the Rise of a New Yorker* (New York: Charles Scribner's Sons, 1926), pp. xiv–xviii.

15. Alexander Woollcott, review of *In a Garden, New York World* (Nov. 17, 1925).

16. Brooks Atkinson, "Lunt and Fontanne, Comedians," *New York Times* (Nov. 29, 1931), sec. 1, p. 1.

17. Although *Brief Moment* is obviously constructed as a vehicle for its leading lady, an unusual event colored the critical reception of the first production. Reviewer and personality Alexander Woollcott was signed to make his professional stage debut in the supporting role of Harold Sigrift. The resultant flurry of excitement over this casting skewed perceptions of the play, and largely overshadowed Ms. Larrimore's performance. See Gross, *S. N. Behrman*, p. 21.

18. S. N. Behrman, *Brief Moment* (New York: Farrar and Rhinehart, 1931), p. 7. Subsequent references are cited in the text.

19. Philip Barry, *In a Garden* (New York: Samuel French, 1929), p. 68. Subsequent references are cited in the text.

20. Frank Goheen Bradley, *The Collapse of Dialogue and the Phenomenon of Social Drama: Ten American Plays of the Twenties and Thirties,* unpublished Ph.D. diss., Cornell University, 1989, p. 60.

21. For examples, see Woollcott's review as well as the anonymous reviews, "Beauty in Metaphysical Rebellion," *New York Times* (Nov. 22, 1925), sec 8, p. 1, and "Critique: The Theatre," *New Yorker* (Nov. 28, 1925), p. 15.

22. S. N. Berhman, *The Burning Glass* (London: Hamish Hamilton, 1968), title page.

23. Robert Sherwood, *Reunion in Vienna* (New York: Charles Scribner's Sons, 1932), p. 205.

24. John Mason Brown, *The Worlds of Robert E. Sherwood: Mirror to His Times, 1896–1939* (New York: Harper and Row, 1965), p. 278.

25. Qtd. in Brown, *Worlds,* p. 26.

26. Walter J. Meserve, *Robert E. Sherwood: Reluctant Moralist* (New York: Pegasus, 1970), p. 80.

27. Robert Dawidoff, *The Genteel Tradition and the Sacred Rage: High Culture vs. Democracy in Adams, James, and Santayana* (Chapel Hill: U of North Carolina P, 1957), p. 2.

28. Richard Hofstadter, *Anti-intellectualism in American Life* (New York: Knopf, 1963), p. 407.

SIX

Remembering the Disremembered: Feminist Realists of the Harlem Renaissance

Patricia R. Schroeder

When Angelina Weld Grimké's realist play *Rachel* was first produced by the NAACP's Drama Committee in 1916, it became something of a cause célèbre in the African-American theatrical community. The program notes from the 1916 production, which proclaim the play as "the first attempt to use the stage for race propaganda"[1] provoked what one recent critic has called a "cultural war . . . [fought] over accurate depictions of the African-American community."[2] Central to this conflict over representation, which affected both female and male theatre practitioners and became one of the defining motifs of the Harlem Renaissance,[3] were the competing aesthetic theories of W. E. B. Du Bois and Alain Locke.[4]

For Du Bois, all art was propaganda. Defining a "Negro theatre" that would be centered in African-American experience and written by African Americans, Du Bois espoused "race" or "propaganda" plays that would depict racial discrimination realistically, demonstrate its detrimental consequences on worthy black Americans, and so prove to white audiences that African Americans deserved a chance at material success and social equality.[5] The other camp, led by Alain Locke, vehemently disagreed with this agenda, arguing that individual expression—art for its own sake—was the only appropriate goal of creative endeavor.[6] Together with Montgomery Gregory, and in direct reaction to the 1916 production of *Rachel,* Locke resigned from the NAACP Drama Committee and began to develop the alternative dramatic form that would become the hallmark of his soon-to-be-formed Howard Players: the folk play.[7] Focusing on the everyday experiences, customs, beliefs, traditions, music, and language of ordinary black people without emphasizing racial oppression, the folk plays of the 1920s were, in effect, an African-American–centered celebration of daily life in black communities, written primarily for black audiences.

Despite the heated controversy between these two intellectual leaders and the editorial barbs they launched at each other through the competing literary journals, *The Crisis* and *Opportunity*, Du Bois's propaganda plays and Locke's folk dramas shared some largely unrecognized common goals, not the least of which is a common reliance on stage realism. While class differences remained an issue (with Du Bois favoring genteel characters of bourgeois aspirations and Locke promoting working-class folk in their own milieu),[8] both critics saw the black-centered theatre as a place where the prevailing stage stereotypes of African Americans (the demeaning legacy of minstrel shows) could be replaced by representations of human beings. And since both Du Bois and Locke demanded accurate stage portrayals of the African Americans they knew offstage, both obviously accepted the mimetic power of theatre to mirror reality in an unmediated way. For playwrights of this era, before poststructuralism undermined our faith in realism's mimetic capabilities, stage realism, by approximating as closely as possible the life experienced in African-American communities, could vividly protest the oppression of its members (in propaganda plays) and also commemorate black culture (in folk plays).

Working within this dynamic African-American theatrical community of the period were a large number of women playwrights,[9] who faced all the racial tensions and aesthetic conflicts of their male counterparts, with the additional problems of depicting the largely effaced black female experience and of combating degrading sexual stereotypes as well as racial ones. This problem of stereotypical representation was an especially complex one for African-American women of the era. Both in popular culture and in literary and theatrical texts of the period, black women were routinely depicted as either stolid matriarchs or wanton whores, with "no equitable variations in between."[10] In a poignant 1925 essay on then current images of black women, Elise Johnson McDougald explained the psychological dam-

age done to women who could not help but absorb the false but ubiquitous representations of them: "Even in New York, the general attitude of mind causes the Negro woman serious difficulty. She is conscious that what is left of chivalry is not directed at her. She realizes
that the ideas of beauty, built up in the fine arts, have excluded her
almost entirely. Instead, the grotesque Aunt Jemimas of the streetcar
advertisements, proclaim only an ability to serve, without grace or
loveliness. Nor does the drama catch her finest spirit. She is most often
used to provoke the mirthless laugh of ridicule; or to portray feminine
viciousness or vulgarity not peculiar to Negroes. This is the shadow
over her."[11] Given this cultural climate, both on and off the stage, it
is clear that replacing stereotypical images of African-American
women would be of paramount importance to these female playwrights. Realism, with its ability to present coherent and developing
characters who are shaped by and respond to their environments, offered these dramatists a built-in opportunity to assert the creativity
and humanity of black women.

While stereotypes of mammy and whore dominated representations of black women, the reality of African-American women's lives
before the twentieth century had been all but erased from American
history. There are, of course, multiple reasons for such oversight, ranging from poor record keeping by slave owners to a widespread politics
of silence among black women determined to protect their privacy
and middle-class status. Given this secrecy and silence surrounding
African-American women's shared and individual histories, writing
plays to reconstruct their lives was both challenging and important.
As Barbara Christian has pointed out, the concept of remembering
and reevaluating the past "could not be at the center of a narrative's
[or a play's] revisioning of history until the obvious fact that African-
Americans did have a history and culture was firmly established in
American society";[12] without such factual background information,
writers would lack the details necessary to impart authenticity to their
works and audiences would lack a context in which to read or view.
For these women playwrights of the Harlem Renaissance, therefore,
a crucial first step in claiming the stage for a black feminist vision was
to discover and depict the historical and cultural facts that black
women had repressed or to which they had been denied access.

For this task, like the tasks of depicting oppression and overturning stereotypes, African-American women playwrights turned to realism. While their numerous plays dramatize subjects as varied as lynching, poor treatment of black war veterans, gender roles within the black community, and the debilitating effects of poverty, the explicitly feminist issues of reproductive freedom and motherhood appear repeatedly in their works, and will form the focal point for my analysis of their plays. For even within the confines of this one narrow topic, examples abound of black female playwrights turning to realism to protest racial discrimination, to correct degrading stereotypes, and to reclaim something of African-American women's unrecorded history.

An early and obvious example of such a play is Grimké's *Rachel,* which, as we saw above, sparked the furor over dramatic aesthetics that would become one defining element of the Harlem Renaissance. A clear-cut example of the propaganda play that Du Bois espoused, this realist drama takes place behind the fourth wall of the Loving family parlor. The Lovings are a respectable, middle-class family consisting of a mother, a son Tom, and a daughter Rachel. The title character is an ebullient teenager when we first meet her, devoted to her family and her education. Her dominant characteristics are a love for children (especially "the little black and brown babies") and a fervent desire someday to marry and raise a large family of her own.[13] As she matures into a young woman in the second and third acts, however, she learns that her father and an elder brother were killed by a lynch mob, and she suffers when her young adopted son is physically and verbally abused by a gang of white boys. Traumatized by this violent racism, Rachel refuses the marriage proposal of the man she loves, vowing never to marry and bring more black children into the world to be blighted by racial abuse.

In commenting on her motives for writing this play—which some contemporary reviewers saw as advocating genocide[14]—Grimké defines white women as her target audience and motherhood as the hook by which she would enlist their support in black women's causes: "If anything can make all women sisters underneath their skins, it is motherhood. If then I could make the white women of this country see, feel, understand just what effect their prejudice and the prejudice of their fathers, brothers, husbands, sons were having on the souls of the colored mothers everywhere and upon the mothers that are to be, a great power to affect public opinion would be set free and the battle would be half won."[15]

Motherhood is certainly a key issue of the play, and, in fact, a number of critics have complained that Grimké overloaded the play with excessive sentimentality on this topic. These commentators criticize Rachel's frequent effusions about babies and motherhood and the flowery language in which she habitually discusses them.[16] Given Grimké's goal of enlisting white women in black women's causes, however, I am inclined to agree with Judith Stephens, who sees Grimké as *intervening* in the cultural code the play ostensibly espouses. Stephens writes: "In *Rachel,* Angelina Grimké threw the image of idealized motherhood back at white women in an attempt to make them see what meaning this so-called 'revered institution' might hold for black women. . . . In writing *Rachel,* Grimké used the sentimental language of the [era's] dominant gender ideology, which idealized motherhood, but the play does not support or concede to that ideology. Instead, it breaks dominant gender ideology by raising the issue of race and asking white women to consider what black mothers must face."[17]

Despite Grimké's avowed interest in engaging a white female audience, a number of recent critics have asserted, probably correctly, that she also sought a black audience "that needed to see an image of its members . . . as they wished themselves to be."[18] In order to protest the unfair treatment of blacks in a white-dominated society, Grimké consciously created characters to represent (in her words) "the best type of colored people."[19] These characters are middle-class paragons, conscientious about family, work, school, and upward mobility; they speak proper English; in short, they are clear-cut examples of the genteel models advocated by Du Bois.

Grimké's probable interest in engaging two audiences—a white one that needed to be shown the conditions of oppression and a black one that needed to see positive stage images of itself—led her on both counts to employ the conventions of realism. In a letter written about *Rachel,* Grimké mentions reading the realist plays of Henrik Ibsen and the naturalist dramas of August Strindberg and Gerhart Hauptmann.[20] Not surprisingly, she imported a number of their dramatic conventions into her own play. In addition to the fourth-wall set and developing characters already mentioned, Grimké structured her play according to a realistic causal logic: stories from the past and incidents occurring in the present combine to form an unbreakable chain of events that restricts Rachel's options and leads inexorably to her rejection of motherhood.

While partaking perhaps of more sentimentality and melodrama than current taste will accept as credible, Grimké's realist play did have a lasting impact on the black women playwrights who followed her. While "the stark realism and political nature" of *Rachel* startled many of Grimké's male contemporaries,[21] and while the debate over whether writing should be political or simply artistic continued to rage, *Rachel* defined playwriting as a powerful ideological tool for other black women playwrights of the Harlem Renaissance who followed Grimké's lead.

Grimké's influence on other playwrights can be seen as early as 1919, just three years after the original production of *Rachel*, when her close friend Mary P. Burrill published a realist, pro–birth control play in Margaret Sanger's *Birth Control Review*. Unlike Grimké, Burrill created characters who are neither genteel nor upwardly mobile. Instead, they are poor rural women trapped in an endless cycle of childbearing and poverty. What Burrill's *They That Sit in Darkness* shares with *Rachel*, however, is an interest in documenting the anguish of African-American motherhood, a protest agenda, and a realist dramatic form.

Like *Rachel, They That Sit in Darkness* employs the fourth-wall convention, depicting one of the two rooms in the Jasper family's overcrowded rural shack. The action concerns two women: Malinda Jasper, who is the mother of ten children, and her seventeen-year-old daughter Lindy, who is preparing to leave for Tuskegee Institute on a grant. Using a sort of documentary realism, the play depicts the typical events of a day in this mother and daughter's lives. The stark and dingy setting, Malinda's and Lindy's weariness as they struggle over a washtub and with the many unruly younger children, the lack of milk for the baby and food for the others, and Malinda's apparent weakness (she has recently delivered her tenth baby) all vividly illustrate the destitution under which the family suffers and counteract the notion prevalent in the era (and lingering into our own) that poverty is somehow deserved or can be overcome by a willingness to work.

The climax of the play comes with the entrance of Elizabeth Shaw, a white visiting nurse, who arrives to check on Malinda's heart condition. Their brief conversation about birth control is central to the play. When Nurse Shaw naively counsels Malinda to avoid hard work and future pregnancies, the following dialogue ensues:

Mrs. Jasper: But whut kin Ah do—de chillern come!

Miss Shaw: You must be careful.

Mrs. Jasper: Be keerful! Dat's all you nurses say! . . . Ah been keerful all Ah knows how but whut's it got me—ten chillern, eight living an' two daid! You gotta be telling me sumpin' bettertn dat, Mis' Liz'beth!

Miss Shaw (fervently): I wish to God it were lawful for me to do so! My heart goes out to you people that sit in darkness, having, year after year, children you are physically too weak to bring into the world—children that you are unable not only to educate but even to clothe and feed. Malinda, when I took my oath as a nurse, I swore to abide by the laws of the State, and the law forbids my telling you what you have a right to know![22]

This brief exchange manifests many of the conflicts of the play. The contrast in the two women's dialects, for instance, illustrates realistically the differences in class and education that accompany their difference in race. Further, Miss Shaw believes in the letter of the law; she has accepted the privileges her race, education, job, and access to information have afforded her, and will not violate this power structure to help Malinda control her reproductive destiny or her life. The fact that the state prevents health care professionals from providing information that would save women's lives—and that even Miss Shaw thinks they have a right to know—underscores the complex network of unseen authorities that conspire to maintain the darkness of impoverished lives.

The plot, like that of *Rachel,* is structured according to a realistic causality. Miss Shaw's refusal to share information with Malinda leads inevitably to Malinda's death. That the cycle will be endlessly repeated as long as birth control information is withheld is abundantly clear through Lindy's fate. Realizing that she cannot attend college as planned, Lindy relinquishes her dream of improving the family's condition and takes her mother's place as caretaker to the other children.

Burrill was also clearly attempting to refute racist and sexist images in her portrayal of the Jasper women, who defy the traditional stereotypes of black women. Malinda and Lindy are neither stoic maternal figures nor promiscuous whores. Furthermore, they are not passive victims, but actively seek ways out of their entrapment: Malinda wants birth control information and Lindy wants an education. In these two characters, Burrill has created positive images of black women who seek to change their lives; their inability to overcome their victimization is clearly portrayed as society's fault, not theirs.[23] Burrill emphasizes this point in her starkly naturalistic set, which illustrates the power of environment (both physical and social) to control destinies. With its realistic dialogue, naturalistic set, and the inevitable causality that leads to Malinda's death and the loss of Lindy's single opportunity, the play depends upon techniques of stage realism to denounce the law's enforcement of poverty and ignorance that, like the people they enchain, endlessly reproduce themselves. *They That Sit in Darkness* illustrates the strategic use of realism as a form of social criticism, as a way of documenting what is in order to suggest what should be.

Other women of the Harlem Renaissance followed the leads of Grimké and Burrill in writing propaganda plays about current issues like lynching and suffrage. Another group, however, chose to focus on African-American women of the past, writing history plays and dramatic recreations of the lost voices of their female ancestors. Both male and female playwrights of the period took this mission of recovering lost stories seriously and wrote dramas about the achievements of African-American historical figures, presenting them from an African-American viewpoint. Randolph Edmonds's *Nat Turner* (1935), May Miller's *Harriet Tubman* (1935), and Langston Hughes's *Emperor of Haiti* (1936) are all prominent examples of this genre.

Several women playwrights, however, wrote realist plays to reclaim African-American women's history in a general way, by depicting the conditions of those women about whom specific facts are unknown, unrecorded, or simply repressed as unspeakable. In several striking cases, African-American women playwrights turned to a story that, as Toni Morrison comments in her novel *Beloved,* "was not a story to pass on."[24] I refer to the story recounted in *Beloved* and depicted in several plays of the era, that of a mother's killing her child to protect it from a life of racial or sexual abuse.

Georgia Douglas Johnson's 1929 play, *Safe,* exemplifies this genre. Set in a small southern town in 1893, *Safe* presents a double action. Onstage, the plot centers on Liza Pettigrew, happily married and about to give birth to her first child. Offstage, although discussed by the characters and in part overheard by the audience, an angry mob lynches seventeen-year-old Sam, a polite neighbor boy, for slapping the face of a white man who had first struck him. These two events fuse when Sam is heard outside screaming for his mother and Liza's baby is born, identified as a son, and strangled by his distraught mother to keep him (in her words) "safe from the lynchers."[25]

As this summary reveals, *Safe* inherited both its protest agenda and its realist method from *Rachel* and *They That Sit in Darkness. Safe* further illustrates the mutually influential relationship between public issues (the lynching) and private tensions (Liza's maternal fears). Because this double plot skillfully interweaves the political and the personal in a causal chain, the play defines lynching as "*both* a violent crime *and* a pervasive influence in daily life."[26] By bringing the chilling results of lynching into the Pettigrews' peaceful living room, Johnson protested the way racial violence hovered menacingly over even the joyful aspects of African-American domestic life—including the birth of a baby who (unlike Malinda's children) is eagerly awaited.

In addition to the anti-lynch message of this propaganda play, however, Johnson clearly illustrates the way motherhood was intertwined with racial oppression for African-American women. In explaining this connection, scholar Kathy Perkins has written that certain issues of the era "could only be expressed by a black woman. Neither the white nor the black male playwright could express the intense pain and fear a black woman experienced concerning her children—wondering, for instance, if the child she carried for nine months would be sold into slavery, or be a son who might one day be lynched."[27] While I hesitate to endorse the seeming essentialism of Perkins's statement (which implies that the conditions of African-American motherhood are unimaginable to others), within *Safe* Liza's despair does identify motherhood as something unique and terrible for black women of this historical period, a condition that reveals the inseparability of race, gender, and historical context in defining feminist issues.

As Perkins's comment above further suggests, this conflict within African-American motherhood is a particularly distressing legacy of slavery. When a child could be sold at an owner's whim, when a slave woman's behavior could be coerced by threats to her child, when a child was the result of rape, or when a child's inevitable slave status would only perpetuate the institution of slavery, motherhood became a profoundly vexed issue.[28] As a result, an emotionally overwrought mother might actually view infanticide as an act of love and protection, as Liza in *Safe* evidently did when faced with a lynch mob. Moving beyond the era of lynching, deeper into the historical past, playwright Shirley Graham explored the connections between motherhood, slavery, and infanticide in her powerful 1940 drama, *It's Morning.*[29]

Information about actual historical cases of infanticide among slaves is difficult to obtain. While historians like Eugene Genovese claim that slave abortions and infanticide were not a problem for slave owners because "the slaves . . . loved their children too much to do away with them,"[30] oral histories and court records suggest that the infanticide committed by Margaret Garner, the historical slave woman on whom Toni Morrison loosely based her protagonist Sethe in *Beloved,* was not unique.[31] While the handful of documented cases of slave infanticide certainly does not indicate a general trend, surviving slave narratives suggest that those mothers who killed their children acted out of love, motivated by "an understanding of the living death that awaited their children under slavery."[32]

But child killing may simply have been the most extreme example of a widespread, and of course undocumented, female slave resistance to the institution of slavery. Using actions ranging from sexual abstinence to abortion networks to infanticide, these women rejected "their vital economic function as breeders," an opposition with major political and economic implications for the slave owners.[33] After slavery was abolished, a politics of silence arose among black women regarding their past rebellious actions and their own sexuality, a "culture of dissemblance" designed for self-protection.[34] Events like infanticide, then, routinely left out of formal histories and seen in African-American oral tradition as "not a story to pass on," would clearly be of interest to a playwright bent on recovering African-American women's lost history.

Graham's *It's Morning,* the most obvious example of this genre, is set in a slave cabin on the last day of December, 1862.[35] Cissie, a slave mother, has just received word that her vivacious fourteen-year-old daughter, Millie, has been sold to a lascivious creditor. In response to

Cissie's grief, Grannie Lou, the oldest slave on the plantation, recounts two stories to the group of slaves gathered in Cissie's cabin. First, she tells them that Cissie was once as lighthearted as her daughter, until an overseer vowed to break her will and did so with repeated rapes. Second, she narrates the tale of a queenly slave woman from Africa, noted for her strength in cutting down cane stalks, who lined up her three sons to watch the sunrise and beheaded them from behind— with one swoop of her cane knife—to prevent their being sold down river. Cissie overhears this last story and, at dawn on the next day (New Year's Day), kills Millie with a cane knife. The play ends with Cissie's proffering Millie's limp body to the horrified Yankee boy who arrives too late with the news that slavery has been abolished, sug- gesting that the sunrise framing him in the doorway, symbol of a new day dawning for the freed slaves, will never obliterate the ghastly atrocities on which slavery was built.

Despite this rather melodramatic symbolism at the end, the play, like *Rachel* and *They That Sit in Darkness,* depends on techniques of dramatic realism to counteract stereotypes. While Cissie's action can be seen as a mercy killing designed to spare Millie the life of degra- dation that Cissie herself has suffered, murdering her own child as a safeguard against sexual abuse effectively undermines Cissie's status as either nurturing mammy or loose woman. In recreating slave life onstage, however, Graham's realism serves another end, one distinct in both purpose and technique from that used by Grimké and Burrill twenty years earlier or by Johnson in her version of the Medea story. Instead of depicting present conditions to protest them, Graham's play dramatizes a past that has been suppressed. To accomplish this re- creation of the forgotten past, Graham fused the cause-and-effect logic, realistic setting, and upstanding characters typical of propaganda plays with the dialect, oral stories, and music that characterize folk plays. Because of this innovative embedding of African rhythms and culture within a traditional Aristotelian structure, Elizabeth Brown- Guillory has described *It's Morning* as "a major breakthrough in Afri- can-American drama."[36]

Graham's attention to representing African-American slave culture faithfully is apparent from the beginning of the playtext. In the open- ing stage directions, the playwright comments that the diverse dialects in *It's Morning* are intentionally not uniform, but are meant to reflect the various African languages from which slave dialects evolved as well as the changes in pitch and volume that African Americans use to indicate changes in meaning. And by employing realism's linear causality, Graham elucidates the tragic and long-lasting consequences of sexual abuse, which range in this play from spiritual damage to murder.

Yet because of the folk elements incorporated into this conventionally realistic framework, the play offers some hope for cultural survival beyond that suggested by the rising sun of the conclusion. By depicting oral history in action, *It's Morning* makes explicit the importance of keeping the past alive through storytelling. Both Cissie's past and the legend of the noble African woman are communicated to the slave women and to the audience through Grannie Lou's unofficial history, a spoken tale. Despite their lack of formal documentation, Grannie's remembered truths are powerful: they explain Cissie's motives for killing Millie and provide a model (complete with choice of weapon) for the murder. To be sure, without Grannie Lou's oral history Cissie might never have taken her tragic action. However, in the context of the play, Grannie Lou's story emphasizes the heroism of the African mother and suggests the defiance and pride of black people who must use drastic measures to resist their enslavement. Furthermore, without such oral histories and without plays like this one, women like Cissie would be in the same straights as those Morrison described for her character Beloved: "Disremembered and unaccounted for, she cannot be lost because no one is looking for her" (p. 274). Combining a realistic structure with elements of folk drama, Graham could record some of the content of African-American oral history, embody its interactive form, document its authority, and restore voice to long-silenced African-American women.

Arguing convincingly about realism's inherent theoretical limitations, materialist feminists Judith Newton and Deborah Rosenfelt have stated that "literature and cultural production [do not] 'reflect' history in a simple mimetic moment. Since we live within myths and narratives about history, there can in fact be no reflections of it. Literature, rather, draws upon various ideological productions of history or discourses about history to make its own production."[37] Given the widely accepted poststructuralist mistrust of realism's claim to record offstage reality faithfully and objectively, this critique of mimetic representational strategies is hard to quarrel with. But when viewed in the context of the interlocking factors of race, gender, and social oppression faced by the female playwrights of the Harlem Renaissance era, realism was clearly a valuable instrument for protesting conditions as they were and for recording and acknowledging alternative versions of history. In fact, what these early black feminists did was exactly what Newton and Rosenfelt espouse: they questioned the established "productions of history" and replaced them with their own "discourses about history," borrowing realism's referential power to document abuse, to dispute degrading stereotypes, and to resurrect and preserve a facet of herstory that had been disremembered and unaccounted for. Arguing against the use of inherited conventions like realism for African-American feminists, Audre Lorde has stated that the master's tools will never dismantle the master's house.[38] These pioneering African-American realists, however, saw a sledgehammer lying in the master's yard and used it to their advantage. In so doing, they created in American drama a tradition unique to African-American women and left a legacy that we residents of the postmodern cosmos would do well not to disremember.

Notes

1. Cited in Robert J. Fehrenbach, "An Early Twentieth-Century Problem Play of Life in Black America: Angelina Grimké's *Rachel,*" in *Wild Women in the Whirlwind: Afra-American Culture and the Contemporary Literary Renaissance,* ed. Joanne M. Braxton and Andree Nicola McLaughlin (New Brunswick: Rutgers UP, 1990), pp. 89–106, at 91.

2. Wahneema Lubiano, "But Compared to What? Reading Realism, Representation, and Essentialism in *School Daze, Do the Right Thing,* and the Spike Lee Discourse," *Black American Literature Forum* 25 (1991): 263.

3. It is difficult to define the Harlem Renaissance (or the New Negro Renaissance, or the Negro Renaissance) with any precision, since both the name of this African-American aesthetic movement and the exact dates of its influence are currently under debate. "Harlem Renaissance" is the most familiar title, but scholars like Katana Hall (*Reclaiming the Legacy: An Afracentric Analysis of Selected Plays by African American Wimmin Playwrights, 1916–1930,* Ph.D. diss., Bowling Green State University, 1990) have correctly pointed out that this term devalues the contributions of such artists as Alain Locke and Georgia Douglas Johnson, who, like many other writers of the time, lived and worked outside New York (p. 28). Other critics challenge the dates usually assigned, which are based on the end of World War I

in 1919 and the stock market crash in 1929. Abraham Chapman, for instance, contends that certain defining elements of Harlem Renaissance literature were recognizable as early as the mid-1910s in Claude McKay's poetry ("The Harlem Renaissance in Literary History," *CLA Journal* 11 [Sept. 1967]: 44–45), while several other scholars suggest extending the endpoint to coincide with the Harlem riots in 1935 or even into the civil rights era of the 1960s. For overviews of these controversies see Nathan Irvin Huggins, "Introduction," *Voices from the Harlem Renaissance* (New York: Oxford UP, 1976), pp. 3–10; Jay Plum, "Rose McClendon and the Black Units of the Federal Theatre Project: A Lost Contribution," *Theatre Survey* 33 (Nov. 1992): 144–53; and Cary D. Wintz, *Black Culture and the Harlem Renaissance* (Houston: Rice UP, 1988), p. 13.

Whatever the exact title and duration of this Renaissance, the decade of the 1920s saw the emergence of an African-American dramatic tradition that extended beyond the '20s and Harlem and to which both women and men contributed.

4. For a comprehensive overview of the Du Bois/Locke debate, see Samuel A. Hay, *African American Theatre* (Cambridge: Cambridge UP, 1994). This volume contains a discussion of Hay's work and the Du Bois/Locke debate in Bergesen and Demastes's essay on Baraka and August Wilson.

5. W. E. B. Du Bois, "Krigwa Little Theatre Movement," *The Crisis* 32 (1926): 134–36.

6. See Locke's comments about propaganda plays as cited in Huggins, *Voices from the Harlem Renaissance,* esp. pp. 312–13.

7. For details of Locke's reaction, see Leslie Catherine Sanders, *The Development of Black Theatre in America: From Shadows to Selves* (Baton Rouge: Louisiana State UP, 1988), p. 23.

8. The class bias of Du Bois's position has been well explained by Rebecca T. Cureau, "Toward an Aesthetic of Black/Folk Expression," in *Alain Locke: Reflections on a Modern Renaissance Man,* ed. Russell J. Linneman, pp. 77–90 (Baton Rouge: Louisiana State UP, 1982).

9. In 1987 Nellie McKay estimated that during the Harlem Renaissance eleven black women published twenty-one plays as compared to only a half-dozen black male playwrights; see " 'What Were They Saying?': Black Women Playwrights of the Harlem Renaissance," in *The Harlem Renaissance Re-examined,* ed. Victor A. Kramer (New York: AMS Press, 1987), pp. 129–46. However, McKay's estimate has already been shown to be low, especially given the controversy over the ending date of the Renaissance; see Kathy Perkins, ed., *Black Female Playwrights: An Anthology of Plays Before 1950* (Bloomington: Indiana UP, 1989), p. 1. Furthermore, McKay's estimate does not include the many black women's plays that were performed in community schools, auditoriums, and churches, but never published; see her "Black Theater and Drama in the 1920s: Years of Growing Pains," *Massachusetts Review* (Winter 1987): 615–26.

10. Cynthia Belgrave, quoted in Elizabeth Brown-Guillory, *Their Place on Stage: Black Women Playwrights in America* (New York: Praeger, 1988), p. 107. For further examination of these and other persistent literary stereotypes of black women, see

Barbara Christian, *Black Women Novelists: The Development of a Tradition, 1892–1976* (Westport, Conn.: Greenwood Press, 1980), pp. 10–19.

11. Elise Johnson McDougald, "The Task of Negro Womanhood," in *The New Negro: An Interpretation,* ed. Alain Locke (1925; rpt. New York: Arno, 1968), p. 370.

12. Barbara Christian, " 'Somebody Forgot to Tell Somebody Something': African-American Women's Historical Novels," in *Wild Women in the Whirlwind,* p. 333.

13. Angelina Weld Grimké, *Rachel,* in *Black Theater, U.S.A.: Forty-five Plays by Black Americans, 1847–1974,* ed. James V. Hatch (New York: Free Press, 1974), p. 143.

14. See Gloria T. Hull, *Color, Sex, and Poetry: Three Women Writers of the Harlem Renaissance* (Bloomington: Indiana UP, 1987), p. 121, for a summary of these reviews.

15. Qtd. in Jeanne-Marie A. Miller, "Angelina Weld Grimké: Playwright and Poet," *CLA Journal* 21 (June 1978): 517.

16. See, for example, Hatch, ed., *Black Theater, U.S.A.,* p. 138; Fehrenbach, "Problem Play," p. 97; and Hull's summary of this response in *Color, Sex, and Poetry,* pp. 121–23.

17. Judith L. Stephens, "The Anti-Lynch Play: Toward an Interracial Feminist Dialogue in Theatre," *Journal of American Drama and Theatre* 2.3 (1990): 62.

18. Hatch, ed., *Black Theater. U.S.A.,* p. 137; see also Hull, *Color, Sex, and Poetry,* pp. 117–18.

19. Quoted in Miller, "Angelina Weld Grimké," p. 515.

20. In Fehrenbach, "Problem Play," pp. 95–96.

21. Freda L. Scott, "Black Drama and the Harlem Renaissance," *Theatre Journal* 37.4 (Dec. 1985): 429.

22. Mary P. Burrill, *They That Sit in Darkness,* in Perkins, ed., *Black Female Playwrights,* pp. 71–72.

23. McKay, "What Were They Saying," pp. 138–39.

24. Toni Morrison, *Beloved* (New York: Knopf, 1987), p. 274. Subsequent references are cited in the text.

25. Georgia Douglas Johnson, *Safe* (1929), in *Wines in the Wilderness: Plays by African American Women from the Harlem Renaissance to the Present,* ed. Elizabeth Brown-Guillory (Westport, Conn.: Greenwood Press, 1990), p. 32.

26. Judith L. Stephens, "Anti-Lynch Plays by African American Women: Race, Gender, and Social Protest in American Drama," *African American Review* 26 (Summer 1992): 332.

27. Perkins, ed., *Black Female Playwrights,* p. 2.

28. Darlene Hine and Kate Wittenstein, "Female Slave Resistance: The Economics of Sex," in *The Black Woman Cross-Culturally,* ed. Filomina Chioma Steady (Cambridge, Mass.: Schenkman, 1981), pp. 295–96.

29. While the Harlem Renaissance is usually seen as ending before 1940 (the date of Graham's play), she herself was involved in the artistic endeavors of the period and later married W. E. B. Du Bois. Furthermore, as my third note explains, the endpoint of the Harlem Renaissance is open to debate. More to the point of this chapter, *It's Morning* clearly inherited its dramatic conventions and thematic

imperatives from Grimké and other writers of the Renaissance years, so I decided to include it in this discussion of feminist realists of the Harlem Renaissance.

30. Eugene Genovese, *Roll, Jordan, Roll: The World the Slaves Made* (New York: Random House, 1972), p. 497.

31. Raymond M. and Alice H. Bauer, for instance, quote five examples of documented slave infanticides in "Day to Day Resistance to Slavery," *Journal of Negro History* 27 (Oct. 1942): 388–419, as does Deborah Gray White in *Ar'n't I a Woman?: Female Slaves in the Plantation South* (New York: Norton, 1985), with little apparent overlap between the two sets of cases. For the details of documented cases of slave infanticide in the United States, see Bauer and Bauer, "Day to Day Resistance," pp. 416–18; Hine and Wittenstein, "Female Slave Resistance," pp. 291–95; B. A. Botkin, ed., *Lay My Burden Down: A Folk History of Slavery* (Athens: U of Georgia P, 1989 rpt. of 1945 edition), p. 54; Gerda Lerner, ed., *Black Women in White America: A Documentary History* (New York: Random House, 1973), pp. 38, 61–62; and White, *Ar'n't I a Woman?* pp. 87–89.

32. Hine and Wittenstein, "Female Slave Resistance," p. 295.

33. Hine and Wittenstein, "Female Slave Resistance," p. 296.

34. Darlene Clark Hine, "Rape and the Inner Lives of Black Women in the Middle West: Preliminary Thoughts on the Culture of Dissemblance," *Signs* 14 (Summer 1989): 915.

35. Throughout this discussion, I refer to the version of *It's Morning* printed in Perkins's anthology *Black Female Playwrights* and housed (according to Perkins's bibliography) in the Fisk University Library special collection, Nashville, Tenn. A different version of the same play with the slightly different title *It's Mornin'* appears in Elizabeth Brown-Guillory's anthology *Wines in the Wilderness*. While Brown-Guillory cites no manuscript, she evidently bases her version of the play on the 1940 Yale University Theatre production (p. 83). In the Yale version, the story line, many of the characters, and many of the speeches are identical to those in the Fisk version. However, the Yale version dramatizes two things that occur offstage in the version under discussion: the visit of the slave owner, Mrs. Tilden, to Cissie's cabin, and the New Year's party Cissie gives so that Millie may enjoy one final day of happiness.

36. Brown-Guillory, *Wines in the Wilderness*, p. 82. Her comment on the play refers to the Yale version rather than to the one under discussion. However, since her statement refers to elements common to both plays (like Grannie Lou's status as voodoo woman and Graham's use of music), it is equally relevant to the version under discussion.

37. Judith Newton and Deborah Rosenfelt, "Introduction: Toward a Materialist-Feminist Criticism," in *Feminist Criticism and Social Change: Sex, Class, and Race in Literature and Culture,* ed. Newton and Rosenfelt (New York: Methuen, 1985), p. xxiii.

38. Audre Lorde, "The Master's Tools Will Never Dismantle the Master's House," in *This Bridge Called My Back: Writings by Radical Women of Color,* ed. Cherríe Moraga and Gloria Anzaldua, pp. 98–101 (New York: Kitchen Table Press, 1981).

SEVEN

Eugene O'Neill and Reality in America

Frank R. Cunningham

In his essay "Reality in America," Lionel Trilling has written that despite V. L. Parrington's social importance in articulating the American public's sense of the significance of the practical and the ordinary in *Main Currents in American Thought,* his influence upon American culture has not been entirely positive—that Parrington's conception of reality as external, fixed, monolithic, tended to subordinate in artistic importance and value such writers as Melville and Hawthorne, to imply "that part of Hawthorne's insufficiency as a writer comes from his failure to get around and meet people." To Parrington's charge that such private, solitary writers dealt with shadows rather than with reality, Trilling replied, "But shadows are also part of reality and one would not want a world without shadows, it would not even be a 'real' world." Trilling reminds us that well-intentioned literalists like Parrington failed to realize that democratic ideas and values could be increased by creative artists who were nourished rather more by their own subjectivities than by the common-sense pragmatism of most of their countrymen, but he admits that the pragmatic vision of the world remains dominant in America, that Parrington "expresses the chronic American belief that there exists an opposition between reality and mind and that one must enlist oneself in the party of reality."[1]

Just as nineteenth-century writers such as Melville, Hawthorne, and Thoreau fused their shadowed visions with their unique perceptions of reality to forge morally and socially significant depictions of the world far exceeding Parrington's notions of reality, Eugene O'Neill early in the next century saw both his society and literary form in new ways, recognizing the truth of George Orwell's profound assertion, written later in the twentieth century, that "orthodoxy, of whatever color, seems to demand a lifeless, imitative style."[2] In an early letter to drama critic George Jean Nathan, O'Neill wrote, "Damn that word, 'realism'! . . . I [mean] something 'really real,' in the sense of being spiritually true, not meticulously life-like—an interpretation of actuality by a distillation, an elimination of most realistic trappings, an intensification of human lives into clear symbols of truth."[3] Throughout his long career as a dramatist, O'Neill exerted enormous effort in attacking artistic and social assumptions held by the ever-powerful "party of reality"; he continually challenged orthodoxies wherever he found them, in an attempt both to create a more "really real" dramatic literature by subverting commonly accepted literalist notions of dramatic form, and to affect his society by mounting frequent challenges to its complacency, particularly in matters concerning class discrimination and the burgeoning commercialism and materialism in the new American century. Like most of the great modernist writers essentially subversive of established structures, O'Neill was truly a revolutionary in several senses of the word: his lifelong preoccupation with sounding greater spiritual depths within humankind blended into a social concern with overthrowing his materialistic, bland culture's arid, unconsidered conventions and rituals, its unceasing drive toward euphemism and conformity, and the eternally American flight from self-knowledge. Thus his aesthetic concern with creating a more humanly responsive, organic, and imaginative realism merged with a fervently spiritual/social quest (O'Neill would never have termed it "political" or "ideological") to lay bare the often twisted and scarred psyches of his characters which, he implied, were in large part responsible for creating the steadily increasing coarsened and deadening conditions of his culture.

O'Neill's belief that the human condition was improvable has correlatives in realistic thought which, in their critical anthology, *The Modern Tradition*, Richard Ellmann and Charles Feidelson, Jr., have termed "melioristic realism." The editors comment, "This form of realism moves toward ethics. Its eye is always on what life should be."[4] Radical dramatist John Howard Lawson has agreed that social protest and reform are inherent in the nature of realism, that an "ameliorative and humanistic [viewpoint] . . . is the general philosophy of realism, which nourishes the hope that men possess the reason and will to improve their condition, or at least recognize the need of improvement," that the form implies "an ultimate hope of progress toward a more moral and meaningful existence."[5] The humanist critic M. H. Abrams has written that the importance of such a socially embedded view of the world inheres in its dealing with "matters of abiding human concern,"[6] a position with which Marxist critic Georg Lukács is in accord. Lukács sees art as embedded in the world, "saturated with social and moral humanistic problems," and sees representation as "illuminating human conflicts in all their complexity and completeness." In his praise for Balzac as his standard for a great realist writer, Lukács continues that he sees as "the essence of true realism: the great writer's thirst for truth, his fanatic striving for reality—or expressed in terms of ethics: the writer's sincerity and probity." In the industrial age, Lukács feels, "a writer could achieve greatness only in the struggle against the current of everyday life. And since Balzac the resistance of daily life to the deeper tendencies of literature, culture and art has grown ceaselessly stronger."[7]

Even at the very beginnings of his dramatic writing, Eugene O'Neill reveals in his personal letters both the lifelong zeal for truth and the struggle against the conventional and mundane in America that would appear again and again throughout his greatest plays. Writing to his friend Jessica Rippin, in whose family's New London boarding house he lived in the winter of 1913–14, as he struggled with his early one-act dramas, O'Neill stormed: "Sin and its punishment, virtue and its reward; piffle upon piffle . . . I tell you such values are the triumph of the commonplace, the low-browed mob at its zenith with its insolent 'Thou shalt not' . . . To be different and hold oneself aloof from their virtue—that is Good! . . . But . . . to heed their opinions, to harken to their vapid praise of all that is commonplace; to be contaminated by their approval—THAT IS BAD." To newspaperman Louis Cantor he complained, when his play *Diff'rent* was criticized for its bleakness, "The accusation of always seeing things black has been hurled against the best of them in all countries—Ibsen, Strindberg, Hauptmann, Andreyev . . . so I am in good company. It is a very obvious criticism to make, especially in this 100% optimistic country." Unsparing of his own flaws as of his country's, a more mature O'Neill wrote to his son in 1932 on Eugene, Jr.'s college graduation with congratulations yet with a personal lament: "I know a fine life is before you. You make me soundly ashamed of all the years I wasted in stupidity, and whose loss as a background for culture is a handicap that will always make my road tougher to travel." His own father's death in 1920 prompted him to write to producer George Tyler about the almost archetypal American myth of ruination through illusory success:

> My direst grudge against *Monte Cristo* is that, in my opinion, it wrecked my father's chance to become one of our greatest actors . . . he . . . confessed it to me . . . with great bitterness. . . . He had fallen for the lure of easy popularity and easy money. . . . The money was thrown away, squandered in wild speculations. . . . The treasures of *Monte Cristo* are buried deep again—in prairie dog gold mines, in unlubricated oil wells . . . the modern Castles in Spain of pure romance. . . . My father died broken, unhappy. . . . His last words to me . . . were: "This sort of life— here—all froth . . . rottenness!" This after seventy-six years of what the mob undoubtedly regard as a highly successful career! . . . His words [are] seared on my brain—a warning from the Beyond to remain true to the best that is in me though the heavens fall.[8]

That O'Neill heeded his father's warning he indicates in a letter concerning the success of *Beyond the Horizon:* "I am . . . not trying to get too wealthy although, as you can imagine, the opportunities to sell myself have not been lacking of late." And in 1922 when the Theatre Guild offered to finance him for a period so that he could concentrate on his writing, he responded to Lawrence Langner: "I am in no dire straits for money, as you must know. Even if I were, my poverty-stricken years of the past are proof enough that there is no danger of my street-walking along Broadway. I simply ain't that kind of a girl."[9]

The young playwright's personal struggles against what Lukács termed the "current of everyday life" as revealed in the letters blend into reflections on his early reading, on his vision of America in relation to what he considers the mechanical realism of the day, and on his ideas for a more imaginative realism. In letters to Beatrice Ashe in 1914, O'Neill reacts negatively to Gorki's unadulterated naturalism in *The Lower Depths* and praises a less well known drama, the 1907 *King Hunger,* by Leonid Andreyev, whose protagonist at first champions the poor but then betrays them as he serves the rich class. On the closing of *Chris Christopherson,* O'Neill wrote to George Tyler, "At least all [the critics] got the idea that I was trying to do something new and outside of the carpentered flip-flap that constitutes the usual American play. . . . And if the Philadelphia public refuse to be interested in any unconventional form of drama—well, after all, who could expect them to, and in the middle of Lent at that." In an important letter to Malcolm Mollan in 1921, he accuses the critics of *Anna Christie* of misunderstanding realism, of failing to see that a realistic play "is life. Life doesn't end. One experience is but the birth of another." He continues by accusing his society of completely misunderstanding the meaning of happiness, confusing it with "a mere smirking contentment with one's lot," and having no appreciation of the tragic: "Supposing someday we should suddenly see . . . the true valuation of all our triumphant, brass band materialism, see the cost—and the result in terms of eternal verities? . . . Why we *are* tragedy the most appalling yet written or unwritten!"[10]

O'Neill's conception of realism as flexible, of the art of literature as imaginative as well as strictly representational, has distinguished antecedents in the history of commentary about realism. Wellek and Warren remind us that literature must "stand in recognizable relation to life, but the relations are very various . . . it is in any case a selection, of a specifically purposive sort, from life."[11] Perhaps the most significant of the nineteenth-century theorists of realism, Henry James, recognized the complexity inherent in realistic art. In a passage in "The Art of Fiction" which O'Neill echoes in the Mollan letter of 1921, James writes: "Humanity is immense, and reality has a myriad forms. . . . It is equally excellent and inconclusive to say that one must write from experience. . . . What kind of experience is intended, and where does it begin and end? Experience is never limited, and it is never complete." And in a famous passage, James frames the qualities, again imaginative as well as objective-observational and impersonal, that would describe the major realist writers of the new century: their attempt "to render the look of things, the look that conveys their meaning, to catch the color, the relief, the expression, the surface, the substance of the human spectacle."[12]

O'Neill's lifelong quest to render both the appearance and the significance of a uniquely American reality can perhaps best be understood by examining in some detail a play from each of four distinct periods in O'Neill's artistic career: the earliest, sometimes deterministic, short plays, exemplified by *The Web;* the more subtle sea plays, represented by *Bound East for Cardiff;* the middle period of intense and varied theatrical experimentation, combined with realistic technique and a rich social, familial, and historical milieu in the case of *Marco Millions;* and the major late plays of matured realism, illustrated by *Hughie.* In these four works, which have received relatively less critical attention than the more famous plays, O'Neill forcefully expresses his vision of American culture, employing and developing a melioristic realism to delineate weaknesses in our national social fabric, creating drama that "should be a source of inspiration that lifts us to a plane beyond ourselves as we know them and drives us deep into the unknown within and behind ourselves. The theatre should reveal to us what we are."[13]

Few among a writer's very early works drive us so deeply into awareness of the plight of socially marginal people as does *The Web,* O'Neill's first fully developed one-act play, written in the fall of 1913 soon after his release from a tuberculosis sanitarium. The subject and action of *The Web*—concerning a tubercular prostitute and a thief who momentarily breaks the ensnaring structures of American class prejudice and circumstance that ultimately will destroy them both—fulfill the objective presentation of commonplace life traditional for realism, as well as Chekhov's observation that "dung-heaps play a very respectable part in a landscape."[14] While the action is sometimes melodramatic, verging on deterministic naturalism, the depiction of contemporary, alienated urban sufferers ground down by disease and crime attains George Becker's standard of comprehensiveness, the illusion of a fullness of experience, through O'Neill's creativity in the various elements of realistic drama. Setting and spectacle are not merely ornamental but contribute to theme, as in O'Neill's detailed description of the "squalid bedrooms"[15] on the lower East Side; the "open window" (p. 15) crucial to Steve's ironic destruction of Rose and Tim Moran can be observed, as can the "bottle of milk" that rests incongruously on the fire escape, enhancing and complicating Rose's character by foreshadowing her desperate need for her infant, which in such degrading circumstances is all she has to live for. Characters are heightened, individualized beyond mere social types who further action probable for their social station. Even Rose's pimp, Steve, hardened by having been raised in an orphan asylum and by years of drugs and petty crime, can briefly rise beyond gangster stereotype, his "shattered" nerves reacting to Rose's prolonged coughing fits with, "Dammit! Stop that barkin'. It goes right trou me" (p. 17) just after Rose dejectedly has observed of their lives, "I dunno. It's a bum game all round." Tim, himself a hardened criminal, reacts with suppressed humanity at Steve's harsh treatment of Rose, and after forcing the pimp from Rose's flat at gunpoint, then observing the woman soothing her infant, looks "embarrassed, puts the revolver back in his pocket and picking up the table sets it to rights again and sits on the edge of it" (p. 20), his sensitivity prefiguring his loving treatment of her and the child moments later. Rose, far more interesting than the stereotyped golden-hearted whore of melodrama, movingly but cynically speaks to Tim of her serious attempts to find generative work, and of frequent sexist efforts by the hypocritical "who'd drag me back" (p. 22), while candidly thanking Tim for his efforts to aid her with "I ain't worth it" (p. 20).

Dialogue in *The Web* not only forwards the action with efficiency and unobtrusiveness, but in places imaginatively represents character and social theme, approaching a hardened lyricism while preserving functionality typical of realistic language. When Rose attempts to hide her tubercular pallor with garish rouge, Steve yet compares her to a "ghost" (p. 16), thus symbolically indicating her inevitable end. While the functionally clear stage directions themselves suggest meanings beyond their denotative value—the milk bottle; Rose's "gaudy, cheap" (p. 15) hat, suggesting her extremely limited social power—the dialogue can rise to symbol. After the Second Plain Clothes Man is convinced, as a result of Steve's setup, that Rose has murdered Tim, he says casually, "Little sister here attends to business, all right" (p. 26), tacitly confirming through his dismissive sexist reference to Rose her lifelong victimization through male societal structures. Nowhere is this idea more poignantly realized than in the play's final line, after Rose is led away by the police, when the First Plain Clothes Man, cuddling the infant, croons to the crying child, "Mama's gone. I'm your Mama now" (p. 28).

Such ironies are part of O'Neill's subtle structuring of the action; throughout he balances realism's traditional respect for mirrored, relatively unmediated reality with the artist's shaping function toward the chaotic flow of experience. Early on (p. 15) we hear the sound of rain falling on "the flags of the court below" (including probably an American flag); at the end, an ironically counterposed sound is that of the echo of "Rose's hollow cough . . . in the dark hallways" (p. 28). Rose's opening words to a half-hoped-for "Gawd! . . . What a chance I got" (p. 15) are echoed in a hopeless cry (p. 26) before her final words to "Gawd! Why d'yuh hate me so?" (p. 28). O'Neill's imaginative handling of realistic dramatic elements results in a similarly heightened realistic thematic representation, as O'Neill suggests the necessity of improved social conditions for people like Rose and Tim, who dimly recognize that "We can't work out of this life because we don't know how to work. We was never taught how" (p. 22). Rose's "It's a bum game all round" (p. 17) pointedly suggests the validity of Becker's realistic thematic standard that people must be represented as a complex aspect of material causality, subject to, if not determined by, nature's limits.

O'Neill advances toward "poetic realism" in the 1914 sea play, *Bound East for Cardiff,* in which subject and theme reflect James's myriad sense of reality. Here the social milieu from which the oppressed characters emanate is the sea, and the dramatist's extensive personal experience with the vagaries and difficulties of ocean-bound life allow him great accuracy in its description and representation, along with an early expressionistic episode at the moment of Yank's death, which improves in psychological verisimilitude upon O'Neill's earlier such efforts in the primitive sea plays, *Thirst* (1913) and *Fog* (1914). While O'Neill does not describe closely Yank's dying vision of the "pretty lady dressed in black,"[16] he precisely describes in the opening stage directions the enclosing, cramped conditions of the seamen's forecastle on the *Glencairn,* the afar sides so narrow as to function symbolically as the site of Yank's impending death, and the privation represented by the setting materially effecting the oppression of the working class of many nationalities. The characters are, of course, social and national types, but O'Neill individualizes them, especially Yank and his closest friend, Driscoll, whose words of praise for the "hard-featured" (p. 187) Yank suggest a measure of heroism about him; yet Yank fears his mate's departure to go on watch with the men about him "asleep and snoring" (p. 193). He also fears his vague conception of the Divine because of the Cape Town killing in self-defense.

O'Neill particularly individualizes his characters through dialogue, risking what in less skilled hands would be an overdependence on dialect, a seemingly obtrusive medium for realism, yet managing it with his fine ear for rhythm that at times approaches a working-class lyricism. At his mate's fear of God's vengeance, Driscoll replies with a lilt akin to Paddy's in O'Neill's *The Hairy Ape:* "Don't be thinking av that now. 'Twas past and gone" (p. 197), and he advises Cocky "that Yank is bad took and I'll be staying wid him a while yet" (p. 192). Similarly adroit handling of dialect occurs in Driscoll's description of Yank's shipwreck heroism and Yank's lament for the rigors of the sailor's life.

Again, irony functions as a principle of structure, and symbol does as well, as O'Neill's references in dialogue to the oppressive fog both suggest the men's victimization by ship owners and officers and indicate their temporary release from its dangers at Yank's death, a departure that approaches mythic significance. Through artistic structuring of the seamen's chaotic reality (the first third of the drama functions as a sort of prologue to Yank's initial words, a muttered negative), O'Neill suggests Cocky's spiritual progress from teller of racist jokes at the start to awed participant in death's mystery, as his repeated "Gawd" attains a deeper level of reference. Even Yank's moving complaint against ocean life is split into two approximately equal sections of dialogue by Driscoll's brief agreement, "It's a hell av a life, the sea" (p. 195). Yank's discovery that Driscoll has ironically entertained the same dream of a secure land life as he has enhances the thematic probability of the play's meliorative concern for improved working conditions for a working class exploited by "the owners ridin' around in carriages!" (p. 190). Their "starvation ship" (p. 190) renders meaningless an organic life for Americans and other western men alike, as the reiterative blast of the steamer's whistle periodically reminds them all, as Driscoll realizes, that "Such things are not for the loikes av us" (p. 196).

Modern scholars have written that realistic drama's aim "is to cut away an important dimension in the presentation of character—theatricality—in order to gain another quality—the illusion of authenticity."[17] Throughout the 1920s, O'Neill alternated between realism and experimental presentation of his ideas through the media of masks, choruses, asides, and different types of music and monologue.

Perhaps the most interesting of these experiments is *Marco Millions* (1925), in that O'Neill represents his critique of American materialism and vulgarity through both realistic and expressionistic techniques in a drama that contains the most successful realism of the experimental plays, that expands upon the racial considerations of earlier predominantly realistic works such as *The Dreamy Kid* (1919) and *All God's Chillun Got Wings* (1923), and that reveals O'Neill's satire and humor, traits usually more evident in the letters than in the plays. In achieving authenticity of character in the greedy, conformist Marco, O'Neill created both an individual and a type much venerated on Wall Street, heeding Georg Lukács's view that the "criterion of realist literature is the type, a peculiar synthesis which organically binds together the general and the particular both in characters and situations. What makes a type a type is . . . that in it all the humanly and socially essential determinants are present . . . in extreme presentation of their extremes, rendering concrete the peaks and limits of men and epochs."[18] Marco was founded historically on O'Neill's contempt for the financier Otto Kahn; George Jean Nathan reported that the dramatist's meeting with Kahn prompted him to write "the sourest and most magnificent poke in the jaw that American big business and the American business man have ever got."[19]

An O'Neill scholar has recently written that modern American plays "consistently challenge the dominant self-help ethos and aspirations that centre on material and social success."[20] In *Marco Millions*, O'Neill deftly satirizes America's numbing optimism and go-getting through Marco's characterization. Appointed by Kublai as government tax agent, young Marco insensitively overturns decades of Chinese traditions: "I found they had a high tax on excess profits. Imagine a profit being excess! Why, it isn't humanly possible! I repealed it. . . . Every citizen must be happy or go to jail. . . . Here's the way I figure it; if a man's good, he's happy—and if he isn't happy, it's a sure sign he's no good to himself or anyone else."[21] Impervious to Kukachin's love or Kublai's wisdom, the young capitalist takes pride in his efficient administration of cargo loading: "We killed six slaves but, by God, we did it!" (p. 437). His typically American response to philosophical thought is apparent in his words to the sage, Chu-Yin: "[R]iddles. . . . Keep on going ahead and you can't help being right! You're

bound to get somewhere!" (p. 438). His sole motivation for travel beyond Venice is to "become really big and important" (p. 393), and
during the expressionistic scenes early in his travels when he is confronted by the ages-of-man tableaus in many cultures, he represses
recognition of aging and death with a fervor that predicts his unen-
lightenment throughout the action.

Character is forwarded and revealed with functional dialogue that
is at once frequently ironic and expressive of meditative lyricism. Not
all westerners are fools in O'Neill's meliorative vision: the Papal Leg-
ate, Tedaldo, counterpoints the Polo family's idiocy. When informed
that Kublai requests Rome to send a hundred wise men to discuss with
him world religions, Tedaldo mutters, "This Kublai is an optimist!"
(p. 395), and wisely sends Marco as his emissary after he is chosen
to be Pope: "Let him set an example of virtuous Western manhood
amid all the levities of paganism, shun the frailty of poetry . . . and I
will wager a million of something or other myself that the Khan will
soon be driven to seek spiritual salvation somewhere!" (p. 399).
O'Neill's American critique is advanced also through the meditative
dialogue of Kublai and Chu-Yin, even in the realistic scenes: in an
exchange following Marco's initial sales pitch, Kublai says, "Did their
Pope mean that a fool is a wiser study for a ruler of fools than a hundred wise men could be? This Marco touches me, as a child might,
but at the same time there is something warped, deformed . . . " and
his sage replies, "Let him develop according to his own inclination and
give him every opportunity for true growth if he so desires. . . . At
least, if he cannot learn, we shall" (pp. 415–16).

Over the twenty-three years of the action, O'Neill employs parallel
structure in setting and characterization to represent his ironic theme
of western moral and spiritual bankruptcy. Throughout his financial
career Marco is seen reacting to many nonwestern cultures, with approximately equal fatuity. Whether with Donata, the mythic prostitute, or Kukachin, he is similarly spiritually defunct. Though he is
exposed expressionistically in the play's prologue to hypocritical behavior by western Christians, to Kublai's realization that the West
must "devour itself" (p. 451), and in the epilogue to Kublai's final
tragedy, he is found to be utterly without understanding of all he has
seen this night at the theatre, conforming to crowd reactions, "sure

of his place in the world," and as he enters his limousine, "Marco Polo, with a satisfied sigh at the sheer comfort of it all, resumes his life" (p. 467).

The antitheses of Marco's moral passivity, and very much in the spirit of the early 1940s when O'Neill was writing the late major plays of a matured realism, including *Hughie* (1942), are Lukács's words in his essay, "The Ideology of Modernism": "But in life potentiality can . . . become reality. Situations arise in which a man is confronted with a choice; and in the act of choice a man's character may reveal itself in a light that surprises even himself. . . . The literature of realism, aiming at a truthful reflection of reality, must demonstrate the . . . potentialities of human beings in extreme situations of this kind."[22] Common to the final plays, from *A Touch of the Poet* through *A Moon for the Misbegotten*, is an uncertain character, a wanderer in an isolated wasteland, seeking some tenuous connection, attempting to form an authentic self, and, in Sartrean terms, thus responsible not only for himself but for the destiny of humankind.[23] In such an urban milieu, the lonely Erie Smith gropes toward selfhood, and beyond, trying to confront a terrifyingly flexible reality and echoing O'Neill's own artistic boundary situation as "a teller of tales,"[24] ironically a role that suits the ever fantasizing Night Clerk equally well. The setting functions to disclose character in the play, as O'Neill's descriptions early on convey the results of urban decay early in the century, particularly upon insecure and socially marginal members of society. The hotel, perhaps like these two present inhabitants, "*began as respectable second class but soon* [was] *forced to deteriorate in order to survive*" (p. 831). For Erie the decline has taken the form of incessant talk in order to try to evade his isolation, to avoid the confrontation with choice of which Lukács writes. For the Night Clerk, ruin lies in sentimental fantasies of the city night's illusory excitements, which O'Neill realistically suggests through some memorable inner dialogue. As he deludes himself with thoughts of garbage collection—"*I'd bang those cans louder than they do! I'd wake up the whole damned city!*" (p. 837)— Charlie's thoughts reflect his own sense of meaningless desolation. And "*the noise of a far-off El train. It's approach is pleasantly like a memory of hope; then . . . the noise pleasantly deafens memory . . . recedes and dies. . . . But there is hope . . . each* [El] *passing leaves one less to pass, so the night recedes, too, until at last it must . . . join all the other long nights in*

Nirvana, the Big Night of Nights" (p. 838). Charlie's deadened verbal responses to Erie prior to Erie's venturing a truth suggest that, indeed, these are *"the obsequies of night"* (p. 838).

Spoken dialogue is inextricably a part of character. Erie's introduction of himself to the Night Clerk with but one word, "Key" (p. 832), suggests both his and contemporary urban man's simultaneous need for connection and avoidance of bespeaking that need. Similarly, Erie's references to Hughie as "one grand little guy" (pp. 838, 839) reveal his unconscious need, at this point, to minimize his need for Hughie and for future social communion. Charlie's uncertainty about his age (p. 834) shows his nearly unbridgeable distance from an authentic selfhood, as does Erie's continual bravado. While Erie, though his class has disallowed much education, reveals verbal nuance at times, when describing Hughie's marital state as "happy enough. . . . Well, not happy. Maybe contented. No, that's boosting it, too. Resigned comes nearer" (p. 842), he is unaware of the irony behind his " 'no guy can beat that racket' " just before (p. 840). He is also unaware of a change in the structure of his flow of thought after he admits his loneliness to Charlie, begins to speak of his conning Hughie, and asks plaintively, "If every guy along Broadway who kids himself was to drop dead there wouldn't be nobody left. Ain't it the truth, Charlie?" (p. 846). When their mutually extreme situations then induce Charlie to approach "Truth?" (p. 846), and to venture to connect his Arnold Rothstein fantasy with this palpable gambler before him, both are joined in verbal risk as Erie repeats the "racket" metaphor, accepting Hughie's permanent absence, and Charlie makes concrete a past fantasy with, "Yes, it is a goddamned racket. . . . But we might as well make the best of it . . . you can't burn it all down. . . . There's too much steel and stone" (p. 848). Talk of gambling leads to the further risk of the act itself as both men are bonded through the empowering choices of suspending some self-delusions and simultaneously assuming roles that may enhance their confidence to confront future situations that demand their freedom.

In assuming some responsibility for the other, both men in *Hughie* reveal O'Neill's melioristic realism as one infused both with subjective, imaginative genius as well as with social concern useful in a democracy. Georg Lukács, writing in 1948 and seeking an end to all species of fascism, could hope, "Never in all its history did mankind so urgently require a realist literature as it does today. . . . There is today in the world a general desire for a literature which could penetrate with its beam deep into the tangled jungle of our time . . . could play the leading part, hitherto always denied to it, in the democratic rebirth of nations" (p. 360).

Notes

1. Lionel Trilling, *The Liberal Imagination* (New York: Doubleday/Anchor, 1953), pp. 19, 20, 21. Somerset Maugham drily observed the dominance of similarly shadowless notions of the real in less provincial cultures contemporaneous with Parrington's America, describing the realism of much Edwardian drama as "the sudden arrival of a stranger who comes into a stuffy room and opens the windows; whereupon the people who were sitting there catch their death of cold and everything ends unhappily" (qtd. in Sylvan Barnet, Morton Berman, and William Burto, *Aspects of the Drama: A Handbook* [Boston: Little, Brown, 1962], pp. 246–47).

2. George Orwell, "Politics and the English Language," in *A Collection of Essays* (New York: Doubleday/Anchor, 1954), p. 172.

3. Letter to Nathan, May 7, 1923, in *Eugene O'Neill: Comments on the Drama and the Theater: A Source Book*, ed. Ulrich Halfmann (Tubingen: Gunter Narr Verlag, 1987), pp. 174–75.

4. Richard Ellmann and Charles Feidelson, Jr., eds., *The Modern Tradition: Backgrounds of Modern Literature* (New York: Oxford UP, 1965), p. 232. The editors include as a representation of melioristic realism Dostoyevsky's 1869 letter to Strachen which includes, "What most people regard as fantastic and lacking in Universality, *I* hold to be the inmost essence of truth. Arid observation of everyday trivialities I have long ceased to regard as realism" (p. 310). In a June 6, 1931, letter to critic Barrett Clark, O'Neill, minimizing Freud's influence upon his writing, commented, "He has had none compared to what psychological writers of the past like Dostoyevsky, etc., have had" (Travis Bogard and Jackson R. Bryer, eds., *Selected Letters of Eugene O'Neill* [New Haven: Yale UP, 1988], p. 386).

5. John Gassner and Edward Quinn, eds., *The Reader's Encyclopedia of World Drama* (New York: Thomas Y. Crowell Co., 1969), pp. 704, 705. Noting the flexibility of the realistic form, Lawson distinguishes it from naturalism, which "tends to regard emotional instability, selfishness, and moral blindness as inherent in the nature of man" (p. 704). William W. Demastes underscores this distinction: "Realism . . . can succeed at reflecting . . . a variety of outlooks or perspectives on, and philosophies of, existence" (*Beyond Naturalism: A New Realism in American Theatre* [Westport, Conn.: Greenwood Press, 1988], p. 15).

6. M. H. Abrams, "Literary Criticism in America: Some New Directions," in *Theories of Criticism: Essays in Literature and Art* (Washington, D.C.: Library of Congress, 1984), p. 30.

7. Georg Lukács, from *Studies in European Realism* (1948), in Ellmann and

Feidelson, eds., *The Modern Tradition*, pp. 351, 352, 354, 356. Interpreting Lukács's Marxist/realist thought, Terry Eagleton writes: "A 'realist' work is rich in a complex, comprehensive set of relations between man, nature and history. . . . The task of the realist writer is to flesh out . . . those latent forces in any society which are . . . most historically significant and progressive . . . in sensuously realized individuals and actions; in doing so he links the individual to the social whole" ("Marxism and Literary Criticism," in *Criticism: The Major Statements*, ed. Charles Kaplan [New York: St. Martin's Press, 1986], p. 550).

8. Letter to Jessica Rippin, May 7, 1914; to Louis Cantor, Jan. 28, 1921; to Eugene O'Neill, Jr., May 13, 1932; to George Tyler, Dec. 9, 1920. In Bogard and Bryer, eds., *Selected Letters of Eugene O'Neill*, pp. 22–23, 146, 394–95, 143.

9. Letter to Nina Moise, Aug. 29, 1920; to Langner, Jan. 10, 1922, in *Selected Letters*, pp. 137, 164.

10. Letters to Ashe, Nov. 2, 1914 and Oct. 8, 1914; letter to Tyler, March 17, 1920; to Mollan, Dec. 1921; in *Selected Letters*, pp. 36, 30, 120, 159. An amusing letter to Tyler discloses O'Neill's impatience with literalistic realism urged upon the producer of *The Straw* by the Boston child labor agency: "The play cannot be played without real children. To use midgets would simply turn the whole thing into farce" (April 7, 1920, in *Selected Letters*, p. 126). In a 1924 essay called by Travis Bogard "perhaps O'Neill's most personal critical statement," O'Neill calls for an overturning of the old realism in favor of a new "super-naturalism": "We have endured too much from the banality of surfaces" ("Strindberg and Our Theatre," in *The Unknown O'Neill: Unpublished or Unfamiliar Writings*, ed. Travis Bogard [New Haven: Yale UP, 1988], pp. 386–87).

11. René Wellek and Austin Warren, *Theory of Literature* (New York: Harcourt, Brace, 1956), p. 202.

12. James E. Miller, Jr., ed., *Theory of Fiction: Henry James* (Lincoln: U of Nebraska P, 1972), pp. 34–35, 36. For additional background on theories of European realism, see Ellmann and Feidelson, eds., *The Modern Tradition*, pp. 229–328, and George Becker, *Realism in Modern Literature* (New York: Ungar, 1980), pp. 78–96. In *American Realism and American Drama, 1880–1940* (Cambridge: Cambridge University Press, 1948), pp. 24–49, Brenda Murphy discusses American realistic dramatic theory.

13. Qtd. in Virginia Floyd, *The Plays of Eugene O'Neill: A New Assessment* (New York: Ungar, 1985), p. xxv.

14. Anton Chekhov, "Letter to Kiselev" (1887), in Ellmann and Feidelson, eds., *The Modern Tradition*, p. 245.

15. O'Neill, *The Web*, in *Eugene O'Neill: Complete Plays, 1913–1920*, ed. Travis Bogard (New York: Library of America, 1988), p. 15. Subsequent references are cited in the text.

16. O'Neill, *Bound East for Cardiff*, in *Eugene O'Neill: Complete Plays*, p. 198. Subsequent references are cited in the text.

17. Henry F. Salerno and Conny E. Nelson, eds., *Drama and Tradition: The Major Genres* (New York: American Book Co., 1968), p. 434.

18. Lukács, *The Modern Tradition*, p. 351.

19. Qtd. in Halfmann, ed., *Eugene O'Neill: . . . Source Book*, p. 80.

20. Jean Chothia, "The Real Thing: American Drama's Search for its Natural Voice," *Times Literary Supplement* (May 7, 1993): p. 6.

21. O'Neill, *Marco Millions,* in *Eugene O'Neill: Complete Plays, 1920–1931,* ed. Travis Bogard (New York: Library of America, 1988), p. 425. Subsequent references are cited in the text.

22. Georg Lukács, "The Ideology of Modernism" (1956), in *The Critical Tradition,* ed. David H. Richter (New York: St. Martin's Press, 1989), p. 600.

23. Doris Falk, *Eugene O'Neill and the Tragic Tension* (New Brunswick: Rutgers UP, 1958), pp. 34–35; Travis Bogard, *Contour in Time: The Plays of Eugene O'Neill* (New York: Oxford UP, 1972), p. xvi.

24. O'Neill, *Hughie,* in *Eugene O'Neill: Complete Plays, 1932–1943,* ed. Travis Bogard (New York: Library of America, 1988), p. 830. Subsequent references are cited in the text.

EIGHT

"Odets, Where Is Thy Sting?" Reassessing the "Playwright of the Proletariat"

John W. Frick

In a 1964 interview with the *New York Times,* playwright William Gibson, a protégé and personal friend of Clifford Odets, ended an assessment of his late mentor with the claim that "the theater did not want Clifford Odets."[1] The significance of Gibson's simple statement is remarkably easy for the casual reader to overlook; yet the underlying implication cuts to the very heart of Odets criticism. In effect, Gibson was saying that the playwright who, in 1935, was dubbed the "White Hope" of the American theatre, who had four plays running simultaneously on Broadway, who was widely acknowledged as the playwright of the downtrodden and disenfranchised, and as the "Voice of the Thirties," had been rejected by the theatre he served and to this day is still neither fully understood nor appreciated.

While Gibson admittedly was alluding to Broadway's unwillingness (or inability) to support Odets financially, his statement, examined in light of Odets criticism, has wider and considerably more serious implications. In his own time, Odets had the disturbing knack of polarizing the critics. His admirers hailed him variously as "the boy wonder," "the poet of the Jewish middle class," "the proletarian Jesus," another Chekhov, and, as Richard Watts trumpeted in the *New York Herald Tribune* on March 31, 1935, "the most exciting [writer] to emerge in the American Theater since the flaming emergence of Eugene O'Neill."[2]

At the other end of the critical spectrum, reviews ranged from the vitriolic (Frank Nugent's "Odets, Where Is Thy Sting?" in which Nugent possesses a "surer knowledge" of dramatic composition than does the "playwright of the proletariat," and Joseph Wood Krutch's infamous review of *Paradise Lost*, "The Apocalypse of St. Clifford," in which he accuses Odets of losing "his reason . . . from too much brooding over the Marxian eschatology") to the smug (the critic for the *New York American* dismissed *Awake and Sing!* as a "stirring *little* play") to the downright obtuse.[3] In the latter category Grenville Vernon's obsession, publicly exhibited in review after review in the *Commonweal*, with having Odets declared nothing more than another "Jewish" playwright, is a striking example.[4]

Historically, however, the most common tendency of the critics in the 1930s was simply to label Odets as a political writer, as a revolutionary, and examine him or dismiss him in that context. Unfortunately, this tendency applied not only to mainstream critics like Brooks Atkinson—who responded (overreacted, some say) to *Till the Day I Die* with the warning, "If you want to register an emotional protest against Nazi polity, Mr. Odets requires that you join the Communist brethren"—but also to left-wing critics, who alternately praised Odets when he furthered their cause and scolded him when he failed to remain strictly doctrinaire.[5] In the opinion of Edward Murray, "unhappily, Odets has been tagged with *Waiting for Lefty*, while his best work has been largely forgotten. Odets was too often applauded for the wrong things in the thirties [namely his political 'message'] and [is] ignored today chiefly for the same reasons."[6] Michael Mendelsohn concurs, calling *Lefty* and the famous "Stormbirds of the Working Class" speech the "ghosts" that Odets could not escape, and stresses the fact that, because of his first four plays, Odets "became known as a vigorous critic of American society, a reputation that was not completely deserved" and a reputation that has evolved into a commonly accepted view that has severely hindered impartial study of an important American playwright.[7]

While book-length studies such as Mendelsohn's, Murray's, Harold Cantor's, and more recently Gerald Weales's *Odets: The Playwright*, Margaret Brenman-Gibson's *Clifford Odets: American Playwright*, and Gabriel Miller's *Clifford Odets* have done much to dispel the myths and misconceptions that haunt Odets, misapprehensions unfortunately persist. In a widely read book on the 1930s, for example, Odets is regarded simply as "the most skillful theatre propagandist of an age of propagandists," and in a recent reference work, he is characterized as much for being "the radical American dramatist of the depressed thirties, who sold out to Hollywood, and even named names to the House Unamerican Activities Committee" (HUAC) as he is for having possessed a marvelous ear for speech and for creating vivid, dynamic characters.[8] Considering the persistence of assessments of Odets as reckless and superficial as these, it is little wonder that students regard Odets as a communist first and a playwright second or that his contributions to the American theatre and to a general understanding of American culture continue to be devalued. Considering remarks such as these, Gibson's declaration that the American theatre did not want and still does not want Odets takes on additional significance.

While there may be widespread disagreement on Odets's overall merits as a playwright and his eventual place in the history of the American stage, there is what amounts to a consensus among critics regarding Odets's ability to write stage dialogue that was once described as being "ungrammatical jargon . . . and constantly lyric . . . composed of words heard on the street, in drugstores, bars, sports arenas, and rough restaurants. . . . It is the speech of New York."[9] Alfred Kazin, recalling the dialogue of *Awake and Sing!* in his book *Starting Out in the Thirties*, describes it as a "lyric uplifting of blunt Jewish speech, boiling over and explosive, that did more to arouse the audience than the political catchwords that brought the curtain down. Everybody on that stage was furious, kicking, alive,—the words [were] always real but never flat, brilliantly authentic like no other theater speech on Broadway."[10]

Like Kazin, the average theatregoer in the thirties recognized and reveled in the "Odetsian line," the working man's witticism, the defensive wisecrack, the lively kitchen repartee. Adopting the stance of others before me, that it is easier to recognize an Odets line than to characterize it, I offer the following sampler: "I shtupped him a ten dollar bill"; "Everything's hot delicatessen"; "What this country needs is a good five cent earthquake"; "The lord so loved the world that he gave them missionaries"; "I wouldn't trade you for two pitchers and an outfielder"; and the following exchanges from *Awake and Sing!*:

Sam: Why should you act this way?
Hennie: Cause there's no bones in ice cream.
Bessie: Where are you going?

> *Hennie:* For my beauty nap, Mussolini. Wake me when it's apple blossom time in Normandy.[11]

Critics and scholars likewise agree on Odets's talents for creating vivid and passionate characters who take on additional life when they leave the printed page and step upon the stage. Joseph Wood Krutch, who ranged the critical spectrum from vehement detractor to ardent admirer, felt that Odets understood the people he wrote about "from the inside out" and consequently created characters exhibiting an intensity of life that "lift[ed] them into another realm" and endowed them with an "extraordinary freshness." Joseph Mersand in an article in *Players Magazine* in 1940 identified more than forty distinct, vibrant characters, all full of vigor and more than mere imitations of life; and Kazin, attending *Awake and Sing!* at the Belasco, watched his "mother and father and uncles and aunts occupying the stage . . . by as much right as if they were Hamlet [or] Lear."[12]

There is also little argument about Odets's role as the spokesman for a class, for a generation, and for a decade, the turbulent thirties. Odets earned those titles with one production of one play, which Richard Watts claimed had "all the qualities of a dramatic machine gun."[13] The event, as any beginning student of American theatre history knows, was the opening night of *Waiting for Lefty* on January 5, 1935, and when the audience stood to join the actors in shouting the final line of the play, "STRIKE, STRIKE, STRIKE," an exhortation which Harold Clurman dubbed "the Birth cry of the Thirties," few would dispute the fact that Odets had voiced the frustrations and longings of the working classes. When, after *Lefty* was moved to Broadway two months later and more bourgeois audiences from Rye and Mamaroneck reacted at the Longacre Theatre the way workers had at the Fourteenth Street Theatre, there could be little doubt that Odets was echoing the sentiments of a significant proportion of the American populace and that, more than perhaps any other playwright, he intuitively sensed the tenor of the era.

Discussions get considerably less congenial when the question of whether Odets's plays transcend the thirties is raised. Although Odets "has always been recognized as an influential playwright—who made contributions to the development of such later writers as Tennessee Williams, Arthur Miller, Paddy Chayevsky, William Gibson and Lorraine Hansberry—his plays are nevertheless regarded as museum pieces. His critical standing among literary scholars has been touched by condescension and distorted by political [and biographical] factors which detract from his genuine literary achievements."[14] Admittedly, Odets gained notoriety in the 1930s because of his much heralded "sellout" and desertion of Broadway for Hollywood in 1936 and for his well-publicized hubris, which led him to brag publicly about being the most talented playwright in New York, to write to Bernard Shaw claiming to be his "playwrighting son," and to send a lengthy letter to the New York press, lecturing them on the meaning of his *Paradise Lost* while comparing his writing to that of Chekhov; but theoretically the passage of time should have assuaged the offended and repaired the damage.[15]

The label of propagandist was not as easy to dismiss. Odets was a member of the Group Theatre, which had leftist leanings. *Waiting for Lefty* debutted in a left-wing theatre and Odets was a member of the Communist Party at the time of the opening, facts that the press stressed in their coverage of the play and the playwright. Ironically, Odets was a member of the party for only eight months and his plays—even *Lefty*, his most overtly political work—were never strictly doctrinaire, a point the left-wing critics were quick to emphasize. John Howard Lawson writing in the *New Masses*, for example, pointed out that almost half of the characters in *Lefty* were middle class and hardly qualified as "Stormbirds of the Working Class" and Edna, while clearly the *raisonneur* of her scene, was most certainly not a communist spokesperson.

Since the 1930s, careful examination of Odets's plays and his personal life have convinced scholars of the political theatre of the thirties that Odets actually knew very little about Marxism; that he was inconsistent in the use in his plays of what he did know; and that, like the surrealists in the 1920s and other theatrical radicals of the twentieth century, he was actually attracted more to the "romance" and the revolutionary spirit of communism and the hope it offered the proletariat than he was to strict Marxist principles. Recent studies, in fact, have confirmed that Odets was emotionally attracted to the idealism inherent in communism, rather than intellectually committed to a fixed, disciplined program, an attitude that Morgan Himelstein and Ira Levine, in separate studies, have found to have been common in the artistic community during the thirties. When questioned in 1952 by HUAC about his Marxist reading and education, Odets admitted that "to study these matters required really months of very serious study which I did not give them," a fact which Harold Clurman, Odets's constant companion during the pre-*Lefty* days, confirms in *The Fervent Years*.[16] In his recent study of Odets, Gabriel Miller reinforces this view of Odets's communism, noting that his "work was never, in any real sense, reformist. It might be more accurately termed personal; at times it was even confessional, an examination of the self."[17]

Writing of this stage of his career, Odets admits that he, like other writers of the period who experienced similar pressures, felt the need to "take some kind of real life I knew and [try] to press it into some kind of ideological mold."[18] Such attempts were not without some costs and Odets freely admits that he damaged some of his plays by trying to remain faithful to ideology rather than to his dramatic instincts. The often-criticized "conversion" endings of *Paradise Lost* and *Awake and Sing!*, for example, have a "tacked on" quality and strain credibility; after all, do we really believe that Ralph in the latter play will read all of Jake's books and change the world, after what we have seen of him for three acts?

If Odets's "message," his political imperative of social reform, were his sole contribution to the American theatre, his work truly would be dated. Fortunately, through the work of Brenman-Gibson, Weales, Miller, and others, we are afforded the opportunity of looking past the political cant of Odets's early works and examining issues of lasting merit, ideas transcending temporal boundaries. The playwright himself helps in this regard. In his words, "All my plays . . . deal with one subject: the struggle not to have life nullified by circumstances, false values, anything. . . . Man is an heroic being if he can only break through to fulfillment. . . . Nothing moves me so much as human aspirations blocked. I see it every day, all over the city girls and boys were not getting a chance . . . in life."[19] Contained in this statement are issues usually ignored in the study of Odets's plays: loss, the need to belong, and the frustration or shattering of dreams.

In *The Fervent Years* Harold Clurman describes how he and Odets, in the early months of 1933, nightly "wandered aimlessly through sad centers of impoverished life" in the streets between Times Square and

Greenwich Village, watching the people and listening to the conversations on street corners. *The Fervent Years* further chronicles how "Odets seemed to share a peculiar sense of gloomy fatality, one might almost say an appetite for the broken and rundown, together with a bursting love for the beauty immanent in people," a people Odets desperately wanted to rise above their present situations; a people severely "affected by a sense of insecurity; [a people] haunted by the fear of impermanence in all their relationships; [a people] fundamentally *homeless*."[20]

As they roamed the streets and ate their meals with the poor at Stewart's Cafeteria on Sheridan Square, it was evident to Clurman that Odets was unconsciously selecting the characters who would later people his plays, characters whose social rank, according to John Gassner, was "not high enough to escape frustration or low enough in the social scale to have its plight taken for granted and regarded as inevitable."[21] Furthermore, as Gassner observes, the problems that Odets's fictitious characters encountered would be the problems faced by the men and women he saw on the streets of New York, and the resultant drama would be a "theatre of frustration" which reflected Odets's own sense of hope clouded by despair.

Critics who ignore the significance of this critical, formative period in Odets's life are likely to overlook totally the intensely personal nature of Odets's identification with his characters, which accompanies his more detached, politicized critique of the American dream. Confronted with newspaper headlines proclaiming sixteen million unemployed, Odets saw not simply a national catastrophe, the breakdown of the American dream, but the shattering of sixteen million individual dreams. Thus, while socioeconomic and ideological questions are raised and scrutinized in Odets's plays, a more central concern is how his characters react to barriers to their achieving their *personal* aspirations—how will Sid and Florrie in the Young Hack episode in *Waiting for Lefty* find the means and courage to marry? How will Ralph, opposed by a domineering mother and a responsibility to help support his family financially, declare his independence and, as the title indicates, awake and sing? How will Joe Bonapart find a world where he is respected and people no longer laugh at him? How does an Olympic caliber athlete cope with the information that he has a weak heart and can never compete again? How will Steve Takis and Fay Tucker in *Night Music* forge a future in a seemingly hostile society? How does an aging actor (in *The Country Girl*) cope with his personal inadequacies and manage to perform night after night? While the plights of these characters may be due in part to social ills and the evils of capitalism (of which the Depression serves as an ever-present symbol in Odets's early works), the root problems the characters must solve—achieving financial security before marrying, declaring independence, attaining and maintaining self-respect, and the loss of a particular vocation and the status it brings—are certainly more than strictly economic or ideological issues.

If achievement of personal, and by extension, national, ambitions is a recurrent motif in Odets's work, his plays are also permeated with a deep sense of loss. Everything that is gained (or, in many cases, retained) in an Odets drama is gained at the expense of something lost. Lefty attains the martyrdom that prompts his union to strike, but he sacrifices his life; Hennie gains freedom and the hope of happiness at the loss of her family; Leo Gordon maintains his values but loses his house and business; Ben Stark in *Rocket to the Moon* gains a spark of insight but pays a price as Clio walks out of his life; Charlie Castle in *The Big Knife* attains wealth and fame but sacrifices his integrity.

The degree to which loss or the fear of loss dominates Odets's writing can be seen by an examination of his directions and comments at the beginning of *Awake and Sing!* Myron, mourning the loss of the "old days," constantly retreats into nostalgia or into vaudeville shows, in 1935 a dying art form; Moe Axelrod has lost a leg in the war, a fact he "seldom forgets"; Schlosser, the janitor, in Odets's words, "lost his identity twenty years before"; Jacob has lost his ability to act on his ideals, if he ever had that ability; Uncle Morty has lost his compassion for others; and Ralph, described as being "ardent, sensitive, romantic and naive," is being set up to lose. Even Bessie's fear of poverty is a fear of losing her home, a fear she allows to slip out when she describes an eviction on a neighboring street—"they threw out a family on Dawson Street today. All the furniture on the sidewalk" (pp. 37–39).

Loss in Odets's works takes many forms: loss of property as in *Paradise Lost;* loss of a job and income, a central concern in *Waiting for Lefty* and *Rocket to the Moon;* loss of status or role—*Till the Day I Die, Awake and Sing! Paradise Lost;* loss of self-respect—*Paradise Lost, Awake and*

Sing! Golden Boy, The Country Girl; lost opportunity—*Awake and Sing! Paradise Lost, Rocket to the Moon;* loss of a loved one or a cherished friend—*Till the Day I Die, Awake and Sing! Paradise Lost, Rocket to the Moon, Waiting for Lefty, The Big Knife, Clash by Night;* loss of life—all of Odets's early plays and many of his later works. No loss, however, was more significant to Odets than the loss of identity that resulted from the sacrifice of one's ideals, a loss which Odets explored in *Golden Boy* and again in *The Big Knife.* As depicted in *Golden Boy,* Joe Bonapart's Faustian bargain to sell his ideals (as embodied in his artistry) for dollars and fame represented to Odets the most serious and pitiable type of loss, one that could only be redeemed by death, and one that Odets's biographers say haunted him personally.

A third characteristic of Odets's dramaturgy has been identified by Joseph Wood Krutch. Writing in 1939, he noted that no dramatist writing at that time could "more powerfully suggest the essential loneliness of men and women, . . . and the powerlessness of any one of them to help the other."[22] What Krutch and others have noted was the almost Chekhovian sense of isolation that caused Americans to remain "alone" even when in a crowd, even if that crowd was the family. In *Awake and Sing!* Sam Feinschriber, described by Odets in the stage directions as a "foreigner in a strange land, . . . a lonely man . . . who wants to find a home" (p. 39), wanders endlessly between his apartment and the Bergers', feeling comfortable in neither environment; Jake is banished to his small cell to listen to Caruso and read Marxist literature; and Myron seems happiest talking to himself. Ernst Tausig begins the play *Till the Day I Die* as a member of a nuclear family and the communist family, but by the end of the play he has been cast out of both to die alone. Charlie Castle feels alone in his Hollywood mansion even though he is adored by millions and loved by a dedicated coterie of friends. And, in *Paradise Lost,* Odets carried the sense of isolation to such an extreme that the dying Julie is allowed to sit in a corner of the stage muttering meaningless stock market quotations to himself for entire scenes while characters endlessly wander in and out of the apartment at random, frequently without speaking to another human being—much to the consternation of the critics, one of whom summed up the situation with the terse note that "home was never like this."

In *Waiting for Lefty,* Odets seemingly solved the problem of belonging by postulating that a man could find his place in a trade union or in the Communist Party; but in *Golden Boy,* a play which some scholars claim contains existentialist overtones, Joe Bonapart, like O'Neill's Yank, finds belongingness only in death. Throughout Odets's work, his characters, like O'Neill's, echo the question asked by Yank in *The Hairy Ape,* "Where do I fit in?" Posed by O'Neill, the question remained metaphysical; but, asked by Odets, it became manifestly social and, on a deeper level, psychological. If, as many believe, O'Neill sought a replacement for his lost Catholicism, Odets, according to Dr. Brenman-Gibson, a practicing psychotherapist as well as a personal friend of Odets, sought a surrogate family. Deprived of a sense of family, Brenman-Gibson hypothesizes, by an overbearing father and a mother who was too weak and too consumed with her own suffering to respond to her son, Odets turned to the Group Theatre and the Communist Party for his support. And it was this personal loneliness that infused Odets's characters with their deep-rooted desire to belong.

If Brenman-Gibson is correct, it was these intensely personal and human concerns, not simply the desire for social reform, that drove Odets to write, and it is his compassion for those like the Bergers, who are engaged in "a struggle for life amidst petty conditions" (p. 37), and for people like Steve and Fay in *Night Music,* who are described as "two lonely, pathetic creatures, needing a home, needing friends, needing assurances of a future in which their small talents are needed and appreciated" (p. 1), that is one of the most recognizable and consistent characteristics of his work and that rendered him a spokesman for a significant portion of American society—the disenfranchised and the abandoned.

These then were the forces that precipitated Odets's rebellion—a personal revolt that was "a persistent and many-sided rebellion of human nature against anything that would thwart it."[23] It started as an individual "tendril of revolt," an isolated act like Joe's protest in *Lefty* against the social forces that threaten his marriage and well-being, and spread from there to encompass all of humanity, all problems, the class struggle. It was this many-sided rebellion that Gassner describes as "theatre of frustration."

Throughout his career there was confusion, not only about what Odets was trying to say but about how he was trying to say it. In

Waiting for Lefty, although Odets maintained that its form was that of the minstrel show with its interlocutor, its endmen, and with its performers seated in a semicircle awaiting their turn to perform, everyone in the audience recognized it as a variation of the agitprop, a mode of left-wing production popular in the early thirties. *Lefty,* like other agitprops, was designed to be produced for working-class audiences in union halls and meeting rooms; the performers were to be dressed in their work clothes so that the workers would readily identify with them; audience "plants" were placed to enhance audience involvement in the action; stylized, cartoonlike characters were employed; the play ended with the harangue, begun on the stage but quickly picked up by the actors in the house and then by the audience itself, to "STRIKE! STRIKE! STRIKE!"; and the play, as John Howard Lawson pointed out, was a series of "conversions."

While there were distinct strains of realism in *Lefty,* obvious enough to prompt some to label the play "realistic agitprop," and some critics at the time noted the many points of departure from the agitprop form, it wasn't until the production of *Awake and Sing!* (actually written before *Lefty*) that the critics noticed that Odets was principally a realistic writer and described his style as "revolutionary realism," "messy Jewish kitchen realism," or "synthetic Jewish realism." Actually, if critics had been more aware of trends within the theatre of protest, they would have been less surprised, for by 1935 the agitprop was rapidly slipping from favor among left-wing groups. Meanwhile, there was a rediscovery and revaluation of realism and at the same time a growing realization of the power of professional acting companies and techniques, previously considered bourgeois.[24]

Perceptive critics, however, saw more than a mere slice-of-life in Odets's dramaturgy and were quick to note allegorical strains in his writing. In this, they were aided by Odets's ill-fated message to the newspapers prior to the opening of *Paradise Lost:* "In 'Paradise Lost' the task was not . . . simple. . . . Here the hero is not the worker with conflicts cleared to the fighting point, the enemy visible, palpable. The hero in 'Paradise Lost' is the entire American middle class of liberal tendency."[25] Looking back, it is possible to view even *Waiting for Lefty* in light of this pronouncement. After all, at the time of *Lefty*'s production, the strike upon which it had been based was long since over and hence the play's appeal could not be said to be a literal call to the barricades. The play had meaning only, in the words of one critic, as a "lyric proclamation of the proletarian revolt"—in other words, as a metaphor for the revolution.

In John Gassner's opinion, "the allegorical method was an almost inevitable procedure for a man who [like Odets] sought significance for his narratives, vents for his explosiveness, and a function for his poetic . . . flare."[26] Furthermore, it put Odets squarely in the mainstream of that segment of the artistic community which rejected the old saw "art for art's sake," in favor of the more current "drama is a weapon"; that rejected realistic *representation* in favor of a more *symbolic* realism.[27]

Critics have noted similar tendencies in the writing of Elmer Rice, John Howard Lawson, William Saroyan, Tennessee Williams, and Arthur Miller, and, if George Jean Nathan can be believed, even in Anderson and Stallings' *What Price Glory?*[28] These writers, like Odets, "succeeded in fusing the contemporary with the poetic, realistic dialogue with symbolic force, anger and despair with warmth, tenderness, and compassion, to forge a unique and remarkable dramatic idiom."[29] In this context, Lawson's *Roger Bloomer* can be read as the "average" (the author's term) American boy's search for personal identity; Elmer Rice's polyglot neighborhood in *Street Scene* can be construed as a critique of the American melting pot; Williams's Amanda and Blanche are viewed as representatives of a dying way of life; and Willy Loman serves as the quintessential middle-class "victim" of a depersonalized, dehumanized social system. In his best plays, as Gabriel Miller observes, when Odets's "dream of transcendence [was] realized in images less tactile and specific, when his poetic imagery . . . grew out of the material at hand rather than being imposed arbitrarily, it [could] be as provocative and mesmerizing as his ability to capture reality" and his dramaturgy, like that of Saroyan, was capable of projecting a "mystical, Whitmanesque tone of democratic utopianism."[30]

Viewing Odets's work symbolically pays immediate dividends. First, reevaluating *Paradise Lost* with an entire class of people as the hero—a concept accepted in Europe before the end of the nineteenth century, but causing American critics of the 1930s no end of confusion—partially explains how one allegedly average middle-class American family could have one son who is terminally ill, a second son gunned down in the street, a daughter who is unable to wed her fiancé because of economic conditions and who hence chooses to become a hermit in her own home, while the family become victims of bankruptcy, eviction, and a seemingly endless series of miscellaneous humiliations, all in the course of just one play. The Gordons as a real family could not credibly suffer so many misfortunes in a single work; the Gordons as a representative of an entire class, however, could take on their backs the misfortunes of that class, a fact Odets's flawed technique unfortunately obscured. Viewed from this perspective, *Paradise Lost* was no more a literal representation of an American family than Elmer Rice's paradigmatic neighborhood in *Street Scene* was an actual New York neighborhood.

Likewise, *Awake and Sing!* has been endowed with added meaning. Since this play was written before *Waiting for Lefty,* Moe's accusation, "It's all a racket—from horse racing down. Marriage, politics, big business. . . . You, you're a racketeer yourself" (p. 71) directed at Uncle Morty, is the earliest example of Odets's creating the Brechtian parallel between the businessman and the criminal. The play abounds in escape images—movies, vaudeville, the Boston mail plane that Ralph hears every day, nostalgia, dreams, Horatio Alger platitudes, music. And the family was created by Odets as the "breeding ground for revolt," as the representative of an entire class, as a microcosm of the social situation, as a miniature of the "fundamental activity [of millions of people], a struggle for life amidst petty circumstances" (p. 17).

Odets's symbolic realism is nowhere more apparent than in his choice of the music played or mentioned in the play. Hennie, in attempting to avoid her mother's relentless questioning, invokes the song "Apple Blossom Time in Normandy" to symbolize her desire for escape, not only from Bessie's probing but from the boredom and meaninglessness of her daily existence; Jake's use of the "lament from *The Pearl Fishers* is a reflection of his own self-pity"; and "O Paradiso," which is paired with Jake's dream of escape to utopia, is contained in *The Best of Caruso* which, Weales has noted, stated in its record notes that "it is music to free the spirit" (pp. 63–66). The most complex example, however, is Moe's song about the "land of Yama Yama." On one level, as Weales points out, it is an "inaccurate rendering of *Yamo Yamo, . . .* a standard longing-for-escape song" written in 1917; but it also may refer to "The Yama Yama Man," a song popular when Odets was growing up. Written in 1908, "The Yama Yama Man" was a bogeyman song ending with the verse, "Maybe he's hiding behind the chair / Ready to spring out at you unaware / Run to your mama / For here comes the Yama Yama Man." During the early thirties there was no more fearful bogeyman than the economic Yama Yama Man that threatened to tear families apart and deposit their belongings in the street (pp. 63–66).

While Odets's symbolic realism, in the cases of *Awake and Sing!* and *Paradise Lost*, may have caused some confusion and may have contributed to Mordecai Gorelik's feeling that "Odets has never been able to strike a balance between his amazing intuitive grasp of the American scene and the oversimplified patterns into which he forces his materials," there were no such problems with *Golden Boy*, subtitled "*an American allegory*."[31] Everyone readily understood that Odets had created an analogy between capitalism and boxing, an endeavor in which one individual tries to "kill" or "murder" another. Not only does Odets provide the audience with Eddie Fuselli, his most misshapen gangster-businessman, but Joe is treated and referred to as being nothing more than property; the fight game and all of the necessary ugliness that it entails is summed up by Moody in the simple statement, "It's a business"; and, if there had been any previous doubt, the point is brutally reemphasized in the final scene of the play when people gather to mourn Joe. Some mourn the death of a human being, while others in the same room mourn the loss of a possession.

In the final analysis, the reasons for undervaluing Odets's dramaturgy, which began in his own time and continue into ours, are too complex for one article. Certainly Odets's haughty demeanor alienated many critics, and his politics triggered a backlash among mainstream reviewers. Possibly, as some have maintained, he was blamed for not becoming another O'Neill. But one fact is certain: Odets's plays are not dated. In an era when we trip over the homeless on the sidewalks of America's cities at the same time as we dodge Ralph Lauren–clad BMW drivers on their way to the store for a case of designer water, I think it is safe to say that Odets's fear of a "life printed on dollar bills" is still very real; and as long as the prizefighter is valued over the violinist, Odets's theatre of frustration is not obsolete. Harold Clurman summarized the issue in the following manner: "What crushes . . . people . . . is not simply the economic situation, . . . but the temper of the society as a whole, of which the Depression of the thirties was only an episode, a wounding symptom. It is . . . humanity which is in constant danger of being destroyed. That has not changed."[32]

Notes

1. Qtd. in Ira Peck, "The Theater Did Not Want Clifford Odets," *New York Times* (Oct. 18, 1964).

2. Margaret Brenman-Gibson, *Clifford Odets: American Playwright* (New York: Atheneum, 1982), pp. 336–38; and Richard Watts, Jr., "Sight and Sound," *New York Herald Tribune* (March 31, 1935).

3. Frank S. Nugent, "Odets, Where Is Thy Sting?" *New York Times* (Sept. 6, 1936); and Joseph Wood Krutch, "The Apocalypse of St. Clifford," *The Nation* (Dec. 25, 1935): 552.

4. Grenville Vernon, *Commonweal* (April 12, 1935): 682; (June 10, 1938): 188; (Dec. 16, 1938): 216; (March 31, 1939): 639–40.

5. Brooks Atkinson, Review of *Till the Day I Die, New York Times* (March 27, 1935).

6. Edward Murray, *Clifford Odets: The Thirties and After* (New York: Frederick Ungar Publishing Co., 1968), p. 24.

7. Michael J. Mendelsohn, *Clifford Odets: Humane Dramatist* (Deland, Fla.: Everett/Edwards, 1969), p. 1.

8. Warren French, ed., *The Thirties: Fiction, Poetry, Drama* (Deland, Fla.: Everett/Edwards, 1967), p. 177; and Peter Thomson and Gamini Salgado, *The Everyman Companion to the Theatre* (London: J. M. Dent & Sons, 1985), p. 286.

9. Harold Clurman, "Introduction," in *Clifford Odets, Six Plays* (New York: Grove Press, 1979), p. xi.

10. Qtd. in French, ed., *The Thirties*, p. 197.

11. Odets, *Awake and Sing!* in *Clifford Odets, Six Plays*, pp. 57, 91. Subsequent references are cited in the text.

12. Joseph Wood Krutch, *The American Drama Since 1918* (New York: Random House, 1939), p. 275; Krutch, "The Apocalypse," p. 552; Alfred Kazin in French, ed., *The Thirties*, p. 197.

13. Richard Watts, Jr., "Sight and Sound," *New York Herald Tribune* (March 31, 1935).

14. Harold Cantor, *Clifford Odets: Playwright-Poet* (Metuchen, N.J.: Scarecrow Press, 1978), p. 1.

15. Gerald Weales, *Odets: The Playwright* (New York: Methuen, 1985), p. 13. Subsequent references are cited in the text.

16. Harold Clurman, *The Fervent Years* (New York: Da Capo Press, 1975), pp. 150–52.

17. Gabriel Miller, *Clifford Odets* (New York: Continuum, 1989), p. 14.

18. Qtd. in Brenman-Gibson, *Clifford Odets,* p. 249.

19. Brenman-Gibson, *Clifford Odets,* p. 73; and R. Baird Shuman, *Clifford Odets* (New York: Twayne Publishers, 1962), p. 40; Clifford Odets in Joseph Mersand, "Clifford Odets: Dramatist of the Inferiority Complex," *Players Magazine* (May 1940): 9.

20. Clurman, *The Fervent Years,* pp. 116–19; Clurman, "Preface," *Night Music* (New York: Random House, 1940), p. viii. Subsequent references to *Night Music* are cited in the text.

21. John Gassner, " 'Paradise Lost' and the Theatre of Frustration," *New Theatre* (Jan. 1936): 8.

22. Krutch, *The American Drama,* p. 272.

23. Krutch, "The Apocalypse of St. Clifford."

24. Ira A. Levine, *Left-wing Dramatic Theory in the American Theatre* (Ann Arbor: UMI Research Press, 1985), pp. 68–69.

25. Clifford Odets, "Some Problems of the Modern Dramatist," *New York Times* (Dec. 15, 1935).

26. John Gassner, *The Theatre in Our Times* (New York: Crown Publishers, 1954), p. 305.

27. Gassner, " 'Paradise Lost' and the Theatre of Frustration."

28. Barnard Hewitt, *Theatre U.S.A.* (New York: McGraw-Hill, 1959), pp. 358–59.

29. Miller, *Clifford Odets,* p. 18.

30. Miller, *Clifford Odets,* pp. 13, 17.

31. Mordecai Gorelik, *New Theatres for Old* (New York: E. P. Dutton & Co., 1962), p. 242.

32. Clurman, "Introduction," *Six Plays,* p. xiii.

NINE

Thornton Wilder, the Real, and Theatrical Realism

Christopher J. Wheatley

Now listen! Can't you see that when the language was new—as it was with Chaucer and Homer—the poet could use the name of a thing and the thing was really there? He could say "O moon," "O sea," "O love" and the moon and sea and love were really there. And can't you see that after hundreds of years had gone by and thousands of poems had been written, he could call on those words and find that they were just worn-out literary words? . . . I'm no fool. I know that in daily life we don't go around saying "is a . . . is a . . . is a . . . " Yes, I'm no fool; but I think that in that line the rose is red for the first time in English poetry for a hundred years.

Gertrude Stein, as quoted by Wilder[1]

Stein's search for a new way to present a living rose requires a disruption of ordinary language. So too, Wilder's attempt to present reality requires a disruption of the dominant "language" of the stage in the twentieth century: realism. While Wilder experiments with realism during his career (usually in an ironic manner), theatrical realism fails for Wilder because it has lost the possible in the probable; moreover, realism has become "soothing" in its assumptions of the causality involved in the construction of human nature and, consequently, has become untruthful. Also, humanity defined by its circumstances seems to Wilder un-American, both because the realist author claims an unjustifiable paternal authority and because Americans, unlike Europeans, construct their identity from actions rather than environment.

Wilder's best and most frequently performed plays are examples of what John Gassner has called the "theatricalist" tradition in American drama.[2] The experimental one-act plays from 1931, *The Long Christmas Dinner*, *The Happy Journey to Trenton and Camden*, and *Pullman Car Hiawatha*, rely on nonrealistic sets and radical distortion of chronological time. *Our Town* (1938) extends these experiments through disregard of dramatic conflict. *The Skin of Our Teeth* (1942) presents the Antrobuses as existing simultaneously in the biblical time of Genesis, the ice age, suburban New Jersey, and a theater in New York; unlike *Our Town*, it presents conflict without resolution, as the play ends with the lines that begin the first act. *The Alcestiad*, renamed *A Life in the Sun* in 1954 for its premiere in Edinburgh, is similar to a Greek tragedy in three parts followed by a satyr play, "The Drunken Sisters." Two of the three plays from *Bleeker Street* (1962), *Infancy* and *Childhood*, externalize the psychomachia of human development.

Nevertheless, the other three one-acts of 1931, *Such Things Only Happen in Books*, *Love and How to Cure It*, and *The Queens of France*, possess at least the trappings of realism, as do the two one-acts of 1957 presented in Berlin: *Bernice*, and *The Wreck of the 5:15*.[3] Moreover, Wilder adapted Ibsen's *A Doll's House* for Broadway in 1938, in a production that starred Ruth Gordon and was directed by Jed Harris; he also worked on an adaptation of *The Cherry Orchard* in the mid 1950s that was to star Montgomery Clift.[4] Wilder's occasional engagement with realism also occurs in his novels. While *The Cabala* (1926), *The Bridge of San Luis Rey* (1928), *The Woman of Andros* (1930), *The Ides of March* (1948), and *The Eighth Day* (1967) all disrupt at least some of the expectations of the realist novel, *Heaven's My Destination* (1935) and *Theophilus North* (1973) present a mostly linear narration of probable characters doing plausible things in real places.

This catalogue of Wilder's literary career indicates that he saw a place for realism. A remark in an interview in 1938 suggests what the limits of realism are: "And I think that Ibsen and Chekhov, after pushing realism as far as it would go, realized that there was insufficient truth in mere copying."[5] Wilder stresses in this interview his admiration for the great realists, but he suggests that realism, when it becomes "mere copying," ceases to reveal "truth." Truth of course is a loaded term in the twentieth century, and Wilder's conception of it indicates the difference between himself and playwrights such as Miller and Williams, a difference that perhaps accounts for Wilder's tenuous critical reputation. In Wilder's *The Angel That Troubled the Waters and Other Plays* (1928), written for the most part while an undergraduate at Oberlin and Yale, lies an attempt to find the truth of religious experience: "I hope, through many mistakes, to discover the spirit that is not unequal to the elevation of great religious themes, yet which does not fall into a repellent didacticism" (p. 98). Wilder's difficulty is that religious truth has also become exhausted: "The revival of religion is almost a matter of rhetoric. The work is difficult, perhaps impossible (perhaps all religions die out with the exhaustion of the language)" (p. 99). Religion, in the twentieth century, has become improbable, while realist drama deals with the probable. Although Wilder's conception of truth is not limited to religious experience, it indicates a kind of truth that, by its nature, cannot be expressed in purely realist terms, since the mystery of faith is an expression about the possible, not the probable. Of course, an essentialist view of truth, whether religious truth or any other kind, in the secular, pragmatic American twentieth century, places Wilder in an anomalous position, and it is worth noting that Eliot also needed to eschew realism in *Murder in the Cathedral*.

The early realist one-act *Such Things Only Happen in Books* examines the limitations of the probable. A young novelist playing solitaire explains to his wife the likely outcome of future games: "Listen to the scores this evening; zero, two, five, three, zero, one four, zero, three, one six, zero, zero, zero, three, zero, six, and now five. The full fifty-two come out every twenty-one times. So that from now on my chances for getting it out increase seven point three two every game."[6] The reasoning on the probable is fallacious. The odds of winning future games of solitaire remain exactly the same no matter what the previous occurrences. But the young novelist's error about probability is reinforced in his life. He is having difficulty writing a story because he is unable to find a plausible plot: "Plots. Plots. If I had no conscience I could choose any one of these plots that are in everybody's novels and nobody's lives" (pp. 92–93). But the tired old stories, that married women have lovers, servants hide brothers escaped from prison, and a murder was committed over an inheritance in their house, are in fact happening all around the novelist; his insistence on the probable keeps him from seeing the possible. After the revelations of the play (to the audience, not the novelist), the play ends where it begins:

> *Gabrielle:* I don't see why that game shouldn't come out oftener. (*Pause*) I don't think you see all the moves.
> *John:* I certainly do see all the moves that are to be seen.—You don't expect me to look under the cards, do you? (p. 100)

Wilder's treatment of realism in this play is ironic. A realist set emphasizes the narrowness of the realistic novelist's conception. The old plots are true but exhausted in John's view. A look under the surface aspects would reveal the repetition upon which the old stories are based and which maintains their dramatic validity.

Elsewhere in his journal (while writing *The Skin of Our Teeth*), Wilder notes the advantage of theatricalist plays in terms of their ability to express truth in the same way that great myths do: "I have one advantage: the dramatic vehicle as surprise. Again by shattering the ossified conventions of the well-made play the characters emerge *ipso facto* as generalized beings. This advantage would no longer be mine twenty years from now when the theatre will be offering a great many plays against freer decors; the audience will be accustomed to such liberties and the impact of the method will no longer be so great an aid to myth-intention."[7] Despite the reference to the well-made play, the more significant target here is the proscenium and the realist set. Both are dated, and Wilder's self-conscious theatricality will come as a surprise to the audience, making the play "new," just as Stein's rose regains a lost presence through the novelty of repetition. Yet even Wilder's theatricalism is connected to a specific literary time; it too will become stale as other playwrights discard the conventions of realism. Mere novelty is insufficient without the generalized truth of myth.

"Myth-intention," Wilder's literary grail, is achieved by Joyce in *Finnegans Wake*, the source of *The Skin of Our Teeth*. According to Wilder, Joyce's deliberately difficult form and language "reveal the extent to which every individual—you and I, the millions of the people who walk this earth—is both sole and unique and also archetypal" (p. 172). Realism can provide the "I" but denies the type, and Wilder's example of this in the same essay is a hypothetical production of *Romeo and Juliet* in 1910 or 1890: "What we see are real chandeliers, real rugs, tables laden with supposedly real food and drink, and it is all boxed in within a picture frame. . . . And what did it convey? It said that these events took place to one set of persons, at one moment in time, in one place. That is the theater of the Unique Occasion" (p. 174). This is not Shakespeare's *Romeo and Juliet* because it suggests that a specific young man and woman, through a series of misfortunes and bad judgments, end up dead. In Wilder's view, while all young men and women live their own tragedies, the theater should (and great modern novelists like Joyce and Stein do) stress the commonality of tragic young love. The realist set distances the audience from that commonality.[8]

The same idea occurs in the introduction to *Three Plays*. Despite Wilder's admiration for plays like *Desire Under the Elms* as compositions, he "didn't believe a word of them": "I began to feel that the theater was not only inadequate, it was evasive; it did not wish to draw upon its deeper potentialities. I found the word for it: it aimed to be *Soothing*."[9] The shock of seeing the author of *Our Town* describe *Desire Under the Elms* as one of a class of plays that are soothing can only be explained with reference to Wilder's rejections of realism: "Every person who has ever lived has lived an unbroken succession of unique occasions. Yet the more one is aware of this individuality in experience (innumerable! innumerable!) the more one becomes attentive to what these disparate moments have in common, to repetitive patterns. As an artist (or listener or beholder) which "truth" do you prefer—that of the isolated occasion, or that which includes and resumes the innumerable? . . . The theater is admirably fitted to tell both truths" (p. 107).

Realist plays, however, tell only the truth of unique occasion. An audience, or Wilder at least, is not shaken by *Desire Under the Elms* because the characters' crimes are the consequence of circumstances in a different place at a different time. If an audience does not regard itself as in the bondage of a puritan work ethic or a repressive New England sexual climate, then the problems of Abbie and Eben are interesting in a sociological way, but not personally relevant: in a word, soothing, since our problems are comparatively minor. Also, the audience is not subject to the same causes and is therefore unlikely to commit the same crimes. This a dubious theoretical proposition. One need not be from New Orleans to be complicit in Stanley's brutal rape of Blanche in *A Streetcar Named Desire;* simply being an American male who regards Blanche as annoying may be sufficient to create a damning self-identification with Stanley. Wilder would presumably respond that such identification would be easier and more forceful without the details of time and place.

In *The Skin of Our Teeth*, Miss Somerset refuses to play a scene involving her character's seduction of Mr. Antrobus: "Well, if you must know, I have a personal guest in the audience tonight. Her life hasn't been exactly a happy one. I wouldn't have my friend hear some of these lines for the whole world. I don't suppose it occurred to the author that some other women might have gone through the experience of losing their husbands like this."[10] In a realist play the problem does not exist, at least in Wilder's view, because the action is safely distanced by circumstance and properties from the audience. But Miss Somerset and Sabina (and, playing them, the tempestuous Tallulah Bankhead actually starring in the double part in the Broadway premiere) are engaged in an interaction with an audience whose presence is acknowledged throughout. Miss Somerset does not want to play the scene, "Because there are some lines in that scene that would hurt some people's feelings and I don't think the theatre is a place where people's feelings ought to be hurt" (p. 109). Despite the comedy, the scene enacts the theater's repetition of common experience, the ever recurring adulteries that are not a consequence of a specific time or place.

Through its use of properties, writes Wilder in his essays, realism invariably places an action in the past, while the stage is the location of the "eternal present": "When you emphasize *place* in the theater, you drag down and limit and harness time to it. You thrust the action into past time, whereas it is precisely the glory of the stage that it is always 'now' there" (p. 108). In the essay "Some Thoughts on Playwriting," Wilder elaborates on this point: "The novel is a past reported in the present. On the stage it is always now. This confers upon the action an increased vitality which the novelist longs in vain to incorporate into his work" (p. 125). In realistic staging, the play loses its immediacy without gaining the breadth of detail that Flaubert and Tolstoy can achieve in their novels. When Sabina complains in *The Skin of Our Teeth* that "the author hasn't made up his silly mind as to whether we're all living back in caves or in New Jersey today" (p. 73), she indicates Wilder's belief that the stage should be able to show both in an eternal present.

The eternal present occurs because of the commonality of knowledge. Wilder, heavily influenced by Stein, claimed that great art succeeded not by convincing the audience of anything, but by the audience's recognition of the artist's moment of recognition, both recognitions coming from a sudden awareness that all knowledge is universal.[11] The audience's approval of the act of creation is explained by Stein—through Wilder—in terms of apprehension: "They *say* that they agree with you; what they mean is that they are aware that your pages have the vitality of a thing which sounds to them like someone else's knowing; it is consistent to its own world of what one person has really known" (p. 203). That what one person really knows is known by all people is mentioned by Wilder in a reminiscence of conversations with Stein: "She was never tired of saying that all real knowledge is common knowledge; it lies sleeping within us; it is awakened in us when we hear it expressed by a person who is speaking and writing in a state of recognition" (p. 204).

Common knowledge cannot be explained, only perceived. The Stage Manager's soliloquy in the cemetery in *Our Town* is an example: "Now there are some things we all know, but we don't take'm out and look at'm very often. We all know that *something* is eternal. And it ain't houses and it ain't names, and it ain't earth, and it ain't even the stars . . . everybody knows in their bones that *something* is eternal, and that something has to do with human beings. All the greatest people who ever lived have been telling us that for five thousand years and yet you'd be surprised how people are always losing hold of it" (p. 52). Our knowledge of the eternal is remarkably difficult to describe. For the most part, the Stage Manager asserts such knowledge and circumscribes it by a series of negations describing what is not eternal. The test of the claim is the third act of *Our Town;* audience response to the act is, presumably, the recognition of the eternal onstage in the present.

The Skin of Our Teeth enacts several examples of Wilder's belief that the audience need not "understand" what is being presented, but need only recognize the act of knowing. In the first act when Moses and Homer present their "knowledge," they speak in Hebrew and Greek respectively. There can be no question of most audiences understanding what is said. What is important is the placing of the achievements of the past in a situation where they have no practical use. Wilder regards these truths as having universal validity; if the scene is dramatically effective, then the audience will recognize this without needing to understand the specifics. Donald Haberman perceptively points out the process involved in the first act of *The Skin of Our Teeth*, a process that I think is operant in most of Wilder's nonrealist drama: "This primitive emotional reaction is emphasized by the passages in Greek and Hebrew. The foreign words recited dramatically, precisely because the audience do not understand their meaning, touch something in the audience that is deeper than rational argument could go."[12]

Presented with passages stripped of context and familiarity, the audience responds to wisdom (represented by Homer and Moses) as something that is recognized, rather than as something that is explained. Another example of this principle is the speeches of the hours at the end of the play. These speeches do have an intellectual context within the play that they help to explicate, but this is only clear when reading the play, because the speeches, drawn from Plato, Aristotle, and Spinoza, are too complex to be fully grasped upon one hearing, which is all one gets when one sees the play. Again, it is the insistence dramatically upon the author's and the audience's recognition of their validity outside of understanding that makes the speeches effective.

Francis Fergusson writes that "Brecht, Wilder, and Eliot do not expect the audiences to share their intimate perceptions, whether 'realistic' or 'poetic.' "[13] On the other hand, the realist author presupposes a knowledge and perception that can be communicated to the audience but is not present in the audience prior to the theatrical enactment. Williams, for instance, in the introduction to *Cat on a Hot Tin Roof*, says, "I want to go on talking to you as freely and intimately about what we live and die for as if I knew you better than anyone else you know."[14] Williams's subject is private and can only be conveyed personally: "I want you to observe what I do for your possible pleasure and to give you knowledge of things that I feel I may know better than you, because my world is different from yours, as different as every man's world is from the world of others" (p. vii). Each person's world is inherently different because of circumstance. There are some things, consequently, that Williams knows better than the rest of us—the South, homophobia—and he can explain his "lyrical" understanding to us. On the other hand, Sabina says in her first long speech, "I hate this play and every word in it. As for me, I don't understand a single word of it, anyway" (p. 73). However, she later says, "Now that you audience are listening to this, I understand it a little better" (p. 76). Wilder's bare stage is not something he knows better than we do, because it is everyone's world; moreover, what he knows can only be understood communally. Fundamentally, Wilder thinks that each person's world shares important repetitions that an audience recognizes.

In *The Alcestiad*, Tiresias announces that Apollo is one of four herdsmen come to serve Admetus. One of the four herdsmen responds in disbelief: "If there had been a god among us, would I have not known it?"[15] Since he has traveled with the others thirty days, he assumes superior knowledge based on specific knowledge: "We have drunk from the same wineskin; we have put our hands in the same dish; we have slept by the same fire. If there had been a god among us, would I not have known it?" (p. 29). Eventually, the herdsman comes to see from conversation with Alcestis, who is looking for a sign that the gods exist so that she may know whether or not to marry Admetus, that the messages of the gods are incommensurable with human experience: "But if they did exist, these gods, how would they speak to us? In what language would they talk to us?" (p. 31). The herdsmen's new understanding surpasses the seer's: "Now, maybe that foolish old man got his message wrong. Maybe he was supposed to say that Apollo is divided up among many people—us four herdsmen and others!" (p. 31). Even the new formulation, however, is tentative; "maybe" Tiresias is wrong. But Alcestis recognizes the presence of the god and marries Admetus confidently, because she now knows that the gods exist, even if it is never made clear how. The realist playwright is a kind of seer who claims a knowledge of the causes of things. Wilder's characters, and by extension his audience, achieve a recognition of what they already know. Emily, in the third act of *Our Town*, knows her life. What she sees only in death is the beauty and importance of the mundane: "I didn't realize. So all that was going on and we never noticed" (p. 62). In Wilder's view, the playwright does not show you something he understands better than you do, but something that you knew but did not realize. The nonrealistic staging presents the familiar stripped of the inessentials (i.e., the causal circumstances that account for the familiar to a realistic novelist or playwright) and thus Emily's life becomes the audience's.[16]

Arthur Miller's lengthy interjections in *The Crucible* about the economic and personal circumstances of the characters reveal how much more he knows about the Salem witch trials than we do; he knows the historical and psychological forces that caused the disaster: "Since 1692 a great but superficial change has wiped out God's beard and the Devil's horns, but the world is still gripped between two diametrically opposed absolutes. The concept of unity, in which positive and negative are attributes of the same force, in which good and evil are relative, ever changing, and always joined to the same phenomenon—such a concept is still reserved to the physical sciences and to the few who have grasped the history of ideas."[17] The truth of relativism is apparent only to the few, and, presumably, the play will make it clear to an audience that has not previously understood this point because they have not studied physics and the history of ideas. Miller's realist drama, at least in the printed version, needs to explain why events occurred as they did. The tendentious nature of Miller's interjection—with its assumption of commensurability between physics and ethics—indicates that he is trying to convince us of something. Wilder, on the other hand, usually does not explain the frequent allusions to philosophical and religious works (Ivy's explanation about the hours in *The Skin of Our Teeth* is an exception to this claim), because he regards it as paternalistic—and this is despite the fact that Wilder is almost certainly the most learned of American playwrights, especially if one excludes Eliot as English.

In the speech "Culture in a Democracy," presented in Germany in 1957, Wilder argues that the great problem of European history has been an identification of God as father, and, by analogy, the aristocracy as possessing parental authority: "One of the principal evils of this confusion was the image of the son. No man has a father after twenty-one" (p. 71). Americans have rejected this formulation in Wilder's view, not only politically but in the realm of intellectual authority. In the introduction to his Norton lecture, "Toward an American Language," presented at Harvard in 1950, Wilder draws a distinction between European and American lectures: "In the Old World a lecture tended to be a discourse in which an Authority dispensed a fragment of the Truth. . . . An American lecture is a discourse in which a man declares what is true for him" (p. 5). The realist writer has assumed this paternal role and encased an event in historical determinism: "The problem of telling you about my past life as a writer is like that of imaginative narration itself; it lies in the effort to employ the past tense in such a way that it does not rob those events of having occurred in freedom. A great deal of writing and talking about the past is unacceptable. It freezes the historical in a determinism. Today's writer smugly passes his last judgment and confers on existing attitudes the lifeless aspect of plaster cast statues in a museum."[18] A realist writer assumes the role of European lecturer explaining a fragment of truth. The theatre, occurring in the present tense, should escape determinism and authority by presenting being in action. The fortune teller in *The Skin of Our Teeth* cryptically presents the disagreement between Wilder and realism's past tense: "I can't tell the past and neither can you. If anybody tries to tell you the past, take my word for it, they're charlatans! Charlatans! But I can tell you the future" (p. 100). The future we project from the action we see, but we know that it is free and dependent on choice. We cannot, however, describe the past from the vantage point of the present, because inevitably in the past tense, the element of freedom is lost.

Even explanations in Wilder's plays tend to revolve around central mysteries. In *The Matchmaker,* Cornelius, having fallen in love with Mrs. Molloy, describes first her beauty and then her incomprehensibility: "Golly, they're different from men. And they're awfully mysterious, too. You never can be really sure what's going on in their heads. They have a kind of wall around them all the time—of pride and a sort of play-acting: I bet you could know a woman a hundred years without ever being really sure whether she liked you or not" (p. 177). Miller knows why Abigail acts as she does in *The Crucible,* and despite Williams's claim in *Cat on a Hot Tin Roof* that characters should be mysterious (p. 85), he knows why Maggie is a cat: "It is constant rejection that makes her humor 'bitchy' " (p. 20). Cornelius does not understand Mrs. Molloy, nor does he need to, any more than Alcestis ultimately needs to understand Apollo. Mrs. Antrobus throws a bottle into the ocean containing "all the things a woman knows": "We're not what you're all told and what you think we are: We're ourselves. And if any man can find one of us he'll learn why the whole universe was set in motion" (p. 114). Knowledge is present in the bottle, but we are not told what the bottle contains. This is not evasion on Wilder's part, since any statement of what a woman knows would be reductive and presumptuous; rather, Wilder relies on the audience to intuit what a woman knows with reference to what an individual in the audience knows and through the enactment of what the Everywoman onstage experiences.

Ultimately, Wilder writes that realism is un-American, not merely because it assumes a paternal author with superior knowledge but because it denies a basic character trait in Americans:

> "I am I," says the European, "because the immemorial repetitions of my country's way of life surround me. I know them and they know me."
>
> An American can have no such stabilizing relation to any one place, nor to any one community, nor to any one moment in time.
>
> Americans are disconnected. They are exposed to all place and all time. No place nor group nor moment can say to them: We were waiting for you; it is right for you to be here. Place and time are, for them, negative until they act upon them, until they bring them into being. (p. 14)

The vast spaces of the American landscape shape American consciousness as much as the hills and valleys shape European consciousness, but the effect is a dissimilar sense of identity. Europeans know themselves because of the circumstances of geography, religion, history, and custom that surround them. Realism makes sense for Ibsen and Chekhov since the causality of environment is a part of European consciousness. But Americans, rootless and oriented toward the present and future, have an identity only in action. The deracinated American is perhaps most clearly apparent in Wilder's novels: the American Samuel interacting with the European members of the Cabala in Rome; the traveling salesman George Brush on a pilgrimage through the Midwest in *Heaven's My Destination;* Theophilus North arriving in Newport to heal the sick and moving on at the end of the novel.

However, *Our Town*'s bare stage is itself emblematic of the American's existence in action rather than as a part of an environment. The Stage Manager says, "This is the way we were: in our growing up and in our marrying and in our living and in our dying" (p. 21). The copy of the play placed in the cornerstone of the new bank will exist in the past tense as an object. The play itself is a series of gerunds, "growing," "living," "marrying," "dying," verbs becoming nouns through enactment. The residents of Grover's Corners are not identified by a past (as in, for instance, *The Iceman Cometh,* where in the present the characters are all self-deluding drunks distinguishable only by accent and appearance) but by their actions in the stage's eternal present. In *The Long Christmas Dinner* Charles says, "Time certainly goes very fast in a great new country like this," and Cousin Ermengarde responds, "Well, time must be passing very slowly in Europe with this dreadful war going on."[19] The Americans are also vulnerable to disasters like war, as Charles's son Sam immediately "goes briskly out through the dark portal" that indicates death, but time does indeed go quickly nonetheless as ninety years are condensed to thirty minutes. The past is something that has no hold on Americans in Wilder's plays.[20] Charles claims that the family history is written in a book someplace, and Genevieve denies this: "Nonsense. There are no such books. I collect my notes off gravestones, and you have to scrape a good deal of moss—let me tell you—to find one great-grandparent" (p. 19). The house is ultimately deserted as the generations disperse around the country and the globe.

I am not claiming that Wilder denies a value to history; his two best novels, *The Ides of March* and *The Eighth Day,* are both historical fictions. But Wilder's realist one-act *The Queens of France* shows that for Americans a focus on the past is destructive when characters attempt to find their identity in their antecedents. A con man, M'su Cahusac, makes his living convincing women in New Orleans that they are the true heirs to the throne of France, and that they must buy various heirlooms lest the Historical Society that seeks to establish their claim in the eyes of the world be forced to sell them to defray expenses incurred in their search for documentation. The play is a comedy—the last gull we see is far too old to be the daughter of the lost boy who was the true heir—but the women are transformed for the worse by their delusion of noble ancestry. Mme. Pugeot, for example, denies her husband any place in her new life: "He has chosen to scoff at my birth and my rank, but he will see what he will see. . . . Naturally I have not told him about the proofs that you and I have collected. I have not the heart to let him see how unimportant he will become" (p. 35).

The delusion cannot last as the gulled women eventually run out of money buying back Bourbon treasures before the essential last document is found. Mlle. Pointevin describes the final result: "It is all very strange. You know, M'su Cahusac, I think there may have been a mistake somewhere. It was so beautiful while it lasted. It made even school-teaching a pleasure, M'su. . . . Will you have the Historical Society write me a letter saying that they seriously think I may be . . . the person . . . the person they are looking for? I wish to keep the letter in the trunk with the orb and . . . with the scepter. You know . . . the more I think of it, the more I think there must have been a mistake somewhere" (p. 44). On some level, Mlle. Pointevin knows she has been deceived, yet she prefers the deception to her real life. The worthless forgeries and the letter are properties more important than her own life. The play's realist set ironically comments on the appeal of realist drama. The American characters are conned into preferring somebody else's life to their own through a superficial trail of plausibility. Emily's anguished question to the Stage Manager, "Do any human beings ever realize life while they live it?" (p. 62), helps to explain the problem of the Queens of France; they are focused on things and other places, not on living itself. The bare stage of *Our Town* is an attempt to take the focus off objects and place it on actions, living.

Ultimately, Wilder has had little influence on the American stage, except perhaps in the avant-garde theatre that accepts his practice while rejecting his metaphysics.[21] This has not affected Wilder's popularity with American audiences. *Our Town* remains the most frequently produced American play, and the 1988 production on Broadway won the Tony Award for best revival of the season. *The Skin of Our Teeth*, while panned in 1975 in Washington and New York as dated, has been successfully revived in New York in 1991 and in Washington in 1993. The three experimental one-acts of 1931 have been successfully produced in New York in 1992–93 by the Willow Theater Group.

Yet Wilder's star is currently in critical decline. The chief difficulty with Wilder seems to be the difference between what he writes and how he writes it. Modernists like Joyce and Stein had a relatively new philosophical perspective to go with their structural and stylistic innovations: namely, the idea that truth is additive rather than an ideal achieved by subtracting the subjective from personal perspective.

Wilder does not agree with this; fundamentally he does believe in a teleological universe and that there are eternal verities (apparent in masterpieces of literature and philosophy), and it seems to create a problem for many educated viewers when they find neoclassical philosophy in twentieth-century trappings. Even Wilder's portrait of Americans shows the influence of nineteenth-century writers such as Emerson and Whitman;[22] Wilder has singularly little in common with his contemporaries O'Neill, Miller, and Williams. It is also interesting that the chief influence on Wilder's conception of American consciousness, Gertrude Stein, made her pronouncements on the American character from Europe. Wilder's plays do tend to look European; their theatrical affinity is with Brecht and Pirandello (despite the enormous differences in attitude and subject matter) rather than with the main line of American drama.

But after all, why not? Wilder is not terribly interested in changing anyone's mind—just in keeping his audience awake and reexperiencing life through his plays. Ultimately, one always has the feeling, reading Wilder criticism, that his chief dramatic crime is that he does not have a tragic view of life, and it seems somehow hard to condemn a playwright because he is optimistic about the future of the human race. This is undoubtedly a function of Wilder's background in that he was born to a well-educated family, which, while never affluent, was never poor either. Safely white and middle class, financially secure after the success of *The Bridge of San Luis Rey*, Wilder had little experience with the grimmer aspects of American industrial capitalism. Still, American life does not comprise only exploited salesmen, dysfunctional families, and destroyed southern romantics. Wilder's idealism reflects a strand of American mythology to which audiences respond, however much critics may deplore it.

Notes

1. Thornton Wilder, "Introduction," *Four in America* (New Haven; Yale UP, 1947); rpt. in *American Characteristics and Other Essays* (New York: Harper & Row, 1979), p. 194. Unless otherwise noted, subsequent quotes from Wilder, other than playtexts, are from this volume and are cited in the text.

2. John Gassner, *Directions in Modern Theatre and Drama* (New York: Holt, Rinehart, and Winston, 1966), pp. 138–42.

3. *Bernice* and *The Wreck of the 5:15* have never been published but exist in typescript at the Beinecke Library at Yale University.

4. See Gilbert A. Harrison, *The Enthusiast: A Life of Thornton Wilder* (New York: Fromm International Publishing Corporation, 1986), pp. 162–64, 262.

5. John Hobart, "Thoughts from a Novelist in the Throes of Stage Fever," *San Francisco Chronicle* (Sept. 11, 1938); rpt. *Conversations with Thornton Wilder,* ed. Jackson R. Bryer (Jackson: UP of Mississippi, 1992), p. 29.

6. *Such Things Only Happen in Books,* in *The Long Christmas Dinner and Other Plays in One Act* (New Haven: Yale UP, 1931), pp. 92–93. Subsequent references are cited in the text. This play was not included in the Harper & Row edition of 1963 or the Bard Avon edition of 1980.

7. Wilder, *The Journals of Thornton Wilder, 1939–1961,* selected and edited by Donald Gallup (New Haven: Yale UP, 1985), p. 22.

8. Thomas E. Porter argues in *Myth and Modern American Drama* that Wilder's "truth" is the ideal in the group mind and that his plays consequently approach pure ritual (Detroit: Wayne State UP, 1969), pp. 200–24.

9. Wilder, "Introduction," *Three Plays,* rpt. in *American Characteristics and Other Essays,* pp. 104–5.

10. Wilder, *The Skin of Our Teeth,* in *Three Plays* (New York: Avon Bard, 1976), p. 109. References to *Our Town* and *The Matchmaker* are also to this edition and will be cited in the text.

11. For discussion of Stein's influence on Wilder see John Malcolm Brinnan, *The Third Rose: Gertrude Stein and Her World* (Boston: Little, Brown, 1959), pp. 338–53; Rex Burbank, *Thornton Wilder* (New York: Twayne Publishers, 1961), pp. 82–87; Frederick W. Lowe, *Gertrude's Web: A Study of Gertrude Stein's Literary Relationships* (Ann Arbor: University Microfilms, 1972), pp. 261–64; Linda Simon, *Thornton Wilder: His World* (Garden City, N.Y.: Doubleday, 1979), pp. 104–37; Donald Haberman, *Our Town: An American Play* (New York: Twayne Publishers, 1989). I am particularly indebted to Haberman's examination of the relationship between Wilder's essays and Stein.

12. Donald Haberman, *The Plays of Thornton Wilder* (Middletown, Conn.: Wesleyan UP, 1967), p. 72.

13. Francis Fergusson, "Brecht, Wilder, and Eliot: Three Allegorists," *Sewanee Review* 64 (1956): 544.

14. Tennessee Williams, *Cat on a Hot Tin Roof* (New York: Signet, 1985), p. x.

15. Wilder, *The Alcestiad* (New York: Harper & Row, 1977), p. 29. Subsequent references are cited in the text.

16. Robert W. Corrigan argues in *The Theater in Search of a Fix* that Wilder's theatrical experiments come from a lack of faith in an ultimate perspective (New York: Delacorte Press, 1973), p. 244. While I am sympathetic to this view in that I think Wilder rejects realism's assumption that actions are explainable in terms of an environment (and, in fact, determined by that environment), I am arguing that Wilder thinks that the audience recognizes a common perspective in the pure being of the stage that renders an ultimate perspective not only impertinent but unnecessary.

17. Arthur Miller, *The Crucible* (New York: Penguin, 1976), p. 33.

18. Interview with Richard H. Goldstone, from *Writers at Work: The Paris Review Interviews* (New York: Viking Press, 1958); rpt. in Bryer, ed., *Conversations with Thornton Wilder*, p. 68.

19. *The Long Christmas Dinner*, in *The Long Christmas Dinner and Other Plays in One Act* (New York: Bard Avon, 1980), pp. 19–20. *The Queens of France* is also in this edition. Subsequent references are cited in the text.

20. Peter Szondi argues that time itself is the theme of *The Long Christmas Dinner;* the dramatic montage estranges sequential time from consciousness and thus time is experienced as something new (*Theory of Modern Drama,* ed. and trans. Michael Hays, in *Theory and History of Literature,* vol. 29 [Minneapolis: U of Minnesota P, 1987], pp. 83–91). This estrangement, in my view, eliminates a sense of time as something that is "past" and "passed" from the play.

21. See David Savran, *The Wooster Group, 1975–1985: Breaking the Rules* (Ann Arbor: UMI Research Press, 1986), pp. 9–45; and Michael Vanden Heuvel, *Performing Drama/Dramatizing Performance: Alternative Theater and the Dramatic Text* (Ann Arbor: U of Michigan P, 1991), pp. 132–41.

22. C. W. E. Bigsby points out the similarity between Whitman and Wilder in his three-volume *A Critical Introduction to Twentieth-Century American Drama* (Cambridge: Cambridge UP, 1982), vol. 1, p. 260. Thomas P. Adler argues that Wilder is influenced by Emerson in *Mirror on the Stage: The Pulitzer Plays as an Approach to American Drama* (West Lafayette, Ind.: Purdue UP, 1987), p. 123.

TEN

Into the Foxhole:
Feminism, Realism,
and Lillian Hellman

Judith E. Barlow

Realism has been under attack almost since it become the dominant mode of playwriting around the turn of the century—whether from Eugene O'Neill, who claimed that "most of the so-called realistic plays deal only with the appearance of things,"[1] or Thornton Wilder, who complained that realism robs drama of its magic by binding it to a particular "time and place."[2] But realism has come under perhaps its greatest assault in recent years from materialist feminist critics who, following a variety of postmodern theories, question the nature and value of both representation and narrative. Sue-Ellen Case has presented the point perhaps most strongly: "Cast the realism aside—its consequences for women are deadly."[3]

This attack would seem to sound the death knell for Lillian Hellman's work; in fact, at one point Jill Dolan refers to the "realist, Hellmanesque model of" Jane Chambers's early plays, thus making "Hellmanism" virtually a synonym for realism.[4] Elin Diamond sums up the anti-realist argument when she writes that "realism, more than any other form of theater representation, mystifies the process of theatrical signification. Because it naturalizes the relation between character and actor, setting and world, realism operates in concert with ideology. And because it depends on, insists on a *stability* of reference, an objective world that is the source and guarantor of knowledge, realism surreptitiously reinforces (even if it argues with) the arrangements of that world."[5] From this perspective, realism can never be used as a tool for social criticism because its very methods undermine the goals of such criticism.

If the assault on realism sounds an ominously prescriptive and elitist note for present and future women dramatists (and their audiences) by defining how women should or should not write,[6] it is even more problematic for writers of the past. Realism was the preeminent theatrical mode in this country for the first half of the twentieth century, and a wholesale rejection of realism means the dismissal of three generations of women dramatists—from Rachel Crothers to Lorraine Hansberry—as well as of the audiences to which they appealed. Hellman's work, realism with a strain of melodrama, stands squarely in this now despised tradition.

Without denying that realistic drama has sometimes—inadvertently as well as intentionally—served to reify the very society it would indict, I would like to suggest that many of the criticisms of the realistic mode underestimate author, text, and audience. Realism invokes a far more complex worldview than its detractors acknowledge, and its usefulness as an instrument for societal change is much greater than they recognize. Hellman's most famous play, *The Little Foxes,* and especially its protagonist Regina Giddens, offer a provocative test case for examining the contemporary critique of realism.

It may be well to begin with Demastes's warning that "the term 'realism' is one that many claim to understand but few have been able to define, a fact that has played into the critical hands of its opponents and often hurt its advocates" (p. 1). In her study of realism on the American stage, Brenda Murphy explores the conflicting definitions of realism that abounded even in its earliest days, when William Dean Howells and Henry James offered substantially different interpretations of this new theatrical trend.[7] The final definition of stage realism at which Murphy arrives is useful:

a representation of the playwright's conception of some aspect of human experience in a given milieu, within the fourth-wall illusion and in the low mimetic style. It should have characters who were individuals as well as social types, a setting that aimed at producing the illusion of the milieu as fully as possible rather than simply importing "real" objects onto the stage, thought that expressed the social issues of the milieu and the psychological conflicts of the characters in dialogue they would naturally speak, a form that was derived from the human experience being depicted, and a structure designed to produce the fullest illusion for the audience that the action onstage was taking place in reality. (p. 49)

Even so extensive a definition, however, leaves vast room for interpretation. (How much detail makes a character an "individual," for example?) We must also acknowledge that all critical labels force artificial groupings among diverse works that will inevitably fail to fit comfortably into the categories in which we attempt to entrap them. Perhaps most important, we must be aware when a term—*realism, expressionism, melodrama,* whatever—is being used as a device to illuminate the characteristics of literary works and when it is being used primarily as a stick to beat them.

As a first step in exploring the current critique of realism, it is useful to acknowledge that realism in theory and what actually happens in the theatre often do not coincide. Realism may aim to "naturalize the relation between character and actor"—that is, ask the audience to believe that character and actor are one—but few if any spectators fail to distinguish between player and role, between Bette Davis's interpretation of Regina Giddens and Tallulah Bankhead's. The 1981 revival of *The Little Foxes* enjoyed among the biggest advance sales in history because prospective viewers knew exactly who would be *playing* the part of Regina: Elizabeth Taylor.[8] In a paper given at the ATHE (Association for Theatre in Higher Education) conference in 1991, Lynda Hart aptly referred to realism as "the most naive of illusions." Why then are we so willing to believe that audiences are naive enough to succumb to that illusion, to believe that what they are watching onstage is an unclouded mirror of some coherent world outside the theatre—or actually is that world? Jacob H. Adler may claim that Hellman's plays include "real people speaking real language and carrying out real actions in a real world,"[9] but audiences know that the Hubbards are fictional characters whose razor-sharp repartee is carefully constructed stage dialogue distinctly *un*like what they hear over their breakfast coffee.

While realism does not suppose spectators as innocent as Royall Tyler's Jonathan, who thought he was looking "right into the next neighbour's house"[10] as he sat in the playhouse gallery, Elin Diamond is correct in observing that "mimesis, from its earliest and varied enunciations, posits a *truthful* relation between world and word, model and copy, nature and image or, in semiotic terms, referent and sign" (p. 58). Hellman herself saw plays like *The Little Foxes* as deriving their force from that very mimesis, from the viewer's ability to iden- tify—and identify with—the characters on the stage. Writing in *Pen- timento,* she insists, "I had meant the audience to recognize some part of themselves in the money-dominated Hubbards; I had not meant people to think of them as villains to whom they had no connec- tion."[11] What critics of realism often fail to acknowledge, however, is not only how complex the relationship between referent and sign is in the theatre but that neither the referent nor the sign is itself simple or stable. Martin Esslin makes this point when he argues that "reality itself, even the most mundane, everyday reality, has its own symbolic component. The postman who brings me the telegram which an- nounces the death of a friend is also, in a sense, a messenger of death, an Angel of Death. . . . What the stage gives us is an enhanced reality that itself becomes a sign, a metaphor, a dramatic symbol."[12] Teresa L. Ebert adds still more elements to the equation when she observes that the "features, effects, and uses" of mimesis vary among historical pe- riods "and are determined by class, gender, and race. . . . Thus what is realistic—commonly assumed to be faithful to everyday experi- ences and consciousness—to one group may seem quite unrealistic to another."[13] Simply put, no two groups' (or individuals') "realities" are ever identical.

The relationship between model and copy is further problematized when the copy—the play—offers us a fragmented mirror-world char- acterized by lying, chicanery, and masquerade. In *The Little Foxes,* "truth" is the province of the best liar and every character—from the most pitiable to the most loathsome—is practiced at fabricating sto- ries. Birdie lies about her twisted ankle and headaches, Leo about opening the safe deposit box; Ben and Oscar lie about stealing Horace's bonds, while Horace willingly agrees to play along with their ruse. Indeed, deception is so clearly the lingua franca here that audience members—like the characters—are stunned by Birdie's impropriety in honestly telling Horace how ill he looks.

Moreover, chicanery in *The Little Foxes* is clearly set in the context of theatricality: the medium is the subject. The long first scene is a play-within-a-play carefully directed to impress Mr. Marshall, the visiting capitalist; Birdie and Leo even have to be "cued" when they misplay the roles assigned to them. Katherine Lederer points out that both Regina and her brother Ben are consummate actors,[14] and the battle for supremacy between the two offers a powerful subtext about gender roles that necessarily draws audience attention to all the levels of role playing inside the theatre and out. Once again this self-reflexivity foregrounds the complexity of the relationship among actor, character, and some referent outside the text. Ben repeatedly prompts his sister in her social role as a woman, invoking tradition and their mother as arbiter and ideal. "For how many years have I told you a good-looking woman gets more by being soft and appealing?" he asks; "Mama used to tell you that."[15] Regina, however, needs no coaching. Taking the part of both actor and playwright, Regina wins the competition by threatening a bravura performance of poor helpless female ("You couldn't find a jury that wouldn't weep for a woman whose brothers steal from her") and adding "what's necessary" to fabricate a convincing narrative for her auditors (p. 196). As in Brecht's *The Good Woman of Setzuan,* a Shen Te metamorphoses into a Shui Ta and back again with amazing grace and speed, and nothing is certain except pretense. And if this slippery world of games and changing scripts is a "copy" of some "model" outside the play, it would appear that neither model nor copy has quite the coherence or stability that critics claim they have.

With its attention to gendered role playing, *The Little Foxes* seems to answer Janelle Reinelt's demand that feminist drama include "active and engaged struggle with gender inscription [which] must accompany the recognition that gender opposition is a false construct."[16] Yet the presentation of sex roles is at the heart of still another materialist feminist accusation against realism, one that categorically denies the possibility that realism can critique these very roles. In her indispensable book *Feminism and Theatre,* Sue-Ellen Case charges: "Realism, in its focus on the domestic sphere and the family unit, reifies the male as sexual subject and the female as the sexual 'Other.' The portrayal of female characters within the family unit—with their confinement to the domestic setting, their dependence on the husband, their often defeatist, determinist view of the opportunities for change—make realism a 'prisonhouse of art' for women."[17] While it is absolutely true that realism and domesticity have historically been linked—the realistic domestic drama is the quintessential American play—the two are not necessarily joined; the bond between form and content in this case is descriptive, not prescriptive. Even more important, to demand that women playwrights eschew the domestic setting is to place a severe constraint on any female dramatist who would expose societal ills, many of which are rooted in that site. Ironically, the materialist feminist attack on realism and its bond with domesticity echoes a complaint lodged in 1937 by Joseph Mersand in his condescending essay "When Ladies Write Plays." Deploring "women dramatists for their emphasis on realism,"[18] he complains that "they know how to reconstruct for us on the stage our own little houses, and our own little, petty lives, with our worries and cares, and few moments of laughter" (p. 28). Mersand too confuses the subject (domestic life) with the form (realism) to the detriment of women dramatists; since women's concerns are by definition "little" and "petty," any reenactment of them onstage merits wholesale dismissal. Mersand sweeps aside three decades of plays by Rachel Crothers—concerning issues like the double standard, marital infidelity, and unequal career opportunities for men and women—as "Much ado about nothing" (p. 8). Blanket attacks on realistic presentations of the domestic sphere, when they fail to discriminate among the widely divergent forms such presentations take, come uncomfortably close to replicating Mersand's condescension, however different the reasoning behind those attacks may be.

When we turn to *The Little Foxes*, we see how Lillian Hellman's "portrayal of female characters" actually interrogates conventional notions of women's domestic roles—onstage and off. While the alcoholic Birdie has clearly given up hope of escaping from the tyranny of her husband and son, has there ever been a literary character less defeatist or determinist than Regina, who declares: "There are people who can never go back, who must finish what they start. I am one of those people"?[19] Sharon Friedman rightly notes that the Giddens home "is the setting for business negotiations" in *Foxes*.[20] By locating *Foxes* in the home, Hellman demystifies the relationship between the domestic on the one hand and the economic and political on the other. The hypocrisy of excluding the women from direct participation in business negotiations is foregrounded as Birdie, Alexandra, and Regina are bought, sold, or traded in this domicile of capitalism.[21] Even the befuddled Birdie is aware that marrying her was the "price" Oscar paid to obtain Lionnet, and she vows to prevent her niece from being a pawn in a similar transaction. Hellman's commentary on the gender relationships spawned by capitalism, in sum, virtually necessitates the play's location in the domestic sphere, a sphere inseparable from economic and political realms.

Still another objection to realism is lodged by Catherine Belsey in her influential essay "Constructing the Subject: Deconstructing the Text." Belsey argues that "the classic realist text moves inevitably and irreversibly to an end, to the conclusion of an ordered series of events." Classic realism, she contends, involves "the dissolution of enigma through the re-establishment of order, recognizable as a reinstatement or a development of the order which is understood to have preceded the events of the story itself."[22] On one level, of course, all drama reaches closure: the curtain (if there is one) comes down, the lights come up, the audience leaves. Closure in the sense of the reinstatement of an ordered world, however—a "correction" of the problem presented in the play—is precisely what most modern drama, realistic or otherwise, *lacks*. As Katherine Lederer observes, "Hellman ends her plays on an indeterminate note" (p. 44).[23] Renaissance authors and audiences could believe in such a return to "normality," whether political stability in tragedy or marriage in comedy, but most serious twentieth-century dramatists cannot even conceive of what terms such a reestablishment would take. Alexandra Giddens is no Fortinbras, and she has no army to reestablish stability in the disordered state of the turn-of-the-century South.

The last moments of *Foxes* owe more to the agitprop theater of the 1920s and 1930s in the United States than to the well-made play, and may even be—as Timothy J. Wiles suggests—closer still "to Brecht's dramaturgy."[24] Without breaking the frame of realism, Hellman turns the play outward to the audience for a resolution of the problems exposed during the previous three hours. Alexandra stands up to her mother and the greed and deceit she represents, vowing, "I'm not going to stand around and watch you do it. I'll be fighting as hard as he [Ben]'ll be fighting . . . someplace else" (p. 199).[25] She will not, however, be fighting to reestablish the Old South, a world that lives on only in Birdie's alcoholic imagination. This conclusion points not toward the reinscription of some previous social structure but to the hope of creating a new order—still undefined—based on sharply different values.

The scene is further complicated by the fact that the challenge to capitalist hegemony is uttered by a very young character whose strength has barely been tested, and by the chronological gap between play and audience: the action is set in 1900, thirty-nine years before opening night. Reeling from a decade of economic depression, audience members knew perfectly well that Zan had lost the fight to the Hubbards, and they knew what the consequences of that loss spelled in terms of human misery. Jeanie Forte complains that realistic plays yield "the illusion of change without really changing anything."[26] On the contrary, it is clear that little was altered when power passed from Ben to Regina—a reversal that may be temporary, as Ben's threat suggests, if he can gain the evidence to blackmail his sister as she is blackmailing him. More importantly, Hellman makes explicit that the responsibility for genuine change is lodged squarely with the audience. It is they who must conceive a way to fight the cupidity symbolized by the Hubbard clan. As we have already seen, the role of that audience looms large in critiques of realism. Catherine Belsey takes the issue still one step further: "Classic realism . . . performs . . . the work of ideology, not only in its representation of a world of consistent subjects who are the origin of meaning, knowledge and action, but also in offering the reader, as the position from which the text is most readily intelligible, the position of subject as the origin both of understanding and of action in accordance with that understanding" (pp. 51–52).[27] Belsey's contention is that the realist text—fiction or drama—creates *one* vantage point from which the text makes coherent sense, that the author coerces the spectator into believing that she has reached this position on her own when in fact she has been "written" into her role as spectator by the author, whose singular point of view the spectator is forced to share. I would counter, however, that all plays have designs upon the viewer, are acts of coercion attempting to gain our agreement with the author's "truth" even if that "truth" is that there is no truth at all. In Terry Eagleton's words, "every literary text intimates by its very conventions the way it is to be consumed, encodes within itself its own ideology of how, by whom and for whom it was produced."[28]

Moreover, any work of literature is open not to one but to a myriad of "truthful" readings. How do we account, to take one example, for the fact that critics have dubbed Regina Giddens everything from "a kind of single-handed Lady Macbeth"[29] to a "hateful woman [who] has to be respected for the keenness of her mind and the force of her character"[30] to the logical product of a sexist, capitalist system who "could compete in a male-controlled society only by pursuing her own self-interest, and by being more manipulative than the men around her"?[31] The subject position of the audience member is not infinitely elastic, to be sure, but neither is it quite so narrow as some theorists would suggest. It also clearly varies over time—as recent, more sympathetic views of Regina suggest. Are all but one reading somehow subversive because they are not the interpretation encoded by the author in the work and inscribed in the subject position we imagine we occupy? Belsey's notion of encoding seems to imply that the writer has complete control over the meanings of her text, an assertion most creative writers would challenge. In an interview, Hellman claimed to have been "extremely surprised that anybody thought" *The Little Foxes* was a critique of the industrialization of the South and of the spread of capitalism, but she conceded that "I don't think that what writers intend makes very much difference. It's what comes out."[32] Hellman is certainly being coy here, and her appropriate warning against the intentional fallacy must be balanced against a notion of authorial responsibility. Still, the attack on the way realism "performs . . . the work of ideology" tends unfairly to chastise the realistic text for what all texts do, at the same time as it underestimates the complexity of the composition process and the multiplicity of audience positions from which the characters and events onstage may be rendered comprehensible. Theatrical performance—the intricate interaction of director, actor, designer, and so forth—yet further complicates the question of just who is controlling audience response to a given play at a given moment.

We must also wonder whether readers and spectators are really unable to recognize and criticize the realist author's designs on them. Do all realist playwrights try to hide their presence in the text, as Jill Dolan suggests when she writes that realism "masks the ideology of the author, whose position is mystified by the seemingly transparent text"?[33] It may well be that the melodramatic elements Hellman builds into her text—the elaborate business about protecting Horace's medicine bottle, Regina's verbalized hopes that her husband will meet an early death—are Hellman's way of reminding us that there is a designer at work here manipulating not only plot but audience as well. Yet even without these melodramatic trappings, Hellman's ideology is scarcely masked in her presentation of such characters as the wily Ben, the physically and morally crippled Horace, or the speeches about "people who eat the earth . . . [and] other people who stand around and watch them eat it" that echo through the last act. Finally, Hellman's decision to set her play in "a small town in the South" at the dawn of the new century is still one more attempt to show that *Foxes* is not, as Thornton Wilder would complain, about "one time and place." The year 1900 symbolizes nearly forty years to come, and what we witness is the South turning into the North, trading its tradition for a promise of prosperity. The double lens of history through which Hellman views a turn-of-the-century story in the moral and social terms of the late 1930s is still one more distancing device (one Hellman shares with Bertolt Brecht, among others) that reminds us of the deliberate artifice at work in the not entirely "transparent" medium of realistic drama.[34]

Without question there are limitations—sometimes dangerous ones—in the traditional realistic forms favored by women dramatists early in this century (as well as by many writing now), and we have an obligation to identify and acknowledge these. Materialist feminist theorists have done an important job of locating and articulating these limitations. To return to Catherine Belsey: "In its attempt to create a coherent and internally consistent fictive world the [realistic] text, in spite of itself, exposes incoherences, omissions, absences and transgressions which in turn reveal the inability of the language of ideology to create coherence" (p. 56). In *The Little Foxes* the most crucial "absence," to use Belsey's terminology, is the character of Addie. The realistic framework of the drama does indeed mask the fact that while Addie may be the moral center of the work—the one who points out the dangers of both active villainy and passive complicity—she is the only major character denied a story. It may be a comforting thought for white liberals that the black women who work for them are devoted solely to their white "families," have no ties to their own families or African-American communities, but it is a dishonest fiction grounded in a racist worldview—something Hellman herself implicitly acknowledged many years later in *An Unfinished Woman.*[35] Although realism as a theatrical style certainly does not *demand* that Hellman ignore the anger a character like Addie, born into slavery, would likely have felt toward whites like Horace Giddens who still control her life, it may well facilitate such gaps. At the very least, it fails to call attention to them.

Moreover, as Vivian Patraka convincingly argues, Hellman can use and has used realism to reinforce the status quo, to reify the most "traditional model of gender relations, including female subservience wedded to conjugal bliss and family devotion."[36] In *Watch on the Rhine,* Patraka points out, Hellman uses the realistic mode to chastise American complacency and naivete in the face of fascism, at the same time defining fascism in the most patriarchal terms: "an evil based on its opposition to the nuclear family" (p. 139). This does not, however, negate the very forceful questioning of gender roles that appears in similarly realistic works like *The Little Foxes* and *Another Part of the Forest,*[37] as well as *The Children's Hour, The Autumn Garden,* and even *Toys in the Attic.*

Jeanie Forte proposes that "the challenge for feminist dramatic criticism is one of empowerment, for women writers, performers and reader/spectators" (p. 125). Forte is not naively asking that feminist critics and theorists become cheerleaders for any and all works by women, but rather that we find and acknowledge the strengths and successes, as well as the limitations and failures, in our dramatic legacy. We have an obligation to women playwrights of the past—Rachel Crothers, Zona Gale, Lillian Hellman, Georgia Douglas Johnson, May Miller, Rose Franken, Maxine Wood, Alice Childress, Lorraine Hansberry, to name just a few who mined the ore of realism—to understand the value and power of their work as art and as protest against a society marked by racism, sexism, poverty, greed, and war. In her introduction to *Strike While the Iron is Hot,* Michelene Wandor argues that "historically, artistic movements which seek to represent the experiences of oppressed groups reach initially for a realistic and immediately recognisable clarity."[38] Building on Wandor's comments, Patricia Schroeder adds that "perhaps this appropriation of the devices of realism will turn out to be only a small step in the history of feminist drama, but it is a step that should not be overlooked or undervalued. Depicting what is can help create what should be."[39]

The works of Georgis Douglas Johnson, Shirley Graham, Mary P. Burrill, May Miller, Alice Childress, and Lorraine Hansberry—written from the doubly oppressed position of women of color—are obvious cases in point. Interestingly, some of the very same scholars who attack realism in theory still praise realistic plays by women of color. Sue-Ellen Case, for example, admires Childress's *Trouble in Mind* (p.101)—a drama that, like virtually all of Childress's works, is clearly cast in the realist mold. *Trouble in Mind,* indeed, is *about* realism, about a black actress's refusal to play a dramatic role that falsifies how "real" black women would feel and act. If female playwrights are writing against the societal notion that women have no story—no lives of their own separate from the lives of the men they serve—denying them the use of narrative threatens to undermine the very project of affirming women's existence. This battle for a story and voice of one's own is a central issue in *The Little Foxes,* where Birdie is literally silenced by her husband. "Miss Birdie has changed her mind," Oscar announces in the opening scene, blithely canceling her order to a servant (p. 136). When simple contradiction does not suffice, he uses physical violence to keep her from talking. Regina, in contrast, spends much of the play shouting. However questionable her goals, Regina is determined to be heard, to write her own story, to shape a narrative for herself beyond the boundaries set by her husband, brothers, and the patriarchal society in which she lives. Regina, in many ways, is a realist playwright.

We may finally speculate that realism is the ideal mode for a writer who is more interested in what one does than in why one does it, and who believes that there is no such thing as an innocent bystander. Hellman's primary concern is neither with personal psychology nor with action for its own sake (as some who label her works "melodrama" imply) but with individuals' behavior: no excuse, no fear for the safety of loved ones, can justify Alex Hazen's attempts to appease the Nazis in *The Searching Wind,* Mrs. Tilford's destruction of two women's lives in *The Children's Hour,* or Horace Giddens's past dealings with the Hubbards in *The Little Foxes.* In perhaps her last words on the subject of moral inertia, the conclusion to the 1979 revision of *Scoundrel Time,* Hellman writes: "I never want to live again to watch people turn into liars and cowards and others into frightened, silent collaborators. And to hell with the fancy reasons they give for what they did."[40] While Hellman is recalling the McCarthy witch-hunts here, the lines sum up the philosophy that undergirds all her work: she uses realistic stagecraft to show not only what people do but the consequences of their actions. As Doris V. Falk observes, "realism assumes that there is a certain logical connection between events; that all actions have consequences."[41] Hellman biographer Carl Rollyson puts it another way: "She required a realistic and unambiguous form in order to attack the appeasement of iniquity" (p. 12).

Like many of her female colleagues in the theatre in the first half of this century, Hellman used realism as a tool to explore and expose a capitalist society with narrowly inscribed gender roles, and to counter the demeaning portraits of women typically proffered by male playwrights. Materialist feminist theorists have done an important job of showing the pitfalls in this theatrical mode, the ways in which it may undermine the very criticism of society that it attempts to promulgate. But to dismiss utterly the usefulness of realism to women as an instrument of social commentary and change is to erase a large part of our theatrical heritage and to deny future women playwrights still one more valuable weapon in their dramatic arsenal.

Notes

1. Qtd. in Barbara and Arthur Gelb, *O'Neill* (New York: Harper & Row, 1962), p. 520. O'Neill made this statement in the early 1920s. The great plays he wrote in his last years are, ironically, fundamentally realistic works.

2. Thornton Wilder, "Preface" to *Three Plays by Thornton Wilder* (New York: Bantam, 1958), p. x. See also William W. Demastes, *Beyond Naturalism: A New Realism in American Theatre* (Westport, Conn.: Greenwood Press, 1988). Demastes identifies "a critical thread that has historically reviled realism as a form whose dominance in the late 19th and 20th centuries has limited theatre (and other literary fields as well) to restrictive and reductive presentations of complex thought and feeling" (pp. 1–2). Subsequent references to Demastes are cited in the text.

3. Sue-Ellen Case, "Toward a Butch-Femme Aesthetic," in *Making a Spectacle: Feminist Essays on Contemporary Women's Theatre*, ed. Lynda Hart (Ann Arbor: U of Michigan P, 1989), p. 297.

4. Jill Dolan, " 'Lesbian' Subjectivity in Realism: Dragging at the Margins of Structure and Ideology," in *Performing Feminisms: Feminist Critical Theory and Theatre*, ed. Sue-Ellen Case (Baltimore: Johns Hopkins UP, 1990), p. 52.

5. Elin Diamond, "Mimesis, Mimicry, and the 'True-Real,' " *Modern Drama* 32.1 (March 1989): 58–72, at 60–61. Subsequent references are cited in the text.

6. Sue-Ellen Case, in the Introduction to *Performing Feminisms,* p. 9, acknowledges that the charge of elitism might be leveled against those who repudiate representation.

7. Brenda Murphy, *American Realism and American Drama, 1880–1940* (Cambridge: Cambridge UP, 1987). See especially chap. 2, "Realistic Dramatic Theory." Subsequent references are cited in the text.

8. Gerald Clarke, "The Long Way to Broadway," *Time* (March 30, 1981): 76.

9. Jacob H. Adler, *Lillian Hellman* (Austin: Steck-Vaughn Co., 1969), p. 7.

10. Royall Tyler, *The Contrast,* in *Dramas from the American Theatre, 1762–1909,* ed. Richard Moody (Boston: Houghton Mifflin, 1966), p. 47.

11. Lillian Hellman, *Pentimento,* in *Three: An Unfinished Woman, Pentimento, Scoundrel Time* (Boston: Little Brown, 1979), p. 482.

12. Martin Esslin, qtd. in Demastes, *Beyond Naturalism.* Demastes quotes the passage to make the point that certain "reductive assessments of realism by its opponents [are] unfortunate and misleading" (p. 2).

13. Teresa L. Ebert, "Gender and the Everyday: Toward a Postmodern Materialist Feminist Theory of Mimesis," in *"Turning the Century": Feminist Theory in the 1990s,* ed. Glynis Carr (Lewisburg: Bucknell UP, 1992), p. 104.

14. Katherine Lederer, *Lillian Hellman* (Boston: Twayne Publishers, 1979), p. 41. Subsequent references are cited in the text.

15. Hellman, *The Little Foxes,* in *Lillian Hellman: The Collected Plays* (Boston: Little, Brown, 1972), p. 195. Subsequent references are cited in the text.

16. Janelle Reinelt, "Feminist Theory and the Problem of Performance," *Modern Drama,* 32.1 (March 1989): 52.

17. Sue-Ellen Case, *Feminism and Theatre* (New York: Methuen, 1988), p. 124. Subsequent references are cited in the text.

18. Joseph Mersand, "When Ladies Write Plays: An Evaluation of Woman's Contribution to American Drama," *Players Magazine* 13 (Sept.–Oct. 1937): 26. Subsequent references are cited in the text.

19. Hellman deleted these lines—originally near the end of Act III—when she edited *The Little Foxes* for *The Collected Plays,* but they are an apt summary of Regina. Presumably Hellman cut the lines because they are too obviously apt, hence unnecessary.

20. Sharon Friedman, "Feminism as Theme in Twentieth-Century American Women's Drama," *American Studies* 25.1 (1984): 82.

21. Gayle Austin discusses the similar use of women as commodities in Hellman's *Another Part of the Forest.* See Austin's *Feminist Theories for Dramatic Criticism* (Ann Arbor: U of Michigan P, 1990), pp. 51–55.

22. Catherine Belsey, "Constructing the Subject: Deconstructing the Text," in *Feminist Criticism and Social Change,* ed. Judith Newton and Deborah Rosenfelt, pp. 45–64 (New York: Methuen, 1985), pp. 55, 53. Subsequent references are cited in the text.

23. Lederer notes that, by contrast, the movies made from Hellman's films tend toward closure. Hollywood is apparently less comfortable with open-endedness than Broadway is.

24. Timothy J. Wiles, "Lillian Hellman's American Political Theater: The Thirties and Beyond," in *Critical Essays on Lillian Hellman*, ed. Mark W. Estrin (Boston: G. K. Hall, 1989), p. 102. Wiles concurs that the concluding moments of *Foxes* transfer "the solution to this play's problem to the audience," and finds a similar refusal of closure in *Days to Come*.

25. This line was revised for the 1972 *Collected Plays*. In the original (1939) version, Alexandra's line is slightly longer but only marginally less vague. In the earlier rendering she vows "I'll be fighting as hard as he'll be fighting . . . some place where people don't just stand around and watch."

26. Jeanie Forte, "Realism, Narrative, and the Feminist Playwright—A Problem of Reception," *Modern Drama* 32.1 (March 1989): 115–27, at 117. Subsequent references are cited in the text. The specific play to which Forte refers here is Marsha Norman's *'night, Mother*, but she is making a general point about realistic drama. Perhaps we need to talk about "realists" and to distinguish precisely what the dramatic equivalent of Belsey's "classic realism" might be. Most materialist feminist theorists working with drama, however, seem to use *realism* as a monolithic term. Sue-Ellen Case makes a similar complaint about the "closure of . . . realistic narratives" in "Toward a Butch-Femme Aesthetic," p. 297.

27. Belsey concedes that "this process is not inevitable, in the sense that texts do not determine like fate the ways in which they must be read. I am concerned at this stage primarily with ways in which they are conventionally read" (p. 53). My argument is that even the "conventional" reader's or viewer's position is more flexible than Belsey acknowledges.

28. Terry Eagleton, quoted in Michele Barrett, "Ideology and the Cultural Production of Gender," in Newton and Rosenfelt, eds., *Feminist Criticism and Social Change*, p. 77.

29. Otis Ferguson, "A Play, A Picture," *New Republic* (April 12, 1939): 279.

30. Brooks Atkinson, "Miss Bankhead Has a Play," *New York Times* (Feb. 26, 1939) sec. 9, p. 1. Writing several decades after Atkinson, Hellman biographer William Wright gives a very similar interpretation of Regina. He is, however, disturbed by the ambiguity of the character, by the fact that audiences "can applaud" a woman who allows her husband to die. Not only have critical interpretations of the character and the play varied widely, but what one critic sees as a strength another may see as a flaw (*Lillian Hellman: The Image, the Woman* [New York: Simon and Schuster, 1986], p. 153).

31. Mel Gussow, "Women Playwrights: New Voices in the Theater," *New York Times Magazine* (May 1, 1983): 30.

32. *Playwrights Talk About Writing: 12 Interviews with Lewis Funke* (Chicago: Dramatic Publishing Co., 1975), p. 105. In the famous *Paris Review* interview, Hellman also admits her "great surprise" that audiences saw the play's conclusion as "a statement of faith in Alexandra, in her denial of her family. I never meant it that

way. She did have courage enough to leave, but she would never have the force or vigor of her mother's family." Here again, however, Hellman adds a crucial qualification: "That's what I meant. Or maybe I made it up afterward" (John Phillips and Anne Hollander, "Lillian Hellman: An Interview"; rpt. in Estrin, ed., *Critical Essays on Lillian Hellman*, p. 232).

33. Jill Dolan, *The Feminist Spectator as Critic* (Ann Arbor: UMI Research Press, 1988), p. 84.

34. In her later years—long after writing *The Little Foxes*—Hellman became an admirer of Brecht's work. For a discussion of similarities between Hellman's plays and Brecht's, see Wiles, "Lillian Hellman's American Political Theater," pp. 90–112 passim.

35. Hellman, in her portrait of Helen, an African-American woman who worked for her, acknowledges "the hate and contempt" as well as the "old, real-pretend love" for white people that Helen had brought with her from the South. See *An Unfinished Woman* in *Three*, p. 251. Interestingly, in early drafts of *The Little Foxes*, Addie apparently played a larger role and had at least one family member, a daughter named Charlotte. In the final version, however, her concern and devotion are wholly directed toward Alexandra, and she seems to have no reservations about leaving her home in order to shepherd her young white charge. For discussions of these early drafts, see Richard Moody, *Lillian Hellman, Playwright* (New York: Bobbs-Merrill, 1972), pp. 105–8, and Carl Rollyson, *Lillian Hellman: Her Legend and Her Legacy* (New York: St. Martin's Press, 1988), pp. 128–29. Subsequent references to Rollyson are cited in the text.

36. Vivian M. Patraka, "Lillian Hellman's *Watch on the Rhine*: Realism, Gender, and Historical Crisis," *Modern Drama* 32.1 (March 1989): 130.

37. For a thoughtful, sympathetic reading of *Another Part of the Forest*, see Gayle Austin, *Feminist Theories for Dramatic Criticism*, pp. 51–55.

38. Michelene Wandor, "Introduction" to *Strike While the Iron is Hot: Three Plays on Sexual Politics* (London: Journeyman Press, 1980), p. 11.

39. Patricia R. Schroeder, "Locked Behind the Proscenium: Feminist Strategies in *Getting Out* and *My Sister in This House*," *Modern Drama* 32.1 (March 1989): 112. Subsequent references are cited in the text.

40. Hellman, *Scoundrel Time*, in *Three*, p. 726.

41. Doris V. Falk, *Lillian Hellman* (New York: Frederick Ungar, 1978), p. 32.

ELEVEN

Tennessee Williams's "Personal Lyricism": Toward an Androgynous Form

Thomas P. Adler

—The author who uses written words only has nothing to do with the theater.
Antonin Artaud, The Theater and Its Double[1]

Tennessee Williams has said that "the androgynous is a myth . . . an ideal. You can seek it but never find it. However, the androgynous is the truest human being."[2] If the ultimate endpoint of androgyny is not the total erasure of otherness and difference, at the very least it involves the destruction of a binarism that explicitly presupposes fragmentation and implicitly justifies hierarchy and inequality. In discussions of dramatic form, the chief binary has been the dichotomy between realistic and nonrealistic plays and the ascendancy and valorization in modern drama in English of stage realism. In a daring strategy, Tennessee Williams begins *The Glass Menagerie* by posing this binary in lines that are unique in classic American drama for being explicitly theoretical, demanding that an audience process dramaturgical concepts before becoming caught up in the action. Williams's authorial character/narrator, Tom Wingfield, opens the play by confiding directly to the audience, "Yes, I have tricks in my pocket, I have things up my sleeve. But I am the opposite of a stage magician. He gives you illusion that has the appearance of truth. I give you truth in the pleasant disguise of illusion."[3] Tom's lines pointedly distinguish realistic from nonrealistic theatre. The first, representational or illusionistic drama, demands that its audience make believe they are not making believe, that they accept the imitation for the real thing. The

172

second, nonrepresentational or nonillusionistic drama, challenges its audience to revel in the conventions of make-believe; yet, at the same time, to recognize that illumination *about* life can come clothed in an illusion not necessarily true *to* life.

Because of the myriad devices that *Glass Menagerie* employs to violate the "fourth wall" between stage and auditorium so that, as Stanley Cavell would say, "the *audience* vanishes" in the very act of being recognized,[4] Williams christens his work "nonrealistic." Since Williams consistently calls attention to his plays as theatre, Esther Merle Jackson believes that neither in theory nor in practice is his "highly abstract" form realistic. She prefers to consider him a romantic or an expressionist, or some hybrid of the two, while more recently— though perhaps less convincingly—David Savran rejects the expressionist-realist designation all together in favor of surrealist and postmodernist.[5]

For most drama in English (and for most English-speaking audiences), the chief evidence of stage realism resides in the handling of character. If characters are fully dimensioned and treated with psychological probity, then playgoers—no matter how "unreal" the stage setting on which those characters live and move—tend to designate the play "realistic." In virtually all of Williams's works, delineating and probing character psychology takes precedence; his is an attitude and conception of character enshrined in Method acting, as practiced by trainees from the Actors Studio under the direction of theatre practitioners like Elia Kazan, to achieve what has been called "heightened emotionalism." When Williams does veer away from a representational style, he does so primarily for dramaturgical reasons rooted in an urge to universalize or mythicize his material. In his essay, "Critic Says 'Evasion,' Writer Says 'Mystery,' " Williams proclaims: "My characters make my play. . . . I always start with them, they take spirit and body in my mind. . . . They build the play about them like spiders weaving their webs, sea creatures making their shells."[6] Williams's realism, then—as distinct from that of virtually every one of his American contemporaries, such as William Inge—resides in a tension and, finally, accommodation or reconciliation between characters conceived for their psychological verisimilitude and in a setting, what he terms the "webs" or "shells," almost invariably handled nonrealistically or even expressionistically.

In the production notes preceding *Glass Menagerie,* Williams offers a manifesto for the theatre no less important than Strindberg's on naturalism in his preface to *Miss Julie,* or Brecht's in his essay "Theatre for Learning," where he distinguishes between the dramatic and epic forms. Questioning the continued ability of the "straight realistic play" to probe beneath the surface any longer, Williams underlines "the unimportance of the photographic in art: that truth, life, or reality is an organic thing which the poetic imagination can represent or suggest . . . only through transformation, through changing into other forms than those which were merely present in appearance." Citing the need for "unusual freedom of convention" to achieve "a closer approach to truth," Williams calls for "a new, plastic theatre which must take the place of the exhausted theatre of realistic conventions if the theatre is to resume vitality as a part of our culture" (p. 7).

Arthur Miller has dubbed the resultant style "theatre of gauze"; Jackson has referred to it as "American formalism . . . in which [Williams] has rewoven the complete fabric of the performing arts";[7] while Williams himself has named it—as incorporated into the original productions of his plays by such influential American scenic designers as Jo Mielziner and Boris Aronson—"personal lyricism," linking it with his recurrent thematic emphasis on the need to move from isolation to community: "Personal lyricism is the outcry of prisoner to prisoner from the cell in solitary where each is confined for the duration of his life" (p. 76). No matter its name, it is a theatre heavily dependent upon visual symbolism. The stage has always had, as Tom Driver once remarked, a natural tendency to turn things into symbols. For his part, Williams claims that all "art is made out of symbols the way your body is made out of vital tissue," concluding that "symbols are nothing but the natural speech of drama . . . the purest language of plays. . . . Sometimes it would take page after tedious page of exposition to put across an idea that could be said with an object or a gesture on the lighted stage" (p. 66).

Jackson finds literary ancestors for the notion of "a 'plastic symbol' " in both the French symbolist and the American imagist poets; and she traces back to Wagner the "revolt against the word-dominated theatre of the nineteenth century" that was to be replaced by "a synthetic symbol [that would] restore to drama a textural language—a theatrical grammar—which could give expression to irrational contents in experience" (p. 93). An equally rich analogue, however, for the notion of plasticity as well as for distrust of the supremacy of dialogue can be found in Antonin Artaud's *The Theatre and Its Double* (1938), a treatise that employs the word "plastic" several times. Decrying the artificial dissociation of "the plastic world" from "the analytic theater" as sheer "stupidity," Artaud proposes the theatrical superiority of a "poetry of senses" or a "poetry in space" to a language composed only of words addressed to the intellect.

While Williams would not subscribe to the complete elimination of a narrative in which action progresses on social, psychological, and moral levels, or to transforming the stage into a director's rather than a writer's theatre, he would assent to Artaud's propositions that "on the stage, which is above all a space to fill and a place where something happens, the language of words may have to give way before a language of *signs* whose objective aspect is the one that has the most immediate impact upon us," and that "the esthetic, plastic part of theater [ideally] drops its role of decorative intermediary in order to become, in the proper sense of the word, a directly communicative *language* [with] a kind of intellectual dignity" (p. 107). Williams's plays challenge those who admit into the canon of literature only the text to be spoken and dismiss as inferior the equally crucial nonverbal text the dramatist imagines for the theatre space. Thus Williams echoes Artaud's position, in both theory and practice, that the scenic and other plastic elements of shape and noise and gesture are a legitimate "theatrical language [having] the power, not to define thoughts but to *cause thinking*" (p. 69).

The distance between Artaud and Virginia Woolf may seem unbridgeable; yet the French theoretician's insistence that "spoken language or expression by words" should not dominate to the degree that it displaces "everything which affects the mind by sensuous and spatial means" (p. 71) may not, finally, be all that removed from the British novelist's belief that a work must appeal to both the male and female sides of the brain. Woolf's now famous work, *A Room of One's Own*, which began its life as a series of lectures in 1928 (ten years before Artaud's *Theater and Its Double*), proved a prescient work, raising issues and setting directions decades before they became solidified in the agenda of feminist criticism. If Woolf points to the way history has never been *her*story, to the way e(wo)mancipation is consistently met by retaliation and backlash, and to the way women are "seen only in relation to the other sex"[8] even when they are the supposed subject of literary works, more recently Sue-Ellen Case, for example, has suggested the innate limitation of the realistic mode when considered from the perspective of feminism: "Realism, in its focus on the domestic sphere and the family unit, reifies the male as sexual subject and the female as sexual 'Other.' "[9]

In her concluding chapter, Woolf, fixing on the sudden sight of a man and a woman merging from opposite sides of the street to enter a taxicab, muses on whether there might not be some "natural fusion" of the "two sexes in the mind" as well. Her conclusion that the mind must be androgynous, either "man-womanly" or "woman-manly," if it is to be "naturally creative" she ascribes specifically to Coleridge: "I went on amateurishly to sketch a plan of the soul," she writes, "so that in each of us two powers preside, one male, one female. . . . If one is a man, still the woman part of the brain must have effect; and a woman also must have intercourse with the man in her. . . . It is when this fusion takes place that the mind is fully fertilised and uses all its faculties. Perhaps a mind that is purely masculine cannot create, any more than a mind that is purely feminine, I thought" (p. 102). Although the tendency to conceive of existence in terms of binaries is now itself suspect, Woolf proposes that the male side of the brain gravitates toward the measurable, in that it deifies facticity; the female toward the imponderable, in that it elevates the poetic. She concludes, "It is fatal to be a man or woman pure and simple. . . . Some collaboration has to take place in the mind between the woman and the man before the act of creation can be accomplished" (p. 108).

In his plays, Williams attempts to effect such a consummation through what might be seen as an *androgynous form*. According to Caroline Heilbrun, who sees androgyny as "a spirit of reconciliation between the sexes"[10] that often coexists with homosexuality and can rightly be seen as a hallmark of civilization, the period immediately after World War II when Williams came to the fore witnessed a subversion of the "extraordinary feminization of . . . vision" earlier undergone by both the novel and the drama: "Women characters had become, as they largely still are, events in the lives of men" (p. 50). Commentators have long noticed the appearance of androgynous characters in Williams, such as the "ethereal" Hannah Jelkes in *The*

Night of the Iguana. And they have long recognized the existence of the androgynous artist; recently, in fact, the Flaubert scholar Jan Goldstein has suggested that writers who admit to experiencing the classic symptoms of hysteria in the act of literary creation—as Williams does in comparing himself with Blanche DuBois—are making an "implicit assertion of androgyny."[11] Yet the concept of an androgynous dramatic form, one that marries realistically handled, prosaic characters in a structure of rising action and climax/resolution with a nonrealistically handled, poeticized stage space that impacts kinesthetically on the audience's senses, has so far remained unexplored.

Theodore Roszack once commented that the woman most desperately in need of liberation is that woman every man has locked up in the dungeon of his own psyche. Williams releases the female imprisoned inside himself through his drama, and specifically through its poetically handled, often nonrealistic, elements, as will be seen by looking briefly at five of his plays (*Glass Menagerie, A Streetcar Named Desire, Cat on a Hot Tin Roof, Sweet Bird of Youth,* and *Out Cry*) and in greater length—because it is less often examined—at *Battle of Angels/ Orpheus Descending.* The lyrical moments of these works, frequently nonverbal in nature, allow him to uncloset those integral aspects of human existence that audiences at the time ordinarily demanded remain hidden on the stage: racial or sexual otherness; artistic creativity as insanity or madness; narcissism and neuroticism; incest and homosexuality.

TOM'S HOUSE OF MEMORY

Although *The Glass Menagerie* (1944) visually does not incorporate elements creating the nightmarish distortion classically associated with expressionism, it remains a wholly subjective play. Williams's visual and aural encoding (transparent scrims; dim atmospheric lighting; legends and images projected on a screen; evocative musical underscore) simulate the vaguely poetic nature of memory and its workings. And yet, because the play likewise constitutes evidence of Tom as apprentice writer—and Williams as burgeoning (autobiographical) dramatist—the world of memory becomes synonymous with the world of art. Such an escape into the realm of mind/art possesses an almost sacramental value. The work's religious iconography (the legend "Annunciation"; the uneaten supper; the shared eucharist-like drink; the candelabrum from the fire-ravaged church) culminates in the central gestural moments, both involving imagery of lighted candles being extinguished. Early in her conversation with the Gentleman Caller, that prosaic emissary from the outside who holds promise, however fleeting, of making real the dream, Laura's face is lit "inwardly with altar candles" (p. 97); his kiss accomplishes her sexual initiation. Yet when he cruelly reveals his engagement to someone else, she is shattered, and "The holy candles on the altar of Laura's face have been snuffed out. There is a look of almost infinite desolation" (p. 108). A final extinguishing of candles occurs at *Menagerie*'s close in response to the pleas of her brother Tom; to escape the ghostly figurative touch of her hand that haunts him at every turn, he has turned—in what provides, along with the nightly furtive meetings at movie houses, the most overt hint of his otherwise closeted homosexuality—to other escapes ("companions" in "strange cit[ies]"), searching for "anything that can blow [her] candles out" (p. 115) and so release him from guilt over having deserted mother and sister.

When the Laura-in-his-mind accedes to his plea, it appears that his act of remembering has been therapeutic and that she has forgiven him so that his world can open out; whereas hers will close in upon her emotionally, psychologically, and even sexually, since the extinguished candle, like the unicorn's broken horn, is phallic. And yet, Laura's blowing out the candles is not part of Tom's memory of things past but pure projection, a figment forged in the solipsistic world of a guilty imagination that refuses to speak its real guilt. Perhaps Williams here had in mind an earlier theatrical command for darkness to overtake light. When Shakespeare's Othello goes to Desdemona's bedchamber to smother her, he orders himself, "Put out the light, and then put out the light" (V.ii.7), the first being the physical torch he carries, the second the light of her radiant being. The extinguishing of Laura's light means that she is destined to remain, like Desdemona, forever virginal, unfulfilled—the possession of her brother, if not in body as he unconsciously desires, yet frozen still in an immaterial world of illusion as simultaneously inspiration and object of his art. Tom's only truly adequate atonement might therefore be to eschew that art. Incestuous desire remains, however, as permanently sublimated in Williams's art as homosexual desire would for a long time be closeted. And Laura's loss of "art"—her fragile world of mythical animal and high school hero—may prove a first step toward madness for her.

BLANCHE'S THEATRE

If Laura retreats into a world of illusion, Blanche in *A Streetcar Named Desire* (1947) theatricalizes the world around her, continually reinventing the self. From one perspective, Blanche acts the central role in a play she writes, produces, designs, and directs. She treats her sister and brother-in-law's apartment as her theatre; their bedroom, separated from the front room by a curtain, becomes the stage for her illusions. As an actress, Blanche carries her costumes and props in a trunk, including the rhinestone tiara she dons at the opening of scene ten to crown her "soiled and crumpled white satin evening gown and a pair of scuffed silver slippers,"[12] temporarily losing herself in a dream of the past. In the face of impermanence and flux, the only thing guaranteed to endure is art/illusion, into which Blanche incessantly escapes. Yet such self-theatricalization easily breaks down when confronted by the telltale mirror. By pulling Blanche back from absolute faith in illusion's ability to shield her from the present (Stanley's return from the hospital to rape her), Williams presages the final scene when reality again takes hold and Blanche realizes that the doctor, accompanied by the threatening notes of the Varsouviana that pronounce her guilty for failing to act compassionately toward Allan, is not the gentlemanly courtier of her romantic imagination proffering safe asylum. Significantly, the most threateningly expressionistic moments in *Streetcar* emanate from the area behind the scrim that forms the back wall of the apartment, which will be Blanche's exit route to the sanatorium.

The easily destroyed Chinese paper lantern over the naked bulb not only functions as a symbol of her vulnerability and subjugation to time's decay but is analogous to the imaginative or creative act that protects one from the grimness and cruelty of reality. When Mitch, and later Stanley, tear the lantern off the bulb, it is as if they are attacking Blanche herself and destroying her world of illusion/art. For Blanche there exists an order ("wayward flashes" of "revelation") higher than the merely factual, whereas for Stanley there exists only empirical facticity, underscored by the roar of the locomotive that is blind, mechanistic progress on the move, a premonition of entropy and return to primal chaos. Blanche's insistence on truth through illusion—"I don't want realism. I want magic!" (p. 145)—and her conviction of the moral imperative of art to raise humankind beyond what it is by showing "what *ought* to be true" are Williams's credo, too.

Williams indicates through the convergence of clothing imagery and religious symbology at *Streetcar*'s close that the physical and psychic violence done to Blanche atones for her guilt and reasserts her gallantry. With her apparel mirroring a spiritual transformation, she emerges radiant from the last of her ritual expiatory baths in a "Della Robbia blue [jacket], the blue of the robe in the old Madonna pictures" (169). Blanche leaves the stage as a violated Madonna to enter another house of illusions, blessed by whatever saving grace insanity/ illusion—however short-lived they may prove—can provide. The closed world of her mind (madness tempering pain) is akin to the world of theatrical artifice (magic offsetting reality). Art and imagination, dramatized through visual symbols, become a kind of sacrament, not only in the scheme of Blanche's redemption but for the audience as well: art makes the word flesh so that the audience can share pain and perhaps experience epiphany.

BRICK'S CLOSET

As he will in *Sweet Bird of Youth*, Williams makes "a big double bed" the focal point of the setting in *Cat on a Hot Tin Roof* (1955). Yet in *Cat* "the bed-sitting room," rather than an anonymous hotel suite, is a bedroom with a past; once it had been "shared . . . all their lives together" by the plantation's original owners, Jack Straw and Peter Ochello. These homosexual lovers, mentioned by Big Daddy in his long Act II confrontation with Brick, accumulated the economic power that was passed on as patrimony—together with an unusual sympathy for and valorization of their relationship—to Big Daddy, and that now in turn awaits transference to Brick. The precise nature of Straw and Ochello's relationship is, however, mostly erased from the play, and present mainly in Williams's "Notes for the Designer": "the room must evoke some ghosts; it is gently and poetically haunted by a relationship that must have involved a tenderness which was uncommon."[13] Also absent from the play is Skipper, whose confession of homosexual love Brick rejected and now attempts to erase, along with any open admission of his own sexual identity, through drinking until he hears the "click"—a crutch not unlike the literal one that supports a leg broken in a futile display of manly prowess and power. Furthermore, even Brick is decentered by not being referenced in the work's title, which constitutes another form of absence.

Although, as Brenda Murphy argues, the Broadway production that the director (Elia Kazan) and the designer (Jo Mielziner) gave *Cat*—with its "recitatives" by the three main characters directly to the audience breaking through the proscenium and "foregrounding [the] production's theatricality"[14]—was finally not as realistic as the playwright wanted, Williams's notes to the play indicate a set in which "the walls below the ceiling should dissolve mysteriously into air; the set should be roofed by the sky" (p. xiv). John Clum interprets the walls that dissolve as symbolic of the "liberation of the Straw-Ochello relationship" that stands "counter to the compromised heterosexual relationships" in the play.[15] This poeticized bedroom that was Straw and Ochello's closet is Brick's closet as well, where what happens on the bed after the final curtain will be, in Savran's terms, a "perpetuation of a homosexual economy and [witness] to the force of Maggie's fetishistic appropriation of Skipper's sexuality" (p. 109). The ambivalence in Brick's characterization—what Williams preferred to justify at the time as "mystery"—reflects the enforced closeting of Williams's own sexual orientation. It might even be said that *Cat*, as well as *Streetcar* and *Menagerie* before it, are Williams's own closet, from which he makes tentative yet subversive steps at coming out primarily through the kinesthetic elements of sight and sound so integral to the design conception of his plays.

ALEXANDRA AND CHANCE'S HALL OF MIRRORS

When, at the close of *Sweet Bird of Youth* (1959), Chance Wayne asks from the audience "your recognition of me in you,"[16] he begs not that they exonerate or condone him; rather, he raises the issue of their perception, pleading for a moral insight so that they might see and respect him as the Princess does at his best moment, as someone in whom, despite his failures, the instinct toward good has not suffered total eradication. That the act of looking and seeing and judging constitutes a central aesthetic and ethical concern is borne out by Williams's intricate system of dramatic structure (spotlighted monologues), theatrical space (forestage, auditorium), and scenic images (the imagined "mirror in the fourth wall" [p. 13], "the big TV screen, which is the whole back wall of the stage" [p. 106]) that makes the audience conscious of themselves as watchers and also aware of themselves as players. The Heckler, whose indignation over Boss Finley's racist demagoguery the audience should share, insinuates himself into the political rally as their representative; so his position in the play is privileged, giving added import to his conviction about "the absolute speechlessness" of God. Metaphorically, he is linked with the play's protagonist as well: if Chance faces literal castration at play's end, the Heckler suffers an allied fate when Boss's men render him speechless, denying him the voice that gives him purpose.

For the Princess, gazing at oneself on a screen—where time is arrested in the fixity of art—and looking at oneself in a mirror can become deeply obsessional, and Williams links them with the self-absorbed, and usually self-exonerating, impetus behind first-person narration. Being consumed with self, using and abusing the other as a commodity (Chance using Alexandra as entrée into a Hollywood career; Alexandra using Chance sexually to forget time's erosion of her beauty) prevents salvific bonds that recognize one as a person rather than an object, as when Chance's little act of grace in responding to Alexandra's plea for oxygen awakens in her heart a feeling she thought herself no longer capable of experiencing. Chance's guilt over Heavenly's sterility, in some ways analogous to Tom's over Laura's absolute aloneness, suggests that even love cannot turn back time, or, by extension, compensate for diminishing artistic creativity or restore lost innocence. To battle time's passage by retreating into selfishness, egoism, narcissism finds its visual equivalent in compulsively gazing into mirrors and conversing with oneself. Stage mirrors and dramatic monologues, potentially agents for truth telling, in *Sweet Bird* reveal themselves instead as means of effecting the obsessive self-absorption and solipsism that have always been inimical to breaking down barriers between people.

CLARE AND FELICE'S ASYLUM

Williams's *Out Cry* (1973)—which might well have been called, after Pirandello, "Two Characters in Search of an Ending"—features a brother and sister acting team, the androgynously named Felice and

Clare, who are locked in a theatre that may be an asylum, preparing to perform a deeply autobiographical but as yet unfinished script by the brother, *The Two-Character Play*. When Clare understands that Felice intends to take the rest of their lives to be written irrevocably as drama, she begs him to "come out of the play" which is "a little too personal, too special, for most audiences."[17] This introduces a level of the metacritical into *Out Cry:* the dramatist apparently realized (as the epigraph from the *Song of Solomon*—"A garden enclosed is my sister . . . "—intimates) that most audiences would discover in it deep and unrealized hints of his own autobiography. Again, the poeticized setting shadows forth the meaning. During performances of the play-within-the-play, Felice asks the audience to "imagine that the front of the house . . . is shielded by sunflowers" (p. 55), with the projected image of the phallic "two-headed sunflower taller than a two-story house" (p. 29) meant to suggest, along with the "huge, dark statue upstage, a work of great power and darkly subjective meaning" (p. 7), the "Abnormality!" of this brother and sister's life.

For Felice to close the play and their lives through a murder/suicide that would replicate their parents' end would be to imprison their lives in the realm of art. When Felice runs frantically from exit to exit pounding to escape "this building . . . windowless as a casket" (p. 66), Clare recognizes a macabre correspondence between the fact of their lives as actors and the denouement he desires for them as characters: no exit. Yet there might be, as the concluding stage direction indicates, transcendence of both life and death through art. Perhaps Clare's inability any longer to find the dividing line between illusion and reality offers the one saving grace open to her, and to reside forever in the world of illusion/art constitutes a blessing; as was true for Blanche, art and life have now completely fused for Clare, for whom "magic," as Felice says, "is the habit of our existence" (p. 72). As Bigsby suggests, "both [the artist and the insane] exist within the shadow of artifice" (p. 49).

MYRA'S GARDEN

As everyone knows, Williams was an inveterate reviser and adapter of his own works; almost twenty years intervene between the initial production of *Battle of Angels* (1940) and its final stage incarnation, *Orpheus Descending* (1957); there would be a film version, *The Fugitive*

Kind, in 1960. Jackson draws a distinction apropos of the present discussion by noting a different level of realism that arises through Williams's more integrated and expressive handling of symbolism in the second version: *Orpheus,* she writes, "does not . . . represent the same quality of imitation [as *Angels* had]. For in *Orpheus Descending* Williams gains dramatic power by allowing his symbols to connote many of the contents to which he gave extended explanation in the earlier work" (p. 39).

Williams's first handling of the material in *Battle of Angels* seems overwrought and apocalyptic, tending to the gothic and baroque; and yet it possesses considerable power. Moreover, the work introduces virtually all of the motifs that become central in the Williams canon: a romantic valorization of the poetic misfit or dispossessed outsider; an almost Manichean duality in the patterning of imagery and symbology, particularly of the forces of dark and light, body and spirit; a consideration of the vocation of the artist, and his/her near sacred function within the community; the place of illusion and dreams in life; the relationship between madness and vision; an emphasis on repressed sexuality and fanaticism or neuroticism, and an elevating of sexual love to (some would argue confusing with) redemption; the necessity for breaking free from the shell of self and responding with compassion to others; the movement from guilt to expiation; a discussion of the way that societal mores and economic dependency constrict individual freedom, victimizing and ostracizing the other; and a focus on the need for civilization to be feminized and humanized as a counter to masculine strength and power.

In "The Past, the Present and the Perhaps," an essay originally published as a preface to *Orpheus Descending,* Williams termed the play in its various permutations "the emotional record of his youth," referring specifically to *Battle of Angels* as "a lyrical play about memories and the loneliness of them."[18] Specific autobiographical references do arise in the play: the wandering Val is a writer who composes on shoebox lids, as his creator did; and the artist Vee paints her canvases the way she "feels" them, impressionistically, an apt commentary on how Williams himself sometimes imagines and adorns his theatrical environment. But, in a more basic sense, *Angels* and its descendant *Orpheus* might be considered memory plays, insofar as the past to which their heroine desires to return materializes on stage as each work progresses. In drama, the memory structure itself, because it depends on and is even tied not only to a more imagistically evocative language but also to certain poetic and nonrealistic theatrical devices, might be seen as a female mode of discourse, in contrast to the more patriarchically embedded male texts that comprise narrative history.

Williams attempts to objectify the subjective memories of Myra in the setting for act three, recapturing the past through memory. Already in the prologue, two of the townswomen reveal that for Myra, "the mercantile store . . . was reality, harsh and drab, but Myra's confectionery . . . was where she kept her dreams"; to provide a visual verification of this, "the confectionery blooms into a nostalgic radiance, as dim and soft as memory itself."[19] In act three, the back room of the store has been transformed physically into her father's garden, which Myra associates with youth and love and life—in contrast to the space associated with buying and selling, formerly a male province, that she now inhabits because of the illness of her husband: "The walls have been painted pale blue and have been copiously hung with imitation dogwood blossoms to achieve a striking effect of an orchard in full bloom [perhaps directly alluding to Chekhov]. The room is almost subjective, a mood or a haunting memory beyond the drab actuality of the drygoods department. Its lighting fixtures have been covered with Japanese lanterns so that, when lighted, they give the room a soft, rosy glow" (p. 77). This room at the rear of the set becomes, in effect, another of Williams's theatres on the stage, a house of illusions/art.

In what may be a not too veiled reference to the forces of darkness unleashed by World War II, Myra's husband, Jabe—who had killed her father (and thus ended her innocence and expelled her from the garden) and then "bought" her for his wife, and whose incessant knocking on the ceiling has interrupted quiet moments of potential communion—stalks in as "a living symbol of death," "the very Prince of Darkness" (pp. 111, 113). Masculine hate and aggression destroy feminine softness and reverie. Jabe's shots kill Myra and Val's love child, thus ending generativity, except on the level of the myth to which Williams, straining somewhat, here tries to raise his protagonists. In Williams's version of the American myth, the pursuit of and faith in Edenic innocence has been undercut and routed by a rejection of difference and an exploitation of the weaker that are seen as threatening the American grail of economic success and cultural domination. Violence has invaded the garden. Specifically, Jabe sets fire to this realm of art and the spirit, just as he had earlier led the vigilante group that burned down the immigrant Papa's taverna for serving blacks. And the main location in the stage setting, the store, is symbolic of the mercantile nature of human relationships, of individuals buying and using and abusing one another. This, in turn, is one reason for the general human condition of loneliness and unconnectedness, for everyone being "sentenced . . . to solitary confinement inside our own skins" (p. 50).

Several major plays intervene by the time Williams revises *Battle of Angels* as *Orpheus Descending;* certainly his dramaturgical strategies as he moves the material further from imitation of externals to revelation of the interior life show the imprint of a growth in craft. Williams had called attention to *Angels* as a fictive construct by framing past action with an expository prologue and a recapitulative epilogue set in the present. For *Orpheus,* he specifies a much more nonrealistic stage setting and introduces in the prologue (the epilogue has disappeared) an expository monologue addressed directly to the audience from the proscenium arch, which "should set the nonrealistic key for the whole production" (p. 15). Williams, however, here employs this narrative device much less consistently than in *Glass Menagerie,* using it just once more, and only cursorily, late in the play.

Along with increasing the use of colors, sounds (especially from nature and animal life), and lighting effects—particularly those that make vertical, cagelike lines dominant—and handling these elements more expressionistically, even surrealistically, Williams foregrounds the theatre on the stage, giving the make-believe orchard considerably greater prominence in his setting. The confectionery is now analogous to Blanche DuBois's longed-for "magic," a world of illusion/art that Myra chooses to inhabit over "truthful" realism. The sense of a diminished, fallen world, one that has lost its connection with its spiritual roots and become deadened by human evil and modern technology, is made explicit. In a motif carried over from *Angels,* civilization, in trying to tame and control the wild, the elemental and primitive in man, actually routs it out and destroys it, rendering Val more the corrupted, branded, dispossessed outsider, decrying the senselessness of society's pervasive violence. All anyone can do in the face of a metaphysical emptiness and a universe that refuses to provide an answer about the "why" of existence is to "go on" with a kind of Beckettian endurance. Now the expulsion from paradise is complete: Lady "points to the ghostly radiance of her make-believe orchard . . . and looks about it as people look for the last time at a loved place they are deserting" (p. 142). The destroyed orchard is as much an image of herself as is the dead child.

Williams's greatness as a playwright, a large part of his characteristic signature, rests in part on the flexibility that he has always demanded of, even forced upon, the realistic mode. Art in Williams means playing with opposites, finding beauty in unlikely places, discovering the light in the dark. Perhaps this might be seen as analogous to the resurrecting of the lost or repressed feminine from the grip of a masculine mindset that, for too long in the modern theatre, has seen poetry as weakness rather than strength, resulting in a drama where sociology or psychology dominates over aesthetic vision. The realist playwright Lillian Hellman, for at least part of her career one of Williams's contemporaries in the theatre, has claimed, "The theatre has limitations: it is a tight, unbending, unfluid, meager form in which to write. And for these reasons, compared to the novel, it is a second-rate form."[20] Williams, a greater dramatist by far, has given the lie to this assertion. As his chief contemporary, Arthur Miller—who acknowledges the influence of *Streetcar Named Desire* upon the structure and style of *Death of a Salesman*—more rightly asserts: "What was new in Tennessee Williams was his rhapsodic insistence that form serve his utterance rather than dominating and cramping it."[21] In his hands, the dramatic form, specifically what has here been called the androgynous form, bends and is fluid, open once and for all to the fullness of reality, particularly able to re-present through a lyrical use of visual imagery and theatre space those elements of personality and facets of the human condition that society ordinarily demands remain closeted.

Notes

1. Antonin Artaud, *The Theater and Its Double,* trans. Mary Carol Richards (New York: Grove Weidenfeld, 1958), p. 73. Subsequent references are cited in the text.

2. Qtd. in C. W. E. Bigsby, *Modern American Drama, 1945–1990* (Cambridge: Cambridge UP, 1992), p. 47.

3. Tennessee Williams, *The Glass Menagerie* (New York: New Directions, 1966), p. 22. Subsequent references are cited in the text.

4. Stanley Cavell, *Must We Mean What We Say?* (Cambridge: Cambridge UP, 1976), p. 157.

5. David Savran, *Communists, Cowboys, and Queers: The Politics of Masculinity in the Work of Arthur Miller and Tennessee Williams* (Minneapolis: U of Minnesota P, 1992), pp. 92, 98. Subsequent references are cited in the text.

6. Tennessee Williams, *Where I Live: Selected Essays*, ed. Christine R. Day and Bob Woods (New York: New Directions, 1978), p. 72. Except where noted, material by Williams, other than playtext material, refers to this volume and is cited in the text.

7. Esther Merle Jackson, *The Broken World of Tennessee Williams* (Madison: Univ. of Wisconsin P, 1965), p. 156. Subsequent references are cited in the text.

8. Virginia Woolf, *A Room of One's Own* (New York: Harcourt Brace, 1957), p. 86. Subsequent references are cited in the text.

9. Sue-Ellen Case, *Feminism and Theatre* (New York: Methuen, 1988), p. 124.

10. Caroline G. Heilbrun, *Toward a Recognition of Androgyny* (New York: Knopf, 1973), p. x. Subsequent references are cited in the text.

11. Qtd. in Ellen K. Coughlin, "Research Notes," *The Chronicle of Higher Education* (August 14, 1991): 87.

12. Tennessee Williams, *A Streetcar Named Desire* (New York: Signet, 1947), p. 151. Subsequent references are cited in the text.

13. Tennessee Williams, *Cat on a Hot Tin Roof* (New York: Signet, 1955), p. xiii. Subsequent references are cited in the text.

14. Brenda Murphy, *Tennessee Williams and Elia Kazan: A Collaboration in the Theatre* (Cambridge: Cambridge UP, 1992), p. 109.

15. John M. Clum, *Acting Gay: Male Homosexuality in Modern Drama* (New York: Columbia UP, 1992), p. 156.

16. Tennessee Williams, *Sweet Bird of Youth* (New York: New Directions, 1975), p. 124. Subsequent references are cited in the text.

17. Tennessee Williams, *Out Cry* (New York: New Directions, 1973), p. 62. Subsequent references are cited in the text.

18. Tennessee Williams, *Orpheus Descending*, in *Tennessee Williams: Four Plays* (New York: New American Library, 1976), pp. vi, viii. Subsequent references are cited in the text.

19. Tennessee Williams, *Battle of Angels*, in *The Theatre of Tennessee Williams*, vol. 1 (New York: New Directions, 1971), pp. 8–9. Subsequent references are cited in the text.

20. Lillian Hellman, "Introduction," *Six Plays* (New York: Modern Library, 1960), p. x.

21. Arthur Miller, "Tennessee Williams's Legacy: 'An Eloquence of Amplitude and Feeling,' " *TV Guide* (March 3, 1984): 30.

TWELVE

Arthur Miller:
Revisioning Realism

Brenda Murphy

> *The fifties became an era of gauze. Tennessee Williams is responsible for this in the main. One of my own feet stands in this stream. It is a cruel, romantic neuroticism, a translation of current life into the war within the self.... The drama will have to find its way back into the daylight world without losing its inner life. I sometimes long to see a set with a ceiling again. The drama will have to re-address itself to the world beyond the skin.*
>
> Arthur Miller, 1960[1]

Throughout his career, Arthur Miller's work has exhibited a preoccupation with the fundamental conflict between the individual's subjective experience and the individual's social responsibility, both to the family and to the larger human community. This bifurcated interest in subjective experience and social responsibility has partly engendered the formal complexity that makes his work unique. As both his creative and his critical statements testify, the conflict between self-actualization and social responsibility is deeply embedded in Miller's consciousness. He said of his position during the House Committee on Un-American Activities hearings of the fifties: "I should have exulted in my aloneness and taken heart from Ibsen's signature line in *An Enemy of the People*—'He is strongest who is most alone.' But the Jew in me shied from private salvation as something close to sin. One's truth must add its push to the evolution of public justice and mercy, must transform the spirit of the city."[2]

Miller has spent fifty years trying different formal solutions to his essential bifurcation. In general, his plays have been most successful when he has been able to convey the tension between the protagonist

189

as experiential subject and the protagonist as citizen directly through dramatic form, as in *Death of a Salesman*. Here the form of the play reflects the disintegration of Willy Loman's ability to distinguish between subjectivity and objectivity, but it is a disintegration that is caused by his failed attempt to be a responsible social being. In order to convey his protagonist's experience, Miller, with the help of director Elia Kazan and designer Jo Mielziner, worked in a new stage idiom, that of subjective realism, a form of drama that juxtaposed the protagonist's purely subjective experience with the objective, social reality that is the experiential field of representational realism. This play is Miller's most successful because, as he pointed out, its form is central to the conflict it represents.

Raymond Williams has said that *Salesman* "is an expressionist reconstruction of a naturalist substance, and the result is not a hybrid but a powerful particular form."[3] The development of subjective realism was no accident. It had its origin in the production of *A Streetcar Named Desire* that was designed by Mielziner and directed by Kazan, and which Miller had seen with Kazan in 1947.[4] Mielziner's new staging techniques—the use of light and transparencies to suggest that the audience was seeing the world subjectively, as the protagonist saw it, rather than to suggest that the stage represented objective reality— were exactly what was needed to give physical reality to the idea that Miller had for his play about Willy Loman.

Miller's statement in the introduction to his *Collected Plays* (1958) that he had first conceived of the play as an enormous face, the height of the proscenium arch, which would open up to reveal the inside of Willy's head, is well known. He went on to say that he wanted to create a form which, "in itself as a form, would literally be the process of Willy Loman's way of mind" (p. 136). This notion of form exploded all the dramatic conventions about structure and tension and suspense, as well as the realistic conventions about the characters' place in time, space, and action. What Miller wanted was "a bloc, a single chord presented as such at the outset, within which all the strains and melodies would already be contained. . . . If I could, I would have told the whole story and set forth all the characters in one unbroken speech or even one sentence or a single flash of light . . . it was to hold back nothing, at any moment, which life would have revealed, even at the cost of suspense and climax" (pp. 136–37).

Miller's desire as a dramatist was to combine two different representational modes on the stage at once. He wanted to represent the "two logics" of a man who "can no longer restrain the power of his experience from disrupting the superficial sociality of his behavior . . . he is literally at that terrible moment when the voice of the past is no longer distant but quite as loud as the voice of the present. In dramatic terms the form, therefore, *is* this process, instead of being a once-removed summation or indication of it" (p. 138). In other words, he wanted to ground his play in the conventions of realism enough to make his audience believe that Willy's experience takes place in their world, but he wanted to represent the experience of Willy's mind, a subject usually left to the conventions of expressionism, concurrently with it. What was needed for the production, then, was a way to represent what Miller called a "mobile concurrency of past and present" (p. 138) through a new mode of drama that would somehow integrate the conventions of realism with the conventions of expressionism to suggest both objective and subjective reality.

Miller was extremely fortunate in having two willing collaborators who understood his artistic desire, and who had probably a better sense than he did of how the language of the theatre could express it. Miller's original script contained no suggestion for the staging of the play, only a note stating: "The scenic solution to this production will have to be an imaginative and simple one. I don't know the answer, but the designer must work out something which makes the script flow easily."[5] According to Mielziner, the original script implied at least nine separate settings or locations, and in several cases, two or three of them were to be used simultaneously. Obviously, conventional realistic staging would make it impossible to represent the play in this way and at the same time to realize Miller's goal, immediately embraced by Kazan and Mielziner, of a mobile concurrency of time in the production. After analyzing the script, Mielziner's solution was to make the house the main set and to play the other scenes on a forestage, making the action continuous, and indicating shifts in both time and space through lighting effects. This decision meant substantial revision of the script for Miller, as well as a reconceptualization of the whole production for Kazan and a need to develop new lighting techniques for Mielziner.

Once this major decision had been made, however, the theatrical idiom for depicting Willy's subjective reality simultaneously with his social reality began to take shape. The major collaboration between Kazan and Mielziner involved the creation of a set for the house that would signify an abstraction from realism for the audience; the use of light to signify changes in time and place as well as the altered state of Willy's mind; and the combination of realistic props with the abstract set to establish the new theatrical idiom that they were trying to develop. As the central material signifier for Willy's life, the house was to be the dominant object in the production. As a set, it also had to allow both for quickly shifting action, such as that between Willy in the kitchen, Linda in her bedroom, and the boys in their bedroom in the opening scenes, and for more difficult shifts in time as Willy's consciousness slips from the social reality of 1949 to the subjective reality of 1932. Mielziner settled on a partly abstracted house, with "the frame outline of the house forming an open skeleton. Some of the doors were simply open framework; arches and windows were cut-outs of wood, but were drawn and painted with a good deal of quality in their line" (p. 36).

Mielziner decided to signify the passage of time onstage by creating two environments for the house through lighting. When the set was first revealed, the audience saw a muslin backdrop, lit from behind to show the oppressive apartment houses towering over the fragile house. When the scene shifted to the past, the lights behind the backdrop were dimmed out, and the buildings faded out as soft light and images of green leaves were projected onto the backdrop from the front. Combined with the flute music that Miller indicated in the script, this lighting change brought the audience effectively into the past along with Willy.

The major decision in Kazan's direction of the actors involved the treatment of the scenes from the past. Interrupting the action of the present with flashbacks was an already established expressionist technique in both drama and film, but this convention also signified to the audience that it was entering the realm of fantasy or madness. Kazan's decision was clear: "There are no flashbacks!" he wrote in his notebook.[6] Instead, he tried to find a new theatrical idiom to suggest to the audience that the action on stage was not fantasy but subjective reality—that the spectator was experiencing empirical reality *through* Willy, and seeing things as Willy saw them. With Miller, Kazan believed that the play dramatized the process in Willy's mind, and that the scenes in the past were "DAYDREAMS. And daydreams are an action. What Willy is doing in these daydreams is justifying himself." The style, then, had to be "an activization in physical equivalents of the events of Willy's mind for the last 24 hours of his life. So it is *all* unrealistic, since it all happens *Willy's way*—as Willy feels it, experiences it" (p. 49).

Kazan established that the most important element in the characterization of Linda and the boys, and Charley and Bernard, was the contradiction between what the audience saw of their social reality in the present and the vision that Willy carried of them in the past. Kazan had to achieve both psychologically believable characterizations from his actors in the scenes of the present and distorted characterizations in the scenes in the past, characterizations that had to be recognized as the creations of Willy's subjective vision of them. Again the demands of the script created the opportunity for artistic development, and the juxtaposition of two conventions created a new language for expressing the reality of human experience. Kazan's subversion of realistic conventions allowed for greater depth as well as breadth in theatrical representation. The production of *Death of a Salesman* opened up its new idiom for the theatre through the juxtaposition of two seemingly contradictory styles, and allowed for the representation of the two forms of experience that Miller sought to depict—the subjective and the social—at once on the same stage.

Despite its particular success, *Death of a Salesman* did not provide a global solution to Miller's aesthetic dilemma. As Miller has pointed out, *Salesman*'s subjective realism solved a specific aesthetic problem, the dramatization of the protagonist's disintegrating mind in the context of his family's, and the larger society's, response to that disintegration. Miller objects to the imposition of the idiom of subjective realism on subject matter to which it is not suited, however. In his introduction to the *Collected Plays,* he wrote that "the way of telling the tale . . . is as mad as Willy and as abrupt and as suddenly lyrical" (p. 138). He believes that "the subsequent imitations of the form had to collapse for this particular reason. It is not possible . . . to graft it onto a character whose psychology it does not reflect." Miller has not used subjective realism since 1949 because "it would be false to a more integrated—or less disintegrating—personality to pretend that the past and the present are so openly and vocally intertwined in his mind. The ability of people to down their past is normal, and without it we could have no comprehensible communication among men" (p. 138).

In many ways, it was history—both personal and public—that impelled Miller to move on from the dramatization of the subjective, psychological conflict between the private and the social that he achieved in *Death of a Salesman*. His particular position as an individual and as a citizen demanded both a private and a public response to the activity of the House Committee on Un-American Activities and its consequences and implications. The seeming impossibility of combining the private and the public modes of experience in one dramatic idiom led Miller to a close critical examination of the forms of expression available to the American theatre in the fifties. In a series of essays during the fifties, Miller laid out his ideas on the relationship between dramatic form and the conflict between what he called the "private" or familial and the "social" life of the individual. In "The Family in Modern Drama" (1956), Miller posited an inherent formal relationship between realism and the private on one hand and non-realistic techniques and the social on the other: "It has gradually come to appear to me over the years that the spectrum of dramatic forms, from Realism over to the Verse Drama, the Expressionistic techniques, and what we call vaguely the Poetic Play, consists of forms which express human relationships of a particular kind, each of them suited to express either a primarily familial relation at one extreme, or a primarily social relation at the other" (p. 69).

In "On Social Plays" (1955), Miller argued that the bifurcation between the public and the private, the social and the familial, that he saw at the root of the formal question of realism expressed a fundamental societal conflict: "Each great war has turned men further and further away from preoccupation with Man and thrown them back into the family, the home, the private life and the preoccupation with sexuality. It has happened, however, that at the same time our theater has exhausted the one form that was made to express the private life—prose realism. We are bored with it; we demand something more, something 'higher,' on the stage, while at the same time we refuse, or do not know how, to live our private lives excepting as ego-centers" (pp. 56–57). The theatre of the fifties, Miller contended, was jaded, bored with the stage idiom and the private concerns of realism, but was unable to find a satisfactory theatrical idiom for the articulation of the public and the social. The new experiments with staging, such as his own with *Salesman*, he thought, merely disguised the fundamental problem: "By means of cutout sets, revolving stages, musical backgrounds, new and more imaginative lighting schemes, our stage is striving to break up the old living room. However, the perceiving eye knows that many of these allegedly poetic plays are Realism underneath, tricked up to look otherwise" (p. 71).

The obvious answer to the need for a theatrical idiom in which to address social and political concerns in the fifties was expressionism. The mainstay of German social rebellion in the twenties and of agit-prop in the thirties, it was the most immediately available public theatrical language. Miller broadened its definition to include essentially all presentational theatrical idioms as opposed to purely representational realism: "The technical arsenal of Expressionism goes back to Aeschylus. It is a form of play which manifestly seeks to dramatize the conflict of either social, religious, ethical, or moral forces *per se*, and in their own naked roles, rather than to present psychologically realistic human characters in a more or less realistic environment" (p. 75). For Miller, the advantages of a nonrepresentational theatrical idiom for addressing social issues were immediately clear: "The moment realistic behavior and psychology disappear from the play all the other appurtenances of Realism vanish too. The stage is stripped of knicknacks; instead it reveals symbolic *designs,* which function as overt pointers toward the moral to be drawn from the action. We are no longer under quite the illusion of watching through a transparent fourth wall. Instead we are constantly reminded, in effect, that we are watching a theater piece. In short, we are not bidden to lose our consciousness of time and place, the consciousness of ourselves, but are appealed to through our intelligence, our faculties of knowing rather than of feeling" (pp. 75–76).

Most importantly, Miller claimed that the two stage idioms were perceived in fundamentally different ways by the audience: "This difference in the area of appeal is the difference between our familial emotions and our social emotions. The two forms not only spring from different sectors of human experience but end up by appealing to different areas of receptivity within the audience" (p. 76). Miller argued that there was "a natural union of the family and Realism as opposed to society and the poetic" on the grounds of perception: "What we feel is always more 'real' to us than what we know, and we feel the family relation while we only know the social one. Thus the former is the very apotheosis of the real and has an inevitability and a foundation indisputably actual, while the social relation is always relatively mutable, accidental, and consequently of a profoundly arbitrary nature to us" (p. 81).

Whatever one may think of the validity of Miller's psychological and epistemological analyses, there is no doubt that the distinctions he delineated held true for *him*. For Arthur Miller, throughout the fifties, "the difficulty in creating a form that will unite both elements in a full rather than partial onslaught on reality [was] the reflection of the deep split between the private life of man and his social life" (p. 81). The realism of the previous half-century, he thought, "could not, with ease and beauty, bridge the widening gap between the private life and the social life," while expressionism "evaded it by forgoing psychological realism altogether and leaping over to a portrayal of social forces alone" (p. 82).

By 1958, when he wrote the introduction to his *Collected Plays,* Miller was ready to blame "realism's hold on our theatre" for what he considered the moral vacuum in American plays. In light of the playwrights' and audiences' inability to agree on "the pantheon of forces and values which must lie behind the realistic surfaces of life," he believed that "realism, as a style, could seem to be a defense against the assertion of meaning" (p. 160). Reflecting on the irony that the realistic style had, in the hands of playwrights like Ibsen seventy years earlier, been "the prime instrument of those who sought to illuminate meaning in the theater" (p. 161), he posed a rhetorical question: "Was it that we had come to fear the hard glare of life on the stage and under the guise of an aesthetic surfeited with realism were merely expressing our flight from reality? Or was our condemned realism only the counterfeit of the original, whose most powerful single impetus was to deal with man as a social animal?" (p. 161).

One of the reasons for dramatic realism's failure to encompass a wider and deeper segment of human life, he suggested, was the imposition of naturalistic philosophical and sociological assumptions, such as environmental and biological determinism, on realistic stage language: "The idea of realism has become wedded to the idea that man is at best the sum of forces working upon him and of given psychological forces within him" (p. 170). In opposition to this determinism, Miller asserted that "an innate value, an innate will, does in fact posit itself as real not alone because it is devoutly to be wished, but because, however closely [man] is measured and systematically accounted for, he is more than the sum of his stimuli and is unpredictable beyond a certain point" (p. 170). A play that stopped at "the point of conditioning," he asserted, "is not reflecting reality" (p. 170). What was needed was a new dramatic form in which "a new balance has been struck which embraces both determinism and the paradox of will" (p. 170).

In the introduction to his *Collected Plays,* Miller stated very clearly: "If there is one unseen goal toward which every play in this book strives, it is that very discovery and its proof—that we are made and yet are more than what made us" (p. 170). It is in fact the conflict of individual will with both familial and social constraints that unites all of Miller's work during the late forties and fifties, a consistent view of the human condition which he persistently tried to find an effective means of expressing.

Despite his discovery of subjective realism and his belief that expressionistic idioms were inherently linked to the dramatization of public issues, Miller continued to use realism as a way of representing a protagonist's social responsibility, and used it most effectively, as in *The Crucible* (1953), when he wanted to present a protagonist with a clear moral dilemma involving the conflicting responsibilities of the family member and the citizen and to lead his audience to a clear rhetorical choice between the two. John Proctor must choose between bowing to an unjust law, and thus providing for his family materially, and maintaining his integrity against injustice, and thus doing his higher duty as a citizen and leaving his children a heritage, his "name," which he considers more important than farmland. Miller's didactic social message in a time of political oppression was conveyed in a stark, realistic idiom.

On the other hand, Miller's most subjective play, *After the Fall* (1964), takes place literally inside the protagonist's mind. It is pure subjective experience, but the conflict it represents is intensely moral and social. How is a man to make choices that are morally right and socially responsible after he has recognized the evil within himself, and the evil that seems to pervade all human cultures? Framed by Quentin's direct communication with an unnamed "Listener," representational realism is used here to convince the audience, the real listeners, or witnesses, of the validity of Quentin's moral conclusions. Unlike the distorted events in an expressionist play, or the events that happen in the memory of Willy Loman, the events Miller shows us from Quentin's life must appear objectively real, or his choice will be meaningless. The reality of Quentin's experience implies that the moral imperative he discovers holds for the audience as well.

During the early nineties, Miller's theatrical idiom has continued to be informed by a series of dialectics—between realism and expressionism, the subjective and the objective, the public and the private, individual will and public or familial responsibility. In two years, Miller had three new plays in major new productions: the expressionistic *The Ride Down Mt. Morgan* (1993) in London and two realistic plays, *The Last Yankee* (1993) in New York and London and *Broken Glass* (1994) in New York. Among them the three plays conduct a revisiting of the major issues that have pervaded Miller's work since the forties. Like *Death of a Salesman, The Last Yankee* is informed by a family struggle, a struggle between the wife's "success mythology which is both naïve and brutal" and the husband's "incredibly enduring love for her, for nature and the world."[7] At issue is the wife's sanity, and, Miller implies even more forcibly than in *Salesman,* that of American society. *The Ride Down Mt. Morgan* revisits the issues examined in *After the Fall:* sin and guilt, sexual fidelity, and family responsibility. While it strikes new ground in its treatment of Jewish self-hatred, *Broken Glass* also places the dynamics of sexuality and family relationships in the context of cultural and societal expectations.

Concomitant with this creative revisiting of Miller's perennial thematic concerns has been a reexamination of his aesthetics. He included in the published volume of *The Last Yankee* an essay entitled "About Theatre Language," which is essentially a chronicle of his own relationship with theatrical realism in the context of the American theatre's development since the thirties. He contends there that serious dramatists of his generation detested "the realism of Broadway—and the Strand and the Boulevard theatre of France" (p. 80) because of what it had become: "a play representing real rather than symbolic or metaphysical persons and situations, its main virtue verisimilitude, with no revolutionary implications for society or even a symbolic statement of some general truth" (p. 81). He writes that he found it "confusing" at the time that realism in the hands of an earlier generation—that of Ibsen and Chekhov and Strindberg—had meant "opposition to the bourgeois status quo and the hypocrisies on which it stood" (p. 81). His conclusion is that "conventional realism was conventional because it implicitly supported the conventions of society, but it could just as easily do something quite different" (p. 81).

Miller articulates clearly in this essay how his own realism combines this desire to assail the bourgeoisie and to effect social change with a distinctly modernist aesthetic: "A real play was the discovery of the unity of its contradictions; the essential poetry was the synthesis of even the least of its parts to form a symbolic meaning. . . . Ideally, a good play must show as sound an emotional proof of its thesis as a case at law shows factual proof" (p. 85). While the earlier plays perhaps exhibit these characteristics unconsciously, they are written into the very design of *The Last Yankee* and *Broken Glass*. The products of a formal experiment that began with *A View from the Bridge* (1955) and *Incident at Vichy* (1964), they are fundamentally rhetorical plays, whose through-line consists of a case to be argued, a problem that demands both a personal and a social solution. The dialogue and the characterization in both are recognized as clearly, almost aggressively, realistic, but, as Miller notes, "it is always necessary to employ the artificial in order [to] arrive at the real" (p. 96).

Significantly, *The Last Yankee* contains the most minimal of stage directions ("*The visiting room of a state mental hospital*" [p. 7]). In striking contrast to the complex theatrical semiosis of *Salesman,* in neither *Yankee* nor *Broken Glass* does the staging matter very much. Both are fundamentally dialogic plays, which can be played either on an almost bare stage or on the most realistic of sets without violating their integrity. Like *Incident at Vichy,* both *The Last Yankee* and *Broken Glass* are static plays in which the action consists of a carefully structured, rhetorical dialogic series. In the first scene of *Yankee,* the dialogue between John Frick and Leroy Hamilton, as they wait for their wives in the visiting room of the state mental hospital, sets up the "social setting" for the disease from which their wives suffer by exhibiting the success myth and the pressure for material success to which all Americans are subject. It also sets up Leroy's rebellion against these pressures. Both wives are the victims of severe depression. Frick feels betrayed that this should happen despite the material success he has attained; Hamilton is afraid that it has happened partly because of his own rebellion against the pressures for material success.

Scene two, which takes place in Patricia Hamilton's room, consists of two dialogic duets and a quartet: first, Patricia and Karen Frick exhibit their illnesses, providing the spectator with some insight into the social and familial pressures that caused them; then Patricia and Leroy analyze Patricia's condition, coming to an understanding about their own relationship that provides some hope for the future; then the two couples come together, contrasting the dysfunctional relationship of the Fricks with the now potentially healthy relationship of the Hamiltons. In the course of the play, Miller states his perennial view of the American success myth quite clearly. As Leroy says of his wife's family: "You all had this—you know—very high opinion of yourselves; each and every one of you was automatically going to go to the head of the line just because your name was Sorgenson. And life isn't that way, so you got sick" (p. 49). Replace "Sorgenson" with "Loman" and this is an explanation for Willy's illness too. Strip away every theatrical element but the dialogue, and Miller is using a minimalist realism to make the same critique of American society that he was making in the much more elaborate theatrical idiom of the forties. Our spiritual destitution and our devotion to acquiring the tokens of material success have made us ill.

The use of a real illness to symbolize the sickness of American society is at the heart of *Broken Glass* as well. Here Sylvia Gellburg's hysterical paralysis is brought on by terror of the Nazis, a displacement for the terror she has for her husband, who hates her for being what he is—a Jew. The rhetorical climax of *Broken Glass* is a reprise of the much-quoted rhetorical climax of *Incident at Vichy:* "Each man has his Jew; it is the other. And the Jews have their Jews."[8] In *Broken Glass,* Dr. Hyman tells Gellburg: "I have all kinds coming into my office, and there's not one of them who one way or another is not persecuted. Yes. *Everybody's* persecuted. The poor by the rich, the rich by the poor, the black by the white, the white by the black, the men by the women, the women by the men, the Catholics by the Protestants, the Protestants by the Catholics—and of course all of them by the Jews. I even wonder sometimes if that's what holds the country together!"[9] When Gellburg confronts him with the reality of Hitler, Hyman replies: "Hitler? Hitler is the perfect example of the persecuted man! I've heard him—he kvetches like an elephant was standing on his pecker! He's turned his whole beautiful country into one gigantic kvetch!" (p. 152). This climax is the endpoint of a rhetorical design that connects Sylvia's physical ailment with her terror, her terror with the historical fact of the Holocaust, the Holocaust with the universal human condition.

In his latest revisioning of realism, the rhetorically structured dialogic series in a realistic frame, Miller has found a successful accommodation for his bifurcated and seemingly contradictory agenda, what he calls his "split vision." He wrote of *Yankee* that the vision of the play "is intended to be both close up and wide, psychological and social, subjective and objective, and manifestly so. To be sure, there is a realistic tone to this exchange . . . but an inch below is the thematic selectivity which drives the whole tale" (p. 94). In the same context, Miller has supplied the most apt summation of his complex fifty-year relationship with theatrical realism: "Perhaps it needs to be said that this split vision has informed all the plays I have written. I have tried to make things seen in their social context and simultaneously felt as intimate testimony, and that requires a style, but one that draws as little attention to itself as possible, for I would wish a play to be absorbed rather than merely observed" (p. 94). In 1994, Arthur Miller seemed convinced that realism can accommodate both the most private lives of human beings and the most public, the psychological and the social. His fifty-year search has led him to a stripping away of theatricality, getting his plays down to the essential elements of drama—actors speaking dialogue—in plays that are classical in their simplicity while they compel the audience's belief in their reality.

Notes

1. Arthur Miller, *The Theatre Essays of Arthur Miller*, ed. Robert A. Martin (New York: Viking, 1978), p. 232. Unless otherwise noted, material by Miller, other than playtexts, is from this volume and is cited in the text.

2. Arthur Miller, *Timebends: A Life* (New York: Grove, 1987), p. 314.

3. Raymond Williams, "The Realism of Arthur Miller," *Arthur Miller: A Collec-*

tion of Critical Essays, ed. Robert W. Corrigan (Engelwood Cliffs, N.J.: Prentice-Hall, 1969), p. 75.

4. Miller, *Timebends,* pp. 181–82.

5. Jo Mielziner, *Designing for the Theatre: A Memoir and a Portfolio* (New York: Bramhall House, 1965), p. 24. Subsequent references are cited in the text.

6. Elia Kazan, "Notebooks for *Death of a Salesman,*" in Kenneth Thorpe Rowe, ed., *A Theatre in Your Head* (New York: Funk and Wagnalls, 1960), p. 49.

7. Arthur Miller, "About Theatre Language," *The Last Yankee* (New York: Penguin, 1994), p. 93. Subsequent references to *The Last Yankee* are cited in the text.

8. Arthur Miller, *Incident at Vichy* (New York: Viking, 1965), p. 68.

9. Arthur Miller, *Broken Glass* (New York: Penguin, 1994), p. 152.

THIRTEEN

Margins in the Mainstream: Contemporary Women Playwrights

Janet V. Haedicke

If, as Susan Harris Smith claims, American drama is an "unwanted bastard child" in literary canons,[1] then female-authored plays, excluded by gender as well as genre, are unborn children threatened with abortion by both the academic and theatre establishments. In 1981, Beth Henley's Pulitzer Prize, the first awarded to a woman dramatist in twenty-three years, prophesied a reemergence of women playwrights following second-wave feminism. Indeed, one of the most significant aspects of contemporary American theatre is the fulfillment of this prophecy as Marsha Norman won the Pulitzer in 1983 and Wendy Wasserstein in 1989; the number of prizes to women in one decade thus approached the prior total of five between 1917 and 1981. Still, the victory may be as illusory as the Pulitzer is political: of forty playwrights in Philip Kolin's *American Playwrights Since 1945,* only eight are women.[2] Subjecting female dramatists to the marginalization they protest in literary critics' treatment of drama in general, drama critics have only superficially evolved beyond Joseph Mersand, whose 1937 *When Ladies Write Plays* defended women's contribution to drama with such praise as: "They may not present those 'eternal verities' which seem to be granted to only a blessed few; but they know how to reconstruct for us on the stage our own little houses."[3] The postwar canonical giants to follow staged, of course, exactly those little houses, but presumably these "blessed few" infused them with a universality still widely denied women playwrights.

Equally disturbing, however, is the compensatory stance of many feminist critics. Some storm the masculinist bastion of the canon, casting laurels for the entry of any female-authored play. But, as Jill Dolan insists, their triumphs may actually be capitulations to hegemonic authority in promoting a text weak by feminist standards, while the alternate tactic of framing a feminist canon perpetuates the very exclusionism it strives to counter.[4] Thus, contemporary female dramatists find themselves stranded in a crossfire between a besieged, yet still standing, male canon and an emerging, yet self-limiting, female canon. Even, or especially, those playwrights who have achieved mainstream success remain thus stranded since this validation seems automatically to invalidate a play for feminist critics. Undeniably, the most challenging feminist plays are produced in alternative venues; also undeniably, they reach a limited and already converted audience. Surely it is not heresy to admit the possibility of challenge to masculinism from both within and without the theatrical mainstream. To claim that only marginalized drama can reflect life in the margins reflects a disturbing reverse elitism that threatens to undermine much feminist drama criticism.

At the center of this canon crossfire is the issue of realism, a form which has dominated American drama to a unique extent. Though not alone in the assault on the form, feminists have occupied the front lines in equating realism with a reinscription of dominant ideology. Their rejection of classical narrative, hence of mainstream drama, is grounded in film critic Laura Mulvey's 1975 identification of the "male gaze," a voyeuristic/fetishistic look intrinsic to traditional filmic pleasure, which has been split between active/male "bearer of the look" and passive/female image.[5] Through this Oedipal polarization, epitomized by the narrative pattern of classical Hollywood cinema, the monolithic male gaze objectifies the woman, whose ultimate meaning is sexual difference or castration. In descrying and decrying this binary opposition encoded in realistic representation, Mulvey set the course not only for feminist film criticism but also for feminist drama criticism. Yet, occurring concomitantly was a shift in feminism itself from both a liberal dynamic seeking humanist equality and a cultural or radical dynamic seeking essentialist separatism. Challenged by women of color, many feminists in the late 1970s moved toward a materialist dynamic, which recognized differences rather than difference, attacking the sex-as-gender construct and focusing on women as sociohistorical subjects rather than as Woman. There followed an evolution in film theory to the concept of a vacillating gaze in a noncolonized spectator; however, though even Mulvey has modified her antinarrative stance, feminist drama criticism has thus far elided this evolution, its most notable critics still condemning any realistic play as perpetuating a masculinist, if not pornographic, perspective and as precluding any possibilities of transformation.[6]

Entrenchment in this position means, of course, self-inflicted marginalization. For an American playwright, to forsake realism is to forsake an audience, presumably still a *raison d'être* for drama and politically an imperative for feminist drama. It is certainly no coincidence that the three recent female Pulitzer winners and the increasingly visible Tina Howe turn often to the realistic form. Sharing a form, however, is not inevitably sharing a perspective, and the negotiations with and within that form vary greatly. These playwrights, having emerged during an era of backlash against feminism, do not all effectively challenge dominant power structures; yet the impact of their plays, from either a feminist or a "universal" viewpoint, seems to derive less from form than from epistemology. Robert Brustein's 1978 call for a shift in American drama from the causal to the metaphorical finds response in the Cagean realism (allied with quantum science) which William Demastes perceives as superseding Aristotelian realism (allied with Newtonian science). In feminist terms, Helene Keyssar urges a shift from a drama of recognition to a drama of transformation.[7] The emergence in twentieth-century American drama of a postmodernist epistemology speaks particularly to feminism with its stake in uprooting master narratives and fixated or gendered identities.

Though a postmodern feminist dynamic occurs more obviously in such alternative playwrights as Irene Fornes, I remain convinced that a challenge to dominant (masculinist) ideology can—and must—be mounted before a mainstream audience. This is not to say that the above-mentioned female playwrights all evoke a feminist political epistemology. Notwithstanding the potential of comedy as subversive, Henley and Wasserstein fail ultimately to undermine classical realism's assumptions of linearity, causality, and unity in presenting female quests for a stable identity. Wendy Brown sees such identity politics as symptomatic of a reactionary modernism, which exhibits an antipolitical preference for identity over pluralities, reason over power, discoveries over decisions, and truth over politics, all the while scorning postmodern theory as apolitical. Brown insists that it is actually this reactionary modernism that precludes a feminist alternative politics. Refusing to deconstruct the subject though insisting on gender as a construct, modernist feminism posits Truth in individualized subjectivity: "Since women's subordination is partly achieved through the construction and positioning of us as private . . . , then within modernity, the voicing of women's experience acquires an inherently confessional cast."[8] Such voicing yields only a politics of *ressentiment*— "feminist hesitations" rather than transformative power.

Both Henley and Wasserstein seem to posit only this reactive subjectivity, a *discovery*, through confession, of unity in individual and familial identity, which leaves intact a national identity founded on myths of America triumphant over a feminized object/other. Conversely, Howe and Norman expose such icons as illusory by dramatizing decided rather than discovered identities, multiple rather than unified subjectivity—worlds of possible chaos rather than predictable order in dramas of metaphor rather than causality. Linear or, in feminist terms, Oedipal narrative is subverted as their plays put into play the quest for an identity defined against (m)other, a teleology fostering violence in the male and contradiction in the female. Myths implode when Oedipal polarization within the family emerges as paradigmatic of that binary opposition on which all myths are grounded. The postmodern feminist dramatist can employ the realist form to attract an audience and then to deconstruct rather than "reconstruct . . . our own little houses," where gendered identity is naturalized and differences are encoded as oppositions.

Henley's "breakthrough" play, *Crimes of the Heart*, regrettably does not break through masculinist/modernist assumptions and serves to confirm feminist objections to the realistic form. Jonnie Guerra faults Henley's choice of realism and of the family format as precluding the possibility of autonomy, which should be intrinsic to the female quest tradition.[9] Since a dismissal of realistic family drama implies a dismissal of the major tradition—female or male—in American drama, it seems more fruitful to recognize that family drama, in or out of the theatre, is intrinsically political and that realism is not invariably regressive. If it proves so in Henley's case, the fault lies not in the form but in the perspective. Leaving unquestioned the validity of the quest narrative itself, Henley leaves unquestioned linearity, causality, and autonomy. Both her supporters and her detractors accept these assumptions implicit in the play and focus on the success or failure of the quest.

Set entirely in the Magrath family kitchen, the play concretizes the construction of women in the private sphere and proceeds to validate it. Having been deserted by their father, the three Magrath sisters were brought as children to this, their grandparents' house, where their mother also abandoned them, first psychologically and then physically through suicide, to the patriarchal rule of Old Granddaddy. They have now gathered to face a family crisis: Babe, long "brutalized"[10] by her husband, has shot him after he struck her teenaged black lover. Failing to explore the implications of a battered wife and a beaten black, Henley foregrounds instead female self-destructiveness and an Oedipal plumbing of the past so that order may be imposed on the present. Apparently concluding that Babe's errant sexuality was only an escapist substitute for romantic or familial love, Meg urges her sisters toward a rebirth of identity. Babe survives two farcical suicide attempts to join her lawyer/suitor against her husband; Lenny becomes her "own woman," overcoming the shame of a "shrunken ovary" (p. 48) to telephone a former beau, who is relieved by her confession of barrenness. Most critics concur that each sister is "reborn as an individual as a consequence of redefinition of her identity and rediscovery of her ability to love."[11] Eager to portray the play as feminist, these critics downplay the motif of male-validated identity to emphasize the familial and female bonding at play's end. Celebrating Lenny's thirtieth birthday, the sisters verify Lenny's vision of bonding as does Henley by leaving them framed "in a magical, golden, sparkling glimmer" (p. 72). As Billy Harbin puts it, having confessed their way to "familial trust and unity," they "celebrate a newly discovered fund of strength."[12]

Though comedy—even comic realism, perhaps—demands a resolution, Henley's capitulation here is not so much to form as to a reactionary modernism and a nostalgia for certainty in a universe of increasing uncertainties. If identity can be discovered through recognition rather than decided through transformation, then chaos and fragmentation are merely comical surface phenomena. Thus Harbin praises Henley's seriousness beneath comic distortions, seeing the play's theme as "lost American ideals" of rural stability and "moral certitude" (p. 83). Had the Magrath sisters been reared in a traditional American family, presumably nurturance would have precluded fragmented identities, now made whole only by a quest through chaos to Truth. As Brown points out, this confessional truth and individualized subjectivity (consciousness raising) reflect only *ressentiment* and resistance politics. Nor have Henley's later plays suggested a move beyond this school of feminism, which Joan Cocks terms "a sanctification of powerlessness, a celebration of weakness."[13] *The Miss Firecracker Contest* (1981, 1984) and *The Wake of Jamey Foster* (1982) both convey the same nostalgia for the traditional family and the same admiration for a determined, if pathetic, quest for and celebration of female identity. A hopeless contestant in the "Miss Firecracker Contest," Carnelle was abandoned by her parents and reared by a non-nurturing aunt, a past offered as explanation for her seeking solace in sex and attaining only a tainted reputation and V.D. In perpetuating this Blanche DuBois, this desperate southern-sexpot figure, Henley parodies female sexuality; like Meg and Babe, Carnelle suffers for illicit sex and finds affirmation only in family at play's and quest's end. In *The Wake of Jamey Foster,* the widow has been devastated by her husband's infidelity and finally finds sleep and solace in a song of spoons by a smelly admirer. Though Jamey's widow, Marshael, rejects family, Henley seems to mourn its dissolution and to posit scant possibility of female subjectivity beyond it.

Perhaps even more disturbing is the phenomenal success of Wendy Wasserstein, often lauded as drama's premier feminist voice. Since *Uncommon Women and Others* (1978), Wasserstein, like Henley, has staged female quests for identity as comic realism without challenging the assumptions of the quest narrative or of traditional realism. Though Susan Carlson praises *Uncommon Women* since it "nurtures" female community and complicates the traditional comic resolution,[14] the play still offers only a reactive female subjectivity. Of the five women, ranging from hollowed professional to menses-obsessed feminist, only the married Sam seems to present possibilities. Her concluding announcement of pregnancy can only confirm, in the face of other options presented, American nostalgia for unity of self through family and of womanhood through nurturing. This nostalgia persists through Wasserstein's other plays, striking a national chord as evidenced by the audiences and awards garnered by *The Heidi Chronicles.*

How more safely for critics to navigate the current backlash against feminism than to acclaim a self-proclaimed feminist playwright who actually reinscribes dominant notions of female identity?

Despite its episodic structure, the play presents a traditional quest narrative, its chronicle a history to be mined for causal nuggets of the mother lode of identity. Heidi Holland struggles through twenty-five years of frustrating relationships and failed feminism to emerge as a pitiable facsimile of her literary model. Holding a copy of *The Heidi Chronicles,* the gay soul mate, Peter, questions this Heidi's progress: "Did you know that the first section is Heidi's year of travel and learning, and the second is Heidi uses what she knows? (*Softly.*) How will you use what you know, Heidi?"[15] Her response, a lament of chronic sadness, reflects the tone of *ressentiment* throughout the play. A respected art historian specializing in women artists, Heidi breaks down during a luncheon speech on "Women—Where are We Going?" to confess that she is "just not happy" and feels "stranded" by a feminism that promised "we were all in this together" (p. 62). Wasserstein should certainly not be banished from the ranks for exposing the pitfalls of 1960s and '70s feminism; feminists themselves have recognized the limitations of the liberal goal of individualist equality or the radical goal of essentialist sisterhood, limitations intrinsic to a modernist ethic.

Even, however, if second-wave feminism was as laughably naive as Wasserstein suggests, it assuredly yielded more than the reactionary retreat with which Heidi closes her chronicles. The penultimate scene depicts her 1987 maternalistic reconciliation with Peter ("sweetie"), now AIDS-terrified but still sexually (and stereotypically) promiscuous. The final scene depicts her 1989 reconciliation with Scoop, the intellectual mentor who deemed her not wife material and moved from Eugene McCarthy supporter to *Boomer Magazine* editor. Such outward reconciliations reflect, presumably, inward unity affirmed by the "*Warm afternoon sunlight*" (p. 68) streaming through the windows of the empty new apartment in which Heidi is as snugly ensconced as in her newfound identity. To Scoop's first query as to her happiness, Heidi replies, "Actually, I am seeing an editor I seem to like" (p. 69); to his second, "Well, I have a daughter" (p. 73). Defining herself by a man and by an adopted child, Heidi hopes only for change for her daughter's generation. As Scoop departs to another mistress and a political career as "a man for all genders" (p. 75), Heidi remains in the private realm, singing a 1950s song and rocking her baby as the lights fade. This nostalgic tableau, recalling Henley's finale, reflects the modernist feminism which Brown terms "feminist hesitations." Single motherhood seems compensatory as Heidi's waiting for her daughter to become "a heroine for the twenty-first [century]" (p. 75) implies her own generation's failure. Confirming this stasis, end echoes prologue, where Heidi compared a female in a painting to a female at a high school dance: "So you hang around, . . . waiting to see what might happen" (p. 8).

What has happened dramatically and thematically is a reinscription of female passivity juxtaposed against male activity. Internalizing a constructed male gaze, which Wasserstein leaves unchallenged, Heidi represents a tentative self rather than the tenuous subjectivity which could have subverted paradigmatic male-female hierarchies. Mocking gender yet leaving the construct intact, Wasserstein offers no voice for transformation, no possibility of difference, no performance of multiplicity. Keyssar cites the play as a regrettable verification of Bakhtin's claim that all drama is monologic and incapable of countering dominant discourses: "In its refusal of such a 'decentering,' *The Heidi Chronicles* reveals a national culture that remains 'sealed-off,' 'authoritarian,' 'rigid' and unconscious of itself as only one among other cultures and languages. And it does so to a dangerous degree" (p. 98). Keyssar's use of Bakhtin's monologism-dialogism concept, paralleling Brown's modernist-postmodernist feminisms, underscores the threat to feminism in Wasserstein's capitulation to a hierarchical national identity bolstered by the suppression of difference. Significantly, her latest success, *The Sisters Rosensweig,* recalls Henley's *Crimes of the Heart* as three sisters celebrating a birthday celebrate the illusion of identity reborn through love rather than the transformative possibilities of multiple, even contradictory, subjectivity. Regrettably, these American trios lack the metaphorical resonance of Chekhov's three, pandering to America's demand for discovered wholeness to perpetuate the dictum of *E Pluribus Unum.*

Lest such resolution in sameness be attributed to the criteria of comedy, I turn to Tina Howe, whose plays are generally described, like those of Henley and Wasserstein, as tragicomedies. Howe, however, eschews their resolutions, instead mocking the linearity of the quest narrative by staging identity formation as a performance text. Her plays examine the mediated, tenuous nature of subjectivity and urge recognition of gender as a polarizing construct and sexual differ-ence as one mediator rather than a defining opposition. As contem-porary feminism reflects a postmodern impulse, so Howe's drama-turgy, more so than that of her counterparts, reflects a postmodern theatre, which undermines notions of unity and causality and thus of classical realism. It is doubtless this challenge to classical realism that has rendered her the only one among these playwrights not to be rec-ognized by the Pulitzer committee, all of these writers having also received far more scholarly notice. The American audience's demand for realism to confirm their sense of identity seems even more unre-lenting than normal for women dramatists who, for the most part, have not only obliged but have also softened the form with comedy. Howe, conversely, employs comedy to convolute the boundaries of re-alism when she works within them at all. After a series of failures in the 1970s, Howe consciously conceded to public taste with the con-ventional domestic setting of *Painting Churches* (1983). Still, she insists that the play is "quite off-center" and proclaims: "God help me if I ever write a realistic play."[16] This play and *Coastal Disturbances*, which followed in 1986, nonetheless reflect an undeniable, if reluctant, re-alism that doubtless accounts for their success within Howe's canon. Here, however, is realism with a (Derridean) difference as oppositions are displaced and chaos belies order. Through this postmodern real-ism, Howe exposes representation as complicit in constructing illusory identities and realism as its most suspect form in constructing "always already" constructed reality.

Painting Churches exposes the artifice of the western quest narrative through its common American variation of the return home, which Henley and Wasserstein both validate. Howe seems more closely aligned with Sam Shepard as she demythologizes family—here the family is literally "Church"—and decenters, in this "off-center" play, a culture whose construction of subjectivity is encoded in familial po-larizations. The setting, with its *"play of light,"* which *"transforms"* the interior of the Churches' Boston townhouse, insists on the fluid and fragmented nature of subjectivity, the *"unreality"* of home and of iden-tity.[17] Artist/daughter Mags returns to help her parents move and at-tempts to combat their sexually and emotionally repressive representation of her by painting her own of them, thereby converting her creators to her creations. In preliminary photos, the parents are disempowered by the child's gaze in a freeze-frame at the Church altar, fixated into previously parodied icons—American Gothic (mythic family), the Pietà (mythic motherhood), the Creation (mythic fatherhood). Only by moving from oppositional child to other-oriented artist can Mags create an image which transforms them all. Her nonrepresentational portrait, blurring boundaries between illusion and reality, artist and subject, presents a transformative subjectivity rather than a fixated identity. Inspired by the painting, the elderly Churches dance as Mags watches, familial reconciliation suggesting not discovered oneness but performed connection. Of this resolution, Howe observes: "We all know it's a purely theatrical moment, which is why it's so precious" (p. 232).

The twenty tons of sand onstage for *Coastal Disturbances* concretizes this same unstable territory in which questers seek to discover stable identities even in the face of continental drifts. Most frustrated yet determined are the women characters, each of whom signifies a phase of the female experience, from the child Miranda, terrified of bleeding, to the matriarch M. J. Adams, betrayed and bitter. Poised between is Holly Dancer, a photographer, whose attempt to freeze images and fixate identity is foiled by the lifeguard Leo, an amateur magician. Like Mags, Holly must stumble over her own self-image before the dancer can rise to dance. Howe's beach becomes a site of transformation, where subjectivity shimmers like a dance in shifting sands. No polarizing male gaze but a magician's perspective prevails as subject-object oppositions dissolve within the gauze "Kubla Khan" tent which Leo improvises around the elderly Adamses' beach umbrella.[18] Unlike Henley and Wasserstein, Howe affirms transformation through the perception of difference rather than unity through the reconciliation of opposites; even in romantic or maternal love, subject loving object shifts to self becoming other. Despite an apologetic identification of her concerns as cultural rather than political, Howe's denaturalization of gendered, or otherwise oppositional, identities emerges as a political epistemology.

Though Howe presents the least and Marsha Norman the most serious realism of these playwrights, they seem aligned epistemologically since both convey a postmodern perspective to challenge previous assumptions of realism. In her first play, *Getting Out* (1979), Norman examines the prison of perception as Arlene's first day outside literal prison yields realization of an inescapable figurative prison. Using a split protagonist, Norman dramatizes Arlene's attempt to exorcise Arlie, her violent teenage past; though successful, the psychological process does not bear that fruit of resolution and unification so abundant in America's drama of causality. Beyond being a "prisoner of patriarchal victimisation,"[19] Arlene remains imprisoned in her own expectations of an autonomous new identity. In *'night, Mother*, Norman again presents a prison of perspective, here utilizing the unities of time, place, and action to subvert the very tenets that classical realism upholds. This quintessentially realistic play evolves into metatheatre as Norman stages Jessie Cates's staging before her mother with unrelenting logic an illogical suicide, which denies all possibilities of unity—in time, in place, in action, in identity.

Surface, not subversion, however, rendered to the play its success as Brustein lauded its classical form and the emergence of an "authentic, universal playwright."[20] Those other male critics who followed suit clamored to applaud Norman's candidacy for the canon doubtless because her plays were more serious, thus more "universal," than were those of her counterparts. Feminist critics found themselves in the paradoxical position of either supporting the elevation of a play that represents female defeatism and defeat or undermining one of the rare inroads for female playwrights. Seeking to align feminist considerations with canonical standards, some critics espouse a liberal feminist analysis of Jessie as "a microcosm of the universal human condition"; others reflect a cultural feminist perspective in perceiving a mythic mother/daughter bond.[21] Materialist feminists regard these approaches as naive, faulting the play's realistic form as intrinsically incompatible with a feminist perspective. Jeanie Forte does find qualified redemption in the play's superficial, yet producible, feminism, while Jill Dolan belatedly concedes to it a liberal or cultural feminism, though warning that both are animated by an absent male.[22] Dolan sees *'night, Mother* as epitomizing the exclusionist basis of canonization—dominant or revisionist—and the gender bias in theatre production and criticism. Disparaging Norman's intentional universality and the producers' casting of the overweight Kathy Bates as Jessie, Dolan faults reviewers for focusing on fat rather than epilepsy as the "fatal, tragic flaw" (p. 239).

Ironically, Dolan seems to have returned to the Aristotelian criteria which she impugned in Brustein's review; yet Norman undermines the classical unities by subverting just this notion of an inevitable causal flaw. As the stage clock measures real time, the spectator is seduced into seeking Jessie's motivation for her announced suicide, playing detective with Thelma, who frantically probes the past: the father's death, the epilepsy, the deserting husband, the criminal son. Yet Jessie, with disquieting detachment, discounts each proposed cause, simply insisting on the positive nature of her choice: "I'm *not* giving up! This *is* the other thing I'm trying. . . . *This* will work. That's why I picked it."[23] Insisting on the choice of suicide as her first, if last, foray into proactive subjectivity, Jessie tells her mother of finding an old baby picture: "And it was somebody else, not me. . . . That's who I started out and this is who is left. (*There is no self-pity here.*) That's what this is about. It's somebody I lost all right, it's my own self. Who I never was. Or who I tried to be and never got there" (p. 50). Here Norman exposes the destructiveness of the quest narrative, a standard of traditional American realistic drama and ostensibly of her own play. Jessie's philosophical observation that she "never got there" calls into question the "there"—a unified, fixated, autonomous self safe from seizures or shifts and centered through familial bonding. Though Jessie and Thelma experience an unprecedented closeness on this night, Jessie recognizes that it is prompted only by her choice to die. Their mother-daughter bond represents not feminine oneness but perspectival difference.

The mother's house (and the stage) emerges as an epistemological prison. When Thelma dismisses Jessie's view as only "what you think is true," Jessie, "*Struck by the clarity of that,*" replies, "That's right. It's what I think is true" (p. 26). Her recognition of perceptual truths rather than foundationalist Truth, of decided rather than discovered identities reveals Jessie as embodying a postmodernist perspective, which thwarts Thelma's modernist view. Demastes sees Norman as an exemplar of Cagean realism since she supplants Aristotelian assumptions of causality and reveals the realistic form as only artifice (pp. 114–18). His suggestion that the play be viewed not in terms of feminist social critique but as a philosophical debate on the nature of perception actually echoes the evolution within feminism itself. The concept of the male gaze having placed perception at the center of feminist thought, its modification reflects a move from the strictly social to the philosophical or epistemological. Jessie rejects more than objectification by a male gaze here, saying "No" not only to her own gender-dictated experience but to "it *all*" (p. 49), including the Red Chinese. Norman repeatedly insists on Jessie's suicide as an emblem of choice rather than an act of despair. Affirming as well Thelma's choice to remain, Norman gives us in this nocturnal dialogue not dialectic but the Bakhtinian dialogic for which Keyssar calls in drama. There is no reconciliation, but there is empowerment as Norman stresses Jessie's newfound control, her "peaceful energy" (p. 4), through the abnegation of causality. The play emerges as that vocal metaphor which Nancy Love advocates as signaling an extrafoundationalist "political epistemology [as opposed to the epistemological politics of visual imagery] and, with it, a political transformation. . . . an empowerment/knowledge regime,"[24] which makes democratic discourse possible. In this discourse of difference, bonds may not be sealed but boundaries are displaced as Jessie, abandoning the object position, chooses as subject to abdicate the quest rather than to sanctify powerlessness.

In noting that the first-wave voice of female playwrights eventually modulated into a rarely interrupted silence, Kachur warns: "If history does have an inscrutable way of repeating itself, then the recent signs by Henley, Howe and Norman of moving away from centring women as strong, potent characters intimates perhaps an early sign of attenuation not unlike that experienced fifty years ago" (p. 35). Having castigated feminist scholars for colluding with the male establishment by suppressing female playwrights according to a yet unformulated feminist poetics, Kachur herself seems to locate such a poetics squarely in the tradition of male-dominated American drama: a quest (Oedipal) narrative, wherein past and person are plumbed for a centered, autonomous identity, its elusiveness to be mourned. Such a centering, however, whether of woman or man, serves only to confirm dominant hierarchical assumptions of fixated, hence polarized, identity, and, in feminism, reflects that reactionary modernism which makes icons of such traditions as the family. If only by decentering can drama move to the dialogic, then only by this move can theatre become a voice for transformation. Its failure in the mainstream to resonate as such lies not in the predominance of realism, or more specifically, of realistic domestic drama. America's actual domestic dramas, where violence increasingly engenders and genders roles, seem workshop productions for our international dramas, where force myopically defends the godhead of inviolable identity. So long as America casts a male gaze on the world within and without, no discourse of difference can resound. Those playwrights, female or male, who destabilize that gaze, decenter the quest, and denaturalize gender, as well as other paradigmatic polarization, offer possibilities of alternative worlds. Those who do so by putting into play rather than by rejecting the realistic form—foregrounding its artifice, subverting causality, withholding reconciliation, theatricalizing identity—offer that possibility to a wider, if unsuspecting or resistant, audience. Perhaps some among them will heed the urging to follow Oedipus no longer. Perhaps more among them will realize empowerment in difference and revel in otherness. Perhaps feminists among them will proclaim the possibilities in mainstream theatre of such a political epistemology—*Ex Uno Plura!*

Notes

1. Susan Harris Smith, "Generic Hegemony: American Drama and the Canon," *American Quarterly* 41 (March 1989): 112.

2. Philip C. Kolin, ed., *American Playwrights Since 1945: A Guide to Scholarship, Criticism, and Performance* (Westport, Conn.: Greenwood Press, 1989).

3. Joseph Mersand, *When Ladies Write Plays,* The Modern Woman Chapbooks 2 (New York: Modern Chapbooks, 1937), p. 24.

4. Jill Dolan, "Bending Gender to Fit the Canon: The Politics of Production," *Making a Spectacle: Feminist Essays on Contemporary Women's Theatre,* ed. Lynda Hart, pp. 318–44 (Ann Arbor: U of Michigan P, 1989), p. 320.

5. Laura Mulvey, "Visual Pleasure and Narrative Cinema," *Screen* 16.3 (1975): 11.

6. See Laura Mulvey, *Visual and Other Pleasures* (Bloomington: Indiana UP, 1989); Sue-Ellen Case, *Feminism and Theatre* (New York: Methuen, 1988); Jill Dolan, *The Feminist Spectator as Critic* (Ann Arbor: UMI Research Press, 1988); Lynda Hart, "Introduction: Performing Feminism," in *Making a Spectacle: Feminist Essays on Contemporary Women's Theatre,* ed. Lynda Hart, pp. 1–21 (Ann Arbor: U of Michigan P, 1989).

7. Robert Brustein, "The Crack in the Chimney: Reflections on Contemporary American Playwriting," *Theater* 9.2 (1978): 21–29; William W. Demastes, "Jessie

and Thelma Revisited: Marsha Norman's Conceptual Challenge in *'night, Mother,"* *Modern Drama* 36 (1993): 109–19; Helene Keyssar, "Drama and the Dialogic Imagination: *The Heidi Chronicles* and *Fefu and Her Friends,"* *Modern Drama* 34 (1991): 88–106. Subsequent references to Keyssar are cited in the text.

8. Wendy Brown, "Feminist Hesitations, Postmodern Exposures," *Differences* 3.1 (1991): 73.

9. Jonnie Guerra, "Beth Henley: Female Quest and the Family-Play Tradition," in *Making a Spectacle: Feminist Essays on Contemporary Women's Theatre,* ed. Lynda Hart, pp. 118–30 (Ann Arbor: U of Michigan P, 1989).

10. Beth Henley, *Crimes of the Heart* (New York: Dramatists Play Service, 1982), p. 27. Subsequent references are cited in the text.

11. Laura Morrow, "Orality and Identity in *'night, Mother* and *Crimes of the Heart,"* *Studies in American Drama, 1945–Present* 3 (1988): 38.

12. Billy J. Harbin, "Familial Bonds in the Plays of Beth Henley," *Southern Quarterly* 25.3 (1987): 89.

13. Joan Cocks, "Augustine, Nietzsche, and Contemporary Body Politics," *Differences* 3.1 (1991): 145.

14. Susan L. Carlson, "Comic Textures and Female Communities 1937 and 1977: Clare Boothe and Wendy Wasserstein," in *Modern American Drama: The Female Canon,* ed. June Schlueter (Rutherford, N.J.: Fairleigh Dickinson UP, 1990), p. 215.

15. Wendy Wasserstein, *The Heidi Chronicles* (New York: Dramatists Play Service, 1990), p. 65. Subsequent references are cited in the text.

16. Tina Howe, Interview by Kathleen Betsko and Rachel Koening, *Interviews with Contemporary Women Playwrights* (New York: Beech Tree Books, 1987), p. 228. Except for playscripts, references to Howe come from this interview and are cited in the text.

17. Tina Howe, *Painting Churches,* in *Coastal Disturbances: Four Plays by Tina Howe* (New York: Theatre Communications Group, 1989), p. 131.

18. Tina Howe, *Coastal Disturbances,* 1986, in *Coastal Disturbances,* p. 250.

19. Barbara Kachur, "Women Playwrights on Broadway: Henley, Howe, Norman, and Wasserstein," *Contemporary American Theatre,* ed. Bruce King (New York: St. Martin's Press, 1991), p. 28. Subsequent references are cited in the text.

20. Robert Brustein, "Don't Read This Review!" *New Republic* (May 2, 1983), 25.

21. Kachur, "Women Playwrights," p. 29; see also Katherine H. Burkman, "The Demeter Myth and Doubling in Marsha Norman's *'night, Mother,"* in Schlueter, ed., *Modern American Drama,* pp. 254–63.

22. Jeanie Forte, "Realism, Narrative, and the Feminist Playwright—A Problem of Reception," *Modern Drama* 32.1 (March 1989): 115–27; Dolan, "Bending Gender," p. 336. Subsequent references to Dolan are cited in the text.

23. Marsha Norman, *'night, Mother* (New York: Dramatists Play Service, 1983), p. 49. Subsequent references are cited in the text.

24. Nancy S. Love, "Politics and Voice(s): An Empowerment/Knowledge Regime," *Differences* 3.1 (1991): 86.

FOURTEEN

The Limits of African-American Political Realism: Baraka's *Dutchman* and Wilson's *Ma Rainey's Black Bottom*

Eric Bergesen and William W. Demastes

In 1964 LeRoi Jones/Amiri Baraka broke onto the American theatre scene with *Dutchman* and a series of lesser successes, all displaying the revolutionary fervor of an African American who possessed the growing racial self-esteem that would be a touchstone of the 1960s. Two decades later, in 1984, August Wilson's *Ma Rainey's Black Bottom* received its premiere, beginning a playwriting career that has resulted in Pulitzer prizes and other awards, marking Wilson as the foremost African-American playwright of the 1980s and '90s.

Together, these playwrights represent what Samuel A. Hay has identified as the two divergent trends of the African-American theatre agenda. In his 1994 work, *African American Theatre,* Hay observes an historical trend crystallized in the early twentieth century by the debate waged between William E. B. Du Bois and Alain Locke. According to Hay, Du Bois's "strictly political" school of theatre "required that the drama show people not only as they actually were but also as they wished to be."[1] Locke, on the other hand, wanted to shift the African-American theatre from a theatre of protest to an art theatre, demanding, as Hay observes, "believable characters and situations that sprang from the real life of the people" (p. 3). Hay reports that Locke "recommended that artists lay aside the status of beneficiary and ward, that they become collaborators and participants in American civilization" (p. 4). Du Bois, in turn, charged that artists following Locke's agenda "were being hoodwinked into stopping agitation on the African-American question" (p. 4), specifically arguing in his essay "Criteria of Negro Art" (1926), "I do not care a damn for any art that is not used for propaganda. But I do care when propaganda is confined to one side while the other is stripped and silent."[2]

Hay observes that Du Bois's theatre of protest evolved into a sermonizing brand of theatre, "treatises using highly recognizable stereotypes, plots, and themes" (p. 91), which influenced writers like James Baldwin, who later influenced Baraka, both of whom pursued a racially defined adversarial posture. Says Hay, "Baldwin demonstrates, for example, that racism resulted from white people's fear of and attraction to the sexuality of African Americans" (p. 92). And Baraka thematically focuses on much the same issue in *Dutchman*. What Wilson has written in the 1980s, however, does not focus exclusively on tensions between the races but balances on the dual focus of interracial tensions and tensions within the African-American community itself. While Baraka incorporates the politics of an awakening self-identity and oppositionally focused racial unity, Wilson utilizes the politics of self-reflection and self-adjustment, focusing on "inner" more fully than "outer" life, to use Du Bois's terms.

This difference in thematic focus calls attention to another fundamental distinction between the 1960s art of Baraka and the 1980s–90s art of Wilson. Given that Baraka subscribes to a more "strictly political" theatre agenda, following Du Bois, his engagement in a sort of "sermonizing" has led him progressively farther and farther away from a realist format, engaging instead in a more overtly author/messenger-controlled style of theatre, creating characters less "as they actually were" and more as *he* wished them to be. Wilson, on the other hand, less overtly engaged in "propagandizing" and more like Locke in inclination, has allowed his characters to develop organically without his intrusive hand revealing itself. In sum, realism suits Wilson in ways that it cannot completely suit Baraka.

Dutchman was written just prior to Baraka's full conversion to a political/ideological agenda[3] and was still very likely vulnerable to the agenda of the commercial theatre, which mandated the realist structure. Interestingly, something of the opposite is true of Wilson's first effort. With *Ma Rainey's Black Bottom*, Wilson created a realist product complicated by various staging demands, not the least of which was trying to find actors who were also accomplished musicians. Most of Wilson's later works have been increasingly marketable scripts of a standardly realist nature, requiring simple sets and small casts in keeping with the traditional American process of depicting home and family on the stage. With both of their first efforts, Baraka and Wilson created plays of a type they would to one degree or another eventually move away from, the result of a clearer understanding of their own intentions. But with these first efforts, we see, first, Du Bois and Locke in opposition and, second, the effectiveness of realism tested, put to use in order to fulfill these two agendas.

Despite being written twenty years apart, *Dutchman* and *Ma Rainey's Black Bottom* share several crucial similarities. Both plays confront the fragmented selfhoods of their characters, who are identified as products of competing discourses, and both plays comment on the difficulties facing black artists. Yet Wilson's frank concession that problems exist internally—within the African-American community—is a concession Baraka would criticize as undermining the central oppositional feature of race relations, that dominant, white culture is guilty of oppressing the black minority. A Pulitzer Prize–winning African-American predecessor to August Wilson, Charles Fuller, likewise adopted a double-focused and Lockean perspective in his playwriting, creating, among other works, *A Soldier's Play* in 1981. In his 1983 essay, "The Descent of Charlie Fuller into Pulitzerland and the Need for African-American Institutions," Baraka provided a vituperative response to a theatre and a generation willing to complicate the issue of race relations by implying that blacks, too, must accept some blame for their condition. Echoing Du Bois, Baraka asserts: "An oppressed people demand that all their resources be put to the service of liberating them, no matter what these resources are. Certainly art and culture must be seen in such a light. Either we are trying to fashion an art of liberation, whatever its forms, or we are creating an art that helps maintain our chains and slave status."[4] Fuller—and by extension Wilson—has diluted African-American resources, according to Baraka, and the result is a product that helps further to enslave rather than to liberate.

What Baraka seems unwilling to accept, however, is that this new generation in many ways sees itself as carrying on the activities

Baraka initiated. It appears this new generation is arguing that the Du Bois agenda that was so very necessary in the 1960s, an agenda of drawing simple battle lines in order to produce an introduction to cultural/racial injustice, can now be fleshed out (quite literally) as Locke advocated to reveal the multiplicity—strengths and weaknesses included—of a group of people who earlier needed to be portrayed as a collective unified against a common oppressor. For Fuller and Wilson, Baraka (and Du Bois's school of protest) successfully foregrounded the interracial opposition of the race issue; it was now up to this generation to take up Locke's position and reveal the internal complexities of the African-American camp. To know the opposition is to break down the oppositional barriers. Wilson explains his intentions:

> What I tried to do in *Ma Rainey,* and in all my work, is to reveal the richness of the lives of the people, who show that the largest ideas are contained by their lives, and that there is a nobility to their lives. Blacks in America have so little to make life with compared to whites, yet they do so with a certain zest, a certain energy that is fascinating because they make life out of nothing—yet it is charged and luminous and has all the qualities of anyone else's life. I think a lot of this is hidden by the glancing manner in which White America looks at Blacks, and the way Blacks look at themselves. Which is why I work a lot with stereotypes, with the idea of stripping away layer by layer the surface to reveal what is underneath—the real person, the whole person.[5]

Wilson and Fuller believe that race relations are at a sufficiently advanced stage to move to this second phase; disagreeing with this premise, Baraka refuses to give his blessings, arguing that this "second phase" is not part of a progression but rather of a regression. That Wilson and Fuller have been successful in the theatre of the 1980s when Baraka is no longer commercially productive may at first glance indicate that Fuller and Wilson were right; but one must recall, as Baraka would ask us to recall, that their successes largely indicate the approval of a theatre community comprised primarily of whites. Commercial success obviously does not necessarily entail success at any other level (though neither does it necessarily entail failure). Speaking of the Locke/Du Bois debate and specifically relevant to the Wilson-Fuller/Baraka debate, Hay rightly observes, "Within the particular context of their origins and development, neither school appears more obviously right or wrong, modern or outdated, than the other" (p. 5).

That African-American theatre in large part must depend on the approval of white audiences for survival is not a fresh insight. For example, in the 1928 article "The Dilemma of the Negro Author," James Weldon Johnson comments on the dialectic of aesthetics and politics that is the major source of debate in African-American theater: "I have sometimes thought it would be a way out, that the Negro author would be on surer ground and truer to himself, if he could disregard white America; if they could say to white America, 'What I have written, I have written. I hope you'll be interested and like it. If not I can't help it.' But it is impossible for a sane American Negro to write with total disregard for nine-tenths of the people of the United States. Situated as his own race is amidst and amongst them, their influence is irresistible."[6] Baraka's drama does politically distance, even alienate, itself from the white majority in ways that Wilson's does not. But the fact remains that even for Baraka (the early Baraka, that is) there appears to have been a realization that in order to "succeed," he would be forced to accede to the aesthetic principles of the white hegemony: he would need to produce realism—admittedly an altered, poetic brand of realism, but realism nonetheless. Likewise Wilson acceded to the same critical pressures, albeit much more willingly. In fact, it could arguably be observed that Baraka's post-1960s drama would have been much more openly received had he worked as hard to utilize the realist form as he did with *Dutchman,* rather than experimenting with alternative means of expression as he ultimately chose to do.

In *The Second Black Renaissance,* C. W. E. Bigsby recalls Baraka's 1963 directive: "A writer is committed to what is real and not to the sanctity of his Feelings." Bigsby adds that "there seems little doubt among black writers as to what constitutes the real. The pressure is to see literature as a social act, a moral gesture which, in a sense, requires the minimum mediation by the author."[7] Bigsby has identified in Baraka a central element of the realist form: minimal mediation on the author's part in favor of realistically acceptable probable flow of events/actions. Likewise, Wilson claims that he is subscribing to realism by stripping away stereotypes and thereby uncovering the real. Craft, of course, is very much evident in both playwrights' works, but the effort to minimize theatricality, to minimize personal interferences so that the "real" may reveal itself, is of central concern. Despite claims of objectivity, however, both playwrights reveal the highly personal nature of this form that hides behind claims of impersonality. From this apparent paradox, we come once again to the central element of realism, that it creates the *illusion* of noninterference. Realism ultimately allows each playwright to claim an objective position while creating a subjective agenda. As long as the realist illusion is maintained, the form serves its crafter well; even "propaganda," when realistically cloaked, seems less like an intransigent sermon and more like an almost reluctant confession of truth.

Both *Dutchman* and *Ma Rainey* use the blues as a focal point, but its separate applications in the two plays reveal the playwrights' separate agendas. Wilson offers the blues as a means by which African Americans deal with their troubled world, as he states in his notes on the play: "Thus they are laid open to be consumed by it [the blues]; its warmth and redress, its braggadocio and roughly poignant comments, its vision and prayer, which would instruct and allow them to reconnect, to reassemble and gird up for the next battle in which they would be both victim and the ten thousand slain."[8] While Wilson sees the blues as a source of strength, Baraka sees it as an outlet that releases an energy better directed elsewhere. The agitated Clay of *Dutchman,* coerced finally into speaking his true feelings, observes: "All the hip white boys scream for Bird. And Bird saying, 'up your ass, feeble-minded ofay! Up your ass.' And they sit there talking about the tortured genius of Charlie Parker. Bird would've played not a note of music if he just walked up to East Sixty-seventh Street and killed the first ten white people he saw. Not a note!"[9] In Baraka's world, the blues are a meager substitution for social justice.

It is far from coincidence that Baraka's and Wilson's visions of the blues parallel their distinct approaches to drama. Baraka very likely himself would not have written plays (for ofays) had he had the nerve to kill the first ten white people he saw, and he certainly would never have intentionally written an "aesthetic" play under any conditions. On the other hand, Wilson sees his plays as tools to help reconnect, reassemble, and gird up for the "next battle," one likely more subtle than the civil rights struggles of the 1960s but essential if the advances of the 1960s are to mean anything for future generations.

Both playwrights agree that the blues speaks two different languages, one of aesthetic import to whites that gives them the illusion of participating in black culture, the other speaking to blacks with minimal mediation and a high degree of significance, all under cover of the general aestheticism of the music. Likewise, it appears that both playwrights would argue that there are two layers at work in their plays, one that the white audiences will buy, and the subterranean other message that is accessible to the knowing minority, the black audiences. To this, Wilson would add that white audiences will find understanding as well, something that Baraka is apparently uninterested in doing—at least not as fully as Wilson intends.

Interestingly, if we follow through on the blues/drama comparison, it appears that Baraka would have to concede that his very effort at writing drama—rather than opting for more overt political action (murder or anything else)—is a doomed and nonrevolutionary act. The very act of stepping onto a stage before a white audience—as Bird has done with his music—is an act that misdirects revolutionary energies. In fact, Baraka gives voice to this view in *The Slave,* when his revolutionist, Walker Vessels, observes of himself: "The aesthete came long after all the things that really formed me. It was the easiest weight to shed. And I couldn't be merely a journalist . . . a social critic. No social protest. . . . [R]ight is in the act" (p. 75). Baraka himself has been true to Vessels's words in subsequent years, for, as Bigsby points out, in the past thirty years Baraka has shed all traces of the aesthete to such a degree as to practically exclude himself from the world of theater; according to Bigsby, however, Baraka "obviously believes that what he has lost—the imaginative brilliance of *Dutchman,* the subtle analysis of *The Slave* . . . is adequately compensated for by the historical significance of his new career [as activist]. At the moment it is difficult to endorse that view" (p. 246).

The LeRoi Jones/Amiri Baraka of *Dutchman,* however, was of another opinion (or was without an opinion) on the matter, very intentionally creating a marketable product that embraced the paradoxes of the blues, that was written to be performed in front of a white audience, and that delivered a call to black union even as he entertained his white audiences with a "thoughtful" treatise. Realism appears to have been the optimum vessel for the Jones/Baraka of *Dutchman,* though the play becomes more—or perhaps less—than he apparently intended as a result of that choice. If one looks closely at *Dutchman,* details begin to undermine the Baraka v. Wilson, 1960s v. 1980s oppositions so often assumed to exist. Andrzej Ceynowa, among others, has observed undeniable similarities between *Dutchman* and Edward Albee's starkly realist 1959–60 masterpiece, *The Zoo Story.* But Ceynowa downplays the similarities, arguing that Baraka sought for *Dutchman* "a mere vehicle—sufficiently known to the public to be recognized as such—for carrying a play plotted on an almost purely intellectual, abstract level."[10] The central problem with downplaying this crucial similarity, however, is that one tends to overlook the fact that in the very effort to emulate Albee's popular form, Baraka has fallen into the realist form's trap and runs the risk of losing "didactic" control of his play. In the very effort realistically to minimize authorial mediation, Baraka opened himself to losing central thematic control of his entire play. The result, it could be argued, was the very likely unintentional creation of an American theatrical/*aesthetic* masterpiece.

Simply put, *Dutchman* is open to Baraka's own criticism of Fuller and the theatre of the 1980s. Baraka's confrontational design depends on the very linkage between author's oppositional thought/idea and the play's spectacle/event, a design ultimately diluted in *Dutchman.* To connect his idea with the stage event would require, for example, that Clay be strictly a victim and Lula be strictly an oppressor, the voice of "White America." Ceynowa herself asks: "Why is Baraka on her side, letting her ask all the right questions and fire bull's-eye shots into Clay's defenses? How plausible is it to suppose that a nascent Black Revolutionary Nationalist would allow a character of his who ultimately reduces to a white racist to pass judgment on a Black brother, even one as confused as Clay?" (p. 16). It appears that Baraka's decision to abide by realist standards—resulting in the creation of a flesh-and-blood antagonist—has led him to develop a three-dimensional character, with vices *and* virtues, more fully than his politics would otherwise have preferred. Realism has here perhaps defeated politics and resulted in a play that transcends the didacticism that would inform much of Baraka's later efforts.

Ceynowa's answer to her own above question is that Lula and Clay inhabit many "subroles," pieces of fragmented identities, an argument that supports the claim that the play does much more than merely serve Baraka's political agenda. Ceynowa indicates that Lula and Clay are informed by a common discourse: Clay "draws from the same reservoir of clichés and stereotypes from which Lula seems to be drawing hers. Their minds seem to focus on the same materials, function on the same wavelength" (p. 17). During the verbal territorial assaults each character launches, Clay begins to reveal his internal conflicts about his own identity. But this process is an extended one and is arguably the strongest element of the play, though far less sensational than the conclusion. In order to create a realistically conceived confrontation, Baraka was forced to create a convincing Lula, a Lula who verbally defeats Clay well before she stabs and kills him.

Clay's internal conflicts, brought on by Lula's verbal precision, guarantee his demise, at which point Baraka's political agenda comes into play. But at precisely this moment Baraka abandons his realist *Zoo Story* model. For example, the moment Albee has Peter die, Albee allows Jerry to run away, resulting in an ambiguous ending but adhering to an action consistent with realistic expectations: a person in Peter's position very likely *would* run away at this point. Baraka, however, shifts into expressionistic[11] high gear at the moment Lula decides Clay is to die, placing a heavy hand on the heretofore balanced, realist scales and elevating the murder from being an individual act inflicted by one individual upon another individual to being a collective, conspiratorial moment. The other, nameless white subway riders arise, spurred by an unspoken collective consciousness, and help Lula to dispose of the body. The subway has become the Flying Dutchman of Doom, and the appearance of the young Negro at the play's end solidifies the message, suggesting that the incident between Lula and Clay is not an isolated one, but a pattern initiated and encouraged by a racially motivated, collective urge toward genocide.

The realist exchange between Lula and Clay throughout most of the play is overtaken by the play's expressionistic conclusion, wherein individual actors no longer portray individual characters but become ghostlike automata energized by a spirit not accommodated by an individualist, realist ontology. It is a conclusion that transforms the play's earlier exchanges to a conflict not between two individuals but between two hostile and incompatible collective visions.

But even with this overt authorial mediation apparently warning the black minority against the genocidal tendencies of the white majority, the play still takes on an interpretive life of its own, again very much in opposition to the message/intent of the later (1983) Baraka. Bigsby, for example, chooses art rather than racism or politics as the key to the play: "*Dutchman* is a reflexive work. At its heart is a consideration of the artistic process, a debate over the legitimacy of sublimating social anguish into aesthetic form. It addresses itself to a central problem of the black artist who is alive to the evasion which may be implied in the act of writing" (p. 239). The act of writing, as well as singing the blues, is an act of evading social action. Clay comes close to turning the tables, only to relent at the last moment, because he'd rather be "safe with my words, and no deaths, and clean hard thoughts urging me to new conquests . . . My people. They don't need me to claim them" (p. 35). The Baraka of 1964 is himself something of an evader, though Baraka's more direct confrontation of racial polarities limits the extent of his "evasion" compared to that of Wilson, who has embraced the liberal aesthetic criteria that have made him a successful playwright. Baraka has allowed his art—*Dutchman*—to outdistance his political agenda, implicating blacks as partly responsible for their own victimization in a way that Baraka's later stated political agenda does not condone. The discrepancy between what one sees in *Dutchman* and what one reads in "The Descent of Charlie Fuller into Pulitzerland" may be the result of an artist/activist who has grown and has crystallized his opinions about art, which would finally condemn his own *Dutchman*. Or it may be that the realist roots of *Dutchman* overtook the young polemicist Jones, causing him unwittingly to create a Lula that his politics would not allow but that his realist aesthetic principles required. While the realism of *Dutchman* blurs the simple dichotomies that Baraka's "Descent" attempts to make between his 1960s art and the works of the 1980s, one must concede that Baraka's plays move much more dangerously close to revolution than do Fuller's or Wilson's works, since, as Baraka states, "the victim is getting ready to turn the tables."[12]

Realism, on the other hand, works extremely well for Wilson, who lacks any overt agitprop motives. Invariably setting his plays in the past, he does not allow for the possibility of turning the tables, which could be another reason for his mainstream success—his plays do not threaten his white audiences. His goal is to portray the black experience as having both racially/culturally distinct features and universally identifiable and comprehensible characteristics. Wilson's art simultaneously portrays the black experience as well as black experiences—the collective and the individual.

In the text of *Ma Rainey's Black Bottom,* Wilson introduces each band member with highly individual but also abstract descriptions. For example, Toledo "understands and recognizes that its [the piano's] limitations are an extension of himself," and he "is self-taught but misunderstands and misapplies his knowledge" (p. 20). Toledo's "Africanism" is an intellectual construct on his part that serves as a barrier between himself and the other band members. Toledo's answer to the dominance of whites is found in his theory on stew: "Now, what's the colored man gonna do with himself? That's what we waiting to find out. But first we gotta know we the leftovers" (p. 57). His assertion that "the problem ain't with the white man" (p. 58) demands a retreat from the position held by black revolutionaries. While Toledo does admit the obvious, that white oppression exists, he places the blame for this oppression on other blacks, embodying the assimilationist perspective of the black middle class, which feels that the backward element among blacks is a hindrance to progress. Baraka calls this kind of character the "black-hating negro," of which Sergeant Waters in Fuller's *A Soldier's Play* is another example. Toledo's subjectivity is composed of several often contradictory discourses, an identity that does not lend itself to the kind of unproblematic and scathingly negative interpretation that Baraka employs in divining Fuller's message in *A Soldier's Play:* "Let's look at the scorecard: black folk symbol = dead; black folk symbol–hating negro (openly pathological) = dead; black militant = courtmartialed, locked up" (p. 53). Wilson does resist this kind of signification by creating complex, conflicted characters such as Toledo in an effort to produce a more varied and therefore real black experience.

Baraka notes in his critique of Fuller that middle-class blacks (using Mao's label of "middle forces") know something is wrong but don't know what to do about it. As a result, such people can occasionally be drawn in by reactionary forces during reactionary times. Levee is such an aspiring middle-class black,[13] created to reveal a depth highlighted by paradox that closely parallels Baraka's Clay. Levee "lacks fuel for himself and is somewhat of a buffoon. But it is an intelligent buffoonery, calculated to shift control of the situation to where he can grasp it" (p. 23). Levee is like Clay in that he also assumes the appearance and mannerisms of white artists. In Clay's case, Lula tests him in order to discover what lies under the surface. Bigsby's observations about Clay could easily apply to Levee as well: "As a putative white man, he is wholly knowable, so that Lula can accurately provide him with details about his life and aspirations; as a black man in disguise, he is an enigma and as such, a threat" (p. 238). Clay uses his "enigmatic" strength momentarily to beat Lula into submission, but, says Bigsby, "His anger is deflected into language, his bitterness is displaced into an aesthetic code, and his anarchic potential subsumed in poetic structures" (p. 238), all of which ensures his destruction. Baraka's message seems to be that the black middle class must be led by the masses, not the other way around. Wilson, however, avoids such an ideological showdown. Levee is also "knowable" as a "putative white man," who could also at least momentarily reveal his threatening powers as a black man in disguise. But Wilson does not insist that Levee confront his white oppressors nor that he retreat into his music or "aesthetic code." Rather, Wilson has Levee stab Toledo after Sturdyvant shatters Levee's dream to start his own band because Toledo was unfortunate enough to step on Levee's shoe at the wrong time.

The arbitrariness of the violent act is another softening technique employed by Wilson, only indirectly linking the crime with white oppression. But what likely would concern Baraka even more than the randomness of the murder—a point, however, also related to the murder—involves the fact that Ma senses Levee's ambition and arranges to have him dismissed, ostensibly for causing trouble, but on a deeper level, Ma's ego will not tolerate another artist in the band. As Holly Hill observes: "Levee's swing version of the title song wins the studio boss's approval and Ma's contempt: he is the first example of many in Wilson's work of how a black person is thwarted not simply by whites and/or himself but by other blacks."[14] Baraka's categorical guidelines identify Wilson's sensitivity to the subtle forces at play in *Ma Rainey* as part of the rhetoric of black self-hate. Here the very real, individual emotions of jealousy and thoughts of self-preservation presented by Wilson would be construed by Baraka as representing an abstracting "type" that ultimately is counterproductive for Baraka's political agenda. As has been the case with virtually all of the conflict between Wilson the playwright and Baraka the art-political theorist, one must determine if the probable forces of the realist method are preferable to perhaps less probable—and therefore less realistic—political manipulation that might make Ma Rainey the mother-defender of *all* her brood, even to the point of possibly sacrificing her own self-interest. Simply put, Wilson refuses to reinforce the myth that blacks are united behind a common front.

Baraka's interest in presenting the "pathology created by oppression" (p. 52) is likewise downplayed by Wilson. Early in the play, Ma, Sylvester, and Dussie Mae enter with the police officer who was going to haul them in for threatening a cab driver. The actual offstage events are not entirely clear. After a minor car accident, Ma, Sylvester, and Dussie Mae tried to get into a cab. The cab driver refused to drive them and tried to hasten their exit with a baseball bat. Sylvester apparently made a counterthreat, after which Ma may or may not have knocked the cabbie down. The police officer has accepted the white cabbie's word but finally agrees to bring Ma and company by the studio after Ma tells him how important she is. The officer receives his reward, a bill slipped into his hand from Mr. Irvin, clearing up the whole incident.

Naturally, not all black people have a Mr. Irvin to stand up for them when dealing with the police, but the situation in which Ma finds herself typifies the kind of oppression Baraka would demand be highlighted. The incident, however, largely offers Ma a sensational entrance and secondarily works as an undeveloped reminder that dangers linger outside the supposedly safe haven of the studio. The point is then is dropped, though one cannot help feeling a sort of "residue" of the event linger throughout the play. Subtlety, however, is at work; it does not become a focus, as Baraka would doubtless prefer.

At still another level, Wilson utilizes overt devices to depict racial conflict. The set instructions for the play call for the placement of the music studio on the foreground of the stage. In the back, separated from the studio by a soundproof glass wall, lies the control room. From this vantage point, the white producer and manager can oversee the black musicians in the studio. Visually, the set suggests a hierarchy of power that cannot go unnoticed by the audience. This separation pervasively frames the ensuing events so that the infighting among the band members cannot be detached from the specter of white domination that looms in the background. Wilson again does not impose a racial agenda as strenuously as Baraka does, but he displaces the emphasis on social issues from the textual field to the physical performance of the work. Thus Baraka privileges the linguistic element of theatre, with its ability to shape meaning in a more direct manner, over Wilson's less invasive structural approach, which employs stage movements and the visual to create condensation points— elements that can represent several ideas at once and that communicate through a subtle alliance of several signifying systems.

Wilson reserves the end of the play to provide the most concentrated suggestion of a "pathology caused by oppression"—Toledo's murder. But once again, Wilson sidesteps sending too strong a message by giving the event random or incidental significance. Though the murder raises the question of Levee's motivation—stemming from oppression—Wilson offers no clearly linear, one-to-one answer, blurring the "message." Killing Toledo *may* imply self-hate, but what if a white man (or an Asian American or a Native American) had stepped on Toledo's shoe? Is it not possible that Levee would have lashed out at any "offender" at this point, regardless of race or ethnicity, a natural result of impotent rage seeking an outlet? The mere possibility of these options dilutes any possible direct message of racial self-hate. So while Baraka would likely have found a more direct way to make the connections, Wilson does not. The result is that the ending has been criticized from many camps. But close scrutiny at very least should suggest, as Hill has concluded, that "the ending is a logical growth from character and event" (p. 91). Wilson has striven to be true to the realist conditions with which he began the play. The fact that Levee's explosiveness and his inability to engage in meaningful action lead him to counterproductive violence is not at all an unlikely string of events. This ending does not adhere to a clearly enumerated, positive political agenda, but it does adhere to the probable behavior of a human being confronted with his own total humiliation. And, above all, one must remember that Levee is a human.

Toledo and Levee emerge in something far less than overt or didactic fashion as victims of the dominant white power relations. If one converted the events of the play to Baraka's scorecard, it would not be a result Baraka would approve of: black folk symbol = dead; black folk symbol–hating negro = arrested, locked up for life; everyone else is unscathed. Yet *Ma Rainey's Black Bottom* does indict the system that led to its conclusion. It does so by asking the audience to take some critical leaps: Why does Levee stab Toledo? How do/can blacks gain power? Does the dominant power structure operate in a similar manner today as it did in 1927? That these questions can be reflected upon and can be answered in a way that illustrates the "pathology of the oppressed" is a testament to the richness of Wilson's craft.

Baraka believes that the correlation must be direct and strong, which is the reason Baraka prefers clearly articulated battle lines in his attack on white culture. Nonetheless, Wilson produces a work rife with social revolt while sacrificing nothing artistically. The result is a play that is neither didactic nor polemical, but political nonetheless. It may not offer the full direction a Baraka would demand, but it places before the public issues deserving attention and thought. As Wilson himself insists, "All art is political. It serves a purpose. All of my plays are political. . . . [But] theatre doesn't have to be agitprop."[15]

Baraka's political goals seem to have been undermined by the very decision to use realism in *Dutchman*. Conforming to demands of probability and general credibility, *Dutchman* takes on a life of its own, brought back to its political purpose only by the play's conversion to more fully mediated expressionistic techniques. In the very effort to appear to minimize mediation, Baraka seems in fact to have given up control until the last possible moment. For Wilson, however, the appearance of giving up rights of mediation has resulted in a product that does have its political effect. It is a complex webbing of character and events that reveals an insistence to "eye" the world as one eyes the stage, asking the audience to see what Wilson sees in the world: diversity between *and* within races. Baraka, perhaps less trusting of his audience—and perhaps rightly less trusting—prefers clear and unambiguous presentations of belief. Though he seemed to discover the difficulties attendant to trying to control a realist dramatic event, in *Dutchman* at least, he found a solution by concluding a richly evocative, realist play between two characters with an incantation beyond realism. Finally, what seems most clearly evident is that realism better serves Locke's "aesthetic" African-American theatre agenda than it does Du Bois's "political" agenda.

Notes

1. Samuel A. Hay, *African American Theatre: An Historical and Critical Analysis* (New York: Cambridge UP, 1994), p. 3. Subsequent references are cited in the text.

2. Qtd. in Hay, *African American Theatre*, p. 5.

3. Hay observes that beginning in 1965, "Baraka embarked on finding an ideology for his planned new drama" and shortly thereafter actually "discovered and imposed an ideology on the drama" (p. 96). With *Dutchman*, we see that direction beginning to appear but not with the intentional rigor of his subsequent work.

4. Amiri Baraka, "The Descent of Charlie Fuller into Pulitzerland and the Need for African-American Institutions," *Black American Literature Forum* 17.2 (Summer 1983): 53. Unless otherwise noted, references from Baraka, except for playtexts, are from this article and are cited in the text.

5. Kim Powers, "An Interview with August Wilson," *Theater* 16 (Fall/Winter 1984): 52.

6. James Weldon Johnson, "The Dilemma of the Negro Author," *American Mercury* 15 (Dec. 1928): 481.

7. C. W. E. Bigsby, *The Second Black Renaissance* (Westport, Conn.: Greenwood Press, 1980), p. 38.

8. August Wilson, *Ma Rainey's Black Bottom* (New York: New American Library, 1985), p. xvi. Subsequent references are cited in the text.

9. Amiri Baraka, *Dutchman*, in *Dutchman and The Slave* (New York: Morrow, 1964), p. 35. Subsequent references will be cited in the text.

10. Andrzej Ceynowa, "The Dramatic Structure of *Dutchman*," *Black American Literature Forum* 17.1 (Spring 1983): 16. Subsequent references are cited in the text.

11. The term *expressionistic* is here used very deliberately and formally. J. L. Styan, in *Modern Drama in Theory and Practice*, vol. 3: *Expressionism and Epic Theatre* (London: Cambridge UP, 1981) observes that the realist character "had too many memories . . . to be able to 'externalize' himself; by contrast, the expressionist actor was free to pick out [here Styan quotes Paul Kornfeld] 'the essential attributes of reality,' and to be 'nothing but a representative of thought, feeling, fate' " (p. 6). With the insertion of the puppetlike chorus (another expressionist component), Baraka has signaled a performance shift from realist individuality to expressionist universality, and in the process has assigned the actress portraying Lula the duty of adjusting her acting style accordingly. The result is a shift from apparent objectivity on the author's part (the goal of realism) to a "kind of scripted dream" (p. 4) of an admittedly highly subjective nature (the goal of expressionism).

12. Qtd. in Bigsby, *Renaissance*, p. 243.

13. Ma Rainey is a highly complex character whose problematic identity Wilson does not fully pursue. Though perhaps more in control of her destiny than is Levee (and therefore perhaps more interesting a character), she and Levee do share the important trait of aspiring to middle-class status. But perhaps because Ma Rainey is an actual historical figure invested with factual events that control her characterization, Wilson invests more dramatic energy in Levee than in Ma Rainey, very likely with an eye toward dramatic resolution not fully in his hands if he pursued Ma Rainey as the central character. In other words, Wilson could not have Ma Rainey, for example, kill Toledo, whereas creating a fictional character like Levee allows Wilson far greater liberties. That Ma Rainey and Levee are of a similar type, however, is an important factor. With the above in mind, this essay's discussion of *Ma Rainey's Black Bottom* will operate under the assumption that Levee is the central character.

14. Holly Hill, *Black Theater into the Mainstream* (New York: St. Martin's Press, 1991), p. 89.

15. Qtd. in David Savran, *In Their Own Words: Contemporary American Playwrights* (New York: Theatre Communications Group, 1988), p. 304.

FIFTEEN

Anti-Theatricality and American Ideology: Mamet's Performative Realism

Michael L. Quinn

David Mamet's dramatic writing, for all its apparent seriousness, and the artistic enthusiasm its effects have aroused, has not been very thoroughly explained.[1] That it seems conventionally realistic helps to make it seem familiar, and some of the best criticism of Mamet has been an attempt to recuperate the value of an artistically fluent and culturally sensitive realism.[2] But from the standpoint of meaning, Mamet's apparent lack of a representational strategy—that is, his realism—tends to make his work seem even more opaque. Simple representational realistic explanations of Mamet are too easy, if the vividness of the dramatic effect and the intensity of the intellectual controversies that the plays have aroused are also to be taken seriously by poststructuralist critics. I argue that Mamet's plays use a specific realistic rhetoric to strike a deep but somewhat inaccessible chord in American intellectuals—inaccessible because the critics themselves often participate in the same ideological processes that form the matrix of Mamet's work.[3] Realism is not in this case representational but expressive, focusing on performed actions rather than mimesis, and making judgments of truth a matter of active construction rather than of comparison with an *a priori* reality. As Mamet notes in his own essay on the subject, "In discarding the armor of realism, he or she [the artist] accepts the responsibility of making every choice in light of specific meaning, of making every choice assertive rather than protective."[4]

Mamet's self-proclaimed iconoclasm is a kind of doctrine informed by a system of ritualized liberal dissent in which membership in the national tradition depends upon a declared rejection of the current state of cultural affairs. The principal theorist of this perspective is Sacvan Bercovitch, who points out not only how this pattern manifests itself in a set of texts from the Puritans through the foundational documents of American government to the New England Renaissance, but also how this narrative of American Puritan culture is a deliberate creation of twentieth-century literary historians like Perry Miller and F. O. Matthiessen.[5] Perhaps the crucial figure in this tradition is Emerson, who "had decided, on reconsidering the attacks on individualism, that the remedy was not to abandon it, but to draw out its potential,"[6] that is, the link between individual self-creation and the collective creation of American community. Bercovitch points out that such a closure is virtually impossible, but in working through its visionary demands, American artists have used this political paradox as a basis for constantly renewed visions of authentic American creativity. Bercovitch's thesis also points out how Dennis Carroll's reading of Mamet as an artist of "dichotomy" and "paradox," cohering "in the personality he projects" can be joined with C. W. E. Bigsby's attempts to locate Mamet within an American cultural landscape.[7]

In theatrical history, this pattern of community formation through dissent—the rejection of American culture in the name of American values—is very common. (Consider, for example, the Group Theatre.) Such a cultural pattern, applied in an analysis of Mamet's favorite ideas and artistic techniques, can help to establish a critical context for understanding Mamet's work while also explaining something about his embattled but enthusiastic reception. Americans, like anyone working in the context of a naturalized ideology, often find it very difficult to undertake a culturally based analysis of their own literature; what passes for such criticism usually tends to participate in the politics of empowering denunciation, not theorizing its own implication in the pattern. In Mamet's case, the ideologically effective aspects of dramatic construction are often simply taken for something bold, hardheaded, and realistic, rather than as gestures in a standard romantic ritual of American intellectual culture.

Only a few steps are necessary for a writer like Mamet to position himself in the role of a dissenting, revolutionary artist with a unique perspective. One of the first steps is to identify some orthodoxy that can be decried as ruinous, or perhaps un-American. In Mamet's case, this orthodoxy tends to follow the pattern outlined by his intellectual hero, Thorstein Veblen, of excoriating a greedy bourgeoisie—the class that requires conformity to a way of doing business and administering justice that serves those in power, and ruins the life of the ordinary man.[8] In theatre history, this kind of dissent usually finds its object in Broadway.[9] The decadent commercial theatre is then indicted in a vituperative jeremiad—laden with the rhetoric of the pulpit—which also often outlines a visionary path to redemption through the restoration of neglected moral values: truth, authenticity, selfless commitment to art, reason, etc.[10] In Mamet's case, such public comments are easy to find, especially in his essays and speeches. In "Decadence," for example, he decries the corruption of what he sees as the current dominance of a "theater of good intentions":

> We are in the midst of a vogue for the truly decadent in art— for that which is destructive rather than regenerative, self-referential rather than outward-looking, elitist rather than popular. This decadent art is elitist because it cannot stand on its merits as a work of personal creation. Instead it appeals to a prejudice or predilection held mutually with the audience.
>
> This appeal is political, and stems from the political urge, which is the urge to control the actions of others. It is in direct opposition to the artistic urge, which is to express oneself regardless of the consequences. I cite "performance art," "women's writing" . . . badges proclaiming a position.
>
> Plays which deal with the unassailable investigate nothing and express nothing save the desire to investigate nothing.
>
> It is incontrovertible that deaf people are people, too; that homosexuals are people, too; that it is unfortunate to be deprived of a full and happy life by illness or accident; that it is sobering to grow old.
>
> These events . . . equally befall the Good and the Bad individual. They are not the result of conscious choice and so do not bear on the character of the individual. They are not the fit subject of drama, as they do not deal with the human capacity for choice. Rather than uniting the audience in a universal experi-

ence, they are invidious. They split the audience into two camps; those who like the play and those who hate homosexuals (deaf people, old people, paraplegics, etc.).[11]

Mamet's grouping of banal social realists and the formalist avant-garde may have seemed in 1986 like an unlikely orthodoxy, though it has been repeated often in recent years in denunciations of the "politically correct."[12] What matters for ritual purposes, though, is merely Mamet's ability to construct the current scene as moribund, in a kind of statement that is not argued but rather performed. J. L. Austin would call such a ritualized statement an "illocutionary speech act," a kind of "performative" speech that constitutes some state of affairs through linguistic action; other examples would be things like promises, oaths, and declarations, including the political documents that form the bases of governments.[13] Despite Mamet's often acute consciousness of ritual behaviors, especially within the American contexts of holidays and masculine activities, he does not seem particularly sensitive to his own use of the jeremiad as a tool for his political empowerment.

The second requirement for Bercovitch's ritual of dissent is the construction of a unique individuality, a narrative of genesis and personal growth. Mamet's exceptionalist character is again constructed most clearly in his essays: in personal reflections, descriptions of his unhappy childhood at home, the idealizing influence of Old Chicago, his part-time jobs, his Slavic-Jewish heritage, and comments on the unique progress of his career. In one of the notes from *The Cabin* on Chicago radio, Mamet shows considerable cultural awareness about constructing his personality in this creative political context: "The idea in the air was that culture was what we, the people, did. The idea was—and is—that we were *surrounded* by culture. It was not alien to us. It was what the people did and thought and sang and wrote about. The idea was the particularly Chicagoan admixture of the populist and the intellectual. The model, the Hutchins model, the Chicago model of the European freethinker, was an autodidact: a man or woman who so loved the world around him or her that he or she was moved to investigate it further—either by creating works of art or by appreciating those works."[14]

Many of the exceptional characteristics that Mamet claims for himself, which have found expression in his plays, are tied to one aspect or another of what seem to be perfectly ordinary experiences. Yet the conviction remains in Mamet that the unique combination of experiences—the history of choices and conditions that produces his artistic consciousness—is solely his own, as fully individual as are his inherent human talents. This approach to identity is not representational but expressive; people constitute themselves not by thinking of themselves as copies but rather by thinking of themselves as constituted through actions based in their innate desires and qualities. These actions can then take on a pronounced cultural charge. For example, Mamet often seems so fully identified with the Chicago of the past that his nostalgia strains credibility; though born in 1947, he writes with an acute consciousness of his own "aging," and as if he were himself present at crucial cultural moments like the 1934 Century of Progress Exhibition. Mamet, then, claims exceptional status primarily because he thinks of himself as though he has come from an earlier time: the grittier, more inventive, and more communal Chicago before 1968, the time between Al Capone and Richard Daley (when Chicago writers like Carl Sandburg routinely claimed to represent America, too, by embodying its energy or its history of bootstrap immigrant prosperity). The absurdity of Mamet's wish for this subjectivity only emphasizes its constructed quality, which is even more evident when he folds into it—sometimes even in messianic terms—the ideal of the autodidact and the romantic writer. The title of his second book of essays, *Some Freaks,* is Mamet's way of identifying those individuals, like himself, who are leaders because they "do not fit the norm."[15] Mamet's Chicago is as fully laden with American ideology as was the New England of Henry David Thoreau, whom Mamet imitates in his Vermont cabin.

Typically the American narrative of dissent ushers in a new vision of community, often a political ideal retrieved through personal struggle or travel to a strange place. Mamet treats his ordinary experiences, in French Canada, in a neighborhood pool hall, or at a part-time job, as if they were such struggles or journeys; in any case, they supposedly offered life lessons. In Mamet's life today this ideal community might be Cabot, Vermont, the village where he sometimes lives and writes, or the neighborhood of his Boston row house, before the area was ruined by division into rental units. In Mamet's version of theatre history, such an ideal scene might be something like the Group Theatre's retreat, or the long day in the Slavyansky Bazaar when the Moscow Art Theatre was conceived. But Mamet's broader political vision is never quite so concretely stated; it seems to be conventionally Jeffersonian, though perhaps even more nearly Rousseauian: an American community where politicians tell the truth, friendship is sacred, simple customs are cherished, and men can be men.[16] This sort of sustaining vision underlies many of the plays like an ideological subtext, a wish tacitly shared among sympathetic characters. Yet Mamet's America is rarely dramatized as a place that might actually exist; rather, Mamet's realism is a coming to terms with the difficulty—even the impossibility—of living such ideals.[17]

If the artist and the American individual are free to constitute themselves, to create their visions through the simple action of declaring or performing them, of acting them out, then the negative aspect of Mamet's realism, its paradoxical ideological unveiling, is the dramatic debunking of such constitutive gestures as mistakes of confidence, as willful illusions that the current state of the world cannot sustain. Realism in this context is not a scientific avant-garde, nor even, as Mamet himself notes, is it quite a "scenic truth" in the same way as it was for Stanislavsky; rather, the realistic attitude becomes a skeptical, often physical control on dreams of a better life.[18] This is not exactly the same kind of realism that Jonas Barish would call an "anti-theatrical prejudice," though Mamet often indicts the theatrical when it is abused as a rhetoric of deception in everyday life.[19] Mamet's constant concern in his writings on the theatre, and in his explanations of his style, is with *action*, which he theorizes as a constitutive, authentic movement of the mind and body, as opposed to a less vital, static or mimetic way of living and showing life. In this regard the Method actor is even, for Mamet, an emblem of virtuous life: "When, once again, actors are cherished and rewarded who bring to the stage or the screen generosity, desire, *organic life*, actions performed freely—without desire for reward or fear of either censure or misunderstanding—that will be one of the first signs that the tide of our introverted, unhappy time has turned and that we are once again eager and prepared to look at ourselves."[20] To the extent that Mamet's theatre of action is an attempt not merely to *represent* but actually to *constitute* his vision of a better life, the theatre has special powers. Theatre in such a view does not consciously imitate poetry, but the enactment of vital dialogue might attempt to perform the poetry of life. Theatricality exists in this case in a strange double bind; it can express the truth of things and events, but it can also be used to hide that truth through fantasies or lies. Such an emphasis on action may explain Mamet's preference for a small group of loyal performers, which keeps offstage dramatic intrigue at a minimum.

Consequently the theatrical act within Mamet's work is also, most often, an act of everyday deception, a risky move to create an illusive advantage. Mamet's theatre constitutes an orthodox, illusively realistic world of the play, full of lies, and then these must eventually come undone in an even "more real" scene of social debunking, physical constraint and/or theatrical undercutting. There are a few basic kinds of theatrical scenes in Mamet's work, and these are usually central to what is at stake in the drama. Once these are outlined, I think the anti-theatrical, ideological flow of Mamet's realistic writing will be fairly clear—a dissenting American anti-theatricality, designed to affirm his characters' self-constitutive, performative actions but also to reveal the destructiveness of lies.

THE BUSINESS SCAM

Probably the most famous kind of theatricality within Mamet's dramas, continuing through the filmscript for *Hoffa*, concerns the intrigues of businessmen, whether their purposes are within or, most often, outside of the laws of commerce.[21] In the former case, Mamet seems to criticize the conventional structure of capitalism from the top down; those with the most power and money tend to be able to create situations in which those with the least must scheme for an advantage. When these same ordinary people choose to live outside the law, Mamet's implied criticism falls more directly on the illusions they produce to dupe their victims. In *American Buffalo*, Donny Dubrow is poised on the brink of such a choice. He begins his scheme with Bobby to steal the coin collection as a kind of fantasy, a way of working together with his protégé on an imaginary project that seems to promise more than the poor prospects of his own junk store. Teach forces the scenario, taking the play of theft seriously, and consequently obliging Donny to betray his friend for the sake of the plan.

Glengarry Glen Ross similarly makes financial desperation over into a problem of identity, but it carries the deception two steps further. Shelly "The Machine" Levene built his good name on his ability to close real estate deals, but by the time the action of the play begins, he has failed to maintain the sales record that his self-esteem and his livelihood require. In the first scene Levene asks the office manager, Williamson, to accept a bribe so that he can get better client lists and begin to make more actual sales. Williamson refuses. The second scene does not include Levene, but in it Moss proposes to Aaronow the robbery scam that Levene will eventually enact. The third scene, the shortest of the first act, is an exemplary performance by the most successful agent, Roma, showing how the ordinary business of Levene's firm, the sale of swampland in Florida to gullible investors, requires a rhetorically intense and emotionally exhausting confidence game. In the second act Levene has already robbed the office of its client list and in the meantime believes he has convinced an unsuspecting buyer into signing for "eight units of Mountain View"; he thinks he has reclaimed his identity, but he must sustain himself by performing his own innocence as the break-in is being investigated. In a crucial play-within-a-play scene with Roma, Levene shows the audience that he can still pitch a scam, the two managing to improvise a scene that is designed to put a client off until his check has cleared the bank. As Roma tells Levene, "That shit you were slinging on my guy today was so good . . . it . . . it was, and, excuse me, 'cause it isn't even my place to say it. It was admirable . . . it was the old stuff."[22] It is after playing the old game with Roma, and defending the game itself, that Levene eventually lets slip his crucial knowledge of the contract he saw during the break-in—a lapse of concentration in his double game that causes him to get caught in the robbery scam. A second revelation, that his supposed sale was to a legally incompetent client, only compounds his failure. Levene's performances, as a salesman and an actor in fraud, are what constitute his identity, but when he pushes the illusion a step too far, threatening the profit structure of the business, his whole world comes down around him. Realism in this play is a matter of listening closely, following cues and sustaining the illusion of a seamless performance; when the theatrical self breaks down, reality is felt most acutely by Levene as an absence of achievement, for which he must pay with suffering.

The obverse of *Glengarry Glen Ross* is *House of Games,* Mamet's film about a con game designed to bilk a fortune from a wealthy psychologist, Margaret Ford. After an opening sequence suggesting that psychoanalysis is itself an elaborate scam, Margaret goes to aid a troubled client by confronting Mike, the lender of the con artists, at the House of Games, a gambling room. She is quickly drawn in, ends up teamed with Mike in a poker game, and guarantees his bet; when he loses, she is about to write a check when she notices that the winning player's gun is a water pistol. The first plan to bilk her is revealed. The primary problem for Margaret in the film is the problem of depth, of how many layers of playing a scam might involve, and how many of them she is supposed to see through; the criminals here are performers, who can show or conceal the act of their own playing, so long as they are the only ones who know the limit of the play. The first play with the water pistol, like so many others, turns out to be a setup for the big sting on Margaret, in which she fronts eighty thousand dollars to Mike to replace money supposedly borrowed from the mob and lost. Margaret is sufficiently fascinated by Mike's con games to play with him, to be seduced by him, and to be so hurt by his ultimate betrayal that she murders him. In the end it is Mike who does not know the real limit of playing; when she threatens to shoot him, he calls her bluff, only to discover that the threat was real. Even then he will not stop playing, saying after the second shot, "Thank you, sir, may I have another?"[23]

The world in *House of Games* is as completely theatricalized as in the best modern metadramas, and the problem of authentic action within it becomes the problem of which reality to affirm, which of the performances to accept as true. What Margaret understands, which Mike does not, is that death—not just cash, and not realistic illusion—is only a limit of intentional performance for the one who dies; with his dying breath Mike pleads that he himself never *killed* anyone. In a world so full of lies, the metaphysical distinction is mere hairsplitting. Evil characters, as well as good ones, are constituted by their performances, and Margaret Ford, renowned psychologist, is no exception in Mamet's world. The thrust of realism in such a context, as with *The Verdict* or *The Postman Always Rings Twice,* may be the apparently simple matter of finding out the lie, finding out the theatrical pretense, though this may also eventually involve breaking down the characters' fictions through courtroom melodrama, placing speech under the additional obligations of an oath.

HIDING OUT/UNDERCOVER

Often the theatrical game is not very elaborate in Mamet's work, just a matter of personal preservation through improvisation, or simple flight from a previous life. This latter is the context for Mamet's *Reunion,* in which a daughter seeks out the father who abandoned her and attempts to establish a relationship with him. Bernie, the father, has simply dropped out of his past relationships, drinking and occasionally trying to start again with a new family, which he eventually must leave. By the end of the play Carol, the daughter, seems to have persuaded him to forgive himself and to take a small role in her life that will help to ease her own loneliness.

In *Lakeboat* one of the crew members, Giuliani, is lost, and the remaining fellows invent an elaborate crime story about his adventures, his disappearance, and eventual death, when in fact he had simply overslept and missed the boat. Another character on the boat, Dale, is a sophomore English literature major, simply putting in time on a summer job until he can go back to school; a figure for the author, he becomes an audience for the narratives the crew members tell, allowing them to authenticate themselves while simultaneously reminding the audience, through his presence, that the play is based on the similar experiences of a young Mamet.

The most unusual of the plays that involve hiding out is probably *Lone Canoe,* the musical drama of a stranded English explorer from the early nineteenth century, living with the Athabascan tribe in the Canadian wilderness. More in tune with James Fenimore Cooper than with Emerson, this odd little play's hero, Fairfax, takes an Indian wife but is then discovered by a rescue party. Asked to return to England to explain the fate of his earlier party, Fairfax agrees to leave when a fight occurs between the explorers and natives; the tribal shaman wounds the man who led the English party, Van Brandt, and is in turn wounded by Fairfax. The party leaves, and while they wander through the lake country, Van Brandt dies. His journal reveals that he, not Fairfax, is wanted in England, so Fairfax returns to a forgiving tribe, ready to face a food shortage with the native community. This play draws out the common Rousseauian fantasy of the noble savage and the cultured man who discovers virtuous life in a simpler society. From a theatrical standpoint the plot is virtually transparent; Fairfax is free to choose who he will be by choosing which culture to belong to, and he chooses the more authentic, honest, and virtuous group of people. Fairfax rejects English society because he finds its values exemplified completely by the "natural" community of the Athabascans.

LYING ABOUT LOVE

In the politics of self-creation, one of the most dangerous acts is to give oneself over into dialogue, to admit a relation to another; such relations must, like the created self, be constituted sincerely, in declarations of genuine affection. Consequently Mamet's characters are reluctant to love one another, reluctant to admit it when they do, and apt to be extremely sensitive—hurt, angry, or morally outraged—when they are romantically deceived. It is the seduction more than the money that inspires Margaret Ford to kill her deceiver in *House of Games,* and similar dramas of intimacy are played out elsewhere in Mamet's work.

The early paradigm statement of this anxiety about honesty in relationships is surely *Sexual Perversity in Chicago.* The primary dramatic relationship in the play is between Danny and Deborah, as they struggle to establish their intimacy while simultaneously maintaining the personal identities and friendships that predate their relationship. Love, as a kind of contractual performance, is thus potentially transforming, even in a situation in which both fear of commitment and emotional honesty are obviously ideological, that is, "in Chicago." When Danny confesses his love, and Deborah asks him if love frightens him, he answers that it does; her response, "It's only words. I don't think you should be frightened by words," ignores the performative significance of the declaration, as if it were the same kind of speech as her earlier statement, "I'm a Lesbian," a lie designed to ditch Danny's first proposition. Deborah wants to create a bond hewed on less monumental speech acts, a contact established through the continuity of a dialogue with Danny; their conflict may be a simple difference over communicative preferences, but she, too, seeks authentic declarations:

Danny: I try.
Deborah: You try and try. You are misunderstood and depressed.
Danny: And you're no help.
Deborah: No, I'm a hindrance. You're trying to understand women and I'm confusing you with information. "Cunt" won't do it. "Fuck" won't do it. No more magic. What are you *feeling.* Tell me what you're *feeling.* Jerk.[24]

The italics indicate, here as everywhere in Mamet, a certain pressure on the word that emphasizes its performative significance. Similarly, Danny's curses merely perform anger and aggression theatrically; they have little referential value, yet they do work against any bond of shared understanding. The social alternative to the characters' efforts to constitute romance through authentic speech is a same-sex friendship, which in *Sexual Perversity in Chicago* is almost purely ideological, that is, based on a shared litany of what is supposed in the general culture to be true—in pornography, in child rearing, in casual observation—rather than what might be the case in any particular relationship.

The layers of theatricality and speech are more obvious and contradictory in *The Shawl.* In the first act a supposed clairvoyant, John, meets with a client and convinces her of his psychic talent. In the next act John reveals to his lover, Charles, that his gifts of spiritual vision and prophecy are based on educated guesses, confirmed by the client's wish for his credibility. What seem to be foundational speech actions—prophetic statements and observations of obscure truths—are the result of theatrical technique, and what seems to be dialogue—spiritual contact with the other world—is not. Yet genuine performative speech acts do exist in the play, as when Charles delivers an ultimatum to John: that if he does not convince the client to contest her mother's will and give the money to them, Charles will leave him. In act three when John's seance seems to be going according to plan, the photograph that the client brings turns out not to be a photograph of the mother but rather a test; when John identifies the photograph incorrectly, he puts the whole scam at risk, and can only redeem it through the image of a red shawl. This shawl eventually nets John a fee, though exactly how much the image—a likely guess based on a little simple research in an archive—will net him is not clear. Finally he must lie once again to the woman; in order to get his money, he must tell her he truly saw her mother during the seance. This lie may be a help to the client, and it even seems to coincide with what she remembers, but for John it is too late since Charles has already left, unable to accept the limits of John's vision.

Lying about love is less benign in *Oleanna*, where the title derives from Mamet's choice to write, as he often does, against a literary citation; in this case the framing texts are a quotation from *The Way of All Flesh* on the limits of moral vision and a verse from a folk song in which Oleanna names an ideal land, beyond the misery of the real world. The language of this play is the most fragmentary in Mamet's work—half of a telephone conversation, whole pages of simple phrases that trail off or are interrupted, abrupt and unpredictable changes of topic, etc. It seems to be the case that a confused female student, Carol, unable to understand the course material, gradually becomes frustrated with the male teacher's personal attempts to explain her situation and decides to accuse him of sexual harassment.[25] John's career, marriage, and whole identity eventually turn on her accusations, and by the end of the second short, intense act, he finally becomes violent. Here the quandary of interpreting the play falls upon a choice between two attitudes toward the dynamics of true performance. Was the young woman responding to a sexism situation which, in the final image, is ultimately revealed to the audience as the truth of the teacher's character, or was the teacher forced into a desperate, uncharacteristically violent and hateful act because of the enormity of her false accusations?

Oleanna seems to be written not toward any clear resolution but rather toward what has been called, in various critical arguments, the "proper statement of the question." If real human character exists prior to speech acts and is merely revealed by them, then John would seem to have been harboring criminal thoughts all along, and is perhaps innately guilty of some of the charges. If, however, his character is constituted through performed actions, then his hatred of Carol may be a new aspect of his character, an expression of his suffering and frustration. Similarly, the young woman may always have been constructed as simpleminded, that is, talked down to, in her experiences, like the way she is treated when she asks for help in the first act; her accusation of the teacher may be her new discovery of the power of expressive speech to transform her into a stronger person. Mamet does not presume to decide such conundrums in the play, and seems even to withhold the information that would make the job of interpretation easier for the audience. However, in light of the habit Mamet shows of writing against orthodoxies, and also in view of his often-stated position that women tend to manipulate speech, it would seem that even by problematizing the student's accusation, Mamet is writing against the current social trend toward accepting charges of harrassment without material evidence or convincing corroboration; the professor's life has already been shattered, his reputation and character apparently altered, before such questions of evidence have ever been considered. Mamet seems to attack the harrassment problem from the traditional Americanist perspective of the presumption of innocence and the burden of proof, and to imply that decisions made before such due process are probably unjust; the real truth in *Oleanna,* like the idea of utopia itself, is ultimately deferred.

FORMAL ILLUSIONS/
THE TRUTH OF PERFORMANCE

Mamet also uses perspectives of formal manipulation to reveal theatrical structures. The truth within an illusive dramatic fiction can be revealed as a construction by showing the machinery of illusion making, which Mamet accomplishes not through layered Brechtian techniques but simply by moving the audience's perspective "backstage," showing the action of performance as if it were directed toward some other audience.

The most literal version of this *per angolo* technique occurs in *A Life in the Theatre,* in which scenes in various locations around the backstage of a repertory theater (played toward downstage) alternate with scenes that are supposed to be from actual performances (played toward an upstage drop that looks like a dark theater)—"in effect, a true view from backstage."[26] While the behind-the-scenes action is revealed, the onstage action is shown from a new perspective, in sympathy with the actors' frequent discussions of technique and effect. The play has no story, but the twenty-five scenes cohere in a representative impression of the life of a typical actor. The two characters, one young, one old, gradually reveal their limitations and their depth through everyday actions and their identification with their roles.

Mamet's play flirts with the phenomenology of the theatre, with the paradox of acting and the body of the performer, as the characters continue to build their own identities while building fictional roles together. The drama seems to play especially well when the old actor is cast for closure, as an older, somewhat minor star: Denholm Elliot in London or Ellis Rabb in New York. In these cases the backstage scenes in rehearsal, after a show, or at the makeup table achieve a powerful illusion of authenticity and great sentimental appeal.

Another early Mamet play also debunks the performance by emphasizing its technique; in *The Water Engine* the onstage performance is of a radio play, so that the theatrical audience sees what the radio audience would only hear. Mamet is fond of the imaginative appeal of radio drama and originally wrote the play (about a 1934 Chicago inventor of an engine that runs on distilled water) for a national radio performance; in this case the era of the play's setting and the performance form were an interesting American historical match. When *The Water Engine* was produced theatrically, the conceit of the radio performance was simply placed onstage, and the theatrical audience asked to listen to the drama while they watched the spectacle of its studio production. The play's story is almost a fairy tale of good and evil, as the inventor is destroyed by dark figures from the big business world of automobiles and petroleum. By undercutting standard radio and theatrical techniques, Mamet manipulates form to emphasize the role of the imagination, aligning the audience's experience of imagining the play with the creative imagination of the inventor. The play finally appeals to the nostalgic, naive virtues of radio drama and of the simpler era that so many of Mamet's dramas try to recall. Through imaginative performance both actors and audience create the illusion of life in that era, though in this case everyone participates with full consciousness of the illusion.

The other major anti-theatrical play by Mamet is not about the theater *per se* but rather about Hollywood. *Speed-the-Plow*, written for a minimalist stage, is about the appalling ethics and greed involved in the behind-the-scenes manipulations of film producers and specifically about the arbitrary decision they make of which screenplay to produce. In the first scene, two self-described "Old Whores," Bobby Gould and Charlie Fox, celebrate over having attracted a major star to act in a formulaic sex-and-violence prison movie. Their artistic reasons for producing the screenplay are nonexistent, but they have a clear concept of "wealth." Most of the first act dialogue consists of sharing fantasies that money can fulfill. Hollywood, rather than Broadway, is the powerful commercial orthodoxy that the play condemns, while the only artistic alternative *in* the play is a visionary ecological novel, "The Bridge or, Radiation and the Half-Life of Society."

Mamet's 1983 play *Edmond,* however, remains outside the realm of specific indictments, utilizing a natural framework of American dissent and creating a kind of anti-allegory, a puritan cautionary tale in reverse, where transcendence comes not through a pilgrim's progress but through a spiraling fall, a submersion in the criminal underworld. Toby Silverman Zinman has recognized the Jewish background in *The Disappearance of the Jews* and the other Bobby Gould plays.[27] The strange peace of Edmond Burke in his jail cell at the end of the play is the result of an anti-baptism, a negative apotheosis which is still fully spiritual:

> *Edmond:* Do you think there's a hell?
> *Prisoner:* I don't know. (*Pause.*)
> *Edmond:* Do you think that we are there?
> *Prisoner:* I don't know, man. (*Pause.*)
> *Edmond:* Do you think that we go somewhere when we die?
> *Prisoner:* I don't know, man. I like to think so.
> *Edmond:* I would, too.
> *Prisoner:* I sure would like to think so. (*Pause.*)
> *Edmond:* Perhaps it's Heaven.
> *Prisoner (pause):* I don't know.
> *Edmond:* I don't know either but perhaps it is. (*Pause.*)
> *Prisoner:* I would like to think so.
> *Edmond:* I would, too.
> (*Pause.*)
> Good night. (*Pause.*)
> *Prisoner:* Good night.
> (*Edmond gets up, goes over and exchanges a goodnight kiss with the Prisoner. He then returns to his bed and lies down.*)[28]

The ending echoes that of *The Cherry Orchard,* where Firs lies down to await death. But the inexplicable breaking string of Chekhov has been cut from Mamet's adaptation of that moment, just as the spiritual symbolism of Edmond as everyman has been thrown into doubt.[29] By writing against genre, against religious doctrine, and against a canonical realistic text, Mamet again asserts himself by performing acts of artistic dissent.

Mamet's enormous commercial success in recent years brings a certain pressure to bear on his status as a figure of dissent. While still a relatively young writer, in mid-career, he is also one of the few of his generation to have sustained his project, to develop a distinct way of working and writing that meets with consistent acclaim. A recent issue of the *Dramatists Guild Quarterly* sought to acknowledge this status, though some of Mamet's remarks demonstrate a certain discomfort with his acquired intellectual credibility. About playwriting in general, for example, he argues: "It's a craft which has been practiced down through the ages, in the main, by whores like me; people who didn't know how to do anything else and were wandering around in the dark trying to express themselves, who somehow got good at it or got famous at it (perhaps not both) and so perservered. The purpose of literature is not to do good, but to delight us. That's why the writer writes it; it delights him or her to express it, or to be rid of it, and in some way delights the audience, appealing either to their self-esteem or to their prejudices, creating in them a new, happy understanding of the world."[30] As this statement reflects both on Mamet's talent and on his mission, this public declaration is surely a case of false modesty. Yet such self-deprecation is precisely what Mamet's public position requires, if he is going to maintain his status as an American writer, unique like others and therefore capable of critical self-expression.

In the creation of an illusion, whether of reality or of singular selfhood, the primary compositional technique is still to undercut, to construct an excess which, when pared away, seems to reveal the essential. As Mamet summarizes: "The main difference between somebody who wants to be a professional writer and somebody who doesn't is that the former knows how to cut. If you don't know how to cut, if you're a product of some school that didn't teach you that, you're not serious. If you're unwilling to cut viciously, just on the off chance that the audience might beat you to the punch line, you haven't been watching the audience. And if you haven't been watching the audience watching your plays, you're not a playwright."[31] Mamet's remarks are in the context of a public address, in which he was acutely aware of his audience as a community of American writers.

What Mamet tends to universalize, then, might be more carefully considered as a gesture specific to a particular cultural moment, and an expression which requires as its background a relatively stable cultural symbology. From a technical standpoint his primary advances over the old "selective realism" of the Group Theatre generation would seem to be his recognition of performance as a constitutive act, and his ability to dramatize the moments in peoples' lives when their performances seem to come undone, and so I have tried to suggest a working typology of those moments. Viewed through the critical lens of a theory of representation, a debunked illusion is merely one stage in an infinite regression, and reality is always deferred, always subject to a subsequent deconstruction. Yet viewed in the expressivist mode, which is one the deconstructive theorist often—inconsistently—employs, a gesture of undoing takes on the converse quality of having founded something singularly true. In an American culture that values such creative rejections, Mamet's dramas enjoy a remarkable affective power. But since cultures themselves are far from any security as critical absolutes, estimates of Mamet's significance will almost surely continue to change.

Notes

1. There are four book-length studies of Mamet's work thus far: one reference guide, Nesta Wyn Jones, *File on Mamet;* two general surveys, Dennis Carroll, *David Mamet* (New York: St. Martin's Press, 1987), and C. W. E. Bigsby, *David Mamet* (London: Methuen, 1985); and one treatment of his dialogue, Anne Dean, *David Mamet: Language as Dramatic Action* (Fairleigh Dickinson UP, 1989). No interpretive consensus on the significance of his work has emerged, though Mamet is now read internationally; see Martin Roeder-Zerndt, *Lesen und Zuschauen: David Mamet und das amerikanische Drama und Theatre der 70er Jahre* (Tubingen: Gunter Narr, 1993). My argument here is primarily an extension of the "language as action argument" through speech-act theory into cultural politics.

2. See, for example, William Demastes's chapter, "David Mamet's Dis-Integrating Drama," in *Beyond Naturalism: A New Realism in American Theatre* (Westport, Conn.: Greenwood Press, 1988), pp. 67–94. As regards realism in general I suppose I should admit the undue influence of Roman Jakobson, who thought the

term so overfull of conflicting significance that its use was mostly rhetorical; see "On Realism in Art," trans. K. Magassy, in *Readings in Russian Poetics: Formalist and Structuralist Views*, ed. L. Matejka and K. Pomorska, pp. 38–46 (Ann Arbor: Michigan Slavic Studies, 1978).

3. This, among other things, causes many critics to dislike Mamet. Ruby Cohn, in *New American Dramatists, 1960–1980* (New York: Grove, 1982), repeats Edward Albee's observation that Mamet had "a fine ear, but there was as yet no evidence of a fine mind," and then went on to say that Mamet has a mind "so fine that no idea could violate it" (p. 46). Nevertheless, in the revision of her book she cedes to Mamet a major historical role, linking him with Shepard in the final chapter (*New American Dramatists, 1960–1990* [Basingstoke: Macmillan, 1991]).

4. David Mamet, "Realism," in *Writing in Restaurants* (New York: Penguin, 1986), p. 132.

5. See Sacvan Bercovitch, *The Puritan Origins of the American Self* (New Haven: Yale UP, 1975); his *The American Jeremiad* (Madison: U of Wisconsin P, 1978); and Bercovitch, ed. *Ideology and Classic American Literature* (Cambridge: Cambridge UP, 1986).

6. Sacvan Bercovitch, *The Rites of Assent: Transformations in the Symbolic Construction of America* (New York: Routledge, 1993), p. 311.

7. Bigsby comes close to this reading in the late pages of his chapter on Mamet in *A Critical Introduction to Twentieth-Century American Drama*, vol. 3: *Beyond Broadway* (Cambridge: Cambridge UP, 1985), when he argues that Mamet's realism is rooted in a "myth of decline" (p. 288).

8. Thorstein Veblen, *The Theory of the Leisure Class* (New York: Macmillan, 1899).

9. See for example Herbert Blau's first book, *The Impossible Theatre: A Manifesto* (New York: Collier, 1964).

10. Theatrical manifestoes have a difficult but continuing history; see for example Mac Wellman, "The Theatre of Good Intentions" *Performing Arts Journal* 8:3 (1984): 59–70; or Daryl Chin, "An Anti-Manifesto," *Drama Review* 27.4 (Winter 1983): 32–37, the latter in a special anniversary issue of manifestoes.

11. Mamet, "Decadence," in *Writing in Restaurants*, p. 58.

12. The construction of political correctness as an orthodoxy even allows conservatives, paradoxically, to grasp the rhetoric of dissent, as is evident in *Culture Wars: Documents from the Recent Controversies in the Arts*, ed. Richard Bolton (New York: New Press, 1992).

13. J. L. Austin, *How to Do Things with Words* (Cambridge: Harvard UP, 1962). The principal historian of politics to use this performative method is Quentin Skinner; for an overview see James Tully, ed., *Meaning & Context: Quentin Skinner and his Critics* (Princeton UP, 1988).

14. David Mamet, "WFMT," *The Cabin: Reminiscence and Diversions* (New York: Turtle Bay, 1992), p. 56.

15. David Mamet, *Some Freaks* (New York: Penguin, 1989), p. 3.

16. Rousseau makes his theory perfectly clear in the "Letter to D'Alembert on

the Theatre," *Politics and the Arts,* ed. and trans. Allan Bloom (Ithaca: Cornell UP, 1960); for such a reading of Jefferson see Jay Fliegelman, *Declaring Independence: Jefferson Natural Language and the Culture of Performance* (Palo Alto: Stanford UP, 1993).

17. Mamet theorizes such a shared idealism in relation to the theatre in his "A National Dream Life," in *Writing in Restaurants,* pp. 8–11.

18. See for example his remarks on entropy in "Decay: Some Thoughts for Actors," in *Writing in Restaurants.*

19. Jonas Barish, *The Anti-Theatrical Prejudice* (Berkeley: California UP, 1981).

20. Mamet, "Acting," in *Writing in Restaurants,* p. 129.

21. Henry Schvey, "The Plays of David Mamet: Games of Manipulation and Power," *New Theatre Quarterly* 4.13 (Feb. 1988): 77–89. See also, regarding *American Buffalo,* Thomas King, "Talk as Dramatic Action in American Buffalo," *Modern Drama* 34.4 (Dec. 1991): 538–48, and remember that to "buffalo" is to intimidate (Jack Barbera, "Ethical Perversity in America: Some Observations on David Mamet's *American Buffalo,*" *Modern Drama* 29.2 [Sept 1981]: 270–75).

22. David Mamet, *Glengarry Glen Ross* (New York: Grove, 1984), p. 105.

23. David Mamet, *House of Games* (New York: Grove, 1985), p. 70.

24. David Mamet, *Sexual Perversity in Chicago and The Duck Variations* (New York: Grove, 1978), pp. 57–58.

25. There is a background for this conflict in Mamet's earlier work; see Pascale Hubert-Leibler, "Dominance and Anguish: The Teacher-Student Relationship in the Plays of David Mamet," *Modern Drama* 31.4 (Dec. 1988): 557–70.

26. David Mamet, *A Life in the Theatre* (New York: Grove, 1978), p. 9.

27. Toby Silverman Zinman, "Jewish Aporia: The Rhythm of Talking in Mamet," *Theatre Journal* 44.2 (May 1992): 207–15. In the same issue Carla McDonough reads Edmond in terms of American masculinity rituals ("Every Fear Hides a Wish: Unstable Masculinity in Mamet's Drama," pp. 195–205).

28. David Mamet, *Edmond* (New York: Grove, 1983), pp. 105–6.

29. The sound occurs in act two of Mamet's adaptation but not at the end. Anton Chekhov, *The Cherry Orchard,* adapted by David Mamet from a trans. by Peter Nelles (New York: Grove, 1985). Lue Douthit pointed out this absence to me.

30. Mamet, "Mamet on Playwriting," *Dramatists Guild Quarterly* 30.1 (Spring 1993): 8. Compare Mamet's stature, for example, with that of the playwrights with whom he was first compared in Peter Ventimiglia, "Recent Trends in American Drama: Michael Cristofer, David Mamet, Albert Innaurato," *Journal of American Culture* 1.1 (1978): 195–204.

31. Mamet, "Mamet on Playwriting," p. 12.

SIXTEEN

The Hurlyburly Lies
of the Causalist Mind:
Chaos and the Realism
of Rabe and Shepard

William W. Demastes and Michael Vanden Heuvel

In his essay "Naturalism in Context" (1968), Martin Esslin announced that though the early, turn-of-the-century interest in naturalism in the theatre may since have been replaced by other dramatic forms, naturalism's legacy to those new forms—the key surviving element of naturalism in the theatre today—is "an experimental exploration of reality in its widest possible sense."[1] In "The Experimental Novel" (1893), Emile Zola observed that the naturalist author "gives the facts as he observes them, suggests the point of departure, displays the solid earth on which his characters are to tread and the phenomena to develop."[2] What develops from Zola's agenda is a process in which the author "sets his characters going so as to show that the succession of facts will be such as the requirements of the determinism of the phenomena under examination call for" (p. 5).

Zola's determinist requirements were informed by the dominant episteme of his age, of which Newtonian causation was a primary discourse. Naturalism has thus become a term associated with linear causality, which proceeds from a classical scientific assumption that small and large causes beget effects of value equal to their causes. For the naturalist, where one begins on this solid earth virtually foreordains where and how one will tread upon it.

In the 1950s, following the turmoil of two world wars and under the impact of important new developments in philosophy and the sciences, Europe firmly reassessed the "determinist requirements" of its age. Consequently, a strong anti-realist theatrical movement—the theatre of the absurd—emerged that reflected a growing awareness that neither history nor physics offered adequate proof that determinist elements governed material or human existence. In his *The Theatre of the Absurd* (1961), Esslin argued that, predicated on existentialist philosophy, there arose a uniquely European movement in the theatre, in which a "sense of the senselessness of life, of the inevitable devaluation of ideals, purity, and purpose"[3] replaced the orderly, Newtonian fiction of life adhered to by the period's predecessors. The theatre of the absurd, as Esslin would later argue in "Naturalism in Context," is nonetheless indebted to naturalism in retaining its spirit of inquiry, its use of a closely scrutinizing eye for detail in human events, though with different results. Though the methodology for deriving their conclusions remained intact, the absurdists' conclusions regarding deterministic existence ran in diametric opposition to the agenda of their naturalist predecessors.

These two strongly influential movements—naturalism and absurdism—have polarized western theatre, arguing respectively for a tidy global perspective of human behavior or for an idiosyncratic local vision, in which ultimately no human behavioral patterns can be abstracted. One is left to choose between existence represented as strict linear determinism or as utter randomness.

In 1978 Robert Brustein extended the naturalism-absurdism debate to American theatre in an article, "The Crack in the Chimney: Reflections on Contemporary American Playwriting," in which he chastised twentieth-century American dramatists for their allegiance to tightly causal and linearly constructed works, the logical assumptions of which "belong to the eighteenth century, which is to say the age of Newton, rather than to the twentieth century, the age of Einstein."[4] Brustein agrees with Esslin's observation that absurdism never became a force in American thought or theatre because, as Esslin reports, "In the United States the belief in progress that characterized Europe in the nineteenth century has been maintained into the middle of the twentieth century."[5] American drama for the most part remained linear and progressive, refusing seriously to acknowledge the randomness and stagnation embodied in absurdist drama.

But while Brustein notes the adherence to causal progression of plot in the work of such playwrights as O'Neill and Miller, he also observes a relatively recent (in 1978) trend that seemed intent on overturning the standard methodology and its attendant naturalist philosophy. He cites David Rabe's *Sticks and Bones* and Christopher Durang's parody of Rabe, *The Vietnamization of New Jersey,* as revolutionary American attempts to develop an anti-causal form. Here Brustein cleverly anticipates a direction in American drama, not quite absurdist or naturalist, that has to this day met with critical confusion and audience resistance.

While Brustein does not discuss Rabe's 1976 play *Streamers,* his observation that American drama has taken a new turn nevertheless applies to this work. Though largely conforming to traditional realist assumptions, *Streamers* concludes with a sequence of unexpectedly violent, seemingly senseless and bloody events. Audiences were clearly repelled by the events before them, for reasons explained by reviewer Walter Kerr: "What the audience asks for is a pattern, a design, a shape that will embrace what they are now looking at and place it in significant relationship to what has gone on before and what may come after."[6] The apparent gratuitousness of the concluding events of the play shattered causal expectations and left the audience confused and grasping for unity and design. Whereas an audience may anticipate such randomness from an absurdist play by Ionesco or Genet—with a clearly nonrealist premise, acting style, and set—from a realist format such as the one utilized in *Streamers* (and most American drama), an audience invariably expects Ibsenesque causality. And this Rabe refuses to provide.

Despite violating strict naturalist philosophy in his play, Rabe is nevertheless subscribing to naturalism's legacy of experimentally exploring the realm of reality with a scrutinizing, "scientific" eye. In this particular case, however, Rabe confronts the linear science of Newton and suggests a nonlinear dynamic that is in many ways more closely allied to an absurdist vision. Yet Rabe's presentation is something more than an absurdist embodiment of inexplicable, unpatterned randomness. His theatre presents a hybrid form, something that gravitates between the strict causality of naturalism and the utter randomness of absurdism. The play scatters events that amount to unrelated causes of the play's final effects, but they arise in such a way as to suggest principles increasingly significant in contemporary scientific thought, which fall under the popular rubric of "chaos theory."[7]

Testing laboratory conclusions against less controlled natural events, a recent group of scientific skeptics—not unlike their critical equivalents in the theatre—discovered that scientists often oversimplified the systems they studied, creating "true" results in the artificially closed environment of their laboratories and computer simulations; these results, however, did not incontrovertibly occur in "real" time and space. Like the naturalist playwright, traditional scientists created controlled, artificially closed environments that ultimately guaranteed the behavior they anticipated. What usually emerged in both cases were tidy results that seemed to produce objectively conclusions that were globally applicable. But while such conclusions abstractly argued for perfect consistency between the local and the global, in practice "inexplicable" deviations occurred between them. The chaos scientists discovered, quite simply and conclusively, showed that the kind of order envisioned by the Newtonians and naturalists was impossible. The human desire for such an order conflicted with natural evidence.

Perhaps the first expanded scientific evidence of the extent of this impossibility occurred when meteorologists during the 1960s and '70s concluded that they had amassed sufficient understanding of variable deterministic influences to develop a system of making long-term weather forecasts. But in the process of developing the determinist system, it was discovered that in complex and open systems like the earth's atmosphere, even the most minor and undetectable events thousands of miles away may affect the overall outcome of events. The idea that the movements of a butterfly flapping its wings in China can unpredictably rise to a level of significance and affect the weather in Arizona is the image that led to the popular labeling of the so-called "butterfly effect." Not knowing which events would ripple up to a level of significance undermined any attempt at long-term weather forecasts, leading to an inevitable uncertainty and to imprecise conclusions even when data is precise to a reasonable, scientifically acceptable degree. It eventually became evident that the uncertain results of the butterfly effect impacted upon any number of dynamic systems, from the weather to population growth systems, heartbeat patterns, morbidity patterns among certain populations, even the stock market.

The conclusions to be drawn from these insights are significant. Elements of the absurdist message have been verified by the discovery that it is impossible to realize the scientific/naturalistic goal of discovering deterministic patterns of behavior in a system from which future events can be solidly predicted. This further implies that randomness seems to dominate reality; and so all our efforts at finding order have been mere illusion or delusion. But though chaos theory does conclude that a chaotic system's behavior cannot be strictly predicted, significantly, the theory does not conclude that the world is total randomness, as is often commonly assumed when the term *chaos* is summoned. Paradoxically, chaos theory identifies systems of "unpredictable determinism": there are causes and effects (determinism), but we cannot always know all the causes or even the overall effect arising out of each cause (uncertainty). Because of the proportional uncertainties invested in how causes impact upon effects, predictability itself is uncertain, but because order is present, complete surrender to total randomness is equally untenable.

These scientific breakthroughs have been variously described as deriving from cultural inclinations to revision reality or as influencing cultural thought to reinvestigate its own positions.[8] Whether science influenced culture or vice versa is less relevant, however, than the fact that a convergence of thought occurred, for ideas similar to the chaos paradigm clearly pertain to the kinds of alterations that Brustein identified in American drama. While straightforward naturalism may lead audiences to expect a single line of causality to determine ultimate outcomes, something akin to a butterfly effect intrudes into the events of plays like *Streamers* to produce determined, yet unpredictable, behavior. Hindsight will reveal that causes are indeed present, but attempts to anticipate which causes will have lesser or greater effects will only produce probable conclusions, which finally may or may not occur. This brand of realism in the theatre—a hybrid of naturalism and absurdism—would seem to embody a new vision of reality similar in some respects to that provided by chaos science. What Brustein has identified is the fact that unpredictable determinism, an inconceivable concept for an audience trained to expect causal linearity, has permeated the fabric of popular theatre.

Rabe articulates this concept of unpredictable order in his afterword to *Hurlyburly* (1985) when he describes the " 'realistic' or 'well-made' play [as] . . . that form which thinks that cause and effect are proportionate and clearly apparent, that people know what they are doing as they do it, and that others react accordingly, that one thing leads to another in a rational, mechanical way, a kind of Newtonian clock of a play, a kind of Darwinian assemblage of detail which would then determine the details that must follow, the substitution of the devices of logic for the powerful sweeps of pattern and energy that is our lives."[9] Rabe's notion of causes fluctuating nonlinearly and leading to disproportionate effects echoes the concept of the butterfly effect. What may appear a minor source influence could rise up to unexpected levels of significance not anticipated by Newtonian rationalist expectations. Causal, mechanistic logic may predict linear transfers of force and energy in the material realm (as with one billiard ball striking another), but the quanta of "powerful sweeps of pattern and energy" that Rabe locates in the open system of human life argue against such a model. Note, too, that Rabe nonetheless argues for "pattern" rather than randomness or absurdism; but that pattern is, and will always remain, unpredictable and disorderly.

Despite Brustein's and Rabe's imprecision in articulating ideas which have become more exact in the wake of chaos science, it is clear that science and theatre are fast approaching agreement on new, more sophisticated and subtle ways of viewing and representing the world around them. A crucial aspect of this shift in how to model reality is the way information is conceived. Realism and naturalism have been both praised and damned for the techniques they use to manipulate the knowledge and information they provide. An objective, documentary rhetoric and an emphasis on recording the data of experience with acute detail and verisimilitude is, of course, the hallmark of all realistic art. The question of realism's ontological status as an object of knowledge, a source of information, thus has been crucial in critical assessments of the form. The information that early realist theatre amassed was judged complete and accurate, and the technologies that made the communicative task complete—from stage design to acting technique and appropriately realistic dramatic texts—were lauded for their ability to describe systems of reality exactly and completely, with Newtonian precision.

· More recent critiques of realism, however, have emphasized the duplicity inherent in its claims to objective, complete representation and perfect information. As a recent example, we have William Worthen's insightful critique of realism's attempts to assign a " 'scientific' transparency" to its practices by "attenuat[ing] the medium," thereby positioning the audience as objective and unstaged so as to "legitimate its private acts of interpretation as objective."[10] From this perspective, concludes Worthen, the "realist theatre of disclosure is also a theatre of concealment" (p. 17). Information meant to demystify the world is conveyed, paradoxically, through a technology that dissimulates its own operations and dissembles its own decision procedures.

Realism, then, is a form that renders information as a measure of a system's order. Information about a system is understood to be a message as it is actually communicated, its specified order, and not a chaos of possibilities. Early realist theatre sought to produce complete descriptions of reality in order to eliminate uncertainty, disorder, and complexity. It qualitatively assessed what information was valuable and what information was extraneous "noise," highlighting the former and suppressing the latter so that the data ultimately presented was taxonomic, linear, and transmitted with optimum clarity.

Developments in modern American drama since the advent and subsequent reevaluation of realism share the common notion that reality is not mechanical, simple, regular, predictable, and deterministic. Because the macroscopic world is by definition antimechanistic, one must construct an information technology based, paradoxically, upon the scientific principle that information is inevitably degraded in transmission, and that the receiver of the information will always be left with some degree of uncertainty as to the content of the original state of the message: a "system"—which is defined as an orderly structure—impossibly, in constant disequilibrium. To resolve the paradox, a technology must be created which constructs information not simply as an orderly message but rather out of the woof and warp of noise and message, disorder and order. This appears to be the model which Rabe and other recent American playwrights seek in response to contemporary life.

Lost in the new paradigms is any sense of inherent simplicity to the universe. Instead, emphasis is placed on how physical and cultural systems engage in processes of exchange with their environment, transforming one another and evolving in dynamic patterns similar to the "sweeps of pattern" that Rabe identifies. Chaos science shows that, when they are large enough, systems normally compliant to linear formalization can become highly unstable and begin to fluctuate nonlinearly as they engage in a torrent of information and become susceptible to the butterfly effect. Such systems are prone to erratic and random behavior and are highly sensitive to fluctuations in their initial conditions, a fact which can have system-shattering effects on the whole.

There is no proof that Rabe or any other American playwright is well versed in such recent trends in the scientific community;[11] however, his work suggests that Rabe has intimated the limitations of a dramatic form which carries the burden of reproducing reality in such a way that precedence is always given to clarity and order. His plays explore the possibility that higher levels of knowing are produced when information is unstable and uncertain, when messages degrade and consequently create noise or disorder. While the play's message lacks clarity, from the point of view of the audience, such turbulence creates an increased flow of actual information, because it includes both the original message and the new static or noise created by chaotic fluctuations. Hence audience members are obliged to construct their own responses out of the dynamic torrent of orderly messages and disorderly noise.

This is not to say that the interpretive strategies of new realism have been easily incorporated into the mainstream of American drama. Rabe's work has met with a measure of audience resistance, as evidenced by the reaction to *Streamers* described earlier. In *Hurlyburly,* Rabe even more rigorously assaults naturalist causality, seeing as a necessary substitution for the "devices of logic" the need to exhibit the "powerful sweeps of pattern and energy that is our lives" (p. 162). The words *logic, logical, syllogism, deduction,* and *induction* pervade the play's dialogue, set up only to be undermined by the disorderly sweeps and nonlinear effects that take over the lives of the characters. That the theatre establishment was not prepared for such an assault is evident in the original Broadway production of the play, where significant cuts were made to Rabe's text. Mike Nichols, the director, "cut everything about Phil [a central character] that could make him interesting or complex or vulnerable and tried to turn him into a total creep," according to Rabe.[12] The production was essentially reduced to a linear narrative, more easily accessible to its audience, rather than fleshed out to incorporate the flood of uncertainties and ambiguities present in the text.

Phil is a character struggling to control or understand the chaos that engulfs his life. The other central character, Eddie, utilizes cool abstractions both to explain himself, when possible, and to discard untidy material when it fails to fit his self-conception. Mickey, on the other hand, sees randomness as an excuse to behave as an ethical egoist: what is right is that which provides him with greatest gains. Phil's self-doubts reach their peak in the following exchange, which additionally affects Eddie's own visions:

> *Phil:* I mean, we got these dark thoughts, I see 'em in you, you don't think you're thinkin' 'em, so we can't even nail that down, how we going to get beyond it? They are the results of your unnoticed inner goings-on or my gigantic paranoia, both of which exist, so the goddamn thing in its entirety is on the basis of what has got to be called a coin toss.
> *Eddie:* I can figure it, I can—It's not a goddamn coin toss.
> *Phil:* You think I'm being cynical when I say that? Nothing is necessary, Eddie. Not a fucking thing! We're in the hands of something, it could kill us now or later, it don't care. Who is this guy that makes us just—you know—WHAT? . . . THERE'S A WORD FOR IT. . . . IT'S LIKE A LAW. IT'S A LAW? WHAT THE FUCK IS A LAW? (p. 70)

Eddie's desperate response notwithstanding, the two men are grappling with something that does appear to be an ethical coin toss. Like Einstein insisting to quantum scientists that God does not play dice with the universe, Phil recognizes that something exists besides randomness, that there is an order, even a law, governing existence. But tidy deterministic laws are insufficient. So what law is it? This "guy," this thing that controls us, is a controlling order uncharacteristic of Newtonian expectations but perfectly comprehensible if Phil could learn to embrace a more flexible paradigm of random order. Not as precise as the Newtonian fictions, it nonetheless is capable of making "sense" of the apparent senselessness of existence.

This need to transcend strict linear causality informs the work of other playwrights, including Sam Shepard. Applications of chaos theory to Shepard's work reveal strong affinities between the playwright's expanding vision of the world and science's changing perspective. The titles to Shepard's recent plays (like Rabe's *Hurlyburly*)—*A Lie of the Mind* (1986) and *States of Shock* (1991)—suggest an explicit awareness of the turmoil attendant to this paradigm shift.

The very fact that Shepard has difficulty with closure in his dramas reflects his resistance to the tradition of strict realism: "Endings are so hard. Because the temptation always is a sense that you're supposed to wrap it up somehow. You're supposed to culminate it in something fruitful. And it always feels so phony, when you're trying to wrap it all up."[13] Shepard here seems at least intuitively aware of the scientific fact that information exists in an orderly state only when placed in laboratory-like closed systems, rarely existing in the natural world itself. The result is that Shepard's realism assaults the bastion of traditional, strictly linear and causal realist theatre in an attempt to reveal the indeterminate and chaotic nature of the world.

Shepard's 1986 play, *A Lie of the Mind*, documents the results of a particularly brutal case of domestic violence, in which the husband, Jake, has inflicted wounds on his wife, Beth, to such a degree that she suffers brain damage. Ironically, the damage Beth receives leads her to greater insights into life than her deterministic, linearly obsessed husband and both his and her families can ever achieve. Jake looks very determinedly for the actual cause of his violent eruption, seeking linear connections between his actions and their results. His mother, Lorraine, works as well to verify another linear link between cause and effect by establishing a traditional realist's/naturalist's genetic logic, recalling her husband's (Jake's father's) own violent nature. Jake's brother, Frankie, goes to Beth's family to find answers but falls prey to his own rationalist process and to Beth's family as well. Beth's father, Baylor, works in a business-as-usual manner to conclude that Beth's problems are typically "female"-induced and are evidence of a fundamental incompatibility between the sexes. Beth's brother, Mike, orders events by responding to a code of honor, applying conventional and vengeful responses to the event. Each is, to one degree or another, a deterministic causalist, and, as Shepard presents it, none of their approaches resolves the conflict. The overall result is either to succumb to a traditional interpretation, namely to see the play as filled with meaningless noise—since events do not linearly cohere—or to see the noise from a new perspective, arising from an order not grasped by anyone but, perhaps, the brain-damaged (reason-impaired) Beth.

While there are numerous ways to apply the title *A Lie of the Mind* to the play, one application seems often to be overlooked: that the rational application of deterministically causal patterns to human events is, itself, a lie of the mind, a categorical reduction of reality to fit convenient patterns and responses designed by human desire to explain and even anticipate existence. Causal determinism, in short, is a lie created by humanity in its efforts to delude itself into believing it is in control of its surroundings.

From this perspective, the play fits nicely into Brustein's observations about postmodern American drama. Shepard is clearly revolting against the tyranny of rationalist causal models of inevitability. But he is not merely concluding that existence randomly produces the results that it does. Randomness may have been all that Brustein (and postmodernism in general) could offer in place of causality, a randomness agonized over by many absurdist playwrights or celebrated in the works of many postabsurdists. But Shepard articulates a chaos-informed pattern similar to that created in *Streamers*.

The fact that much of Shepard's dramatic output seems nonlinear has often been ascribed to Shepard's own carelessness as a craftsman. It is more likely that his apparent carelessness is in fact highly crafted. The various dead ends he sets up in his landscape reflect the fact that "noise" is designed to force detours in what Shepard would consider our errant pursuit of linear comprehension.

Unpredictable determinism best describes what Shepard presents, which denies mere randomness as much as it denies the strict causal determinism of the many naturalist predecessors. In scene one, Jake asks, "Why didn't I see it coming?"[14] The answer is simple: there is no exact way to predict future events. An audience may presume that Beth's decision to accept an acting job led to Jake's eruption, and to a large degree it was a cause. But there is no way to presume that Beth's decision predetermined Jake's reaction. In fact it could be a case of Shepard inserting superfluous noise, true static that ultimately has no causal bearing on the subject under scrutiny, despite possible clues to the contrary. Similarly, Lorraine says Jake's genes predetermined his actions; after all, Jake is like his father. But, again, there is no legitimate basis from which to presume that this genetic influence predetermined events. Finally, Mike assumes he has only one course of action, to follow a code of honor and to seek revenge. But the fact that he does subscribe to such conditions does not mean that he must *inevitably* subscribe to the conditions. Nothing, finally, is causally inevitable in the action of the play.

Because of writers like Shepard and Rabe, realism has been forced to confront the fact of its own discursive status, and to recognize that its technologies for communicating information are not objective and absolute but rather culturally determined. This is an important lesson, for as Worthen states, the politics of theatre "emerge not only in the themes of drama but more searchingly in the disclosure of the working of ideology in the making of theatre, in the formation of the audience's experience and so, in a manner of speaking, in the formation of the audience itself" (p. 146). Traditional realism, following ritual and classical theatre, maintains an ideology of mastery over nature which hypostatizes its laws and renders universal and atemporal its description of the systems it delineates. Chaos theory, and the emerging theatre of such writers as Shepard and Rabe, which isomorphically reflects the principles of chaotics, is playing another game, one which has important consequences for the working of ideology in the theatre and for the formation of the audience's experience. Even the acting style Shepard prefers in his work—"controlled anarchy" (p. 4)—argues for a revisioning of audience expectations.

Controlled anarchy, in fact, is a term applicable to most of Shepard's work, a characteristic that distinguishes his work from that of earlier American dramatists whose instincts tend toward visioning a world or culture that *controls* anarchy. That earlier American dramatic sense of a need for order reflects an American cultural desire for control in general, the need to maintain an order in its pursuit of its "manifest destiny," a cultural imposition of a sort of determinism over the events with which it engages. The triumph of this position is evidenced by the triumph of America over its primary foe—nature. America has tamed "the West" and has thus apparently achieved its manifest destiny. That such a victory has borne anything but productive fruit is suggested in *Buried Child* (1978), a play that argues for a readmission of natural processes into the (re)creation of our cultural fabric. America, Shepard seems to be suggesting, must relinquish its grip on control, must allow the natural processes of disorder to reemerge and to revitalize a culture which has become "triumphant" over disorder but which has paid the price of stagnation and sterility. From the perspective of chaos science, however, the reemergence of chaos is inevitable, so America had best adapt and prepare for it by embracing its promise of a reconstituted order.

Shepard's implicit argument is profound and reverberates to the very foundations of our cultural edifice. Reversing American mythic history, Shepard intimates that we must release ourselves from an order that excludes the noise of real experience. The new "order" that Shepard posits is one that sees the necessity of welcoming a dynamic tension between disorder and order, a decentered vision of the notion of order as control. Such unpredictable interferences are inevitable and are therefore actually determinist. Hence the appropriateness for Shepard's turn to realism and an "apparent" naturalism. But, like Rabe's realism, Shepard's realism is not Zola's; it is a chaos-informed realism.

True West is an excellent case in point, the play's very title suggesting its cultural engagement with American myth. Austin and Lee are, respectively, paragons of culturally prescribed order and a "natural" disorder. Separately, the two brothers have stagnated into sterile, unproductive existences. Austin is a product of a culturally triumphant "real" West and Lee of a natural "untamed" West. It should be noted that while several critics have seen the play as a psychological study of two halves of one self, Shepard has rejected such an interpretation because in many ways Austin and Lee are not "selves" at all. Only insofar as Shepard argues for a dynamic interaction between the two can psychology even enlighten the subject. What Shepard argues, more precisely, is that the real West—developed, paved, orderly— must reengage with the untamed West—vital, wild, nonlinear. The fact that Austin and Lee reverse roles suggests that neither position can exist exclusively because the reversal ultimately reifies the oppositional difference and satisfies neither brother. Instead of an either/or choice, Shepard suggests a both/and proposition. The dynamic between order and disorder, culture and nature, provides the necessary vitality for continued cultural *and* natural health. The play's conclusion, with the two brothers embraced in a death grip, can be taken two ways. If the two men do not derive an understanding for their need to allow order and disorder to interact, they will destroy each other in an effort to eradicate the other. If, however, they accept their interactive differences and realize the mutual interest in necessary co-existence, a new vitality will rise up. As with the haunting, ambiguous ending of *Buried Child*, *True West* offers no single resolution, leaving open the possibility of a self-destructive decision to fight or a regenerating decision to embrace a new vision. The conclusion could lead to a triumph of the real West wherein the entire landscape turns into a Palm Springs development and the vitality of the wild is eradicated. Or it could lead to a triumph of the untamed West wherein the resistant real West is ultimately overrun by a patient but persistent natural cycle. Or—the hope of Shepard—the standoff could lead to the revelation that both opponents need to reengage in a dynamic interchange and an evolving pattern of order/disorder.

Culturally speaking, it is not entirely surprising that such reevaluations of American mythic suppositions occurred during and after the Vietnam War. That era saw America reassessing its linear assumptions regarding its historically unchallenged belief in its universal "rightness" within the world community. Rabe's plays, of course, comment directly on Vietnam. Even *Hurlyburly* has a tentative Vietnam connection, offering a threatening, jungle-like landscape just outside the apartment set: "The house is completely surrounded by wild vegetation" (p. 13). While all of Shepard's drama can be said to be a product of a Vietnam-era spirit of reassessment, in *States of Shock* (1992), Shepard, too, brings Vietnam—or a suggestive facsimile thereof—to the stage.

In *States of Shock,* Shepard argues that America can no longer adhere to its rationalist, Newtonian vision of reality and behavior, certainly not in a post-Vietnam, post–Cold War, post–Desert Storm world. The chaos, randomness, and uncertainty of the current world (dis)order is pervasively inserted into the play by way of an upstage scrim, from which we hear the efforts of two percussionists and through which the silhouettes of scenes of war invade the action taking place in Danny's family restaurant. In the restaurant sits a "West Palm Beach" couple, well-off, "civilized," generally imperturbable, but subject to the poor service of the waitress and rude behavior of the other pair on the stage. This other pair consists of a wheelchair-ridden veteran of some unnamed war, Stubbs, who has had the middle third of his body blown away in battle by a shell which passed through him and apparently killed the son of the other member of the pair, the Colonel. The Colonel has taken Stubbs from his hospital to this restaurant on the first anniversary of his son's death, ostensibly to uncover the truth about the events that day.

Stubbs's mental capacities have been damaged as well as his body; the Colonel explains, "He's suffered a uh—kind of disruption. Temporary kind of thing, they say. Takes some time to unscramble."[15] A thorough American, the Colonel intends precisely to unscramble Stubbs's mind, by way of rational inquisition: "I want to reconstruct everything up to that moment. . . . What I'm trying to figure out is the exact configuration. The position of each element. A catastrophe has to be examined from every possible angle. It has to be studied coldly, from the outside, without investing a lot of stupid emotion. . . . What we're after is the hard facts" (pp. 13, 14, 15). Stubbs, of course, cannot review his catastrophe free from "stupid emotion," and his conclusion is that on that day "America had disappeared" (p. 20). The Colonel immediately responds: "DON'T TALK FOOLISHLY! That's a blasphemous thing to say! It's a disgrace to the memory of my son!" (p. 20). Clearly for the Colonel, America could not have been in error, and the truth should verify his point. Blending nationalism with an apparently interchangeable rationalist fervor, the Colonel adds: "The principles are enduring. You know that. This country wasn't founded on spineless, spur-of-the-moment whimsy. The effects are international! UNIVERSAL!" (p. 20).

But this insistence on order, reason, manifest destiny is immediately undermined by the play's stage action: "*Immediately the percussionists and war sounds join in full swing. The cyclorama explodes with bombs, missiles, and blown-up planes*" (p. 20). Order, quite simply, finds no place in war; fear limits the possibility of reason to dominate. However, the Colonel wants exactly that kind of control over the events of the war. He wants coolly calculated explanations, although he can accept momentary chaos, "as long as we can always come back to our senses. That's the important thing." Such equilibrium, he adds, is "a blessing. . . . It's a gift. An American virtue" (p. 20).

Shepard essentially gives us two characters who respectively see the events of that day, on the one hand, as reflecting the randomness of existence and, on the other, as demonstrating the potential for an eschatology of order and purpose. Stubbs is the living result of randomness, ironically observing throughout, "I was the lucky one," while the Colonel strives to overlay meaning onto the thus far meaningless event. The Colonel insists on control, believing no action goes wasted in the grand design; what he seeks to uncover is how his son's life was invested in that grand design.

That the Colonel understands chaos only as an obstacle to be overcome is evidenced in a speech he gives to the waitress, Glory Bee, who is having trouble balancing water glasses while delivering food orders. He shows her how to balance the glasses, and then explains: "Always [remind] yourself that the human body is little more than a complex machine and, like all machines, can be trained and programmed to fulfill our every need. Through repetition and practice" (p. 32). To this mechanistic perspective of life, reminiscent of neo-Newtonian conclusions, the Colonel adds: "Repetition and practice. Slowly, a pattern begins to emerge. Slowly, through my own diligence and perseverence, this pattern takes on a beauty and form that would have otherwise been incomprehensible to my random, chaotic laziness. Now I become master of my own destiny. . . . I understand my purpose in the grand scheme of things. There's no longer any doubt. Fear takes a backseat to the certainty and confidence that now consumes my entire being. I am a God among men!" (pp. 32–33).

The Colonel understands chaos only to a limited degree. In his mechanistic understanding of human action, chaos is an undesired other, the enemy that he must destroy. Constantly set up in oppositions—friend or foe—the Colonel's worldview sees order as friend and chaos as foe. Once he "orders" his laziness, he can control the randomness apparent in the world out there. It is a simple concept and one that Shepard appears to ascribe to the American psyche throughout his work, whereby ordering the wilderness into civilization is conceived to have been our singular task and triumph. What is missing in the Colonel's view, however, is the idea that one must allow order to *arise* out of chaos—and allow the opposite to occur as well—rather than working to *impose* order upon chaos. The natural processes of a rising order have been superseded by an impulse to control, to be "gods" dictating order to nature. The result of this impulse is to place nature in the role of "enemy" and, ironically, to place ourselves in the path of self-destruction, destroying both nature and ourselves in our very attempts to redeem both.

In essence, claims Shepard, today we have become victims of "friendly fire." Just as Stubbs concludes that his wounds came from friendly fire, so too does Shepard suggest that America's decline has been the result of friendly fire, namely a debilitating unwillingness to see the world in any way other than oppositionally. Even Glory Bee suggests that we've been hit by our own friendly fire: "The thing I can't get over is, it never occurred to me that 'Danny's' could be invaded. I always thought we were invulnerable to attack. The landscaping. The lighting. The parking lot. All the pretty bushes. Who could touch us? Who would dare?" (p. 40). This triumph over nature has instilled in Glory Bee a sense of invulnerability. But the invasion is internal, another instance of friendly fire, since the domestic assaults of which she speaks can only actually be metaphorical. She even muses, "I missed the Cold War with all my heart" (p. 41). References to clearly defined oppositions were instrumental in maintaining a rationalist control over all the ethnic, racial, and nationalist disorders lurking beneath the oppositional surface. With the thawing of the Cold War, however, a chaos pattern has resurfaced.

Before his accident, Stubbs, too, thought like Glory Bee and even the Colonel. On the assault beach, he worked to control both his fears and his growing sense of meaninglessness in ways the Colonel's eschatology would fully endorse. Says Stubbs of his recollections on the beach, rather ironically spiced: "Keep thinking of 'home.' That's the way to pull through this. . . . Think of what we've achieved! The 'Trail of Tears'! The Mississippi! Samuel Clemens! Little Richard! The Dust Bowl! The Gold Rush! The Natchez Trace! It's endless! A River of Victory in all directions! Flooding the Plains! Hold to an image! Lock onto a picture of glorious, unending expansion! DON'T LET YOURSELF SLIP INTO DOUBT!! Don't let it happen! You'll be swallowed whole!" (p. 38). Stubbs saw himself as part of a greater purpose and perhaps would have continued to believe so except for the friendly fire that destroyed his body, along with his beliefs in the value of what he has just catalogued. He also has suggested the standard means of explaining failure, that his own *will* to succeed was insufficient and therefore that his failure was his own fault. However, through the course of the play he becomes remasculated literally (by recovering his ability to have an erection) as well as figuratively (by a growing realization that he did not fail the vision but that the vision failed him).

Similarly, the Colonel's control over his world crumbles. Shortly after his speech on laziness, the Colonel loses both Stubbs and the girl he dreams of marrying (Glory Bee). More significantly, he never recovers a satisfactory explanation of his son's death. He cannot accept the friendly fire explanation, and he will not accept any suggestion of cowardice. Responding to the possibility that Stubbs will leave him, the Colonel observes: "I can easily do without. It's a question of training. Repetition and practice. All those days. All those horrible long days without the enemy. Longing out the window. Staring at the stupid boredom of peacetime. The dullness of it" (p. 39). Wedded to an oppositional perspective on life, war is the only place the Colonel comes alive. The subtle complexities and nuances of peace are incomprehensible to him; in fact, it is apparent that through "repetition and practice" he has interpolated himself into a mechanistic existence void of any life-affirming qualities. He does not engage; he can only confront ("Aggression is the only answer" [p. 39]).

Stubbs, however, has begun to reenter life. He makes contact—yet again, literally and figuratively—with Glory Bee, and together they become a pair searching to fathom the mysteries of a world no longer fitting the mold of the old American, rationalist, pre–Cold War frame of thought. Stubbs cannot dismiss his own confrontation with randomness; his emotional attachment to those events forces him to comprehend a pattern that cannot be reformed, as the Colonel insists. Chaos, we learn through Stubbs, cannot be ignored or dismissed. And it can no longer be overpowered or subdued. Rather, its reality and inevitability must be accepted, and new strategies to cope with it must be developed. The Colonel is absolutely wrong in his last speech when he takes an aggressive posture and ascribes it to his own version of American isolationism, which even he appears no longer fully to accept: "We've got to keep our back to the mountain, Stubbs. At all costs. You can see our position. We've got a perfect vantage point from here. We're lucky in that respect. There are certain advantages to isolation. After all, we're not in exile. This is our domain. We've earned every inch of it. Surrounded by water. Engulfed by the prairies. Marooned. (*Pause.*) MAROOOOOOOOONED!!" (pp. 44–45).

He has perhaps a perfect vantage point from which to *observe* life, but he is indeed marooned, not only by geographical realities but by an overweening fear of embracing uncertainty. Stubbs and Glory Bee embrace that uncertainty; they appear willing to accept the patterns of nature, to look for an orderly disorder, and in the process, to live. When Stubbs blasts out his last "GOD BLESS THE ENEMY" (p. 46), he speaks it differently than on the other occasions, in that this final blast is an ironic speech of thanks for an enemy who has blasted him out of his incapacitating ignorance. Shepard's ultimate, unanswered question is whether or not America can follow Stubb's insight.

Thus, that Brustein missed the precise point of Rabe's work and that audiences often miss the point of both Rabe's and Shepard's works is not entirely surprising. When audiences do not see causal, determinist patterns, they often conclude that only one consequent can replace the pattern—randomness (or absurdism). So too, Brustein rightly observed the new allegiance to noncausality in recent American drama, but he concluded imprecisely that randomness or absurdism is the only alternative. What chaos theory has taught us is that the law of excluded middle does not apply to open systems. It is not the case that events are either deterministically causal or absurdly random. There is a third option, one explained by chaos theory as unpredictable determinism. The fact remains that contemporary theatre, science, and culture in general are undergoing profound paradigm shifts not yet fully digestible by the general community. And the "realism" debate—in theatre and science—seems to be central to the issues under scrutiny.

Realism is not obsolete by any means, but the definition of its task— to provide a scientific description of reality as it is experienced by human beings—has been altered by the dynamics of modern life and by what science now makes possible. In the wake of the new chaos science, even the understanding of "description" has been changed by the increased awareness of the benefits that accrue when certainty is mixed with uncertainty, when information is a function of both order and disorder, message and complexity. "History," writes Michel Serres, "is the locus of full causes without effects . . . the river of circumstances and no longer the old orbit of the mechanists."[16] American new realist playwrights are discovering that to turn away from the linear causality of the mechanists and to wade into the "river of circumstances"—the dynamic, nonlinear, and evolving chaos of "the powerful sweeps of pattern and energy that is our lives"—may provide them with a more accurate depiction of life.

Notes

1. Martin Esslin, "Naturalism in Context," *Drama Review* 13.2 (Winter 1968): 67–76, at 72.

2. "The Experimental Novel" (1893), trans. Belle M. Sherman, in *The Naturalist Novel,* ed. Maxwell Geismar (Montreal: Harvest House, 1964), p. 5.

3. Martin Esslin, *The Theatre of the Absurd* (London: Eyre and Spottiswoode, 1961), p. 17.

4. Robert Brustein, "The Crack in the Chimney: Reflections on Contemporary American Playwriting," *Theater* 9.2 (1978): 21–29; rpt. in *Images and Ideas in American Culture,* ed. Arthur Edelstein (Hanover, N.H.: Brandeis UP, 1979), p. 148.

5. Esslin, *The Theatre of the Absurd,* p. 230.

6. Walter Kerr, "When Does Gore Get Gratuitous?" *New York Times* (Feb. 22, 1976), sec. 2, p. 7.

7. For a readable (though necessarily reductive) version of chaos theory breakthroughs, see James Gleick, *Chaos: Making a New Science* (New York: Penguin, 1987); and John Briggs and F. David Peat, *Turbulent Mirror* (New York: Harper & Row, 1989).

8. N. Katherine Hayles, in *Chaos Bound: Orderly Disorder in Contemporary Literature and Science* (Ithaca: Cornell UP, 1990), argues that, as with artistic innovation, so too scientific discoveries are culturally motivated. As a culture's perspective changes, so does scientific motivation to pursue different perspectives and derive conclusions consistent with the cultural model. Well supported, Hayles's work does much to undermine common assumptions about the "objective" nature of scientific enquiry and places its efforts clearly in a cultural context, the two overlapping and mutually influencing one another.

9. David Rabe, *Hurlyburly* (New York: Grove, 1985), p. 162. Subsequent references are cited in the text.

10. William B. Worthen, *Modern Drama and the Rhetoric of Theatre* (Berkeley: U of California P, 1992), p. 17. Subsequent references are cited in the text.

11. Interestingly, however, in the published text of *Goose and Tomtom* (New York: Grove, 1986), Rabe quotes from the quantum physicist Werner Heisenberg— "Not only is the Universe stranger than we think, it is stranger than we can think"—suggesting that Rabe may be more aware of such trends than one suspected.

12. David Savran, *In Their Own Words: Contemporary American Playwrights* (New York: Theatre Communications Group, 1988), pp. 200–1.

13. Carol Rosen, " 'Emotional Territory': An Interview with Sam Shepard," *Modern Drama* 36.1 (March 1993): 6. Subsequent references to Shepard are from this interview and are cited in the text.

14. Sam Shepard, *A Lie of the Mind* (New York: Plume, 1986), p. 2.

15. Sam Shepard, *States of Shock,* in *States of Shock, Far North, Silent Tongue: A Play and Two Screenplays* (New York: Vintage, 1993), p. 6. Subsequent references are cited in the text.

16. Michel Serres, *The Parasite,* trans. Lawrence Schehr (Baltimore: Johns Hopkins UP, 1982), p. 20.

Selected Bibliography

The following is a selected secondary bibliography of general studies in American drama and theatre. Please refer to chapter notes for references relating to single authors or for matters not directly related to drama and theatre.

Adler, Thomas P. *Mirror on the Stage: The Pulitzer Plays as an Approach to American Drama.* West Lafayette: Purdue UP, 1987.

Artaud, Antonin. *The Theater and Its Double.* Trans. Mary Carol Richards. New York: Grove Weidenfeld, 1958.

Austin, Gayle. *Feminist Theories for Dramatic Criticism.* Ann Arbor: U of Michigan P, 1990.

Becker, George. *Realism in Modern Literature.* New York: Ungar, 1980.

Belsey, Catherine. "Constructing the Subject: Deconstructing the Text." In *Feminist Criticism and Social Change: Sex, Class and Race in Literature and Culture,* ed. Judith Newton and Deborah Rosenfelt, pp. 45–64. New York: Methuen, 1985.

Berkowitz, Gerald M. *American Drama of the Twentieth Century.* London: Longman, 1992.

Bigsby, C. W. E. *A Critical Introduction to Twentieth-Century American Drama.* 3 vols. Cambridge: Cambridge UP, 1982–85.

———. *Modern American Drama, 1945–1990.* Cambridge: Cambridge UP, 1992.

———. *The Second Black Renaissance.* Westport, Conn.: Greenwood Press, 1980.

Blau, Herbert. *The Impossible Theatre: A Manifesto.* New York: Collier, 1964.

Brown-Guillory, Elizabeth. *Their Place on Stage: Black Women Playwrights in America.* New York: Praeger, 1988.

Brown, Wendy. "Feminist Hesitations, Postmodern Exposures." *Differences* 3.1 (1991): 63–84.

Brustein, Robert. "The Crack in the Chimney: Reflections on Contemporary American Playwriting." *Theater* 9.2 (1978): 21–29; rpt. in *Images and Ideas in American Culture,* ed. Arthur Edelstein, pp. 141–57. Hanover, N.H.: Brandeis UP, 1979.

Case, Sue-Ellen. *Feminism and Theatre.* New York: Methuen, 1988.

———, ed. *Performing Feminisms: Feminist Critical Theory and Theatre.* Baltimore: Johns Hopkins UP, 1990.

Chothia, Jean. "The Real Thing: American Drama's Search for its Natural Voice." *Times Literary Supplement,* May 7, 1993.

Clum, John M. *Acting Gay: Male Homosexuality in Modern Drama*. New York: Columbia UP, 1992.

Clurman, Harold. *The Fervent Years*. New York: Da Capo Press, 1975.

Cohn, Ruby. *New American Dramatists, 1960–1980*. New York: Grove, 1982.

————. *New American Dramatists, 1960–1990*. Basingstoke: Macmillan, 1991.

Corrigan, Robert W. *The Theater in Search of a Fix*. New York: Delacorte Press, 1973.

Demastes, William W. *Beyond Naturalism: A New Realism in American Theatre*. Westport, Conn.: Greenwood Press, 1988.

————. "Reinspecting the Crack in the Chimney: Chaos Theory from Ibsen to Stoppard," *New Theatre Quarterly* 10.39 (Aug. 1994): 242–54.

————, ed. *American Playwrights, 1880–1945: A Research and Production Sourcebook*. Westport, Conn.: Greenwood Press, 1995.

Diamond, Elin. "Brechtian Theory/Feminist Theory: Toward a Gestic Feminist Criticism." *The Drama Review* 32.1 (Spring 1988): 82–94.

————. "Mimesis, Mimicry, and the 'True-Real.'" *Modern Drama* 32.1 (March 1989): 58–72.

————. " 'Lesbian' Subjectivity in Realism: Dragging at the Margins of Structure and Ideology." In *Performing Feminisms*, ed. Sue-Ellen Case, pp. 40–53. Baltimore: Johns Hopkins UP, 1990.

————. "The Violence of 'We': Politicizing Identification." In *Critical Theory and Performance*, ed. Janelle G. Reinelt and Joseph R. Roach, pp. 390–98. Ann Arbor: U of Michigan P, 1992.

Dolan, Jill. "Bending Gender to Fit the Canon: The Politics of Production." In *Making a Spectacle: Feminist Essays on Contemporary Women's Theatre*. ed. Lynda Hart, pp. 318–44. Ann Arbor: U of Michigan P, 1989.

————. *The Feminist Spectator as Critic*. Ann Arbor: UMI Research Press, 1988.

Eaton, Walter Prichard, *At the New Theatre and Others*. Boston: Small, Maynard, and Co., 1910.

Elam, Keir. *The Semiotics of Theatre and Drama*. London: Methuen, 1980.

Esslin, Martin. "Naturalism in Context." *Drama Review* 13.2 (Winter 1968): 67–76.

————. *The Theatre of the Absurd*. London: Eyre and Spottiswoode, 1961.

Forte, Jeanie. "Realism, Narrative, and the Feminist Playwright—A Problem of Reception." *Modern Drama* 32.1 (March 1989): 115–27.

Freedley, George, and John A. Reeves. *A History of the Theatre*. New York: Crown, 1941.

Gassner, John. *Directions in Modern Theatre and Drama*. New York: Holt, Rinehart, and Winston, 1966.

————. *Form and Idea in Modern Theatre*. New York: Dryden Press, 1956.

————. *The Theatre in Our Times*. New York: Crown Publishers, 1954.

Gelderman, Carol. "Hyperrealism in Contemporary Drama: Retrogressive or Avant-Garde?" *Modern Drama* 26 (1983): 357–67.

Goldman, Michael. *The Actor's Freedom: Toward a Theory of Drama*. New York: Viking Press, 1975.

Gorelik, Mordecai. *New Theatres for Old*. New York: E. P. Dutton & Co., 1962.

Grimsted, David. *Melodrama Unveiled: American Theatre and Culture 1800–1850*. Berkeley: U of California P, 1968.

Hart, Lynda, ed. *Making a Spectacle: Feminist Essays on Contemporary Women's Theatre*. Ann Arbor: U of Michigan P, 1989, pp. 1–21.

Hay, Samuel A. *African American Theatre: An Historical and Critical Analysis*. New York: Cambridge UP, 1994.

Herne, James A. "Art for Truth's Sake in the Drama." *The Arena* 17 (Feb. 1897): 361–70. Rpt. in Downer, Alan S. *American Drama and Its Critics*. Chicago: U of Chicago P, 1965: pp. 1–9.

Hill, Holly. *Black Theater Into the Mainstream*. New York: St. Martin's Press, 1991.

Himelstein, Morgan Y. *Drama Was a Weapon: The Left-wing Theatre in New York, 1929–1941*. New Brunswick: Rutgers UP, 1963.

Kachur, Barbara. "Women Playwrights on Broadway." In *Contemporary American Theatre*, ed. Bruce King, pp. 15–39. New York: St. Martin's Press, 1991.

Kaplan, Charles, ed. *Criticism: The Major Statements*. New York: St. Martin's Press, 1986.

Kiper, Florence. "Some American Plays from the Feminist Viewpoint." *Forum* 51 (1914): 921–31.

Kolb, Deborah S. "The Rise and Fall of the New Woman in American Drama," *Educational Theatre Journal* (May 1975): 154.

Kolin, Philip C., ed. *American Playwrights Since 1945: A Guide to Scholarship, Criticism, and Performance*. Westport, Conn.: Greenwood Press, 1989.

Krutch, Joseph Wood. *The American Drama Since 1918*. New York: Random House, 1939.

Levine, Ira A. *Left-wing Dramatic Theory in the American Theatre*. Ann Arbor: UMI Research Press, 1985.

McConachie, Bruce A. *Melodramatic Formations: American Theatre and Society, 1820–1870*. Iowa City: Iowa UP, 1992.

McKay, Nellie. "Black Theater and Drama in the 1920s: Years of Growing Pains." *Massachusetts Review* 28 (Winter 1987): 615–26.

Mielziner, Jo. *Designing for the Theatre: A Memoir and a Portfolio*. New York: Bramhall House, 1965.

Moses, Montrose J. *The American Dramatist*. New York: Benjamin Blom, 1939.

Murphy, Brenda. *American Realism and American Drama, 1880–1940*. Cambridge: Cambridge UP, 1987.

Porter, Thomas E. *Myth and Modern American Drama*. Detroit: Wayne State UP, 1969.

Reinelt, Janelle. "Feminist Theory and the Problem of Performance." *Modern Drama*. 32.1 (March 1989): 48–57.

Sanders, Leslie Catherine. *The Development of Black Theatre in America: From Shadows to Selves.* Baton Rouge: Louisiana State UP, 1988.

Savran, David. *In Their Own Words: Contemporary American Playwrights.* New York: Theatre Communications Group, 1988.

Shafer, Yvonne. *American Women Playwrights, 1900–1950.* New York: Peter Lang, 1994.

Schroeder, Patricia R. *The Presence of the Past in Modern American Drama.* Rutherford, N.J.: Fairleigh Dickinson UP, 1989.

Scott, Freda L. "Black Drama and the Harlem Renaissance." *Theatre Journal* 37.4 (Dec. 1985): 426–39.

States, Bert O. "The Actor's Presence: Three Phenomenal Modes." *Theatre Journal* 35.3 (Oct. 1983): 359–79.

Stowell, Sheila. "Rehabilitating Realism." *Journal of Dramatic Theory and Criticism* 6 (1992): 81–88.

Strindberg, August. "Author's Foreword to *Miss Julie.*" Trans. Elizabeth Sprague. In *Playwrights on Playwriting,* ed. Toby Cole, pp. 171–82. New York: Hill and Wang, 1961.

Styan, J. L. *Modern Drama in Theory and Practice,* vol. 1: *Realism and Naturalism.* Cambridge: Cambridge UP, 1981.

———. *Modern Drama in Theory and Practice,* vol. 3: *Expressionism and Epic Theatre.* London: Cambridge UP, 1981.

Sunquist, Eric J., ed. *American Realism: New Essays.* Baltimore: Johns Hopkins UP, 1982.

Szondi, Peter. *Theory of Modern Drama.* Ed. and trans. Michael Hays. In *Theory and History of Literature,* vol. 29. Minneapolis: U of Minnesota P, 1987.

Vanden Heuvel, Michael. *Performing Drama/Dramatizing Performance: Alternative Theater and the Dramatic Text.* Ann Arbor: U of Michigan P, 1991.

Ventimiglia, Peter. "Recent Trends in American Drama: Michael Cristofer, David Mamet, Albert Innaurato." *Journal of American Culture* 1.1 (1978): 195–204.

Wellek, René. "The Concept of Realism in Literary Scholarship." In *Concepts of Criticism,* ed. Stephen H. Nichols, Jr., pp. 222–55. New Haven: Yale UP, 1963.

Wellman, Mac. "The Theatre of Good Intentions." *Performing Arts Journal* 8:3 (1984): 59–70.

Wilmeth, Don B., and Tice L. Miller. *Cambridge Guide to American Theatre.* Cambridge: Cambridge UP, 1993.

Worthen, William B. *Modern Drama and the Rhetoric of Theater.* Berkeley: U of California P, 1992.

Zola, Emile. "Naturalism on the Stage." Trans. Samuel Draper. In *Playwrights on Playwriting,* ed. Toby Cole, pp. 5–14. New York: Hill and Wang, 1961.

Contributors

Thomas P. Adler is professor of English and associate dean of Liberal Arts at Purdue University, where he has taught dramatic literature and film since receiving his Ph.D. from the University of Illinois at Champaign-Urbana twenty-five years ago. His more recent publications include a monograph entitled *"A Streetcar Named Desire": The Moth and the Lantern,* and Tennessee Williams figures prominently in his new critical history of American drama from 1940 to 1960.

Judith E. Barlow is associate professor of English and of Women's Studies at the State University of New York at Albany. She is the author of *Final Acts: The Creation of Three Late O'Neill Plays,* as well as editor of *Plays by American Women, 1900–1930* and the forthcoming *Plays by American Women, 1930–1960.* She has also written essays on women playwrights from Rachel Crothers to Tina Howe.

Eric Bergesen is a graduate student at Louisiana State University, Baton Rouge, and editorial assistant for the *Henry James Review.*

Frank R. Cunningham, formerly Senior Fulbright Lecturer at the University of Cracow, is professor of English at the University of South Dakota, where he teaches late nineteenth- and early twentieth-century American literature and has been cited for distinguished teaching. He serves on the editorial boards of *Eugene O'Neill Review* and *Literature/Film Quarterly.* He recently published *Sidney Lumet: Film and Literary Vision* (1991), which includes a chapter on O'Neill, and his writings have appeared in *Sewanee Review, American Literature,* and elsewhere. He is currently writing a book on O'Neill's literary art in the light of modern tradition.

William W. Demastes is professor of English at Louisiana State University, Baton Rouge. He is author of *Theatre of Chaos* (forthcoming), *Clifford Odets: A Research and Production Sourcebook* (1991), and *Beyond Naturalism: A New Realism in American Theatre* (1988). He is also editor of *American Playwrights, 1880–1945* (1995) and *British Playwrights, 1956–1995* (1996), co-editor of *British Playwrights, 1880–1956* (1996) and *Irish Playwrights, 1880–Present* (1996), and has published articles on theatre/drama in *Comparative Drama, Modern Drama, New Theatre Quarterly, Theatre Journal,* and the *Journal of Dramatic Theory and Criticism,* among others.

Patricia D. Denison teaches in the English Department and Theatre Department at Barnard College. She is currently completing a book on Arthur W. Pinero and editing a collection of essays on John Osborne. She has articles published or forthcoming on Pinero, Robertson, and Shaw.

John W. Frick is associate professor of Theatre at the University of Virginia. He is author of *New York's First Theatrical Center: The Rialto at Union Square;* co-editor of *The Directory of Historic American Theatres* and of *Theatrical Directors: A Biographical Dictionary;* and has published articles and reviews in the *Drama Review, Theatre Journal, Journal of American Drama and Theatre, Yearbook of Interdisciplinary Studies in the Fine Arts, Performing Arts Resources, Southern Theatre, Marquee, American National Biography,* and the *Encyclopedia of New York City.*

J. Ellen Gainor is an associate professor of Theatre Studies at Cornell University. Her books include *Shaw's Daughters: Dramatic and Narrative Constructions of Gender* (1991) and the forthcoming *The Plays of Susan Glaspell: A Contextual Study.* She is also editing three essay collections, *Imperialism and Theatre, Theatre and Reproductive Rights,* and *Performing America: Cultural Nationalism in American Theatre.*

Robert F. Gross is director of Theatre and associate professor of English and Comparative Literature at Hobart and William Smith Colleges. He is the editor of *Christopher Hampton: A Casebook,* and the author of *Words Heard and Overheard* and *S. N. Behrman: A Research and Production Sourcebook.*

Janet V. Haedicke is an assistant professor of English at Northeast Louisiana University in Monroe. Having published articles on contemporary drama in such journals as *Modern Drama* and the *Journal* *of Dramatic Theory and Criticism,* she is currently working on a feminist study of American domestic drama.

Brenda Murphy is professor of English at the University of Connecticut, Storrs. She is author of *Tennessee Williams and Elia Kazan: A Collaboration in the Theatre* (1992), *A Realist in the American Theatre: Selected Drama Criticism of William Dean Howells* (1992), *American Realism and American Drama, 1880–1940* (1987), and, with George Montiero, *John Jay—Howells Letters* (1980), as well as of articles and reviews in such journals as *Modern Drama, American Literature, American Literary Realism, Theatre Annual, Comparative Drama,* and *South Atlantic Quarterly.*

Michael L. Quinn was assistant professor in Dramatic Theory and Criticism at the University of Washington School of Drama. His articles, reviews, and translations have appeared in *Theatre Survey, Modern Drama, New Theatre Quarterly,* the *Journal of Dramatic Theory and Criticism, Theatre Journal, Essays in Theatre, Theatre Research International,* and several other journals and collections. His book *The Semiotic Stage: Prague School Theater Theory* is forthcoming from Pittsburgh Studies in Theater and Culture, as is a study of Vaclav Havel's plays for Cambridge University Press. A terrible loss for friends and colleagues, Professor Quinn passed away on August 27, 1994.

Brian Richardson is assistant professor of English at the University of Maryland, College Park. He has published on drama and theatre in such journals as *Comparative Drama, Essays in Literature,* the *Eugene O'Neill Review,* and *Philological Quarterly.*

Patricia R. Schroeder is professor of English at Ursinus College, where she teaches American literature and modern drama. Her publications include *The Presence of the Past in Modern American Drama* and essays on a variety of contemporary American playwrights. She has been an officer of the Women and Theatre Program since 1990. Her latest book, *The Feminist Possibilities of Dramatic Realism,* is forthcoming.

Yvonne Shafer is currently teaching in the Theatre and Dance Department of the University of Colorado, Boulder. She has published widely on American, British, and continental drama.

Michael Vanden Heuvel is associate professor of English and Interdisciplinary Humanities at Arizona State University. He is the author of *Performing Drama/Dramatizing Performance: Alternative Theater and the Dramatic Text* (1991) and *Elmer Rice: A Research and Production Sourcebook* (1996). His articles on drama and theatre have appeared in the *Journal of Dramatic Theory and Criticism, New Theatre Quarterly, Theatre Journal,* and *Theatre Topics.*

Christopher J. Wheatley is an associate professor in English specializing in drama studies at the Catholic University of America. He is the author of *Without God or Reason: The Plays of Thomas Shadwell and Secular Ethics in the Restoration* (1993) and is currently co-editing with Kevin Donovan a collection of plays from seventeenth- and eighteenth-century Ireland.

Index